DUBLIN AND THE GREAT IRISH FAMINE

DUBLIN AND THE GREAT IRISH FAMINE

edited by

Emily Mark-FitzGerald, Ciarán McCabe and Ciarán Reilly

UNIVERSITY COLLEGE DUBLIN PRESS
PREAS CHOLÁISTE OLLSCOILE BHAILE ÁTHA CLIATH
2022

First published 2022
by University College Dublin Press
UCD Humanities Institute, Room H103,
Belfield,
Dublin 4

www.ucdpress.ie

ISBN 978-19-1-08207-73

CIP data available from the British Library

Typeset in Dublin by Gough Typesetting Limited
Text design by Lyn Davies
Printed in Scotland on acid-free paper by Bell & Bain Ltd,
Burnfield Road, Thornliebank, Glasgow, G46 7UQ, UK

Contents

SECTION IV: THE FAMINE IN CULTURAL HISTORY

Acknowledgements

The genesis of this volume was a workshop held in University College Dublin in June 2019, co-organised by the three editors and sponsored by UCD's College of Arts & Humanities, and the UCD Humanities Institute Research Series 'Media, Encounter, Witness: Troubling Pasts'. We are especially grateful to our funders for this support, and to Noelle Moran, Conor Graham and their colleagues at UCD Press who responded so warmly to the subsequent edited volume.

The essays in this book are the fruit of rigorous scholarly research, drawing on a diverse range of sources and written from a variety of disciplinary perspectives and methodological approaches. We are grateful to our authors for their contributions, and for their persistence and patience over the past few years, as the global Covid-19 pandemic delayed this project's final realisation. We would also like to express our thanks to Professor Cormac Ó Gráda (UCD) for contributing the book's opening overview, and to Professor Peter Gray (QUB) for his support of this project at various stages.

Ciarán McCabe would also like to acknowledge and thank the Irish Research Council (IRC) and Dublin City Council for jointly funding an IRC Enterprise Partnership Scheme postdoctoral fellowship, held at UCD's School of History between 2018–20.

The kind support of the NUI Publication Grant is greatly appreciated.

Emily Mark-FitzGerald, Ciarán McCabe and Ciarán Reilly
July 2022

List of Contributors

Brian Crowley is employed as a curator by the Office of Public Works and is responsible for the museum collections at Kilmainham Gaol Museum and the Pearse Museum. He was also involved in the reinterpretation of Daniel O'Connell's home in Derrynane. He has published several historical essays and an illustrated biography of Patrick Pearse entitled *Patrick Pearse: A Life in Pictures*.

Declan Curran is Associate Professor of Economics at Dublin City University. Previous publications include *Famines in European Economic History: The Last Great European Famines Reconsidered* (Routledge, 2015).

Joe Curran is an Irish Research Council Postdoctoral Fellow at Trinity College Dublin. He is researching Dublin Castle's economic and social connections with Dublin city between 1801 and 1923.

Christopher Cusack is a postdoctoral researcher and lecturer at Radboud University in the Netherlands. He has published widely on the Great Famine and the Irish diaspora, and is currently researching the role of local colour in Irish American and German American writing.

Rob Goodbody is a building conservation consultant and is a member of the Historical Committee of the Religious Society of Friends in Ireland. Previous publications include *A Suitable Channel: Quaker Relief in the Great Famine* (1995).

Philomena Gorey is a historian of childbirth, midwifery and puerperal fever. Her doctoral thesis, completed at UCD's School of History, examined the regulation of midwifery in Ireland from the seventeenth to the early-twentieth centuries. She is working on her monograph *From Birth Attendant to Midwife: A History of the Regulation of Irish Midwives, 1615–1918.*

Peter Hession is Assistant Professor Faculty Fellow of Irish History at Glucksman Ireland House, New York University. His research focuses on technology and famine in the mid-nineteenth century.

Georgina Laragy is the Glasnevin Trust Assistant Professor in Public History and Cultural Heritage at Trinity College Dublin. She is a historian of suicide, poverty and institutions in nineteenth- and twentieth-century Ireland, and her forthcoming works include (co-written with Olwen Purdue) *Poverty, Children and the Poor Law in Industrial Belfast, 1880–1918* (Liverpool University Press).

Emily Mark-FitzGerald is Associate Professor in the School of Art History and Cultural Policy, where she specialises in the visual culture of the Irish Famine, poverty, migration and diaspora, from the nineteenth century to the present. Her previous books include *Commemorating the Irish Famine: Memory and the Monument* (2013) and *The Great Famine: Visual and Material Culture* (2018).

Ciarán McCabe is a historian of poverty and welfare in nineteenth-century Ireland and Britain, and author of *Begging, Charity and Religion in Pre-Famine Ireland* (2018). He lectures in Modern Irish History at Queen's University Belfast.

Kathryn Milligan is an art historian specialising in nineteenth- and twentieth-century Irish art. Her first book, *Painting Dublin, 1886–1949: Visualising a Changing City*, was published by Manchester University Press in 2020.

Cormac Ó Gráda is Professor Emeritus, School of Economics, UCD. His famine-related publications include *Black '47 and Beyond* (Princeton, 1999), *Famine: A Short History* (Princeton, 2009), and *Eating People is Wrong: Essays on the History and Future of Famine* (Princeton, 2015).

Ciarán Reilly is a historian of nineteenth- and twentieth-century Ireland based at Maynooth University and is author of *The Irish Land Agent* (2014) and *Strokestown and the Great Irish Famine* (2014).

List of Illustrations

List of Abbreviations

DEM	*Dublin Evening Mail*
DEP	*Dublin Evening Post*
DEPC	*Dublin Evening Packet and Correspondent*
DMA	*Dublin Mercantile Advertiser, and Weekly Price Current*
DMR	*Dublin Morning Register*
DWN	*Dublin Weekly Nation*
DWR	*Dublin Weekly Register*
FJ	*Freeman's Journal*
NAI	National Archives of Ireland
NLI	National Library of Ireland
RDS	Royal Dublin Society
SN	*Saunder's Newsletter*
WDWM	*Warder and Dublin Weekly Mail*

Dublin and the Great Irish Famine: Introduction

EMILY MARK-FITZGERALD, CIARÁN MCCABE AND CIARÁN REILLY

Among the most striking features of the writing of Dublin's history has been the lack of attention paid to the Famine years in the city. Rural Ireland, especially the western seaboard, has long attracted the most historiographical attention and popular associations. This is understandable. The impact of the Famine was most severely felt in the rural south and west of the island, where dependency on the potato was greatest. Indeed, the most evocative images of the Famine are set in the rural context: the labourer and cottier class largely dependent on a single crop; the fields filled with rotten potatoes; the country roads swarmed with migrating, and starving, peasants; and evictions of persons from small landholdings. It is certain that Dublin did not suffer the horrors of the Famine to the same extent as the island's peripheral regions; for instance, an estimated 'excess death rate' for Dublin of 5 per cent places the city, in William Smyth's judgement, 'at the bottom end of the national pattern of fatalities'.[1]

Yet, the city and its population witnessed considerable levels of Famine-related distress, sickness and mortality. Dublin's inhabitants – natives and migrants – lived through increased mortality rates, public health crises, the overwhelming of welfare institutions, and the unprecedented movement of persons into and out of the city, migrating from impoverished rural areas, seeking relief, employment or passage to foreign lands. These experiences warrant historiographical attention, yet despite being the capital city, the location of the largest concentration of persons on the island, the hub of central administration (especially in respect of Famine relief, through the Poor Law Commissioners, the Relief Commission, the Board of Works and the Central Board of Health), and the location of the first confirmed identification in Ireland of the new potato blight (*Phytophtora infestans*) – in the Botanic Gardens at Glasnevin on 20 August 1845 by David Moore – the city has long lacked detailed scholarly analysis. As is evident from this volume into an underexplored chapter in Dublin's history, this dearth has not been for the want of research topics or sources. This book re-locates the capital at the centre of enquiry, exploring the effects of the Famine on Dublin, but also the effect of Dublin on the Famine nationally. Its chosen title – *Dublin and the Great Irish Famine* – signals our interest in analysing a relationship moving in both directions.

The neglect of urban Famine histories is not limited to Dublin city. Other large urban centres, such as Cork and Belfast, while not without some historiographical attention, await detailed scholarly analysis of the impact of the crisis in the late-1840s.[2] One wonders whether the historiographical and popular neglect of Famine Dublin arises somewhat from a wider suspicion of the urban context within the Irish historical experience. Throughout the late nineteenth and into the twentieth century, the 'true Ireland' was increasingly seen as being located in the countryside, most notably along the western seaboard. Large cities, especially Dublin, were often seen and vilified as cradles of English and Protestant customs, as well as socialism and depravity. The 'anti-urban philosophy' of the post-Famine decades held, according to Mary Daly, that 'the city was essentially an alien institution'.[3] As such, the suffering evinced within the city during the period of the greatest social and demographic upheaval within modern Irish history could be seen as being less 'deserving', and less pertinent to nationalist teleologies, than the suffering of the 'true' Irish of the rural peripheries.

The most significant contributions to the history of Famine Dublin have been essay-length studies by Cormac Ó Gráda – namely, one chapter (on responses to the Famine in Dublin city) published in his *Black '47 and Beyond* (Princeton University Press, 1999) and two later essays (on mortality in the North Dublin Union and the trade in potatoes in 1840s Dublin) included in *Ireland's Great Famine* (UCD Press, 2006).[4] The historiographical gap has not been lessened by David Dickson's 2014 history of Dublin which, while illuminating the city's history through a masterful broad survey, devotes relatively little space to the Famine years.[5] More strikingly, a brief, yet useful, analysis by William Smyth constitutes the only dedicated consideration of Dublin city in the *Atlas of the Great Irish Famine*.[6] Short discussions of social conditions and relief measures are to be found in the work of Jacinta Prunty, Audrey Woods and Deirdre Lindsay,[7] but, aside from Ó Gráda's aforementioned work, few extended studies have been previously published by historians on relief measures in the city. The efforts of the Catholic archbishop of Dublin Daniel Murray in orchestrating relief measures not only in his own archdiocese but throughout Ireland – efforts which, in Liam Kennedy's opinion, 'surely border on the heroic and maybe even the saintly' – are also noted by Donal Kerr and Christine Kinealy.[8] Maria Luddy's important works on women and children in nineteenth-century Ireland and Dublin have frequently set Famine-era experiences in dialogue with a wider chronological scope, especially in the area of philanthropy.[9] Relatively little on Dublin's position as a political and cultural hub during the Famine has appeared, although a 2018 essay by Ciarán Reilly contrasted the Dublin Castle-based Relief Commission's role in public administration and crisis relief (1845–7) with the Castle's uninterrupted function as a site for pomp, ceremony and elite indulgence.[10] Turning to more popular books, we see that mention of the Great Famine is almost completely absent from Douglas Bennett's *Encyclopaedia of Dublin*, E. E. O'Donnell's *Annals of Dublin* and Tom Kennedy's edited volume on *Victorian Dublin*.[11]

However, more recently, historians of the Famine throughout Ireland have increasingly turned their attention away from the obvious focus on poverty, starvation, disease and mortality, and, instead, explored the ways in which, for many, everyday life in the 1840s went relatively undisturbed. Such research has demonstrated how continuities of social, cultural and economic life were not necessarily anomalous, but should be considered part of the spectrum of Famine-period experience.[12] Recent examples of this approach are Brian Griffin's study of sport during the Famine years and Ciarán Reilly's analysis of the Joly family of King's County (Offaly).[13] Reilly applies this approach in his contribution to the present volume, wherein his exploration of the social worlds of Elizabeth Smith and John Plunket Joly reveals his sample subjects' excursions to Famine-era Dublin for consumerist pursuits amidst the mass influx of impoverished rural migrants. In her recent monograph on animals and urbanity in nineteenth-century Dublin, Juliana Adelman diverts our attention to a previously-neglected avenue of research – namely, the evolving relationship between humans and animals in the city during the Famine years. The concerns of sanitary reformers in 1840s Dublin were shaped by, among other factors, social class and this is evident in the zealous focus on pig-keeping in the city and the parallel absence of concern over the keeping of horses and cattle.[14]

This collection of essays breaks new ground and reconsiders the Famine and its historiography by locating Dublin city and its inhabitants at the centre of its focus. A recurring theme that runs through this collection of essays, and which warrants a stand-alone study in its own right, is the migration of the rural poor into Dublin city and the impact of this influx on governmental administration, relief provision and everyday life in the city. Historically, towns and cities have been magnets for the rural poor at times of crisis, as urban centres offer increased opportunities for employment, relief or migration. During the Great Famine, while the island's population as a whole fell by up to 25 per cent, towns and cities throughout Ireland saw a surge in the number of their inhabitants.[15] Within Dublin, the influx was largely concentrated on the city's north side, due to the proximity of the port, the main access roads from the north and west, and the Bow Street night asylum, among other reasons. The rural poor settled in the slums, laneways and cellars; Dublin became, in Maurice Craig's well-known assessment, 'a gigantic refugee camp'.[16]

This volume of essays, containing work by established and emerging scholars, is novel in its opening up of new avenues of research into the history of the Great Famine in Dublin. The book opens with an invited contribution from Cormac Ó Gráda – whose pioneering work has been central to Famine studies – providing here a statistical and demographic overview of the crisis in the city, and reflections on these essays' contributions and the current state of scholarship in the field. The book's core chapters are then divided into four thematic sections. The continuation of business life in the city is examined both by Ciarán Reilly and Declan Curran, building on their respective earlier published work on everyday life and the Irish banking sector during the Famine.[17] Peter Hession's analysis of advances in seafaring technology places Dublin at the centre of an evolving 'political ecology', promoting integration and transformation throughout the Irish Sea. The city's charitable scene is the subject of three contributions. The vibrant and complex philanthropic landscape of mid-nineteenth-century Dublin is explored by Joe Curran, who usefully discusses that realm of voluntary social activism to contrast the Dublin instance of a city in decline with contemporary Edinburgh's confidence and strength. In his study of charitable societies in Famine Dublin, Ciarán McCabe discusses how the inflow of rural poor imposed additional burdens on welfare mechanisms: when the city's two workhouses were closed to new admissions, Dublin's new poor inevitably fell back on the city's charitable societies, whose finite resources were also stretched to capacity. The admirable efforts of the city's Quaker community are explored by Rob Goodbody, who argues that the success of Quaker initiatives, such as international fundraising and the running of localised relief projects, such as the Charles Street Soup Kitchen, rested on Friends' organisational skills and experience, and their networks of friends, family and co-religionists.

The sufferings of the poor in Dublin's wretched slums was an important context, Georgina Laragy convincingly argues, for the suicide of parochial visiting (relief) officer Patrick Bardin in the height of the notorious winter of 1846–7. However, Laragy's study of the tragic death of Bardin says much about the relationship between Famine suffering and trauma, suicide and social cohesion within urban communities. The poor – and specifically poor women – are the focus of Philomena Gorey's chapter on maternity and childbirth in mid-nineteenth-century Dublin. Gorey considers not only the experiences of expectant mothers within the city's working classes but also the administrative and clinical efficacy of Dublin's maternity hospitals, whereby state inquiry into charitable medical institutions exposed significant shortcomings and drove reform through the Dublin Hospitals Regulation Act, 1856 and the establishment of the Board of Superintendence of Dublin Hospitals.

Among the impacts of the influx of rural poor, many of whom failed to secure adequate housing or relief, was the upsurge in crime and public disorder. Ciarán Reilly's depiction of the world of commodities in Famine Dublin includes revelations on occurrences of bread rioting, in which 'country beggars' were believed to have been prominent. The fallout of this upsurge in crime was increased committals to prisons, such as Kilmainham Gaol and the newly-built Mountjoy Gaol, a phenomenon exacerbated, as McCabe reminds us, by the impact of the 1847 Vagrancy Act. However, the increase in committals brought about by that act was somewhat driven, Brian Crowley demonstrates in his chapter, by an increasing desire by central government to utilise the prisons for basic relief provision for the destitute, at a time when workhouses were overwhelmed. This situation was complicated by the criticism by the inspectors-general for prisons of this policy, as well as by the poor's conscious use of agency in endeavouring to be imprisoned for minor crimes for the very purpose of obtaining succour.

The relative neglect by scholars of Famine Dublin is also evident in twentieth- and twenty-first-century Famine literature, Chris Cusack argues. Yet, where the city does appear in modern fiction, it usually takes the form of the manifestation of urbanism and modernity in tension against the history and tradition so encapsulated in rural society. Cusack deploys the imagery and discourses of political economy to suggest that Famine memory unjustifiably neglects Famine suffering in the city. Kathryn Milligan also explores cultural representations, yet in the context of fine art exhibitions in late-1840s Dublin. The flourishing of 'exhibition ecosystems' in the city reflects the continued vibrancy of the exhibition of fine art, which emerged relatively unscathed from the Famine years having survived through commercial need and robust public demand. As such, Milligan's chapter complements Curran and Reilly's contributions in deepening our understanding of those Famine experiences defined not by cataclysmic upheaval but, instead, a relatively undisturbed continuation of 'the ordinary'. Finally, Emily Mark-FitzGerald's epilogue considers the visibilities of Famine memory in Dublin and its surrounds, suggesting how the palimpsestic nature of cities renders Famine residues in sometimes declarative, but often oblique, ways.

This volume represents the latest research on Famine-era Dublin by a selection of scholars, addressing a number of core themes. As with most edited collections, it is representative of current scholarship though not fully comprehensive in scope, and throughout, reference is made to topics that still require further exploration and that would reward the engaged scholar. More work is needed on the records of the North and South Dublin Union workhouses to investigate, where possible, the lived experiences of those who resorted to the Poor Law system for subsistence, building upon the important work already conducted by Cormac Ó Gráda and Timothy Guinnane. Georgina Laragy's contribution to this volume demonstrates the value that a single case study can hold out for broader research projects and reflects the need for a greater understanding of the impact of the Famine on public officials, those tasked with the allocation of resources to the most distressed. A greater understanding of the workings during these years of public institutions such as the Metropolitan Police and the Poor Law Commissioners, and their officials, would broaden the path marked out by Laragy. Dublin in the mid- to late-1840s was the scene of events of national importance, most notably, the funeral procession in August 1847 of Daniel O'Connell from the Metropolitan Church (Pro-Cathedral) on Marlborough Street to Glasnevin, which attracted crowds estimated to be in the hundreds of thousands, and the royal visit two years later of Queen Victoria. The role that Dublin played in the planning for the Young Ireland rebellion of 1848 has yet to be fully explored, as has the municipal crisis within Dublin Corporation that led to the creation of the independent Rathmines township in 1847. The Famine years saw the dissolution in 1851 of the Wide Streets Commission, under the 1849 Dublin Improvement Act, and much is still to be learned about the efforts of officialdom to 'improve' the city, its streetscape and the 'condition' of its inhabitants, especially, in an era of heightened concerns over public health. The death of the Catholic archbishop of Dublin, Daniel Murray, in 1852 saw the transfer of Paul Cullen from the Armagh see to that of Dublin, ushering in an era of Catholic revival: the impact on Catholic-Protestant relations within the city caused by the death of the affable and ecumenical Murray and his succession by the Tridentine Cullen would constitute a fruitful field of research, deepening our understanding of post-Famine Dublin.

Studies of the Great Famine have arguably constituted some of the richest and most extensive scholarship of nineteenth-century Ireland in recent decades: the publication of the monumental *Atlas of the Great Irish Famine* (Cork University Press, 2012) and its popular dissemination in 2020 via an RTÉ television documentary ('The Hunger', Tyrone Productions) and related online resources[18] are but one bellwether of continued scholarly and public attention. And yet neither this historiography, nor the present volume, are definitive. This book's essays make an important contribution towards redressing our understanding of Dublin's people, buildings and landscape, economies, politics, institutions and cultural legacies during this critical period of history. Most emphatically, we hope its interdisciplinary focus, diverse primary sources, and expansive approaches will inspire future work on Dublin and the Great Famine.

EDITORIAL NOTE

Throughout this volume, 'famine' refers to food scarcities in a general sense, while 'Famine' is used when referring to the Great Irish Famine (1845–*c*.52).

Dublin and the Great Famine: An Overview

CORMAC Ó GRÁDA

During the Great Famine, public policy relied for the most part on market forces to direct food from where prices were relatively low to where they were relatively high. Forms of market intervention practiced as recently as 1799–1800[1] in Ireland — bans on distilling, bounties for boats bringing food to markets, reduced rations for army horses, reduced tolls on shipments by canal, officially sanctioned moral suasion — were no longer acceptable in Whitehall. However, in the 1840s unfettered markets were neither a panacea for famine, as followers of Adam Smith predicted, nor the main cause of suffering, as their critics alleged. During the Great Famine Irish towns and cities suffered, but they were spared its worst horrors, partly because they were more commercialised and partly because even their poorest citizens relied less on the potato than the rural masses. Yet, one should not over-generalise. Based on data on population change between 1841 and 1851 and on workhouse populations on census day in 1851, the impact of the Famine on Irish cities ranged from rather mild in Belfast and Derry to severe in Waterford, Kilkenny, Galway, Limerick, and Cork, with Dublin placed in-between (see Table 1). That said, another perspective on the Famine in Dublin is David Dickson's informed guess that mortality in the city in 1847 may have been less than in 1817.[2]

As the three papers in Part 2 of this innovative contribution to the history of the Famine make plain, Dublin city already had a strong philanthropic infrastructure when the potato failed. The city's almanacs listed well over a hundred charities on the eve of the Famine.[3] That is after excluding proselytising societies, and the lists are by no means exhaustive. While Dublin's charitable institutions had been founded mainly to help its permanent residents, the Famine occasioned a considerable inflow of rural dwellers seeking charity and employment. Many of the bodies mentioned worked hard at helping these unfortunates too. The role of the Society of Friends, already well known, is further explored by Rob Goodbody in his essay; to this may be added the part played by the likes of the Carmelite friar John Spratt, who laboured tirelessly for the south city poor during the Famine.[4]

Table 1. Irish City Populations 1841–51

City	**Population** 1841	**Population 1851**	**Increase (%) 1841–1851**	**Workhouse population 1851**
Dublin	232,726	246,679	6.0	5,484
Belfast	75,308	97,784	29.8	1,815
Cork	80,728	82,625	2.3	1,631
Limerick	48,391	48,785	0.8	2,048
Galway	17,275	20,055	16.1	2,789
Waterford	23,216	22,979	-1.0	1,420
Derry	15,196	19,727	29.8	0[5]
Kilkenny	19,071	15,257	-20.0	4,165

Source: W. E. Vaughan and A. J. Fitzpatrick (eds), *Irish Historical Statistics: Population 1821–1971* (Dublin, 1978); *The Census of Ireland for the Year 1851. Part VI. General Report,* H.C. 1856 [Cd 2134], xxxi.

The growth in the population of Dublin city from 232,726 in 1841 to 246,679 in 1851 was the by-product of increasing destitution outside it, not rising affluence inside it. The number of Dubliners born elsewhere in Ireland rose by three-fifths, from 56,397 to 90,350, so that by 1851, that group accounted for more than one-third of the population, up from less than a quarter ten years earlier. The migration into Dublin from elsewhere in Ireland was heavily female, yet the female proportion of the population fell from 55.0 to 53.9 per cent.

During the Famine, there was a perception that Dublin was like 'a gigantic refugee camp'[6] and, indeed, the Famine's first casualties in the city were rural immigrants from the west.[7] But the scale of permanent internal migration within Ireland was too limited to matter much, and not of the kind that would have made much difference to conditions in the worst-affected areas.[8] Most of the permanent migration into Dublin during the 1840s was from elsewhere in Leinster, not from the worst-hit counties of the west and the south: most emigrants from the west who arrived in the city had Liverpool as their destination, and so they were refugees en route to somewhere else. Data on county-to-county flows are lacking but county-of-birth data in the 1841 and 1851 census provide an indication of the size of inter-county flows. Table 2 proxies the inflows from two counties on Dublin's doorstep, Meath and Kildare, on the one hand, and two counties worst hit by the potato failure, Mayo and Clare, on the other. The important take-away is that relatively few of the famine victims of Mayo and Clare found asylum in the city; urban Ireland offered no safety valve for the famine refugees of the 1840s. Table 3 helps explain why Dublin was not fit for this purpose: the city already contained a significant underclass living in housing not much better than that available in Clare or Mayo. Whereas the Famine caused the number of households living in fourth-class (i.e. single-room) accommodation to plummet in Mayo and Clare, it rose marginally in Dublin. And Dublin at this time, after all, was said to be the 'worst sewered, lighted, cleaned and watered city in the empire'.[9]

Table 2. Migration into Dublin 1841–1851

	1841		1851		Difference (%)	
Where born	**M**	**F**	**M**	**F**	**M**	**F**
Elsewhere in Ireland	27,409	28,988	41,315	49,035	50.7	69.2
Adjoining counties	8,795	10,165	13,545	18,462	54.0	81.6
Other counties in same province	8,633	9,591	13,009	15,907	50.7	65.9
In other provinces	9,981	9,282	14,661	14,666	46.9	58.0
Mayo	351	315	540	508	53.8	61.3
Clare	375	282	610	544	62.7	92.9
Meath	3,137	3,450	4,240	5,581	35.2	61.8
Kildare	2,626	2,926	3,849	5,190	46.6	77.4

Table 3. Percentages of households in Dublin City and Mayo living in third- and fourth-class accommodation in 1841 and 1851

Dublin	**3rd class**	**4th class**
1841	24.8	46.9
1851	25.0	48.9
Mayo		
1841	33.0	61.3
1851	61.3	27.0
Clare		
1841	31.7	56.0
1851	56.1	16.4

Source: *Report of the Commissioners Appointed to Take the Census of Ireland, for the Year 1841*, pp 21, 163, 403, H.C. 1843 [Cd 504], xxiv, 133, 275, 515; *1851 Census, Part V. General Report*, pp xxxi, 25, 218, 574.

Most impoverished refugees from the worst-hit areas of rural Ireland were accordingly determined not to stay in Dublin but to seek relief further afield. The number of Irish-born living in Great Britain rose from 415,000 in 1841 to 727,000 in 1851; the vast majority of these settled in Britain's industrialising cities and towns. The increase in Liverpool's Irish-born population between 1841 and 1851 almost matched the influx into Dublin. Indeed, in England, Merseyside was the main destination for those fleeing the Famine, resulting in significant increases in the region's deprivation and excess mortality figures.[10] Some summary details are given in Table 4. Importantly too, however, many of those who made it to Liverpool were intent on travelling further, Liverpool being the main port of embarkation for those crossing the broad Atlantic.

Table 4. Famine migration into Dublin and four British cities

Year	1841	**1851**
Born elsewhere in Ireland (% of total city population)		
Dublin	56,397 (24.2)	90,350 (35.0)
Born in Ireland (% of total city population)		
Liverpool	49,639 (17.3)	83,813 (22.3)
Glasgow	44,345 (16.1)	59,801 (18.1)
Manchester/Salford	33,490 (11.1)	52,504 (13.1)
London	73,133 (3.9)	108,548 (4.6)

Source: Neal, *Black '47*, p. 9; *1841 Census*, pp 18, 447; *1851 Census, Part V, General Report*, pp 742–4.

The Famine is etched in the records of two famous Dublin institutions: Kilmainham Gaol on the city's western edge and, to a lesser extent, the Rotunda Lying-In Hospital on Parnell (then Rutland) Square. The huge increase in the number of admissions into Kilmainham in the late 1840s — from an annual average of 1,750 on the eve of the Famine to 6,888 in 1848 and 9,034 in 1849 — was in part a reflection of an increase in (mostly petty) criminality, but mainly of a huge increase in the numbers committed for vagrancy (over two-thirds of those committed in 1851). The latter increase sprung mainly from the Vagrancy Act of 1847 which, as Brian Crowley states in his essay, 'effectively saw the criminalisation of poverty'.[11] Whether this transformation in the prison population's intake also influenced its physical stature is a question prompted by a recent anthropometric study of Kilmainham prisoners by Mathias Blum, Chris Colvin and Eoin McLaughlin.[12] They reckon that Kilmainham inmates born in Dublin during the Famine period (defined rather liberally as 1844–53) were nearly 0.3cm shorter in adulthood than those born before it (1834–43). One might attribute that to the impact of the Famine on their health in the long run, were it not for the fact that those born in the following decade (1854–63) were shorter still, by a further 0.7cm. Whether these somewhat puzzling outcomes reflect the adverse shock of the Famine on adult height or a radical shift in the composition of the prisoners' profile remains a moot point.

In the Rotunda, which catered for poor women from the city's north side, the number of births dipped, while both the number of newly-born infants and of mothers who died rose. As described in Phil Gorey's contribution to this volume, the causes given for 227 premature births between 1845 and 1853, with another 265 unexplained, highlight not so much the impact of the Famine as the plight of Dublin's poor throughout this period. Before the sanitary reforms introduced by Master Arthur Macan (1882–9) the Rotunda was a very unsafe place to be born in and, particularly, to give birth in. Puerperal peritonitis was an abiding issue and must have deterred many poor women from giving birth there. In March 1845, nine patients died of it and the wards were closed to new patients for a fortnight. Further deaths from puerperal peritonitis in the spring of 1847 were, strictly speaking, not Famine deaths, although perhaps some deaths from fever may have been misdiagnosed as such. Puerperal peritonitis was the product, not of hunger, but of poor hygiene on the part of hospital staff. It was much less likely to attack mothers giving births in their own tenement homes.[13]

An increase in suicides is one of the hallmarks of famine and their number almost certainly rose in Ireland during the late 1840s, though they are underreported in the censuses and all but erased from memory. The rise in the number of reported suicides in Dublin city and county from 77 in 1831–41 to 94 in 1841–51 (compared to an increase from 792 to 869 in the country as a whole) is most likely an underestimate. We have it on William Wilde's authority that there was a 'manifest increase' in the number of suicides from 1846 on, although the numbers in his famous Tables of Death in the 1851 census, when compared to those reported in 1841, lend him less than emphatic support. Interestingly, in Dublin county as a whole the reported male share of all suicides rose from 67 per cent in the 1830s to 78 per cent in the 1840s, with the metropolis in both decades accounting for about one-tenth of the total. Given the problematic nature of the data, in her contribution to this volume Georgina Laragy chooses to focus instead on a highly evocative case study – that of a water bailiff who took his own life during the first winter of the Famine. She invokes the well-documented tragedy of a decent man, one Patrick Bardin, to raise broader questions about the psychic impact of the impending crisis on the city's population.

Other chapters probe the impact of the Famine on the capital more obliquely, through the prisms of its shops, its banks, its art galleries, its fishing grounds, and its access to the open sea. Kathryn Milligan shows that neither the demand for fine art exhibitions nor their content were, it would seem, affected by the Famine: for the comfortably-off attracted by them, they offered an aesthetic distraction, if such was needed, from the cataclysm close at hand. Nor, as Ciarán Reilly documents in his contribution, did the Famine affect the frequent shopping expeditions to the capital of people such as Elizabeth Smith, wife of a Wicklow landlord, and John Plunkett Joly, the father of the budding polymath and scientist in King's County (Offaly).

Finally, although the treatment of the Famine in literary fiction has been receiving a good deal of attention in recent decades[14], Dublin features little in what Christopher Cusack calls 'the Famine imaginary'. As he explains, that should not surprise us. Cusack's contribution focuses on the impact of the Famine on the capital as represented in three very different works of literary fiction. None, tellingly perhaps, offers a convincing account of what it must have been like to be poor in Dublin in 1847. In the best-known of the three, Colum McCann's *TransAtlantic* (2013), the US anti-slavery campaigner Frederick Douglass confronts the Famine on a visit to Dublin. This forces McCann to stretch the historical record, since in reality Douglass had left the city before the Famine began to bite and, far from being traumatised by its horrors, described his days in Ireland as 'some of the happiest moments of my life'.[15] Stephens's story, published under the alias James Esse in 1918, has been described as 'an unvarnished tale of a poor Dublin family that withers slowly of starvation because the husband cannot find work or the wife beg relief'.[16] Like the others, it squares poorly with how the Famine is generally remembered, but that is because as Cusack aptly notes, 'The streets of Dublin may be haunted by poverty but they are no Famine roads'.[17]

This ambitious monograph is the first to deal exclusively with the Great Famine in Dublin. It straddles several disciplines and touches on many topics. Naturally, it leaves some bases uncovered. While the contributions of Joe Curran, Ciarán McCabe, and Rob Goodbody in Section II greatly add to our understanding of the role of private charity, more remains to be said about the role of public charity, particularly through the poor law and its workhouses. Most of the Famine-era admission and discharge registers of the North Dublin and South Dublin unions, which serving the city north and south of the Liffey, respectively, survive. They have not yet been subjected to much formal, systematic analysis.[18] The same holds for Dublin's Famine-era Catholic and Church of Ireland parish registers, most of which also survive. The former contain information on baptisms and marriages, though not (with one exception) burials, whereas the latter also include burials.[19]

Another topic worth scrutiny – and here the workhouse registers and parish records should be very useful – is the geography of the Famine across the capital. Why, for instance, did the reported causes of death in the two Dublin unions differ so much? 'Marasmus' (a proxy for severe malnutrition) was responsible for 7.4 per cent of all deaths during the 1840s in North Dublin Union but only 3.3 per cent in the South Dublin Union, whereas cholera accounted for 9.6 and 2.1 per cent of the total, respectively, and diarrhoea/dysentery for 14.3 and 21.5, per cent. Did these striking and puzzling differences reflect different workhouse regimes, different ways of describing the causes of death, or differences in the health of inmates on admission? In principle, analysis of the registers can shed light on such questions.[20] They also can tell us more about the disproportionate impact of the Famine on migrants. For example, between January and April 1847, when migrants were pouring into the city, 55 per cent of the deaths of those aged ten or more in the North Dublin Union were of non-Dubliners.[21]

In this volume, several contributions offer insights into how the Famine impacted on economic activity in the city. This is reflected in Declan Curran's analysis of banking activity and Ciarán Reilly's and Peter Hession's insights on foreign trade. The issue calls for further research, however. Is it not time to revisit claims such as that Arthur Guinness & Co. escaped the Famine virtually unscathed, and that savings banks saw their deposits rise? The scale, location, and timing of protest and food rioting in the city during the Famine is another inviting topic. Finally, the role of municipal politics during the cataclysm would repay further scrutiny.[22] Volumes like this one always whet the appetite for more.[23]

SECTION I: BUSINESS LIFE AND INDUSTRY

'A Little London, All Alive': Some Experiences of the World of Goods and Commodities in Famine Dublin

CIARÁN REILLY

> 'How does dear old Dublin look after our absence – beautiful – less misery in it than I ever saw before, its splendid street thronged with busy crowds, walking, driving, moving as if alive, shops swarming like beehives, women dressed, I was going to say better than French women, but as well certainly, the same good taste in shape and colour and material, and their straw bonnets and their ribbons superior. After the vulgar shewy [sic] taste of the English, the Irish women do look so nice'.[1]

In the summer of 1845, Elizabeth Smith returned to Ireland after a two-year absence and as outlined above she found Dublin bustling with commercial activity. Just over a month later, the first signs of potato blight were reported in Ireland. However, for Smith and her family Dublin continued to provide a world of goods and commodities throughout the Great Famine although it was not unaffected by the ongoing social and economic crisis. Shopping expeditions to Dublin were easily made in a six-hour round trip to their home at Baltyboys, near Blessington in county Wicklow but the family often stayed in the city for a number of days at a time, 'taking rooms' in hotels including Gresham's and Elvidge's. From there the family explored a multitude of shops and business premises where they purchased books, toys, clothes, household items, food and 'sugar plums' for the children.[2] Their return to Wicklow following shopping expeditions generated considerable interest from their neighbours and friends who enquired of the latest fashion and news in Dublin. Describing one such occasion when neighbours visited to view 'the Dublin purchases', Smith remarked:

> the Miss Henry's who were most particular in their enquiries as to what I had purchased in Dublin, for myself, for the children, for the house. I offered to show everything from the new inkstand in the drawing-room and the oilcloth on the back stairs to the children's frocks which were up in my wardrobe, so we began our march, first to the patchwork room and then to my room where not only the new purchases were examined but all my shelves full of fine linen, collars, canzons, tuckers etc. and then all the needlework's etc.[3]

Smith's diaries offer an intimate portrait of life in Ireland during the Great Famine and also for the purposes of this study, the commercial fortunes of Dublin. Her experiences mirror those of the young Trinity College student John Plunket Joly, who likewise enjoyed the vibrant commercial world of Dublin at this time. In July 1847, having disputed for his MA degree at the college, Joly celebrated with a shopping trip in Dublin where he purchased amongst other items a four-key concert flute and a number of books.[4] The son of a Church of Ireland rector in King's County (now Offaly) and later archdeacon of Killala, Joly's personal diaries depict a world of plenty amid the ongoing Famine. During his visits to Dublin, often accompanied by family and friends, Joly frequented a number of the city's leading shops including Andrews, Bewleys, Cranefields, Piggots and Pims where his purchases were similar to the Smiths. The family also regularly attended Dublin markets, bringing 'fat cattle' and wool for sale where they could enjoy better prices than at markets in Kildare and King's County. Like the Smiths, Dublin was also a centre of entertainment for the Jolys, which included visits to the Hibernian Academy, the Queen's Theatre and the Royal Dublin Society.[5]

Neither the Smiths nor the Jolys were totally ignorant of the plight of the poor and what would have been evident to them was that Dublin of the mid-1840s was also the 'worst sewered, lighted, cleaned and watered city in the empire'.[6] It resembled, as Maurice Craig has suggested, 'a gigantic refugee camp' as thousands poured into the city from all across Ireland.[7] Indeed, such was the influx of Famine stricken paupers from the west of Ireland in particular that towns on the approach organised patrols to prevent them from entering, preferring instead to send them onwards to Dublin.[8] Likewise, as Frank Cullen suggests in his study of Dublin in 1847, the city was slowly grinding to a halt and its development idled during this period.[9] However, despite the shock to the social and economic make-up of Dublin, nowhere were the polarities between rich and poor in Famine Ireland more evident. While it may be argued that both the Jolys and the Smiths inhabited a world far removed from poverty, their purchases suggest that a thriving business community was present in the city during the Famine, as millions starved elsewhere in Ireland.

Food exports have long dominated the Famine narrative, but what about goods and commodities that remained in the country or were imported during this time? Who was buying what? While the issue is deserving of a much broader study, beyond the remit of this chapter, it is certain that as ships carrying foodstuffs from across the country were exported they met ships ladened with luxuriant goods on the way in. This chapter examines the world of goods and commodities in Dublin during the Famine, principally through the eyes of two frequent visitors to the city, Elizabeth Smith and John Plunket Joly. The experience of Smith and Joly offer a contrasting vista on life in Dublin to the poverty described by McCabe, Curran and others elsewhere in this volume. To do so, this study has examined a number of sources including personal diaries, trade directories, trade labels and newspaper advertisements.[10] In particular, newspaper advertisements offer a unique insight into the consumption of goods in Famine Dublin, although the authenticity of the claims made in them is open for debate. Moreover, these sources reveal the vast trade networks that were established prior to the onset of Famine and upon which Dublin merchants depended. Indeed, the global humanitarian response to the Irish Famine may well have benefited from the existence of these trade networks.[11]

The foundation for many of these networks had been laid in the previous two decades and by the late 1830s, as Samuel Lewis noted, the diverse international trade that Dublin merchants enjoyed included Russia, Holland, France, Spain and Portugal.[12] There was also trade with the West Indies centred on Jamaica, British Guiana and Trinidad. Trade networks existed too with central Europe, although the circuitous route that goods took often added to their cost. There were also Dublin merchants trading directly with China, primarily in tea, brought back to Ireland via Liverpool. Trade with the US, according to Lewis, had diminished during the decade prior to the Famine; and, as one Dublin newspaper commented, few ships from the US had landed in the city in the previous two decades.[13] Trade extended to several African countries also, indeed in the same month as the potato blight first appeared Elizabeth Smith remarked that she had been recommended 'a newly imported African grain as a breakfast'.[14]

As Peter Hession points out elsewhere in this volume the total quantity of foreign and colonial imports to Ireland increased almost tenfold from 26,345 to 269,134 tons during the Famine, most of which entered the port of Dublin.[15] The sheer quantity of goods arriving in Dublin during 1846, as the second potato crop failed, contradicted the fact that Ireland was starving, although some of this trade was undoubtedly for relief purposes. Between 1 July to 3 November 1846 the following was imported from the port of Liverpool: 18,587 quarters of wheat; 363 quarters of barley; 50,545 quarters of Indian corn, 79,148 barrels of flour and 3,901 sacks of flour. Indeed, the figure would have been greater only that more vessels could not be found to transport goods to Dublin.[16] In the same period more than a dozen ships bringing sugar from South America, Trinidad, Barbadoes and St Lucia arrived in Dublin.[17] In December 3,000 tons of breadstuffs from New Orleans, Trieste, New York and Hamburg arrived. When landing in Cork in the same month, a Captain Taylour of the ship, *Manchester*, stated that he had left behind in New York 73 ships ladened with goods for Ireland.[18] And as 'Black '47' commenced the ships kept arriving. In January 1847 the following ships and goods arrived in Dublin: *Anne*, 400 quarters of Indian corn; *Nimrod*, 500 quarters of wheat; *Camille*, 980 hectolitres of Indian corn; *Edward*, 1,925 quarters of barley; *Alphonselle Estelle*, 550 quarters of buck wheat; *Catherine*, 16,000 quarters of barley; *Statira*, 99 tons of potatoes; *Sophia*, 240 quarters of Indian corn; and the *Speed*, 1,144 barrels of flour.[19] Dublin markets also received other American produce including bacon, with shops such as Michael Smith's in Copper Alley describing themselves as 'a specialist in American (family) provisions' providing novel 'fresh American pork'.[20]

However, during the early months of the Famine there was considerable panic and alarm in Dublin which greatly affected trade.[21] Several stockbrokers it was claimed were 'ruined' following the crash in railway stock, while a number of merchants who had been encouraged to take part in the scheme were also badly affected. According to Elizabeth Smith:

> people were much frightened and this caused a run on the Savings Banks ... the very poorest looking people drawing out their forty's, fifty's, hundreds. The crowds were so immense and so excited that horse and foot police were necessary to guard their lives.[22]

There was also considerable animosity towards those involved in the sale of coal in the city. In November 1846 it was claimed that the provisions trade in Dublin was 'full of animation, and the prices keep up steadily'.[23] The following month there were claims of forestalling and tampering with the markets in an effort to drive the prices up. A 'most wicked combination', it was claimed, between the ship-owners and 'coal factors' prevented ships from entering the city, to keep the prices up. This constituted 'such unprincipled villainy' wrote Smith, who lamented that 'tis the poor that suffer – the rich fill their cellars in summer'.[24] Undoubtedly, there were others who made the most of the times and were happy when there were shortages, provided that they had ample stocks. Here they could charge so-called 'famine prices'. According to the *Freeman's Journal*, only in Dublin were sellers able to keep 'famine price'.[25] Butchers in Dublin were singled out for this behaviour and it was claimed that they were making a 'small fortune' as beef stocks were in short supply.[26] Likewise, prices in Dublin fishmongers regularly increased during Lent, when demand was always greatest.

While these problems obviously curtailed business and trade in Dublin during the early stages of the Famine, they alone were not enough to stop it. Despite the best efforts of Fr Theobald Mathew and the Temperance movement the production, sale and consumption of alcohol continued unabated during this period. Brewing and distilling were the leading industries in the city and provided widespread employment. These included Jameson's in Bow Street and Marrowbone Lane, Power's in John's Lane West and Roe's in Bonham Street which were foremost in productivity, supplying a number of Dublin merchants with their products. This included J. R. Andrew & Company who also imported cider, champagne and wines from across Europe and stocked Irish ales including those brewed in Drogheda and Castlebellingham in county Louth.[27] Robert MacDona advertised 'affordable' sherry 'even for family use' from his premises in Dawson Street, while in Upper Jervis Street, John Gilbert supplied the city and environs with 'Devonshire Cider'.[28] Elsewhere, Dublin spirit and wine merchants such as Kinihan & Smyth of the Carlisle buildings; Francis Faulkner on Grafton Street and John McGauran on Westland Row made significant gains from legislative changes in respect of the importation of rum in 1847.[29] There were a number of importers of wine including the 'well known Conolly Brand' on Camden Street who also boasted marsala and claret wines from Italy and France. Indeed, enjoying a picnic at Luggala in county Wicklow in the summer of 1846 Elizabeth Smith noted that they brought with them wine from Constantia in the Cape of Good Hope (South Africa) which they 'cooled in the lake' before drinking.[30] Dublin brewers, distillers and wholesalers were actively engaged in supplying the demands of provincial Ireland and the continued improvement in rail and canal transport greatly benefited them. Indeed, on the eve of the Famine it was estimated that about 2,500 tons of porter were brought from Dublin to the town of Ballinasloe, county Galway each year.[31]

After the production and sale of alcohol, tea and coffee were perhaps the most popular commodities sold and consumed in Dublin. John Cassells was amongst the largest distributor of tea and coffee throughout the country with a regional network of shops and distributors almost nationwide. For other merchants and individuals, Bewleys had a long established 'tasting shop' where customers could sample 'the finest teas from Canton and Congo' amongst other places. Bewley's imports continued during the Famine, and one sale in March 1846 included over 800 casks of 'middling and fine' tea.[32] Likewise, George Marks offered a variety of teas from the Far East, Barbados and St Lucia. Other tea importers in the city included Wilson and Hardy, while 'The Tea Establishment' on Dame Street specialised in black tea, gunpowder tea, green tea, coffee and sugars from all over the world. It was these shops that the Smiths frequented when they visited Dublin, as they wished to acquire tea and coffee from far-flung destinations. Although gifted a new 'coffee maker' in 1842, Smith preferred to brew 'with the help of a bit of muslin as they do in the West Indies'.[33] Newspaper accounts of the arrival of goods suggest that the Custom House docks heaved with produce and people at this time as auctions were held onsite. Many of these auctions were held next to the ship's cranes as goods were being offloaded; 'Reilly's crane' was one that was noted for its cocoa sales.[34] Those like the aforementioned Bewley preferred to auction tea at the docks such as in November 1846 when more than 580 chests of tea, which had been damaged on the ship *Sarah* coming from Canton, were sold. On the same day over 1,400 chests from the same region, but described as being 'of the best quality', were also sold.[35] The docks were also used for auctioning other goods such as sugar, coffee and fruit before they were dispersed throughout the country. And there was a considerable trade in timber at Dublin docks. In May 1846 Jaffray Barcroft oversaw the auction of 100 tons of 'Rio' rosewood, 200,000 feet of mahogany from Honduras, St Domingo and Cuba, and another 100,000 feet of various timber.[36]

As the Famine crisis deepened across the country, Dublin shops and merchants continued to provide goods and commodities for those of means. The number of clothing establishments in the city was further evidence of this. These included Moses & Company of Dame Street who advertised that they had over 40 different varieties of coats in its shop, while Williams' shop on Lower Bridge Street could boast more than 25,000 yards of cloths and tweeds. Likewise, the 'Foreign and British Shawl Emporium' had over 3,000 scarfs and 'productions of the most distinguished French artists', while the 'Dublin Woollen Warehouse' on College Green had cloths, summer coatings, scotch tweeds, doeskins, vestings and liveries. Other garments for sale in the city included those made in the 'Hibernia Woollen Mills' in Kilmainham. Clothing remained a lucrative trade and some new businesses opened during the Famine. Richard Allen commenced a new business in 1849, as did Bulphin and Company, while P. Rogers returned from Germany, Paris and Lyon with the latest fashions which included 'ready-made' garments intended for the 'country gentleman visiting Dublin'. The evidence suggests that there were regular customers for such products. Richard Allen's 'West of England Woollen Hall' on High Street employed a number of 'first rate workmen' who were 'always on call so as the customers could be fitted without delay'.[37] For ladies, Mrs Sidford's millinery and dress rooms on Nassau Street stocked new bonnets of all kinds with French ribbons and mourning clothes for widows.[38] With such choice on offer it was little wonder that Elizabeth Smith commented that she was 'fagged to death' by 'the busy shopping'.[39]

Everything it seems could be found in Famine-era Dublin and there was much to attract people to the city. Isaac English on Bachelors Walk advertised the sale of figs, almonds, currants and other 'French fruit' and Portuguese oranges,[40] while George Kertland's shop on Lower Sackville Street was popular for perfumery and eau de cologne.[41] The aptly named 'Noah's Ark' on Bachelors Walk was a shop that included exotic songbirds, dogs and rabbits and in general 'a bit of everything'.[42] As alternative methods of agriculture were promoted and the government-backed Land Improvement Scheme commenced in 1849, Dublin merchants began to stock a host of drainage implements, tools and seeds. These included Joseph Berry on 8 Arran Quay who sold garden and agricultural seeds including peas, beans and potatoes. Berry sourced much of his produce from Holland and was a supplier to many land agents across the country. Saunders and Gatchells on Mountrath Street were another who supplied agricultural needs.

A number of Dublin shops and merchants relied on the 'Castle season', when the Lord Lieutenant threw open the doors of Dublin Castle for the gentry and upper classes. When George William Frederick Villiers, fourth earl of Clarendon, took the office of Lord Lieutenant in 1847 his wife Lady Katherine insisted solely on Irish dress for such occasions. Encouraging others to do likewise, in 1849 she ordered a 'superb train … composed of the richest crimson Irish poplin, interwoven in colours of gold', designed by a Mr Reynolds of

Grafton Street, which was said to have been of a 'most costly and gorgeous description'.[43] The visit of Queen Victoria in 1849 additionally provided a huge boost to the shops and businesses of Dublin, none more so than in the purchase of candles as people prepared to illuminate their homes as a mark of respect for the monarch. George Dixon's at Upper Erne Street was amongst the most popular in this respect, while for others taking part in the illuminations, James Kerr & Son on Capel Street and Anglesea Row offered the finest oil lamps for the occasion.[44] However, Elizabeth Smith was not enamoured by the quality of Kerr's products, complaining the following month that 'Mr. Kerr palavered the Colonel into buying a lamp which don't seem to burn well – not bright enough for a room at any rate…'.[45]

This bustling trade meant that people visiting Dublin had to be accommodated and city hotels catered for a variety of needs. The 'Wicklow Hotel' on Wicklow Street offered a 'place of amusement' with the finest cuisine in the city; Fegan's 'Commercial Hotel' on High Street offered a breakfast with steak or a chop and snacks throughout the day, while 'The Prince Of Wales Hotel' beside the GPO offered the 'cheapest' rooms in Dublin. 'The Londonderry Hotel' on Bolton Street catered for 'families of respectability', while most offered collection from the train station or the docks as part of the overall fee. In 1849 Walsh's 'Southern Hotel' on South Anne Street decided to get rid of this service as a means of reducing prices in their hotel. The Burke's, John and Martin, with the 'Cashel Hotel' and 'Shelbourne Hotel' respectively, had been established since at least the mid-1820s, with the 'Shelbourne' declaring that it was the 'largest, best situated, and will be found the cheapest' in Dublin.[46] The Famine did not deter others from commencing business: the 'Royal Arcade Hotel', belonging to Henry Anderson, opened in 1849, while others were extensively remodelled.[47] Not everyone, however, was enamoured by Dublin hotels: Elizabeth Smith complained regularly of the exorbitant prices which they were charged, while in others she found it difficult to sleep.[48] The city also offered a host of restaurants where visitors and residents could dine. Shelly's 'Ship Tavern' advertised that they served the best oysters and 'every delicacy of the season' where Edward Jones, a Welsh piper, performed every evening for guests. The 'Dublin Hotel and Tavern', operated by Michael Johnson, on Marlborough Street offered 'hot joints, with soup for 1*s*. per head', punch 4*d*. per tumbler and malt whiskey of all descriptions.[49]

These restaurants, hotels and others offering lodgings thrived on the variety of entertainment that Dublin organised during the Famine years. Events ranged from exhibitions about African Bosjesmans, or 'bush people', at the Rotunda;[50] to Italian opera in the Theatre Royal,[51] to the concerts performed by the celebrated British performer T. P. Cooke.[52] Crowds flocked to events such as Franconi's Circus in Portobello Gardens where they were enthralled with the 'grace and daring' of a Mr Bell, while Gallaher, a ventriloquist, performed in a number of Dublin venues including the Concert Room in Kingstown (Dun Laoighaire).[53] In the year preceding 1849, almost 65,000 people were recorded as visiting the Royal Zoological Gardens in the Phoenix Park.[54] Mindful of what was occurring both in Dublin and throughout the country a number of performances were given in aid of the poor of the city. In January 1847, for example, a performance of *William Tell* in the Theatre Royal was held for such purposes.[55] Crowds converged on Dublin for other purposes. Elsewhere in this volume, Kathryn Milligan discusses the continued popularity of art exhibitions, including the buying and selling of art, in Famine-era Dublin.[56] Efforts to promote Irish manufacturing included a well-attended exhibition in the RDS in June 1847. Speaking at the prize-giving ceremony Richard Griffith commented on the 'signal success which has attended the late exhibition ... undertaken at a period of unexampled depression and distress, arising from the failure of the potato crop'.[57] It would prove to be the forerunner for a number of successful exhibitions, including Dublin's Great Industrial Exhibition of 1853.

Of course, Dublin merchants did not confine themselves to trade in the city alone and by the middle of the 1840s they controlled much of the flow of produce through provincial Ireland, particularly in the large towns of east Leinster and the midlands. The transport networks operating to and from Dublin, discussed by Peter Hession elsewhere in this volume, were central to this development. On the Grand and Royal canals passage boats fought for space with the barges carrying goods to and from Dublin, which included tobacco, tea, coffee, alcohol and clothing. It was little wonder that towns such as Tullamore in King's County could boast a number of shops that sold the latest 'Parisian fashions'.[58] Indeed, such was the flow of produce that merchants including the Malone brothers of Stephen Street and Christchurch offered free conveyance on water or railway for customers.[59] Elsewhere, the City of Dublin Steam Packet Company which operated from Eden Quay offered the conveyance of merchandise between Dublin and Limerick, carrying goods in under two days. Travelling at night-time they were said to have had the 'greatest despatch and regularity'. Indeed, night-time passage boats were favoured by the Smiths and Jolys travelling to and from Dublin. The Smiths sent servants during the night in order to get the freshest produce and return again in time for the following evening's dinner.

While both the Smiths and the Jolys were a world removed from the poverty that the Great Famine brought, details of their shopping expeditions reveal important aspects about the make-up of Famine-era Dublin. Prior to his trip to Belgium in July 1846 to research his family history, John Plunket Joly spent time traversing Dublin shops and indulged himself by purchasing items that were on display. He also had his portrait (a daguerreotype) taken at Nelson's on Grafton Street, which cost 8*s*. 6*d*.[60] In November, in the same week as his father met with the Catholic priest in Clonbullogue in King's County to help alleviate the plight of the poor, Joly made another trip to Dublin on the night boat arriving at 3.50 am. During his stay, he visited a number of shops, purchasing paint, books, plants and musical instruments.[61] The Jolys were avid collectors of books, thus it was little wonder that when his brother, Jasper Robert, donated over 23,000 volumes in the 1870s, it was the largest collection ever deposited in the National Library.[62] Their Famine time purchases included books such as *The Gardener's Almanack*, *The Vicar of Wakefield*, three volumes of the *Library of Wilful Knowledge on Vegetable Substances*, *Outlines of History* by Lardner, and Smillis's *Philosophy of Natural History.* In January 1848, after the death of his mother, Joly and his brother visited Dublin where once more their purchases were made in J. H. Powell's on Westmoreland Street and in Heron & Co on Sackville Street. This discretionary spending also included a brooch for his sister, Mary, made from black oak.[63] The experience of Elizabeth Smith was similar. While many of the purchases made by the Smiths when in Dublin were used for the upkeep of their house in Wicklow, frequently some were gifts, including when she was surprised by her husband with a writing case during the summer of 1847.[64] The case, 'made of Russian leather, Brahma lock, every convenience in a small compass, very neatly finished', prompted Smith to conclude that 'it is the age of luxury indeed in great things and in small'. Yet, less than a month later on another visit to Dublin she remarked:

> on getting into the suburbs of the town only melancholy evidences of the distress of the nation were to be met with – every second house to let – of those retreats where the Dublin tradesmen lived with their families, neat small places with car sheds beside them, little gardens in front and green fields behind. I began to count the number of shops shut up as we advanced and got to twenty-six by the time we reached Miss Knaggs only at the entrance of the busy part of the City – Pim's which used to be so crowded had very few purchasers in it; the other marts we heard drag on a lazy business too, the shops are deserted.[65]

The changing nature of Dublin with the arrival of Famine poor was probably evident to the Smiths when they visited at Christmas 1847 but they still enjoyed themselves as before, as Elizabeth noted in her diary, 'we went to Gresham's and ordered dinner and then set out to shop. Gloves, shoes, a few other necessaries being required, and some little presents on all sides.'[66] However, on other occasions she noted destitution in the fact that the 'streets being filled by young pretty girls lost for ever to virtue'.[67] It was inevitable that the poor would turn their attention to the shops of the city and the number of crimes that were brought before Dublin courts reflected this. In January 1847 'a large concourse of famished looking country people' attacked Jeffers' 'bread shop' on Church Street as newspapers reported on the fact that 'the city is filled with country beggars'.[68] There were other raids on bread shops (bakeries) on King Street, Pill Lane, Thomas Street, James' Street and other parts of the Liberties.[69] At the same time a group calling themselves 'the hungry mob' and numbering more than 1,000 people had paraded through the Liberties stealing bread from shops and causing disturbance.[70] These of course were crimes of hunger carried out in a world of plenty. Those like John Walsh, who stole cakes from the window of a shop in Sandymount Green for which he was committed to Kilmainham jail for 14 days, had little other choice.[71] In 1847 alone crime affecting Dublin businesses grew alarmingly. Delivery vans, particularly those from bakeries, were frequently targeted. In 1847 four railway labourers, driven by hunger they claimed, robbed a delivery cart at Church Street.[72]

Elizabeth Smith's observations about Dublin point to a decline in the fortunes of many of the inhabitants of the city after 1847, which was exacerbated by other factors. This was true also of 1848 when ongoing fears of rebellion in Ireland (as word filtered through from the continent of revolutionary movements mobilising abroad) stunted trade in the city. According to Smith 'Dublin is like a town in a state of siege, people can't feel quite comfortable because there is no actual security or tranquillity'.[73] These fears curtailed visits to the city for shopping and leisure, although by now the family had themselves fallen on straightened financial times as rents continued to dwindle on their Wicklow estate. While in Dublin Smith commented that the sales offered by the shopkeepers were of little use to her as 'I had to lay out the least possible sum required by our necessities, so had to look on what was tempting with the same eyes as would one dying of hunger on a heap of diamonds'.[74] There were signs elsewhere that country house owners had fallen on hard times with Smith wryly commenting that there 'is going to be a gallery opened in Dublin in the Spring for the exhibition of all these melancholy remains of our ruined gentry, plate, pictures, books, furniture &c. The town is glutted with these riches, and there is no chance of private sale for them'.[75] There was however a much more pressing reason for avoiding

Dublin during 1849, with the spread of cholera, which Smith described as 'frightful, in all ranks'.[76]

By 1851 the middle classes and the 'sturdy famer' class, as they were referred to, had also been hard hit by the Famine, as witnessed by the items that were placed before Dublin auction houses.[77] The sales of Messrs Bentley of Wood Quay, Dublin reflected this –the items auctioned included winnowing machines, jaunting cars and gigs with lamps.[78] Elizabeth Smith's fortunes improved and she was once again frequenting Dublin. In March 1850 Smith noted that 'our whole week in Dublin was one continued pleasure'.[79] For them, and others, the worst excesses of the Famine were deemed to have passed and Smith noted that Dublin was 'full and busy, and people in good spirits'.[80] There was an air of optimism too with the hosting in 1851 of an industrial exhibition at the Royal Dublin Society, where 'strangers' were 'expressing themselves quite astonished at the skill of the Irish'.[81] However, some of the shops that the Smiths had previously visited were no more. Some like their 'old dressmaker, Miss Macpherson' was 'bankrupt, turned out of her house'.[82]

The experiences of both Joly and Smith are at odds with what was happening in the country at the time, although the latter in particular did allude to the suffering of the poor amid her world of plenty. Following one trip to Dublin, she wrote that 'the famine is coming, has begun in the plains and must reach the hills, and though those immediately belonging to our small knot of good landlords may feel little of it, all around are already in misery'. [83] This essay has shed light on Dublin during the Famine and provided an insight into the experiences of two people who frequented the city at this time. This small sampling highlights how, for some, life continued as somewhat normal during the Famine. As Dublin abounded with goods it was no wonder that one visitor in June 1846 remarked that it was 'a little London, all alive, so full of splendid buildings, fine streets and squares, beautiful well dressed women and handsome men'.[84] Yet sight should not be lost of the fact that it was a city which was thronged with famished poor flocking from all across Ireland seeking sanctuary.

'AD LIBITUM BANKING'?: DUBLIN'S ROLE WITHIN THE FAMINE-ERA IRISH BANKING SYSTEM

DECLAN CURRAN

As is perhaps understandable, the experiences of Irish joint-stock banks between 1845 and 1850 have not featured prominently in studies of the Irish Famine.[1] These well-capitalised commercial banks – unlike the many small-scale Famine-era savings banks, loan fund banks, credit unions, and pawnbrokers – managed to emerge relatively unscathed from the Famine onslaught.[2] Irish joint-stock banking, which had emerged as a Dublin-centric banking system centred around Bank of Ireland and had grown to ten banks by 1845 (see Table 1, below), sought to carry out its normal day-to-day business as far as was practicable during the Famine years.[3] Those joint-stock banks that were authorised to issue bank notes continued to do so, but only commensurate to the diminished Famine-era level of economic activity. Joint-stock banks also continued to provide credit to traders by discounting bills of payment, but were particularly wary of exposure to losses arising from grain speculation.[4] Irish joint-stock banks generally catered for upper- and middle-class clientele and their branches maintained a relatively small number of accounts comprised of large average deposits.[5]

The Famine-era fortunes of Irish joint-stock banks may well have been far removed from the everyday life of those hardest hit by the crisis – namely, those landless labourers and cottiers operating largely in a barter economy, in which rent for a plot of land to grow potatoes was paid in terms of days worked for the landowner. That said, in certain instances the world of joint-stock banking did intersect with famine conditions: Bank of Ireland, the government-chartered bank, was appointed by the British treasury in 1846 as its relief agent and was thereby tasked with ordering and distributing through its branch network the silver and gold coin required to pay wages in the public works relief schemes.[6] As well as this, the branch networks of joint-stock banks had extended by 1845 from Dublin to provincial Irish towns with populations of 3,000 and less. For example, National Bank had a branch operating in Castlerea, County Roscommon (population of 1,000 in 1841 census), while Skibbereen, County Cork (population 5,000) – known to have endured great hardship during the Famine – was serviced by both Provincial and National Bank branches. That said, the only joint-stock bank to have established branches prior to 1845 in Strokestown, County Roscommon (population 3,000) and Dingle, County Kerry (population 3,000) was Agricultural and Commercial Bank, which had been wound up in the years prior to the Famine.[7] At a local level, the Provincial Bank annual report of 1847 details the death of its Wexford branch manager from Famine-related fever.[8] However, these encounters with Famine distress were clearly of a limited nature and, for the most part, Irish joint-stock banks were relatively unperturbed by the Famine conditions.

Table 1: Irish joint-stock banks active in 1845

Institution	Est. Date	Branch Network	Note Issue (% of total 1845 bank notes issued)
Bank of Ireland	1783	24, predominantly in larger towns	Yes (59%)
Provincial Bank	1825	37, predominantly in smaller towns	Yes (15%)
National Bank	1834	44, predominantly in smaller towns	Yes (13%)
Northern Bank	1824	12 localised branches (Ulster)	Yes (4%)
Ulster Bank	1836	15 localised branches (Ulster)	Yes (4%)
Belfast Bank	1827	18 localised branches (Ulster)	Yes (4%)
Royal Bank	1836	No	No
Hibernian	1824	No	No
London and Dublin	1842	10 branches	No
Tipperary Bank	1838	9 localised branches (midlands)	No

Sources: *Bankers' Magazine*, vols 4–10 (1846–53); G. L. Barrow, *The Emergence of the Irish Banking System, 1820–45* (Dublin, 1975), pp 215–20 (Appendix 3).

Despite not bearing the brunt of the Famine onslaught, it is argued in this chapter that there is much to learn from studying the role of Irish joint-stock banks in the Irish Famine-era economy. In particular, Irish joint-stock banks offer a lens through which to view the emergence of a particular set of colonial institutions, and the regional variation inherent in the functioning of these institutions, which made up the Irish institutional landscape in which famine conditions unfolded.[9] Irish joint-stock banking was an institution of systemic importance in the Irish Famine-era economy. The authorised bank note circulation of Irish joint-stock banks in 1845 was £6.4 million, with a further £8 million estimated to be held in deposits. In contrast, the total balances of Irish savings banks fell from £2.92 million in 1845 to £1.33 million in 1848, while the aggregate value of loan fund banks fell from £1.87 million in 1845 to £0.72 million in 1848.[10] Not only were joint-stock banks the dominant financial institutions in the Famine-era economy, their formation and subsequent development owed much to the political influence exerted by their promoters and investors. As outlined in this chapter, the emergent Irish banking system in the decades prior to Famine was shaped to a great extent by the Irish colonial context: a conflict of interests between the established, largely Anglican, landed gentry and a growing mercantile community well represented by Catholic, Presbyterian, and Quaker denominations. The colonial imprint on Famine-era Irish banking also took another form: the imposition of regulatory regimes onto an Irish banking system that were designed, first and foremost, as responses to British financial crises. As discussed below, the most egregious of these regulations was the 1845 Bankers' (Ireland) Act, an extension of the Bank Act which had been implemented in Britain in 1844. This far-reaching piece of legislation sought in Britain to tightly control money circulation and to centralise note issue in the hands of the Bank of England. However, in the process, these regulations greatly diminished the institutional role of Irish banking and subsumed it into a wider British banking system, despite the regulations being welcomed by Bank of Ireland as a means for preventing 'the misery and ruin which would have resulted if banking had been *ad libitum*, as it was before'.[11]

Embroidered into this Famine-era institutional setting, of course, was a well-established regional pattern. Dublin – seat of government in the decades before the 1800 Act of Union, home of the government-chartered bank (Bank of Ireland), conduit for flows of rental income from Irish provinces to Britain, and a centre of significant domestic and export-orientated mercantile trade – boasted Famine-era banking facilities and currency circulation of far greater depth than that of provincial Irish towns. As with many socio-economic aspects of 1840s Ireland, regional variation in famine vulnerabilities and experiences are brought into sharp focus via a study of Irish banking during these years. This chapter seeks to illustrate, via an overview of the emergent Irish banking system, this colonial-influenced idiosyncratic institution-building process which would provide the institutional landscape for the Famine. Within this chapter, the regional dimensions of this institution-building process receive particular emphasis: an Irish regional context which contrasts Dublin's banking institutions with those of the rest of Ireland, as well as a wider British context which situates Dublin within a changing British banking landscape on the eve of the Famine.

ORIGINS OF THE IRISH BANKING SYSTEM: CONFLICTING LANDED AND MERCANTILE INTERESTS

The eighteenth-century origins of the Irish banking system have been characterised as being shaped by a conflict of interests between the requirements of the landed gentry for remitting funds and the mercantile need for trade credit.[12] Irish merchant banking had begun to emerge as a source of finance for trading activities between the 1720s and 1750s, with six of the eight Dublin banks active in 1754 being mercantile.[13] These merchant banks had been founded by Catholics, Quakers and Presbyterians rather than by the Anglican ascendency, and represented a challenge to landed interests.[14] However, in the aftermath of a series of merchant bank closures, the political establishment introduced legislation in 1756 which prohibited merchants from conducting banking business.[15] This strengthened the grip of the landed gentry on the Irish banking system. However, as Cullen notes, the issue of notes was of secondary importance to these banks, resulting in a declining Irish note issue that failed to keep pace with the growth of external and internal trade.[16] This prompted the emergence of a small number of specialised merchant discount houses in Dublin, Galway and Belfast in the 1780s, which quickly began to advance considerable volumes of trade credit to merchants and would eventually transform into private banks in their own right.[17]

This prevalence of landed interests in Irish banking would have far-reaching implications both for the subsequent development of the Irish banking system and Dublin's role within that system. Non-merchant banks tended to operate in a more cautious manner than merchant banks. Indeed, McGowan notes that Irish banking in the second half of the eighteenth century failed to display the vigour and innovation evident prior to the 1756 legislation.[18] Rather than seeking to create credit in response to a shortage of capital or to meet the needs of trade, Irish banks now operated primarily as a vehicle through which the landlord classes transferred rents either from the regions to Dublin, or from Dublin to London.[19] Indeed, a number of early Dublin mercantile banks, such as that of La Touche, gradually evolved into landlord banks, becoming increasingly reliant on landed interests for capital and management.[20] Landed banking interests were also intertwined with the political sphere and had good reason to seek political favour: being entrusted with government accounts or remitting government funds – along with transferring rental income from the provinces to Dublin or London – offered banks the prospect of ample liquidity. This pronounced landed dimension in early Irish banking, overshadowing mercantile banking interests, has led Cullen to describe Dublin by the turn of the eighteenth century as 'a capital without a financial class'.[21] This government-affiliated landed banking interest would form the core of what was to become, from its founding in 1783, the dominant force in the Irish pre-Famine banking landscape: the government-chartered bank, Bank of Ireland.

From its inception, Bank of Ireland fulfilled the role of banker to the government: from its head office in Dublin it administered the lodgement of all public monies, received all revenue payments, managed the national debt and provided short-term advances to the Irish exchequer.[22] Bank of Ireland's capital arrangements afforded it a level of government support unavailable to other commercial banks. It had legislative approval to raise capital of £600,000 which it then advanced to the government as a loan with interest to be paid by an annuity of £24,000.The legislation establishing Bank of Ireland stipulated that no other body exceeding six persons could issue bills or notes payable, thereby granting Bank of Ireland an unrivalled position of strength in the Irish banking system.[23] Bank of Ireland's initial legislative charter contained a clause excluding Catholics from serving on its board of directors, an exclusion which the bank's directors removed in 1829.[24] Bank of Ireland's largest initial investors were predominantly gentry, peers and landed banking interests. Four of the La Touche family each invested £10,000 in the initial share subscription (the maximum amount permitted per person), accounting for £40,000 of the bank's initial £600,000 subscribed share capital.[25] The first governor of Bank of Ireland was David La Touche, Junior, holding the office until 1791.[26] A cautious approach to banking instilled in the organisation via this landed banking influence would be the hallmark of Bank of Ireland's banking activity in subsequent decades.

PRE-FAMINE DEVELOPMENT OF IRISH BANKING: A CHANGING ROLE FOR DUBLIN

The decades prior to the onset of famine in 1845 marked a period of rapid transformation for the Irish banking system, both in institutional and commercial terms. Legislative change, set in train by the 1800 Act of Union and the subsequent amalgamation of both the Irish and British exchequers and currencies, would hollow out Dublin's role as an institutional centre of the Irish banking system. This legislative change would also impact upon the commercial landscape, introducing greater banking competition to the Irish banking system and eventually leading to greater coordination of banking facilities from Dublin outwards.

In institutional terms, the first half of the nineteenth century saw the Irish banking system being gradually subsumed into the wider British banking sector, centred on the Bank of England. Political developments were the most obvious catalyst for this change: the 1800 Act of Union, in transferring the Irish seat of government from Dublin to London, led to a shift in the financial centre of power for the Irish banking system. The amalgamation of Irish and British exchequers and public debt in 1817, and the abolition of the Irish currency in 1826, bound Irish banking tightly to a wider British banking framework in which the Bank of England was the central actor.[27] While Irish banks already had pre-existing commercial ties with London in the form of inter-bank agencies and deposit accounts with the Bank of England, the unprecedented British industrialisation of the early nineteenth century in the context of political and economic union led to London inevitably replacing Dublin as the focal point for commercial transactions. A shift towards direct payments between Irish and London merchants rather than commodity exchanges completed via financial intermediaries weakened the position of Dublin banks within an amalgamated financial system.[28] The removal of parliamentary and treasury functions from Dublin further eroded the city's financial power, as illustrated by newly formed joint-stock banks such as Provincial Bank and National Bank (discussed below) situating their head offices in London, notwithstanding their commitment to bringing banking functions to Irish provincial towns. As discussed in the next section, this institutional subsuming of the Irish banking system into a British system centred in the Bank of England culminated in 1845 with the passing of the Bankers' (Ireland) Act.

In commercial terms, the structural deficiencies arising from the landed influence over the Irish banking system exposed the system to near collapse in early 1820s, and from that near collapse ensued a rapid modernisation of the Irish banking system. Irish agriculture had benefited greatly from Britain's involvement in the Napoleonic Wars (1793–1815), both as provisions supplier to the British army and navy, and through its near-monopoly status in British food markets arising from a British blockade on continental food supplies.[29] However, the end of hostilities brought with it severe difficulties for Irish agriculture; as Britain lifted the blockade, grain imports resumed from continental Europe, and the demobilisation of the British army and navy reduced the demand for provisions.[30] As part of its war effort, Britain had suspended the gold standard (the convertibility of paper currency notes into a fixed quantity of gold) with resulting price inflation. In the years after the war, Britain sought to return to the gold standard, a move that required a contraction of the money supply and resulted in falling prices. The negative effects of this challenging economic environment reached a crisis point for the Irish banking system in 1820, as falling agricultural prices eroded public confidence. In the course of a fortnight during May and June 1820, seven of the fourteen banks active in the southern counties of Ireland had collapsed.[31] The main activity of these banks was discounting for the produce export trade through the issue of their own notes, an activity that left them particularly exposed to fluctuations in agricultural prices. Dublin banks, though less reliant on the provisions trade and note issuance, also encountered difficulties and sought accommodation from Bank of Ireland. Bank of Ireland provided assistance to all Dublin banks, apart from one Dublin bank (Alexander's), which had already collapsed.[32] While it also provided help to a small number of country banks, this accommodation was not on a sufficient scale to prevent the wave of bank closures experienced in the south. Banks in Ulster, catering more for the linen industry rather than the provisions trade, were not heavily impacted by the 1820 crisis. While Newry and Lurgan each experienced a bank closure, the three banks operating in Belfast at that time remained intact. Bank of Ireland provided assistance to one of these Belfast banks, Montgomery's, which was subsequently taken over, to form Northern Bank in 1824.[33] Cullen argues that the narrow focus of Irish banking around the remittance of rental income impaired the development of an integrated national banking network linking Dublin to the provincial towns of the south and west, as well as to Ulster.[34] Just as Munster merchants had developed their own banking facilities around the provisions trade, Ulster also developed its own banking network as Belfast's Presbyterian merchants sought to break their dependence on Dublin's predominantly Protestant landed banking interests.[35]

Legislative initiatives to bolster the Irish banking system sought to address the problem of under-capitalisation of Irish banking enterprises and a lack of competition within Irish banking. Central to this legislative response was the curtailment of the monopoly position enjoyed by Bank of Ireland. Given Bank of Ireland's dependence on the government to renew its charter, it had to acquiesce to such legislative changes even though they would drastically circumscribe its privileged status within Irish banking. Legislation introduced in 1821 permitted the formation of banks with more than six partners beyond a radius of 50 (Irish) miles of Dublin. The Irish Banking Act of 1824 repealed earlier legislation that had required the names of all partners to appear on bank notes and had debarred any banker from engaging in import or export trade, while further legislation in 1825 clarified that shareholders and directors of Irish joint-stock banks could reside in any part of Great Britain and Ireland.[36] These legislative changes, which had the effect of triggering the formation of a host of Irish joint-stock banks, were enacted in Ireland before being applied to the English banking system. Indeed, Barrow speculates that their implementation in Ireland was effectively a test of their effectiveness in advance of application in England.[37]

The first of this new wave of Irish joint-stock banks was Hibernian Bank, formed in Dublin in 1824 with a subscribed capital of £1 million.[38] The founders of Hibernian Bank, who were of both Catholic and Quaker denomination, sought to challenge Bank of Ireland's monopoly status within Dublin and establish a more liberal banking entity.[39] Hibernian did not establish a branch network beyond Dublin and, as Hibernian was based in Dublin, it was prohibited from issuing its own bank notes. Its banking activities focussed on the receipt of deposits and discounting of trade bills, with its clientele being mostly Dublin businessmen.[40] However, the strongest challenger to contest Bank of Ireland's dominant position was Provincial Bank, formed in London in 1825, with a paid-up capital of £500,000. It was Provincial Bank that ushered in an era of branch banking into the Irish banking system, which Bank of Ireland reluctantly followed. Provincial was founded by Thomas Joplin, an English timber merchant, and it sought to introduce Scottish banking innovations (such as interest payments on deposits and cash credits for merchants) into Irish banking.[41] Provincial was formed with the stated aim of establishing a branch network beyond Bank of Ireland's 50-mile radius which would serve the principal towns of Ireland.[42] By 1845, Provincial Bank had established 37 branches: 13 in Munster, three in Connaught, 16 in Ulster and five in parts of Leinster that did not reside within the 50-mile radius of Dublin.[43] Of these branches, 26 were located in towns of less than 10,000 residents. By 1845, Bank of Ireland had opened 24 branches, with only seven of them in towns with a population of less than 10,000.[44] As Provincial was not permitted to open a branch within Dublin, La Touche's initially acted as their Dublin agent until Provincial eventually opened an office in Dublin in 1836.[45]

Despite being founded as a competitor of Bank of Ireland, Provincial Bank was seen by its critics as being part of a monopoly over Irish banking to the detriment of Irish nationalist interests. This sentiment can be found in the writings of Daniel O'Connell, nationalist political leader and subsequent director of National Bank of Ireland: 'I have sensibly felt the want of a counter-check to the rascality of the Bank of Ireland and of the Provincial

Bank.'[46] That said, the National Bank prospectus in 1834 was relatively conciliatory towards Provincial Bank, stating that it 'conferred great benefits on Ireland' due to its 'connection with English capital, which inspired great confidence and materially contributed to the development of Irish credit' but that it '[had] not succeeded in becoming, notwithstanding it has been established nine years, a National Bank'.[47] It was Bank of Ireland that drew the strongest opprobrium from O'Connell: 'There never was a more close Orange confederacy than that at the Bank of Ireland ... Dishonest and bigoted they are and have been.'[48]

While the emergence of branch banking has seen the activities of joint-stock banks extend to provincial Irish towns, banking in Dublin was of a different nature to that of the rest of Ireland. As Barrow succinctly states: '[Dublin's] banking facilities were better, money was more plentiful, and it penetrated further.'[49] A second wave of joint-stock bank formation in the 1830s, which saw the emergence of the ill-fated Agricultural and Commercial Bank (1834), National Bank of Ireland (1835) and the Royal Bank of Ireland (1836), was in part a response to regional banking deficiencies. While the Royal Bank of Ireland operated solely in Dublin and, like Hibernian Bank, was prohibited from issuing notes within what was Bank of Ireland's exclusive area, the Agricultural and Commercial Bank and National Bank both sought to establish themselves as 'the bank of the poor man and the small farmer'.[50] The National Bank – with Daniel O'Connell as chairman – located its head office in London but its organisational structure initially involved each branch being set up as a local company in partnership with local shareholders. However, by 1838 all but two branches (Carrick-on-Suir and Clonmel) were absorbed into the parent company.[51] By 1845 it had developed a network of 44 branches: nine in Leinster, 25 in Munster, ten in Connaught and none in Ulster.[52] Of its branch network, 34 branches were located in towns of less than 10,000 residents.[53] National Bank also arranged for Hibernian Bank to act as its agent in Dublin. Agricultural and Commercial Bank also proposed a banking model based on local shareholders providing capital for each branch. However, rapid over-expansion of its branch network coupled with poor management and internal conflict led to the bank ceasing operations in 1840.[54] National Bank and the short-lived Agricultural and Commercial Bank recognised that banking needs in rural Ireland, unlike in Dublin, were tied to agriculture: providing credit to farmers prior to harvest and using local capital to stimulate local economic activity, rather than having savings banks direct local funds towards government stocks and thereby removing capital from local circulation.[55]

IMPACT OF THE 1845 BANKERS' (IRELAND) ACT ON THE FAMINE-ERA BANKING SYSTEM

The surge in new banking formation in the decades preceding the Famine was effectively halted by the 1845 Bankers' (Ireland) Act, which extended the 1844 Bank Charter Act to Ireland. The 1845 Act removed the Bank of Ireland's Dublin-centred note-issuing privileges, with all joint-stock banks with note-issuing functions now allowed to issue their notes within the Dublin region.[56] The note issue of Bank of Ireland was now subject to the same criteria as that of other Irish banks: note issue in Irish joint-stock banks was to be limited to a fixed threshold based on their existing quantity of notes in circulation, with any additional issue required to be backed by specie. The legislation also deterred the entry of new joint-stock companies into the Irish banking system, as note issue was only permitted by those joint-stock banks already in existence when the legislation was introduced in

1845.[57] Once again, Bank of Ireland reluctantly accepted these legislative changes in order to ensure renewal of its charter.[58]

While curtailing Bank of Ireland's privileged position within the Irish banking system and discouraging the emergence of further Irish joint-stock banks, the 1845 act was extending to Ireland a set of banking rules that were designed by British policymakers for British banking conditions. The Bank Charter Act 1844 is regarded as the most significant piece of British banking legislation of the nineteenth century.[59] It was prompted by a series of British financial crises – in 1825 and, to a lesser extent, in 1836 and 1839 – in which Bank of England's gold reserves had been depleted. These large-scale gold outflows – typically triggered by the collapse of speculative investment projects or unexpectedly high expenditure on imported grain in the aftermath of a bad harvest – dented public confidence in the value of banknotes issued by relatively weaker banks and fuelled speculation that the Bank of England would be forced to suspend convertibility of banknotes into gold.[60] By the 1840s the view in government circles was that unchecked expansions in the circulation of bank notes had been a significant causal factor in previous crises. The remedy, as advocated by the 'Bullionist' or 'Currency School', was to require bank note issues to be backed by specie reserves and to have one official or semi-official body serve as 'single issuer'.[61] This rule-based position formed the basis of the Bank Act 1844: the Bank of England was to be split in two, with an Issue department which would circulate a fixed maximum of notes (£14 million) against securities and only issue further notes if backed by bullion, and a Banking Department which would continue to operate as a commercial entity. No new banks of issue were to be allowed and existing banks were to have their maximum issue fixed at their existing levels.[62]

The implementation in Britain of the Bank Act 1844, and its extension to Ireland via the Bankers' (Ireland) Act 1845, established a highly restrictive monetary regime in Britain and Ireland in which currency circulation was to be determined by a mechanistic rule-based approach rather than bank discretion.[63] Its extension to Ireland reflected an acknowledgement by the British government that, within the context of a joint currency area, it would not be possible to enforce a rigid monetary regime via the Bank of England while discretionary monetary expansion was still possible in Ireland. However, the newly introduced regulations differed between Ireland and England: in the English case, the Bank of England was primed to become the sole note issuer within the British banking system. In the Irish case, all six existing joint-stock banks of issue were permitted to issue notes. In this way, the 1844 Act cemented Bank of England's place at the centre of the monetary system, while the 1845 Act stymied Bank of Ireland's trajectory towards becoming a fully-fledged central bank.

As discussed below, the immediate aim of the Bank Charter Act – to restrict bank note circulation – had a negligible impact in Ireland during the Famine years, as Irish banknote circulation fell to a level far below the limit authorised by the legislation. However, the extension of the Bank Charter Act to Ireland in 1845 had far-reaching implications for the structure of the Irish banking system. The act removed the Bank of Ireland's monopoly over the issuing of notes within a 50-mile radius of Dublin and stated that the right of note issue was to operate on the same basis across the six existing Irish banks of issue. The act also prohibited the entry of new note-issuing banks into the Irish banking system, and it placed an upper limit on the note issue of Irish banks that could be backed by government securities.

The initial response of Bank of Ireland to the loss of its Dublin note-issuing privileges was to formalise aspects of its systemic commercial role that it had informally assumed by virtue of being the dominant government-chartered Irish bank. This can be seen in its willingness to expand its role of 'bankers' bank' subsequent to the implementation of the 1845 Bank Charter Act. Bank of Ireland already established itself as a reluctant ad hoc lender of last resort in exceptional circumstances. In 1814 it had provided assistance to three Dublin banks (Robert Shaw and Co., Alexander and Co., and Ball and Co.) and, as noted above, in 1820 Bank of Ireland came to the aid of all Dublin banks and a number of country banks. That said, in the late 1820s Bank of Ireland had been unwilling to provide support to its rival, Provincial bank – a stance that was frowned upon by the Bank of England.[64] In 1845, with the Bank Charter Act now in place, Bank of Ireland offered a more broad-based support to fellow joint-stock banks. It provided the two Dublin-based non-issuing joint-stock Banks (Hibernian Bank and Royal Bank) with overdraft facilities at 2 per cent below the usual overdraft rate. It also accommodated the three joint-stock banks of issue with head offices in the north of Ireland (Northern, Belfast and Ulster Banks) with overdraft facilities of £150,000 on the deposit of bills or securities, at the rate charged by Bank of England. A further consolidation of its 'banker's bank' functions involved Bank of Ireland organising a clearing house for exchanging notes between Irish banks, something which had become particularly important in the Dublin context as other joint-stock banks could now issue notes within the Dublin 50-mile radius.[65] In terms of its branch banking activities, Bank of Ireland gave its provincial local agents (i.e. branches) discretion in advancing specie for short periods to other banks.[66] As well as these engagements with its fellow joint-stock banks, Bank of Ireland also continued to act as agent for the government, and in 1846 Bank of Ireland was designated by the British Treasury as agent for the Board of Public Works in the handling of relief funds.[67]

In institutional terms, the Bankers' (Ireland) Act 1845 fundamentally circumscribed Bank of Ireland's institutional import within the Irish banking system and effectively confined Dublin to the role of regional actor within a Bank of England-centred banking system. The earliest European proto-central banks had typically evolved into this institutional role from a pre-existing position as the dominant commercial issuer of banknotes and banker to the government.[68] These banking entities were supported via government privilege, providing these banks with sufficient scale to support government banking requirements. While monetary stability was crucial to these banks, their priority was ensuring their own liquidity rather than wider macroeconomic concerns. Lender of last resort functions and informal banking supervision arose from commercial strength rather than from a public-good objective. Over time governments would curtail the commercial activities of these banks and instead granted them greater institutional powers. While the 1844 act contributed to this evolution of the Bank of England, the 1845 act impeded a similar progression for Bank of Ireland: it removed Bank of Ireland's note-issuing monopoly, while at the same time encouraging Bank of Ireland to maintain a dominant commercial role. Bank of Ireland's note issue limit was set at 60 per cent of the total Irish authorised note issue. The bank retained its role as government banking agent and was still expected to support the stability of Irish banking system.[69] While it continued to serve as the Irish 'banker's bank' and, to a limited extent, the government's bank, Bank of Ireland's emergence as a Dublin-based central banking institution for an Irish banking system had been stymied.

BANKING AND NOTE ISSUE DURING THE FAMINE

During the Famine years, Bank of Ireland and the other Irish joint-stock banks were confronted with a stagnation of Irish economic activity. The impact of potato failure on wider economic activity was noted in the 1846 annual report of Tipperary Bank: 'the loss of the potato crop, and consequent reduction of the export of agricultural produce, [have] caused almost a total cessation of the greatest branch of business in this country, namely, the discount of bills drawn against the shipment of such produce'.[70] Economic conditions in rural areas were, of course, vastly different to those experienced in Dublin. In remote parts of the south and west, landless agricultural labourers and small tenant farmers (cottiers) operated largely in a barter economy, in which rent for a plot of land to grow potatoes was paid in terms of days worked for the landowner or larger tenant. The deficient potato harvest devastated this rural barter economy and led to a scramble for notes of small denomination and silver coin.[71] The process by which silver coin was drained from circulation was succinctly captured by the *Dublin University Magazine*:

> this silver coin has been extorted from the industrious classes by the severest pressure ... The £400,000 in silver coin, which has forced its way into the banks, and now lies there a dead and unprofitable weight, is withdrawn from the circulation of the country ... Thus it was that the silver coin, which had been, in more prosperous times, kept in circulation in the country was forced upon the banks.[72]

The worsening Irish famine conditions experienced in 1847 coincided with mounting financial pressures within the British economy, with government expenditure directed towards Irish famine relief, as well as the end of the railway investment boom, seen as contributory factors. The *Bankers' Magazine*, for example, pointed to the failure of the potato crop as the catalyst for the prevailing British trade imbalance and gold outflows: 'The present adverse state of the exchanges is unanimously attributed to the failure of the potatoe [sic] crop in Ireland, and the large and extraordinary imports of corn and provisions from America and Northern Europe into this country.'[73] The British monetary system experienced two major crises in 1847: an April crisis triggered by a sudden reversal by the Bank of England of its lax discount policy and an October crisis due to a loss of confidence in the convertibility of bank deposits into Bank of England notes. Ironically, the catalyst for the October crisis was a better-than-expected harvest in autumn 1847, which eased grain shortages and led to a sharp reduction in prices. A wave of business failures ensued amongst corn merchants, who had engaged in speculation via forward contracts to purchase grain at high prices, and discount houses, who had discounted the corn merchants' bills of exchange. The Bank of England's ability to assist the money markets in the face of this crisis was hampered by the rigid monetary rules brought in by the 1844 act. The panic was only relieved when the government sanctioned a temporary suspension of the 1844 Bank Charter Act on 25 October 1847. The 1848 Committee on Commercial Distress was subsequently appointed in order to inquire into the causes of the financial distress experienced in 1847.[74]

Initially, Irish joint-stock banks were somewhat insulated from the ill-effects of this economic turmoil. Robert Murray, general manager of Provincial Bank, gave testimony before the Committee on Commercial Distress in 1848, attributing the banks' resilience, despite the deteriorating conditions, in large part to government expenditure on public relief works:

> The issue of the banks in Ireland was kept up in 1846 almost entirely by the Government expenditure; there was less produce, the growth of Ireland, to sell in 1846 than in 1847, but yet the issue kept up, both of bank notes and of silver in the hands of the lower orders, and in 1847 it was very much diminished in amount by reason of the discontinuance of that expenditure, and the country was thrown upon its own resources.[75]

However, note issue fell well below the authorised limit in 1847, as Irish joint-stock banks took a cautious approach to the provision of credit in an economy diminished by famine conditions. The banks' rationale for this cautious approach, as Murray outlines, stemmed from their fear of exposure to potential losses arising from grain speculation:

> There was a strong impression, from the large supplies of food that must be imported into Ireland, in consequence of the failure of the potato crop, money must become scarce, and that therefore it was necessary to increase the value of it, in order to prevent over-speculation in food; and it was deemed necessary, in the months of November and December, to look very cautiously to all transactions, and, upon particular transactions, to increase the rate of discount, though there was no increased rate of interest generally, till the 26th of January, 1847.[76]

Total Irish note issue remained above the limit (£6,354,494) authorised by the Bankers' (Ireland) Act until May 1847. However, from mid-1847 the total note issue of Irish joint-stock banks contracted rapidly: by August 1849 it had diminished by over one-third, and note issue levels did not approach the authorised limit again until 1853.[77]

Bank of Ireland's approach to issuing bank notes during the Famine years was very much in line with that of the other note issuing Irish joint-stock banks. The testimony of Bank of Ireland governor John McDonnell before the 1848 Committee on Commercial Distress provides an insight into bank's views regarding circulation during the Famine years. When asked if he was aware of any want of circulation in Ireland in 1846 and 1847, McDonnell's responses – 'I think not, I am not aware of any complaint of that sort' (Q6616) and 'as regards accommodation on mercantile paper, I think not; I do not think that any man who had good bills which ought to be discounted was refused money after 1845' (Q6615) – echoed those set out in greater detail by Robert Murray. In keeping with the conservative banking ethos of its origins, Bank of Ireland considered reduced Famine-era Irish circulation levels to be appropriate given the diminished level of trade undertaken during the Famine years.[78]

Simmering within the testimony of the Bank of Ireland governor, however, appears to be one particular grievance: the removal of Bank of Ireland's note issue privileges within a 50-mile radius of Dublin. While welcoming the 1845 act's restriction on the establishment of new banks of issue as 'a very wholesome measure' and one that 'afforded greater protection to the general credit of the country' (Q6644), McDonnell was openly critical of the removal of Bank of Ireland's Dublin note issue monopoly.[79] Indeed, this criticism on the part of the government-chartered bank is all the more surprising given that one of the committee members was Sir Robert Peel, the former Prime Minister who had implemented the 1844 and 1845 banking regulations. When asked by Peel if he had any suggestions to offer with respect to any alteration of the law, McDonnell responded:

> I should suggest, but it is rather of a personal character, as it applies to the Bank of Ireland, that it would have been better if we had not been deprived of the privilege which we possessed before that act passed.[80]

In response to a question from the committee chairman, McDonnell framed his argument in terms of the public good rather than in commercial terms. Describing the 1845 act as 'rather injurious to the public, in throwing the limit open which previously existed', he went on to argue that 'if that privilege had remained, it would have been of more advantage to the country generally. Under the former state of things, the bank had the power, if too full a circulation took place, in some degree of checking it.'[81]

Of course, any sullenness on the part of the Bank of Ireland before the 1848 Committee on Commercial Distress was in vain. The bank had already acquiesced to the 1845 regulations as part of the British government's renewal of its legislative bank charter. Notwithstanding the temporary suspension in 1847 of fixed limits on note issues, the die had already been cast for both Bank of Ireland as an institution and Dublin as a banking centre. Bank of Ireland's systemic importance in the Famine-era Irish banking system had been circumscribed, while Dublin had undergone a *de facto* demotion to subsidiary within a centralised British monetary system.

Taming the Channel: Technology, Liberalism and the Irish Sea, *c.*1845–52

PETER HESSION

Writing at the height of the Famine in 1848, Thomas Carlyle ruefully acknowledged that the Irish 'cannot be prevented from circulating among us ... with an Irish Channel everywhere bridged over by ships, steamers, herring-busses, boats and bomb-ketches'. Until the entire island was somehow 'unanchored' and cast off into the Atlantic, he concluded, such a vast 'bridge' of connections unfortunately precluded them from being 'fenced out'.[1] Writing to his friend, the Young Irelander Charles Gavan Duffy three years later, he again exclaimed how 'Watt's steam engine is worth a million of [Daniel] O'Connells ... making us all into one uniform mess'.[2] Against the backdrop of the Famine, Carlyle could thus indulge several of his foremost anxieties: the threat of 'the uncivilized Irishman' to British society, the 'dismal science' of *laissez faire* for pushing them there, and the impersonal agencies of 'the Machine Age' for accelerating the flow.[3] Yet, the sum of his prejudices capture not only Carlyle's racism or rusticism, but the new complexities of an environmental boundary as well: the Irish Sea.[4]

Muir Éireann or the Irish Sea is bounded to the north by the Irish or North Channel linking east Ulster and Scotland and to the south by St George's Channel connecting Wexford and Pembrokeshire, encompassing an area of 46,007 square kilometers.[5] Despite being a sheltered arm of the North Atlantic, it possesses weather and tidal systems that can produce notoriously difficult sailing conditions.[6] Yet, it was precisely this combination of natural advantages and drawbacks that made it an ideal seeding ground for experiments in steam, hosting the world's first regular sea-faring steam service between Belfast and Greenock in 1818, with cuts in travel times on the Dublin-Liverpool route falling 'from two to four days' to just 14 hours.[7] A corridor which had long been frequented by privateers was rapidly 'civilianised' alongside this explosion of steam, with figures like the Dublin Steam Packet Company's director Charles Wye Williams leading the way.[8] By the mid-1830s half of all steamship tonnage reaching Britain was Irish, with regular weekly crossings soon exceeding one hundred.[9] Mid-century Ireland proved, in Oliver MacDonagh's words, more 'open ... than any comparable nation to the mounting blast of the [steam] revolution'; on the eve of the Famine, its fleet of merchant steamers stood behind only Britain, France, and the US globally in both number and tonnage.[10]

While the global era of steam 'came of age' in the Irish Sea in the 1820s and 1830s, the years immediately preceding and spanning the Famine were also framed by landmarks in international seafaring. These included hosting the world's first transatlantic steamship voyage by Williams's *Sirius* in 1838 and its second submarine telegraph in 1852 linking Dublin to London.[11] To date, historians of Ireland have tended to treat such technological advances in relative isolation from their wider social and political contexts, sometimes evoking 'modernisation' in keeping with an established tradition in Irish historiography. In what follows, I adopt a divergent approach by analysing several of the most 'banal' technologies that undergirded and accompanied the 'steam age' within the critical maritime 'contact zone' connecting Ireland and Britain.[12] Drawing a 'political ecology' of the Irish Sea throughout the Famine, in what follows I reassess the agency of such interventions in terms of the application of *laissez-faire* ideology to Ireland, from fishing boats and 'famine piers' to lighthouses and harbours.[13] As such technologies helped to make the Sea a disruptive 'theatre' of liberal reform throughout the 1840s and 1850s, this essay will argue that they also served to materialise the very distinctions between state and market upon which liberal ideology depended.

'A RICH BUT UNCULTIVATED WASTE': FISHERIES, TECHNOLOGY AND *LAISSEZ FAIRE*

When the American privateer *True Blooded Yankee* was finally captured in 1814, it had single-handedly taken some 27 vessels from Dublin Bay in the space of just six weeks. Yet, it was to prove amongst the last to harass the Irish Sea for the remainder of the century.[14] While the Sea possessed a named fencibles unit until 1810, in the aftermath of Waterloo a long history of maritime incursions came to an abrupt end.[15] The Irish coast continued to be fortified through the building of stations by the nascent Irish Coast Guard following its foundation in 1822 , but this occurred first under the auspices of a Board of Customs partly administered from Dublin.[16] While the Sea was thus in no sense demilitarised, the logic of state intervention had begun to shift from one of defence to 'domestication'.[17] A central aspect of this process was a reconceptualisation of the Sea from being a 'wilderness of waters' – as one writer described it in 1830 – to a realm which might be gradually 'tamed' through technological agency.[18] In this rendering, the Sea came to appear less as a negation of *terra firma* than a vast plain inviting the exploitation of its newly apprehended 'natural resources' – what the *Dublin University Magazine* could describe in 1851 as 'a rich but uncultivated waste'.[19] The 'riches' in question were of course its flora and fauna, with contemporaries often citing the seventeenth-century parliamentarian and second-generation Dubliner William Temple in his belief that fish stocks 'might prove a mine under the water as rich as any under ground'.[20]

On the English Channel, the same peace-time focus on sea fisheries had led to international arbitration and the formal demarcation of maritime boundaries; the 1839 Anglo-French Fisheries Convention made law in 1843 proved the first to ensure that sovereign boundaries were to be replicated via the rights of 'national' fisheries.[21] By contrast, the upshot of what Anna Gambles has termed the 'imperial consolidation' of fisheries astride the Irish Sea involved a distinct political economy combining peripheral integration with *laissez-faire* reform.[22] Here, rather than demarcation based on borders, the Sea would become an 'experimental' precinct of liberal reform where the free flow of capital and competition might flourish free from interference.[23] An 1836 commission of inquiry into Irish fisheries strongly influenced by the incoming Whig chief secretary of Ireland, George William Frederick Howard, the Viscount Morpeth, initiated this shift;

the system of bounties or subsidies to fishermen which had existed under the aegis of the defunct Board of Fisheries (1819–30) was thus categorically rejected, with the report affirming that 'no idea of a renewal of such a system, in any degree, can be admitted'.[24]

The resulting 1842 Fisheries Act saw the repeal of 26 pieces of fisheries law dating as far back as the fifteenth century, and their replacement with a regime that sought to strike a new balance between public and private piscatory rights inland versus offshore. This shift was primarily anchored in changes to the regulation of fishing technologies; whereas rivers and estuaries became subject to more restrictive conservation measures affecting 'ancient' engines such as salmon weirs, the coast and 'open seas' were to be liberated from pre-existing technological restrictions. Here, the 1836 commission singled out in particular the need to free up the use of trawl and trammel nets, decrying the organised resistance of the 'poorer class' of line fishermen to such methods due to 'superstitions or prejudices'.[25] By 1843, the newly appointed Fisheries Commissioners based at Dublin Castle could thus proudly proclaim that while previous laws had allowed 'trawls and trammels to be used as an exception ... the present Act is founded on a different principle and makes the restriction on any mode of fishing in the sea the exception'.[26] To mollify opposition, a ban on the use of trammel nets during daytime hours was added to the act, but this was later watered-down through amendments in 1845.[27]

Trawling – a method of fishing that involves a boat dragging a meshed net through midwater or along a sea bed – possessed a long and controversial history in the Irish Sea dating back to at least the mid fourteenth century.[28] Yet, it was not until advances in manufacturing from the late eighteenth-century that trawling nets came to be limited by law, beginning with Dublin in 1773.[29] Just a year later, however, a manufacturer in the capital was still offering new nets 'far superior in quality to any ever before offered to the Public' including multi-layered 'trammel' or 'gill' nets.[30] The settlement of Devonshire trawlermen at Ringsend in 1818 later ushered in 'a revolution in fishing', where 'beam' vessels were soon regarded as 'the best built and equipped ... in the United Kingdom'.[31] This wave of innovation accelerated alongside the rise of steam and mechanisation, including adaptations by Irish inventors like Thomas Walton which in turn sparked calls for regulation.[32] A new class of trawling enterprises like the Dublin Fishery Company also emerged in this era, utilising new techniques to capture large hauls of Irish Sea turbot, sole, haddock, plaice, hake and whiting.[33] New too were a set of totally novel engines such as the 'bag' or 'stake' net for catching salmon and the 'purse' siene used to target dense schools of midwater fish like tuna and mackerel.[34] By the 1840s, such technologies stood poised to transform Irish Sea fishing.[35]

The 'greater' Irish Sea region, centered on Dublin but stretching from the North Channel to St George's Channel, thus experienced the most vivid extremes of technological development during this period. While the east coast hosted a fifth of all Irish fishing boats in 1845, it made up a quarter of all 'first class' vessels of fifteen tons or more with Dublin standing out as 'the head-quarters of the deep-sea trawlers ... ranging from 30 to 50 tons'.[36] Local fishermen likewise faced heavy competition from British trawlers, with well-equipped vessels from towns like Balbriggan and Skerries (Figure 3.1) also frequently circumnavigating the island to fish off the western seaboard.[37] Yet, this subset of well-equipped Irish Sea fishermen from Ballycastle to Rosslare – 3,322 in total according to the 1841 census – formed a minority within a larger cohort of precarious fishers approximately four times as large on the eve of the Famine.[38] For this group, fishing – especially for herring – represented access to the cash economy, albeit enabled by exorbitantly priced conacre plots rented close to the coastline.[39] Responding to the parliamentary Poor Inquiry in 1836, the parish priests of Howth, Baldoyle and Rush all identified the ending of fishing bounties as a source of 'great poverty' among fishermen, but it was the impact of this upon equipment – gear, tackle and boats – which remained a persistent theme up to the Devon Commission of 1845.[40]

While the 1836 commission had balked at the image of rural fishermen being forced to use their bed clothes to handle fish for want of adequate equipment, the solution to this situation – as well as the wider question of fisheries production – was not to invest in such fishermen directly.[41] Rather, it was to attract investment and new technology through capital-formation and a major restructuring of the entire sector; as the Fisheries Commissioners noted in 1844, fishermen would soon 'find that a more certain and better livelihood is to be obtained for themselves and their families by working with superior means for the capitalist, than by their present independent poor and insufficient measures'.[42] As the fisheries official Herbert Francis Hore noted in 1850, these plans 'contemplated ... relief of the poorer class of fishermen who might be injured by the intended removal of restrictions on improved methods of fishing, of which they had not means to avail themselves, [utilising] a Poor Law for Ireland'.[43] Like others, Hore saw the Famine as accelerating a process of proletarianisation necessary to the 'modernisation' of the sector much like the wider agrarian economy.[44]

It was to be this legal and political reframing of Irish fisheries – as opposed to simply the putative 'backwardness' of the sector – which governed how both the Famine itself and government relief policies were to affect fishing communities. Historians have tended to gloss over what has been variously termed the 'puzzle', 'paradox' or 'extraordinary contradiction' that coastal communities apparently starved in the midst of plenty.[45] There is widespread contemporary evidence, particularly from agents of the Central Relief Committee of the Society of Friends, that fishermen were indeed forced to pawn their equipment; James S. Donnelly's assertion that this was 'almost universally' the case is borne out by statements like that of the engineer Francis Coffee, who noted 'five sixths of ... fishermen were obliged to pawn their nets or part with their fishing tackle for their means of subsistence in 1847 and 1848'.[46] Asenath Nicholson quoted one fishermen as stating that year: 'now the fisheries are lost, we are too poor to keep up the tackle and are all starving'.[47] Cormac Ó Gráda has also analysed the impact of this influx upon pawnshops themselves, detailing how much of this credit system collapsed with the purchasing power of the poor.[48] Yet, the ways in which the Famine served to de-equip fishermen is too often associated with 'under-development' rather than the wider politics of technology at the heart of liberal reform and relief efforts.

Even while those at the highest echelons of the Famine relief bureaucracy – both within and outside government – at times disagreed on specifics, a diverse range of official actors remained firmly invested in the logic underlying the liberal restructuring of Irish fisheries. Charles Trevelyan, the treasury official in charge of relief, was himself satisfied that the only explicit expenditure dedicated to fisheries equipment had been paid for 'without any expense to the public' from the pre-existing Irish Reproductive Loan Fund dating to 1822.[49] On the broader question of investment in fishermen, Trevelyan was candid in stating during 1848:

> The plan of making small loans to fishermen to enable them to equip themselves for their trade, was not resorted to, because experience had proved that the fishermen are induced by it to rely upon others, instead of themselves, and that they acquire habits of chicanery and bad faith in their prolonged struggle to evade the payment of the loans.[50]

A year earlier, Trevelyan lent his support to funding for one of six eventual curing stations intended to aid fishermen before they 'starved and their boats and nets have rotted'.[51] Yet, while he assured the incoming Lord Lieutenant, George Villiers, the Earl of Clarendon, that the courage of such fishermen in 'frail curraghs … leads one to hope that these poor people will turn out well', he soon abandoned even cosmetic relief targeting the re-equipment of fishermen.[52]

Rather, liberal policy was to facilitate well-capitalised trawling enterprises which Trevelyan himself – like the secretary of the British Relief Association, Stephen Spring-Rice, and head of the coastguard, Sir James Dombrain – became personally connected to as managers, investors and public patrons.[53] Even as he privately admitted to finding samples of Irish-cured fish 'execrable', he nonetheless continued to champion them to those financially backing such enterprises throughout 1847–8 and to encourage 'emulation … in the sister country' by sending fishing instructors who might themselves become potential entrepreneurs.[54] Writing to the former chairman of the Board of Works, Major-General John Fox Burgoyne in March 1847, he described the policy as one which frankly sought to 'encourage the deep sea fishing companies' while scaling back 'unproductive works', including – by the following year – the six government curing stations which had been established in the south and west.[55] This dovetailed with Trevelyan's own deep skepticism toward public works which he saw as resulting in 'deserted' fisheries as coastal communities supposedly opted for easier work.[56]

In his book *The Irish Crisis* (1848), Trevelyan justified his approach of overlooking aid to fishermen with an unsourced quote from Burgoyne himself, a man who had played a key role in drafting the 1842 Fisheries Act; the latter had allegedly stated that he 'doubt[ed] being able to get the money [loaned to fishermen] back and I think it so necessary to be firm on this point that I have not made use of a penny [of available funds]'.[57] In reality, Burgoyne's successor as chairman of the Board of Works, Colonel Harry Jones, was at times critical of Trevelyan's policy and parsimony, urging targeted support for re-equipping fishermen as against 'self-interested' applications from landowners seeking to build piers which were unlikely to benefit the community.[58] Indeed, this position reflected criticisms which the board had itself been receiving from local relief administrators as early as 1845. Writing to its secretary that year, a Carlingford-based relief committee member and magistrate complained:

> With respect to the advance for the Fishery gear etc., etc., allow me to remark that on such an occasion as that of impending starvation from want of means of employment any former decisions … not being deemed "politic or prudent" is not the reply expected … I feel fully warranted in such a remark when I look out on the shore under my house and there see ten large fishing smacks lying high and dry on the beach, idle, and no prospect of employment.[59]

Jones complained a few months later that the limited nature of relief would cause 'much disappointment' and voiced doubts that 'free trade, with the employment we can give, [offers] a *succedaneum* for the loss of the potato', particularly in areas where 'there is abundance of fish close to their shore, lying upon the beach and no salt to cure them'.[60]

While Trevelyan sought to downplay Jones's negativity regarding fisheries to Clarendon, both the Lord Lieutenant and Board of Works made moves during 1847 to shift the locus of activism away from the Treasury's purview.[61] It was partly due to this that the Central Relief Committee became especially prominent in relieving fisheries, with both the Board and Dublin Castle actively pressing them to do so.[62] Their relief to the sector amounted to £5,365 between 1846 and 1852, less than 3% of their total outlay, but enough to support five short-lived fishing stations on the south and west coasts and monies to redeem pawned equipment on the east coast in Dublin, Antrim, Wicklow and Waterford.[63] Yet, the committee's own fixation on loans over grants, remunerative investments, 'reproductive relief', private enterprise and the necessity of trawlers, sienes and trammels partly echoed the wider ethos of liberal reform.[64] While their 'micro finance' initiatives were lauded in places like Ring, County Waterford, the committee's efforts to re-equip the sector as a form of investment was largely written-off as a 'difficult and expensive' failure.[65] A Dublin trawler hired to 'instruct' fishermen while operating for profit was thus ultimately attacked by line fishermen, figures who were dismissed by one Central Committee auditor as 'like the red Indian, [who] wait until forced by hunger' to act.[66]

Several such incidences of violent resistance to trawlers during the Famine played a key role in limiting their use in coastal inlet and bay areas.[67] Yet, one major reason why both the vulnerability of fishermen and their resistance remain relatively obscure – particularly in comparison with activities such as inshore poaching – relates to a depoliticised and benign view of technology itself; like their near-contemporaries the Luddites, such fishermen resisted a political ecology in which technology acted as the prime agency of social transformation.[68] By 1846, the Fisheries Commissioners were celebrating their promotion of trawling and proudly declared all opposition 'nearly extinguished'.[69] Yet, just two years later, the Louth fisheries promoter Wallop Brabazon noted: 'the distress among the fishermen on the East Coast is caused by the spawn on the fishing banks being destroyed along with the small fish by the trawlers which has made a great scarcity of fish and its effects have been severely felt by the poor fishermen.'[70] By 1853, a line of coast from Waterford to Down had moved to ban shoreline trawling, but by this point the national fleet had shrunk by a quarter of its pre-Famine level and emerged more firmly dominated by Dublin's trawling fleet than ever before.[71]

If the intersection of technology, ecology and relief had served to sharpen both class and geographical antagonisms within the fishing community, it was a moment created by the Famine – but utilised by the state – which served to accelerate the expansion of a national and transnational market for Irish fish. The phenomenon of larger Dublin-based trawlers sailing to fish off the west coast had become common as early as 1823, when boats from Balbriggan, Rusk and Skerries began to complain of violent encounters with Donegal 'line men'.[72] A decade on they were said to regularly venture 'on chance' to Killybegs where they fished to supply the Dublin and Liverpool markets.[73] And by 1846, such 'fish factors' and 'professional fishermen' had come to symbolise the respectable vanguard of their trade, being welcomed by the Royal Irish Yacht Club at the annual Kingstown Regatta to compete for the special 'Dublin Bay Trawlers' Prize' of £20.[74] The presence at the 1853 National Industrial Exhibition of models representing 'a Claddagh whale boat' (Figure 3.2) and 'Kingstown trawler' side-by-side served to capture the sense of transition from a world of traditional crafts to one of modern technology.[75]

As William Andrews, a Dublin trawling investor noted a year earlier at the close of the Famine, 'the line fishermen of Rush and Skerries ... now [are] but few in number' and seemed close to the fading world of the 'half-bred fishermen, turf cutters and potato diggers'.[76] Yet, overfishing had not only helped to decimate de-equipped poorer fisherman by 1847, it was by then also effecting trawlers as they were 'not making more than the wages of their crews'.[77] As one of city's most prominent 'fish factors', Philip Hoare, noted three years later 'open trawling ground adjacent to Dublin was [so] thoroughly exhausted by incessant trawling' he had been forced to expand.[78] In this sense, trawlers were also responding to pressures anticipated by the Irish Railway Commissioners a decade earlier; during 1849, it was becoming clear that the incipient effect of 'the partial extension of the railways ... [on] the produce of the trawl' was that large quantities of fish were being transported from the coasts to Dublin.[79] This in turn, had begun by 1850 to produce such 'constant and large supplies' that it was noted how 'the Dublin trawlers finding the Dublin market thus so far furnished from a distant place, [they have] repaired there ... some jealousy ... having arisen between rivals'.[80] Just as steam had helped to shrink the Irish Sea a generation earlier, rail served to expand its reach from the late 1840s on.

SECURING THE SEA: INFRASTRUCTURES OF NAVIGATION, VISION AND RISK

While the Famine had thus helped to critically de-equip many poor fishermen, the same period witnessed a boom in limited liability fishing companies akin to railways which were favoured by liberal policymakers from the mid-1830s and later actively supported by Trevelyan and others. Yet, unlike the failure of the state to back railway construction in the ways proposed by the Irish Railway Commissioners or the Tory Protectionist leader George Bentinck in 1847, large-scale fisheries did benefit from major state aid throughout the Famine.[81] This is reflected in the fact that the rush to enter the market in fact accelerated as the humanitarian disaster was reaching its peak; no less than three-fifths of all UK-wide joint stock fishing enterprises registered during the Famine years were connected to Ireland, with a half of these formed in 1847–8 alone.[82] Crucially, these included well-capitalised entities also offering essential technical support services to the sector as a whole, including the repair of piers and harbours, the supply of boats and the construction of curing houses.[83] By 1851, the civil engineer George Preston White saw fit to include an entire chapter on Irish fisheries in his *Three Suggestions for the Investment of Capital*, which reminded readers 'the real cause of the fisheries being neglected is the fact that the people are totally unequipped'.[84] Yet, while White was certain the industry was 'much more likely to succeed if left to private enterprise and capital than by any interference on the part of the Government', he did make an exception: it was, he agreed, the 'imperative duty' of the state to put in place the requisite infrastructure to facilitate the sector.[85]

Provision of this type of infrastructure was, in fact, widely recognised as being essential to developing the kind of capital and technology-intensive zone of commerce and exchange linking Ireland with Britain which many in Westminster desired. Yet, the process of asserting new forms of technical, scientific and physical mastery over the Sea – in effect both 'securing' it for private exploitation and 'freeing' it from natural risk – represented a major challenge to state capacity. This process got underway from the 1820s but coexisted with older structures of state activism until these were gradually scaled back in the 1830s and 1840s.[86] Grants for piers, like the creation of the Fisheries Board in 1819, were prompted by the severe post-war economic depression affecting Ireland and the 'mini-famines' of 1817–19 and 1822 in particular.[87] Throughout the latter decade, Tories like Arthur Wellesley, the Duke of Wellington, approved of such investments in places like Howth as both a 'source of labour' and 'national object' in their own right, claiming many old piers needed replacing.[88] Yet, by the late 1820s, Wellington had to be reminded by his own Canningite President of the Board of Trade, Charles Grant, that other forms of support – such as bounties – had to be scaled back in order to avoid 'the precedent of retracing our steps in any instance.'[89]

Rather than wholescale withdrawal then, the result of this process was a long-term shift in state resources away from local producers to the kinds of national infrastructures which mitigated private risk while facilitating market integration through technological growth. Development thus continued throughout the 1830s and '40s, but its scale and place in the overall mix of expenditure had begun to shift; between 1819 and 1830, the Fisheries Board invested £22,978 – just under a tenth of its total expenditure – in the repair and construction of piers and quays such as those at Balbriggan and Lambay.[90] Its successor, the Board of Works, no longer dispensed any bounties whatsoever but continued to outlay a comparable amount to its predecessor in small-scale pier construction projects annually from 1831 to 1845.[91] Yet, it was not until 1846 that one of the first major famine relief measures could bring maritime infrastructural investment to unprecedented levels: the Piers and Harbours Acts allocated £90,000 in total to the sector buoyed up by charity and local contributions from applicants.[92] Despite much contemporary emphasis on the need for economic development on the Atlantic coast, just under half of all 'Famine piers' including that completed at Rush were built on the eastern seaboard and orientated around the gravitational pull of the Irish Sea.[93]

The case of piers represents just one instance of how 'experiments' in famine administration helped to accentuate existing trends in liberal governance of Ireland. Yet, here, the Irish Sea proved not only a vital site of technology and capital flows in a UK-wide context, but on an increasingly transnational scale as well. With the repeal of the Corn Laws in 1846, suspension of the Navigation Acts in 1847 and reform of the Passenger Acts in 1848, the state sought to facilitate the internationalisation of indirect forms of Irish relief.[94] Between 1845 and 1851, the total quantity of all classes of foreign and colonial imports into Ireland increased by a factor of ten from 26,345 to 269,134 tons, three-quarters of which entered via east-coast ports and close to one fifth through Dublin alone.[95] This increase in turn transformed the capital's maritime hinterland still further, helping to make the Irish Sea a precinct which mediated not only the relationship between Britain and Ireland, but Ireland and much of the rest of the world as well.

Yet, even amidst the growth of steam, the 'open seas' remained 'unruly' and often 'treacherous' ecologies; between the late 1820s and early 1840s, global losses of British and Irish vessels was rarely less than 500 per year and it was estimated that Irish Sea wrecks alone resulted in losses of £5 million from 1845 to 1854.[96] A new focus on civilian maritime safety evident from the 1820s also accelerated with a spate of inquiries into several major maritime disasters beginning in 1847, the year one-in-ten Irish migrants bound for the US and one-in-three for Canada perished at sea or shortly after disembarkation from notoriously over-crowded 'coffin ships'.[97]

Efforts to mitigate the risks of sea travel thus assumed a new and vital significance, with the Irish Sea – and at its heart, the Dublin–Liverpool route – becoming the key focal point for rapidly increasing quantities of Irish-bound corn, outgoing cattle and transiting migrants.[98] In this context, the push for more ambitious interventions to ensure safety at sea gained impetus; building on proposals first set out in ground-breaking select committee inquiries into maritime navigation, security and safety piloted by the Radical Scottish MP Joseph Hume from the mid-1830s, the political and financial support necessary to pursue major infrastructural investments accelerated further under the exigencies of famine.[99] And yet, rather than the more outlandish private schemes to 'fill in' or 'bridge' the Irish Sea which arose in these years, it was the public application of cutting-edge technologies to relatively 'banal' infrastructures which underlay much of this investment.[100] Such deployment ultimately served to socialise the costly burdens associated with embedding a globalising *entrepôt* within the Irish Sea's own complex ecology.

The expansion of lighthouses, often seen as the quintessential 'public good', is indicative of this process.[101] As well as hosting the world's oldest continuous-use lighthouse at Hook Head in Wexford, early Victorian Ireland inherited a relatively comprehensive coastal network; in 1820, it possessed an estimated one-fourteenth of the globe's lighthouses, as many as France on the eve of Augustin-Jean Fresnel's sweeping technological innovations and more than the maritime nations of either Scotland or Sweden.[102] Yet, even while it was later surpassed, Ireland did experience a frenetic period of lighthouse building in the 1840s and 1850s, with a third of all structures put in place during the nineteenth century – 24 in total – emerging in these years.[103] Throughout the Famine, this building was concentrated on the east and south-eastern coastlines with three-fifths of all new lighthouses built up to 1854 situated between Coleraine and Kinsale including the critical 'east' (1847) and 'west' (1852) pier lights which still stand at Dún Laoghaire.[104] The pace of growth was driven by both public investment and liberalisation, with the repeal of the Corn Laws leading to increased revenues from shipping tolls levied by the Dublin Ballast Board, the body responsible for maintaining and building Irish lighthouses; between 1845 and 1852, its annual expenditure doubled to £73,059, while the ports of Kingstown, Howth, Donaghdee and Dunmore absorbed a total of £102,640 on improvements through loans provided by the Board of Works over the same period.[105]

In total, £529,054 was spent by the Ballast Board from 1845 to 1853 before its income fell back to a quarter of its Famine-era average in the late-1850s, an investment comparable in scale to the £1,000,000 outlaid in the 'quasi-nationalisation' of all English and Welsh private lighthouses after 1836.[106] As even John Stuart Mill was willing to concede in his 1848 *Principles of Political Economy*, it was 'a proper office of government to build and maintain lighthouses' on the basis that 'unless indemnified ... there are many scientific researches of great value to a nation... [which] could only be undertaken by few persons'.[107] The impact of such innovation, as Theresa Levitt has argued, ensured lighthouses became truly 'public goods' in both ceasing to function practically on a strictly private basis and by necessitating large-scale public support.[108] Yet, just as investment in UK-wide lighthouses was driven by the need for oil lamps and Fresnel lenses in the 1830s, and later by Michael Faraday's work in photometry, ventilation and electricity, local inventions like Thomas Drummond's lime-light, Alexander Mitchell's screw-pile lighthouse, John Richardson Wigham's gas light and John Tyndall's light pipe ensured this technological momentum ricocheted back and forth across the Irish Sea.[109]

The diverse sources of such development – emanating from industrialists, engineers, scientists and soldiers working across professional and disciplinary boundaries – reflects how technological innovations often transgressed as much as fixing neat distinctions between 'public' and 'private'.[110] Yet, what is striking about the Irish case is that, unlike its counterparts in either England's Trinity House or the Scottish Northern Lights, the Ballast Board was a self-professedly 'public private' oligopoly of mercantile interests.[111] Unlike the 'old corruption' associated with private lighthouse rentiers in England and Wales however, the board reflected wider collaborative arrangements amongst Dublin's merchant class to regulate the intersection of technological with market competition. These included the 'conference system' pioneered by Charles Wye Williams to manage an otherwise destructive competition emanating from the introduction of steam to Irish Sea shipping from the 1820s.[112] The impact of much famine-era infrastructure, including lighthouses, reflected a similar logic; technologies were embedded both inside and outside market structures while helping, in turn, to frame them. The Irish Sea became such an acute focus of technological innovation in the 1840s and 1850s partly because the boundaries of market and state were being so thoroughly reconstituted in those years.

Yet, the tension between 'public' and 'private' technologies in rendering the Irish Sea a stage of free enterprise was often messier than even the case of lighthouses suggest. Such strains frequently arose from the fact that infrastructures which undergirded the growth of maritime capitalism depended upon not only a new 'mastery' of nature, but its effective ordering as well. The development of shipping lanes offers a case in point; here, a system of lights, beacons and signals not only protected vessels from hazards, but did so in concert with the scientific apparatus of cartography, hydrography and ichthyology to co-ordinate movement along preordained routes or within particular regions of water.[113] Alexander Nimmo's pioneering work on marine geology for the Fisheries Board thus led directly to his widely-used manual of sailing instructions in 1832, which in turn fed into the vital mapping work of Ordnance Survey and Admiralty Hydrographical Department throughout the 1840s and 1850s.[114] And here too, the reports of the commission on Tidal Harbours (1845–7) dovetailed with persistent calls for more accurate sea charts by those seeking to 'open' Ireland to trade and commercial development in the midst of the Famine crisis.[115] Yet, moves to 'tame' the Irish Sea in this way inevitably implied distinct political ecologies in their own right, drawing on competing logics of technological capacity and environmental resilience as well as the political priorities of imperial integration, regional development and national security.

Like lighthouses, the development of systemic 'harbours of refuge' in the Irish Sea from the mid-1840s highlights many of the complexities incumbent to such political ecologies, particularly where the technological ordering of private and public sectors overlapped. The first select committee into the topic in 1836 noted a 'great deficiency' of such facilities in the Irish Sea, but established the principle that 'such ports should be formed and kept up at the public expense'.[116] Subsequent inquiries into London and Dublin roads (1836), Irish railways (1838), post office communication (1842) and shipwrecks (1843) narrowed the selection down to two major contenders for a 'national harbour' to connect with Dublin across the Irish Sea, the Welsh villages of Porthdinllaen and Holyhead.[117] Yet, the final choice of the latter in 1847 had, by then, become deeply interwoven with a much wider infrastructural system combining technologies of rail, steam and telegraphic communication into a privileged public-private maritime vein.[118] Holyhead Harbour after 1847, the Chester and Holyhead Railway from 1850 and the Electric Telegraphy Company's submarine cable of 1852 all involved unorthodox forms of state support beyond a cumulative parliamentary vote of £396,260 throughout the Famine years.[119] Yet, more controversially still, they had also served to create conditions of near 'perfect monopoly'.[120] Ultimately, this was justified by both Tories and Whigs on the grounds that it represented the keystone of a wider architecture ensuring order and security to all commerce on the Irish Sea and the deeper political linkage binding Dublin to London.[121]

CONCLUSION

From the perspective of formal sovereignty, the Irish Sea had ceased to be a *res nullius* ('nobody's thing') in the thirteenth century, but its effective status as a *res communis omnium* ('a thing of the entire community') was transformed in the first half of the nineteenth century as the result of political union, international peace and new technology.[122] As this essay has described, the Sea emerged in this context as a critical arena for the application of *laissez-faire* ideology to Ireland in the lead up to, and throughout, the Famine. Yet, it was primarily technology, I argue, which proved both the object and agent of this process. After all, if the Sea was to become a conduit for the social and economic transformation in Ireland, it required the disruptive powers of light, power and velocity to be unleashed across and within it. This process, as I have argued elsewhere in relation to railways, helped to catalyse a 'technocratic' approach central to Victorian liberalism, often deploying emergent technologies reflexively as reified agents of functional 'objectivity'.[123] In reconstructing the impact of technology in the Irish Sea, this essay suggests another significant strand to this story by showing how liberalism became 'durable' in Ireland at the intersection of politics, materiality and the environment.[124]

The Famine is central to this story in a multiplicity of ways, in some cases as an accelerant of existing trends and in others as a spur to experimentation. Furthermore, we can locate Dublin centrally within this shift: the city and its fishermen emerged as an increasingly dominant player in the Irish Sea economy – for instance, as seen in the dominance of Dublin's trawling fleet in this period – while also becoming an increasingly significant bridgehead to Britain, developments fostered by mid-century technological innovations. The focus on technology and ecology throughout this essay has aimed to highlight not only underexamined dimensions of political power and agency, but also to problematise a deeper tendency to divorce and essentialise 'natural' from human actors in relation to the Famine.[125] As the case of fishing highlights, contemporary technologies had the power to reshape work and food entitlements relating to a source of nourishment that was always immune from the potato blight but fully subject to *laissez-faire* reform. Yet, approaching the Irish Sea as a complex theatre of governance in its own right also recognises it as a dynamic space, transforming through a gradual process of domestication and civilianisation into an arena of global exchange on an unprecedented scale. Such changes, in turn, inevitably required massive public investment; the combined expenditures of the Dublin Ballast Board including 24 new lighthouses, the Board of Works outlay on 54 piers, and parliamentary votes for the renovation of systemic harbours at Port Patrick, Kingstown and Holyhead alone amounted to £1,009,508 from 1845 to 1852 – a sum equivalent to all private charity and a tenth of total Treasury expenditure on all famine relief.[126]

Political ecology has recently been summarised as an approach that 'examines winners and losers, is narrated using ... contradiction, and surveys both the "objective" status of nature as well as stories about the status of nature'.[127] In keeping with this formulation, the foregoing analysis has highlighted the apparently opposing – but in fact complimentary – functions of technology as both unfettering private enterprise and securing it from environmental risk through public intervention. The case of reforms to trawlers and trammel nets, the liberalisation of maritime trade and the infrastructural emplacement of piers, lighthouses and harbours emerge here as coeval instruments of a single political ecology, that of a *laissez faire* promoting integration and transformation through the Irish Sea. In recognising the political 'work' of such technologies, not only do 'winners' and 'losers' become more clearly evident, but so too do the roles and culpability of the non-human mechanisms which helped to facilitate such change. Yet, if technology emerges here as an ambivalent agent of liberalism, it does so in ways resonant of the moral and political 'grey zones' in Famine-era society alluded to by Breandán Mac Suibhne, serving as both the scaffolding and sinew of market and state alike.

SECTION II:
CHARITY AND PHILANTHROPY

'The Metropolis of the Poor': Charity and Perceptions of Dublin on the Eve of the Great Famine

JOE CURRAN

In 1842 the lord lieutenant, Earl de Grey, commissioned a report into certain charitable institutions in Dublin hoping to ascertain why they received annual grants from Westminster, when charities elsewhere did not. The resultant document sheds light on contemporary views of Dublin, claiming: 'Immediately after the Union, Dublin, it may be said, ceased to be a metropolis as regards the wealthy, while it continued a metropolis as regards the poor; and in no inconsiderable degree it has remained so since.'[1] It argued that since the departure of the Irish parliament in 1801, the aristocrats and gentry who had frequented the city during the eighteenth century had deserted Dublin, but the city continued to attract the poor as before.

The above quotation was underpinned by several contemporary assumptions about the nature of a capital city. It was believed that a capital should house a substantial wealthy population and be able to support the many poor people attracted to it because of its metropolitan position. Implicit in this was the idea that a capital city, as part of its national leadership role, should be able to provide for some of the poor people who migrated to it. In reality, city authorities made considerable efforts to evade this responsibility, but such migration and an associated duty of care were still seen as a metropolitan fact of life. It was believed that the economic characteristics of a capital city – a critical mass of wealthy people creating demands for services and funds for charities – enabled the poor to be supported.[2] The quote also reflected the view, widely held among Dubliners, that the Union had been detrimental to the city, and that there was a time before the Union when Dublin was a metropolis of both rich and poor, as a capital city should be. As David Dickson has argued, nostalgia for a now-lost pre-Union 'golden age' coloured much discussion about Dublin in the 1830s and 1840s.[3]

By investigating these years further and by examining how philanthropy shaped the city's reputation on the eve of the Famine, this chapter provides perspectives useful for contextualising Dublin during the Famine. Drawing on contemporary comment in newspapers, official reports, and other sources, it examines how activities, structures and events associated with charity reinforced the ways in which the city was perceived by the elite and middle classes. These perceptions did not always reflect Dublin society as it 'actually was' but rather how it was believed to be.[4]

In particular, this chapter will analyse the interactions between charitable endeavour and Dublin's position as 'stateless capital': an urban centre that was not home to a parliament but still performed many of the functions of a national capital.[5] The concept of 'stateless capital' adopted in this essay has been derived from the work of Graeme Morton on Edinburgh. As we will see, Morton indicated that nineteenth-century Edinburgh maintained its position as Scottish metropolis, despite losing its parliament in 1707. Reflecting on two cities that in principle shared a similar position within the United Kingdom provides a way of assessing the overall impacts of philanthropy on how Dublin was perceived.

Nineteenth-century urban centres were complex entities characterised by a variety of social relations, economic interactions and cultural assumptions. Rosemary Sweet, writing about perceptions of the English town between 1680 and 1840, has noted tensions in contemporary views of urban life: for some, towns were beacons of civilisation, for others they were places of degradation and immorality. Sweet argued that the latter view became prevalent with the rise of the industrial town in the early nineteenth century.[6] Yet, in the midst of the growing gloom about urban environmental and moral decay, perceptions of the large town in the British Isles during this period continued to be shaped by many different factors, which often affected their reputation in contradictory ways.

In a fascinating study of civic identity and rivalry in Glasgow and Edinburgh between 1752 and 1842, Helen M. Rapport examined how contemporary writing about these two cities, including the writing of civic histories, helped to shape their reputations (ironically encouraging the view that Glasgow was a more 'modern' place than Edinburgh, despite its long history).[7] Rapport and others have highlighted how a multitude of other factors also influenced the development of a city's reputation during the nineteenth century, including the physical appearance and shape of the city: its prominent public buildings, statues and monuments, as well as new physical infrastructure such as roads and bridges. The ways in which people used the physical space of the city, and how they related to it, could also be significant in shaping how urban reputations were created. Simon Gunn, for example, has discussed the powerful but ambiguous role of civic ceremony in influencing perceptions of English industrial towns.[8]

Local newspapers also played an important role by providing insights into the vibrancy of economic, social and cultural life in urban centres, as did city directories, almanacs and guidebooks. The presence of an official institution such as a courthouse or prison, an important voluntary organisation or even the hosting of public meetings could alter, enhance or damage a town's reputation.[9] The nature of inhabitants' religious or political affiliations also helped to define how a town was perceived, while contemporaries believed that economic endeavours and the nature of market relations strongly impacted a town's character. Prominent Scottish thinker Revd Thomas Chalmers's *The Christian and Civic Economy of Large Towns*, for example, included a didactic exploration of the moral effects of different forms of economic production on a town's social relations.[10]

Philanthropy played a central role in shaping a city's reputation during the nineteenth century. Much charitable publicity material was ephemeral: most annual reports produced by philanthropic bodies probably received a cursory glance from those who received them. Yet, it would have been difficult for the nineteenth-century urban dweller to avoid knowledge of charitable activity. Philanthropic institutions were not only obviously present in the built environment but also in the everyday written word. The front pages of local newspapers were filled with notices placed by charitable organisations soliciting aid, advertising fundraising events and describing the proceedings of their governors.[11] These notices often included lists of prominent donors or managers, which suggested that the organisations were strongly embedded in the life of the city. This impression is similarly given by the lists of charities in city directories, almanacs and guidebooks.

Philanthropy occupied a central position in nineteenth-century urban societies. It provided opportunities for rich and poor to interact, albeit mediated in paternalistic ways. Charities also existed in a space between official government activity and citizens' private lives. Though usually the result of voluntary endeavour, when philanthropists decided to ameliorate social problems, they entered the realm of urban governance.[12] In fact, nineteenth-century charitable organisations frequently interacted with official government bodies. Studying charities therefore provides unique insights into nineteenth-century life beyond the specific activities of the organisations themselves, something Maria Luddy has demonstrated to great effect by using philanthropy to provide critically important insights into gender relations in nineteenth-century Ireland.[13]

Philanthropic organisations helped to shape how contemporaries perceived the urban centres in which they were located, but their effects were multifaceted. The reputational advantages of charitable endeavour to donors are well-known, but philanthropic activity also frequently added to the prestige of an urban centre through use of the streetscape and the built environment.[14] Prominent charities were often housed in lavish buildings, which were considered part of the town's public architecture, and prominent visitors were taken on tours around such institutions.[15] Descriptions of philanthropic activity and charities' buildings featured prominently in 'The Picture of' genre of writing: part guidebook, part civic history, these works emphasised a town's positive attributes.[16] However, charitable efforts, and the fundraising associated with them, could also injure a town's reputation. If charities wanted to raise money, they had to call attention to the social problems that they were designed to ameliorate. This might mean emphasising the diseases, rotting physical infrastructures, or moral iniquities to which the organisation intended to respond.

Both the 'positive' and 'negative' impacts of philanthropy interacted with and reinforced contemporaries' perceptions of towns and helped to further shape their reputations. This was the case for both Dublin and Edinburgh. In terms of the latter Morton claimed that Edinburgh's capital status was preserved during the nineteenth century because it was home to many national-level institutions including the highest law courts of the distinctive Scottish legal system, and some government departments such as the Scottish Exchequer Office and the Scottish Excise Office.[17] Edinburgh hosted the annual meeting of the General Assembly of the Church of Scotland and the meetings of the Convention of Royal Burghs of Scotland (towns with specific legal rights). These gatherings emphasised the city's position at the centre of Scottish administration. Voluntary associations also helped to ensure Edinburgh's metropolitan reputation. Being home to cultural and philanthropic organisations that claimed to serve all of Scotland helped to reinforce the city's national leadership position even after the Anglo-Scottish Union.[18]

Efforts to emphasise Edinburgh's position as the ancient Scottish metropolis were made with one eye fixed on the city's nearby rival, Glasgow. Glasgow's wealth was growing rapidly at this time and by 1821, the city had surpassed Edinburgh in population.[19] Glasgow could also claim to be central to many aspects of Scottish life: it was home to some of Chalmers's most famous philanthropic experiments, which played a critical role in conversations about urban welfare in Scotland and beyond.[20] Edinburgh's commentators, aware of the changes taking place in Glasgow, emphasised the attributes of Edinburgh that were associated with the professions, education and 'national leadership'. Although Glasgow was an old city, Edinburgh's champions emphasised their city's history and connected this with its capital status.[21] This partly resembled the relationship between Dublin and Belfast, though such similarities became clearer later in the century when Belfast surpassed Dublin in population.[22] In 1845 Belfast was significantly smaller, though this did not prevent its elites from highlighting the problems faced by Dublin and other Irish towns to promote their own town's reputation. Alice Johnson, for example, has indicated that Belfast elites eschewed government aid during the Famine to avoid associating their city with other 'beggarly' Irish towns.[23]

As a capital, Dublin, like Edinburgh, was home to the nation's highest law courts, as well as national-level governance institutions. The city also hosted charities designed to serve all of Ireland. These tended to be educational or missionary organisations such as the Society for Promoting the Education of the Poor in Ireland[24] and the Catholic Book Society.[25] In fact, once every year, Ireland's nationally-focused Protestant missionary societies held a week of annual meetings in the city. These gatherings attracted the praise of their supporters and the ridicule of their critics, but in either case they further emphasised Dublin's claims to be the centre of nationally focused activity.[26]

Discussions about charities in both cities highlighted the recognition that, as metropolitan centres, they would attract poor people migrating to them for many reasons, including to access the specialised philanthropic services available in each. Medical hospitals in both cities claimed to be 'national institutions', as poor patients travelled specifically to benefit from their medical expertise.[27] This was a source of frequent complaint on the part of philanthropists, and charities attempted to evade this responsibility by setting minimum residency requirements for applicants, which were often not adhered to in practice.[28] Similarly, charities tried to raise funds on a regional or national basis, in order to make the areas that 'supplied' patients pay their 'fair share'. Such concerns resembled contemporary debates about the necessity of Laws of Settlement within the Poor Law systems but with a specific metropolitan flavour.[29]

Overall, however, partially providing for poor migrants was grudgingly recognised by elites in both Dublin and Edinburgh as part of the responsibility of capital cities. The argument that Dublin was a metropolis for the poor and not for the rich was invoked by the three Dublin-based Unionists who wrote the 1842 report examining the city's charities quoted at the start of this chapter. This strongly implied that looking after poor people arriving from elsewhere in the nation was part of the role of a capital city.[30] This view was shared by the Edinburgh Police Commissioners, a local government body. In 1836 they complained that Dublin received more exchequer funding than Edinburgh and argued that they were entitled to a similar share since, as the 'northern metropolis', Edinburgh experienced the same kind of difficulties as Dublin, attracting many poor people from throughout Scotland.[31]

At the same time, Dublin and Edinburgh resembled many large towns in nineteenth-century Britain, in possessing vibrant philanthropic cultures. Both cities were home to a multitude of charities of diverse sizes and functions, including poor relief organisations, medical hospitals, educational charities, and 'rescue' institutions. City almanacs for 1845 listed 132 charities operating in Dublin and 91 in Edinburgh, and these lists were not exhaustive.[32] Philanthropy in each city had its own unique features. For example, there were a greater number of general medical hospitals and, as might be expected, a greater number of charities with Catholic connections in Dublin, whilst there were several Scottish Poor Law institutions operating in Edinburgh that, unlike their Irish counterparts, relied partly on income raised from voluntary collections, as well as on rates.[33] Overall, though, there was a similar range of charitable organisations operating in both cities and if an inhabitant of one looked at a list of charities from the other, it would have appeared familiar.

Many of these charities were what Robert Morris has called 'subscriber democracies', a governance structure that specified a minimum subscription for membership but in principle had no restrictions on joining other than agreement with the organisations' goals. These associations combined minimum subscription with layers of membership that allowed them to partly reflect existing social hierarchies, while providing some opportunities for those outside traditional elites.[34] Many such charities were operating in Dublin and Edinburgh on the eve of the Famine and members of all the main religious denominations participated in this kind of organisation.[35]

As Morris himself recognised, however, subscriber democracies were not the only philanthropic organisations operating in the early nineteenth century. Martin Gorsky's study of charities in nineteenth-century Bristol indicated that in an urban centre with any history, older charities based on endowments left in trust on the death of a benefactor were frequently operating at mid-century and many had been founded centuries before.[36] These organisations were usually managed by small groups of trustees who held office *ex-officio*, such as local magistrates, or by a self-selecting group. Endowed charities frequently attracted the ire of reformers in the early nineteenth century, who saw them as anti-meritocratic and wasteful.[37]

Nevertheless, endowed charities, and older philanthropic institutions more generally, formed part of a mid-nineteenth-century city's 'philanthropic inheritance'. Richard Rodger argued that as a 'capital city and city of capital, nineteenth-century Edinburgh was shaped by the power of the past', and that endowed charities figured strongly in these processes.[38] Edinburgh was home to several endowed charities known as 'hospitals', most of which were charitable boarding schools. By 1845, several of these had already been in operation for over a century. Some were very wealthy, and their prominent buildings helped shape Edinburgh's reputation as the Scottish metropolis, especially from the 1830s when it became fashionable for the charities to rebuild their institutions in an elaborate, self-consciously 'Scottish' style.[39]

The most influential of Edinburgh's endowed charities was George Heriot's Hospital, a charitable boarding school founded in 1628 (Figure 4.1). This trust was managed by Edinburgh Town Council and the city's Church of Scotland ministers.[40] By the nineteenth century the charity had used its investments to become a major player in Edinburgh's property market. Heriot's did not rebuild its prominent seventeenth-century home, but it had a substantial impact on the shape of the city. In the 1830s Heriot's financed a series of 'foundation schools' throughout Edinburgh (Figure 4.2). These were day schools providing free education for much greater numbers than the original school building could accommodate. The new day schools were designed to look like smaller versions of Heriot's seventeenth-century headquarters, complete with turrets and the school crest. As these buildings spread throughout the city, they served as reminders of how influential

Edinburgh's older charities were.[41] These changes connected past and present, and suggested that the city's historical legacies were shaping a future worth looking forward to. Indeed, they were part of a movement gaining force in Edinburgh from the 1830s where 'traditional' 'Scottish' forms of architecture became favoured over the neoclassical styles that characterised eighteenth and early nineteenth-century public building, further suggesting a city whose present and future were rooted in the Scottish past.[42]

Mid-nineteenth-century Dublin did not possess a collection of wealthy endowed hospital schools but as a city that had long been amongst the largest in the British Isles, Dublin was also home to many older charities and so possessed some sort of 'philanthropic inheritance' on the eve of the Famine. Some of these philanthropic organisations, if not financed entirely by endowments, shared several of the features of an endowed charity. St Patrick's or Swift's Hospital (for psychiatric illness) (founded 1740) and Dr Steevens' (medical) Hospital (founded 1710) were both partly funded by endowments, as was the more recently founded Sir Patrick Dun's Hospital (1791), the purpose-built training hospital for both Trinity College Dublin, and the King and Queen's College of Physicians in Ireland.[43] The financial structures and functions of these charities made them influential in a variety of ways during the Famine. Sir Patrick Dun's endowment was primarily invested in estates outside of Dublin and this partly funded Dun's Hospital.[44] Steevens' Hospital also raised funds from landholdings in King's County and Westmeath.[45] Both, therefore, were landlords during the Famine and both also responded to the direct impact of the calamity on Dublin city through their treatment of victims of the concomitant epidemics.[46]

Older charities also helped to shape how early nineteenth-century Dublin was perceived. St Patrick's and Steevens' Hospitals were architecturally impressive institutions dating from the eighteenth century, as were other older charities, such as the Rotunda Lying-In Hospital, an elaborate complex of ward facilities and entertainment venues designed by Richard Castle in 1745 (Figure 4.3).[47] These hospitals were sometimes looked on as a source of pride by later commentators. In May 1845, for example, the Lord Mayor hosted a dinner of aldermen and a 'select circle of his private friends' at the Mansion House. As they toasted Dublin's medical achievements, they applauded the hospitals founded by medics in the eighteenth century as 'enduring monuments of the philanthropy and kind-heartedness of the medical men of the day'. They claimed that 'there was no capital in Europe in which the benevolence, tenderness, wisdom, and charity of the members of the profession so exhibited themselves to so great an extent as in the Irish metropolis.'[48] Similarly, the author of *London to Dublin*, a travel account published in 1853, discussed Swift's and Steevens' Hospitals to emphasise the charitable nature of contemporary Dublin.[49]

Yet, the residents of early nineteenth-century Dublin did not always use these architectural and philanthropic legacies to rejoice in the current state of their city. This was partly due to how they perceived changes in Dublin more generally. Dun's Hospital opened its doors in 1808 and the Meath Hospital relocated to a new building in 1822, but many of Dublin's most prominent philanthropic buildings predated the Union.[50] As well as the Rotunda, Swift's and Steevens' Hospitals, these included Mercer's Hospital (founded 1734, rebuilt 1759), the Hibernian Marine School (founded 1766) and the King's Hospital or Blue Coat School (founded 1671, new building commenced 1773).[51] In contrast, the buildings of charities founded in Dublin after 1800 did not tend be as architecturally prominent. Indeed, even when based in high-status areas, new charities sometimes appeared to herald decline, as they opted to take over buildings previously used for more prestigious functions, such as the residences of prominent families. Charities in other towns appropriated townhouses for their use, and this too was sometimes associated with loss of prestige.[52]

In Dublin, this lack of architectural ambition served to emphasise what was believed to be the mass exodus of aristocrats from the city following the Act of Union. Dickson has incisively indicated how a sense of decline was thrown into relief by the relationship between charities and architecture. Describing the impact of the Mendicity Association's move into its new home on Usher's Island in 1824, Dickson argued that 'the transformation of Moira House, the old centre of Whig intrigue, into a new asylum for beggars (the Mendicity Institute) was a powerful metaphor' for the perceived degradation of the city.[53] This was reflected in the concerns of a deputation from St Audeon's parish who in June 1822 tried to persuade the charity not to relocate to Moira House. They argued that '[t]he presence of the Institution would force respectable individuals to leave their town houses and would halt improvements now taking place in the area'.[54] Refracted through the lens of the recent Union, the changes in the way Dublin's charities were housed may have also suggested that the city had once been capable of supporting magnificent purpose-built charitable infrastructure but that this lay in the past, part of the lost eighteenth-century 'golden age'.[55] By contrast, Edinburgh's contemporary reputation was enhanced by the city's older charities, some of whose ambitious building projects associated architectural heritage with philanthropic innovation.

In her seminal essay, 'Catholic Dublin: The public expression in the age of Paul Cullen', Mary E. Daly discussed how, in the post-Famine years, Catholics worked to make Dublin look like a Catholic city. This was part of their efforts to demonstrate that the city was no longer the preserve of Anglican elites but rather had been reclaimed for 'the faith'. As Daly has indicated, the building of significant Catholic physical infrastructure, including charitable institutions, was central to this.[56] In the decades before the Famine, Dublin was home to an increasingly confident Catholic middle class spurred on by Catholic Emancipation and O'Connellite associational culture. This encouraged the foundation of many Catholic charities. Although such lively philanthropic activity reflected a rich Catholic middle-class culture operating across Dublin's urban spaces, these charities were not perceived to enhance the city's reputation in the way they would later in the century. The pre-Famine years saw the building of several architecturally significant Catholic churches but Catholic philanthropic architecture tended to be understated.[57]

A comparison between St Vincent's Hospital, established in 1834 by the Sisters of Charity, and the Mater Misericordiæ Hospital opened by the Sisters of Mercy in 1861, is a case in point. The former was situated on the prestigious St Stephen's Green but not in a new purpose-built structure; rather, it re-appropriated the earl of Meath's townhouse. Hence, it provided another reminder of the city's decline in status, as well as the more modest state of the charity's finances. The Mater, by contrast, was a newly-built, imposing edifice in keeping with Cullenite confidence (Figure 4.4). Those fundraising for the Mater's construction in the 1850s claimed it would be 'a permanent monument to the benevolence of the Catholics of Dublin'.[58] In practice plans for the Mater's foundation had begun in the 1840s but it did not have a visual impact on the city until several years after the Famine. In fact, even that hospital's siting speaks somewhat to the perceived decline of Dublin, as it was built in an area once reserved for a 'Royal Circus', a prestigious housing development that was never executed due to the increasing economic problems of its developers.[59]

The German geographer J. G. Kohl noted a similar trend in Edinburgh's Old Town where 'once distinguished' houses had become 'degraded', and the former residence of the Dukes of Queensberry had become 'a beggar's [*sic*] lodging-house' (the House of Refuge and Night Refuge).[60] This was, however, not something that heavily shaped broader perceptions of the city. As Kohl emphasised, conditions in Edinburgh's Old Town rarely received attention and he had only investigated them because he was encouraged to do so by a 'German settled in Edinburgh' who said this was something visitors constantly neglected.[61]

As well as altering the static built environment, charities' temporary appropriation of the public and semi-public spaces of an urban centre could improve a town's reputation. In both Dublin and Edinburgh, prestigious charity fundraising events, such as promenades, enhanced perceptions of the city by associating it with social elites or celebratory public display.[62] Charity processions were used throughout the British Isles and philanthropic schools, in particular, marched their charges through the streets demonstrating to the public how well-cared for their pupils were.[63] Some schools, including institutes for educating deaf and mute children in Dublin and Edinburgh, held public examinations of students to highlight the success of their educational methods.[64] These events were designed to emphasise that the charities were a civic asset and to publicly demonstrate to observers the city's commitment to philanthropy.

Public ceremonies organised to celebrate Edinburgh's hospital schools helped to enhance the reputation of the city and its civic elites. Ceremonies, for example, were held on 'George Heriot's Day' to celebrate the birthday of the founder of Edinburgh's most prestigious charity. These events required significant coordination as local government officeholders took part in the ceremonies alongside pupils from the city's other hospital schools. In June 1844, the *Caledonian Mercury* reported that Edinburgh's chief magistrate (the lord provost), councillors and clerics participated in the ceremonies along with hundreds of children. The newspaper noted that the processions were witnessed by 'several thousands of respectable citizens'.[65] These events provided a way of celebrating, not simply Heriot's Hospital, but Edinburgh itself and the philanthropy, wealth and power of its elites.[66]

Dublin was also the scene of public processions by charitable institutions, and these too sometimes served to enhance that city's reputation. However, as with the contrast between pre- and post-Union philanthropic architecture in Dublin, the relationship between nineteenth-century charitable processions and civic pride was complex and variable. The ability of charity processions to mutually reinforce institutional and civic prestige in Edinburgh was aided by the existence of several venerable hospital schools whose pupils created a 'critical mass of respectability' with which dignitaries could be associated. Dublin, by contrast, lacked a similar number of high-status charities meaning that philanthropic display did not always muster the same level of civic enthusiasm.

Before municipal reform legislation was passed, the then exclusively Protestant Dublin Corporation governed the King's Hospital, one of Dublin's rare seventeenth-century foundations.[67] This charity did not possess the riches of its Edinburgh counterpart Heriot's, but the pre-reform corporation considered it to be of higher status than many of the city's other charities. Corporation members were prepared to use the school to display their own Protestant affiliations, such as when, in 1828, they resolved that its pupils would wear Orange ribbons on 'the usual public days'.[68] They, however, expressed concern when its pupils were invited to attend the annual procession and catechetical examination for charity school children held by the Association for Discountenancing Vice, an organisation that promoted Protestant religious knowledge. The corporation knew that children from significantly 'lower status' charities would take part in the procession and that the hospital could be damaged by association.

In 1828, while somewhat exaggerating the school's wealth, corporation members argued that:

> as the King's Hospital ... is a Royal Foundation possessing ample estates and independent property. – It is the opinion of the Sheriffs and Commons, that it is derogatory to the respectability of that establishment to allow the Boys educated therein to join in processions made by the children of Charity Establishments. And therefore, we request an order to prohibit their attendances in any future processions of Charity Children.[69]

The pre-reform corporation was a staunchly Protestant body that frequently claimed to be dedicated to the promotion of Protestantism.[70] That it expressed qualms about these events highlights how potentially damaging association with 'lower status' organisations was perceived to be for charities with social pretensions. In fact, the school's managers had already worked out a compromise solution: 'the Boys of this House shall not join the other children in procession, but merely that they should proceed to the Cathedral where they would have a separate Gallery to themselves, during Divine service'.[71] The lord mayor would be present with the pupils in this gallery, highlighting the institution's connection with civic elites. This compromise ensured that the school could still claim a role in the defence of Protestantism, while eschewing the taint of pauperism associated with walking alongside the other charity children. In Edinburgh the existence of many prestigious charities which, working together, could use public space to mutually maintain their status meant the attendance of children from lower status charities was unnecessary to bring an impressive number of pupils on to the streets. By contrast, Dublin elites who wanted to demonstrate a commitment to Protestantism were forced to make this compromise.

Even more significant was the Dublin Mendicity Association's use of city space. This organisation's main objective was to take beggars off the streets by providing them with food, work and shelter during the day. It sometimes held fundraising initiatives, such as balls, attended by elite supporters, which newspapers added to their descriptions of exciting events in the city. In May 1828 the Mendicity Fancy Ball, for example, featured in the *Freeman's Journal* 'Fashionable World' column dedicated to cataloguing elite social activities throughout the British Isles.[72] On a number of occasions, however, the society's management decided to hold events of a less 'fashionable' kind: processions of those who used their services. The *Freeman's Journal* argued that these demonstrated the Mendicity's value to observers, by reminding them of what the city had been like before the organisation existed. When discussing one such procession, the newspaper described the Mendicity as 'that Institution which gives such benefit to this city, by keeping of beggars from our shop doors, which are yet even in our recollection'.[73]

Rather than highlighting how well cared-for the marchers were, however, these parades emphasised the poor condition and destitution of those who would be released back on the streets if the society could not raise sufficient funds to survive.[74] They were held when the charity was in particularly dire financial straits and by reminding citizens of the precarious existence of a major charity, they highlighted how Dublin could easily decline further. The reputational impact of these demonstrations was suggested in 1830 when Dublin Castle and the lord mayor contacted the charity to express their strong opposition to its plans to hold a parade.[75] On this occasion the organisation relented but on 16 August 1839 it announced that it would be 'reduced to the melancholy necessity of parading the Paupers through the streets of Dublin' unless sufficient funds were found. It held this procession on 21 August.[76] The *Freeman's Journal* referred to the parade as 'this most disagreeable course'. It noted, perhaps with some embarrassment, that the parade had taken place 'through all the principal streets and leading thoroughfares' of Dublin, and that many of the marchers had been 'reduced the very verge of actual starvation' – a far cry from processions designed to demonstrate the healthy state of a charity's charges, or the generosity of its donors.[77]

Public discussions about charity were used to highlight Dublin's problems by those across the city's political spectrum. In order to present an effective case, Repealers needed to emphasise the problems that they believed the Union was causing and they seized on the opportunities that philanthropy offered to emphasise Dublin's perceived degradation.[78] Significantly, however, when Unionists discussed charitable activity, they sometimes presented a similar picture of the city. This chapter began by considering a quote from an official inquiry into philanthropic funding that was carried out by three Dublin-based Unionists.[79] In their report, they strongly recommended continuation of parliamentary grants to the city's philanthropic institutions, arguing that while Dublin could in time recover, the grants were needed to compensate for the initial damage arising from the Union.[80] Their discussion of the parliamentary grants allowed them to present a bleak picture of Dublin as a town unable to properly look after its social problems. They expressed the hope that in time, with the temporary support of the grants, Dublin would achieve 'the same creditable position as great towns in England, where the hospitals, being unconnected with the poor-law system, are amply supported by the liberality and charity of the inhabitants'.[81] Their praise of large English towns at the height of 'The Condition of England Question', when many commentators damned social conditions in these urban centres, reflected and reinforced a bleak assessment of Dublin's position.[82]

The introduction of the Irish Poor Law (1838) and the reform of the Scottish Poor Law (1845) indicated that, in practice, there was a need to respond more effectively to poverty in both cities. These measures also further 'bureaucratised' poor relief in each city: yet, even these changes enhanced differences between Edinburgh and Dublin. The Irish Poor Law introduced a significant extra layer of representative local government in Dublin, but supervision by appointed Poor Law officials and close connections with the English Poor Law may have further exacerbated a sense of dependence in the city on the eve of the Famine.[83] The New Scottish Poor Law system also introduced central oversight by establishing an Edinburgh-based Board of Supervision. This board, however, allowed some continuity with the Old Scottish Poor Law. The board was independent of the English Poor Law system, it allowed greater local variation in relief provision than permitted in Ireland and even included the Lord Provost of Edinburgh as an *ex-officio* member.[84] All of these features allowed Edinburgh to continue to appear more independent than Dublin.

Nineteenth-century Dublin and Edinburgh had much in common with other large towns in the contemporary UK. In all these places philanthropy had a broad range of effects helping to both simultaneously enhance and damage a city's reputation. Dublin and Edinburgh were marked out from other UK towns by their stateless-capital status, but this meant that the two cities shared many features. The differences between Dublin and Edinburgh were very much matters of degree rather than kind, especially when it came to the impact of philanthropy. Nevertheless, these differences could serve to reinforce contemporary views about each city. In practice Dublin had a vibrant philanthropic associational culture and Edinburgh in 1845 was home to significant poverty. Both cities had a long history of philanthropy associated with impressive public buildings and both cities' charities held eye-catching public events. Viewed through the lens of contemporary hopes and anxieties, however, on the eve of the Famine these features helped to further the idea that Edinburgh continued to draw strength from its past, while in Dublin they helped to reinforce a sense of a capital city in decline.

The Impact of the Great Famine on Voluntary Charitable Societies in Dublin City

CIARÁN MCCABE

Studies of poor relief during the Great Famine have understandably centred on assistance provided through the Poor Law system. Owing to the sheer numbers who were admitted to these institutions, the centrality of the Poor Law system to welfare provision in Ireland at the time and, of course, the wealth of surviving Poor Law records, the workhouse has been central to popular memory and scholarly studies of the Famine. Just as this is the case for locations throughout Ireland, it is also true of the historiography in respect of Dublin during the Famine.[1] However, large portions of Dublin's welfare landscape during the Famine years remain underexplored – the roles played by Catholic religious communities, the Church of Ireland and civil parish vestries, and the plethora of voluntary charitable societies that were already in existence in the city or the new charities that emerged in Dublin during the late 1840s. This chapter examines the third of these topics, focusing on the impact of the Famine on the city's charitable societies, the role of charities in meeting the temporal needs of the rural migrants who flooded into the city and the role of charities in responding to the 1847 Vagrancy Act.[2]

Timothy P. O'Neill's study of charities and famines throughout the nineteenth century examines the relief committees established during the Great Famine and notes the role played by clergy in raising and distributing funds; yet Dublin's pre-existing charitable societies are not covered in his analysis.[3] Dublin city's charitable scene in the early nineteenth century was largely denominationally-based and in a period of heightened tensions between Catholics and Protestants, this sector was characterised by rivalry and suspicion. However, some philanthropists transcended the often-bitter divide. Among the most notable such figures during the Famine years was the Carmelite friar, Revd John Spratt, a towering presence in mid-century Dublin whose charitable work during the Famine has been recounted by Fergus D'Arcy, including Spratt's involvement with the Sick and Indigent Roomkeepers' Society, the Metropolitan Relief Committee for the Poor of the City of Dublin, the relief committee of the Church of Ireland parish of St Peter's and, from May 1849, the General Relief Committee.[4] The Famine work of individual charities is also discussed briefly in Deirdre Lindsay and Audrey Woods's respective case studies of the Sick and Indigent Roomkeepers' Society and the Dublin Mendicity Association, while Joseph Robins's study of 'charity children' in eighteenth- and nineteenth-century Ireland limits its discussion of the Famine to the Poor Law workhouse system.[5] Elsewhere, Cormac Ó Gráda demonstrates the pastoral activism of the city's Church of Ireland clergy through the Dublin Parochial Association, which encouraged and rewarded cleanliness and respectability among the urban working classes.[6]

The charitable landscape in the middle of the century was crowded, competitive and complex, and especially during the Famine years, the main charities that provided material assistance to the poor, in the form of food, shelter, fuel and clothing, filled a gap left by the Poor Law system. Charitable societies operated on a voluntary basis (in their fundraising and their management) and endeavoured to assist the poor according to the discretion of their managing committees. As such, the city's charities played an important role in relieving the local and non-local poor in Famine Dublin at a time when the city's workhouses were overwhelmed and this study illuminates an important, yet largely overlooked, sector of Irish society which contributed to the relief of the poor during the Great Famine.

THE POOR OF DUBLIN

The population of Dublin city totalled just more than 230,000 on the eve of the Famine.[7] According to the apothecary and social surveyor Thomas Willis, whose analysis of the 1841 census outlined the wretched social conditions prevalent in the city, around half of the 45,000 families living in Dublin resided in single rooms.[8] Four decades previously the prevalence of overcrowded and insanitary living conditions for significant numbers of Dublin's poor had been identified and comprehensively charted in Revd James Whitelaw's *Essay on the Population of Dublin* (published in 1805), and was further recorded in subsequent social surveys and reports typically by medical practitioners, the most notable being Barker and Cheyne's nationwide study of the 1816–19 typhus fever epidemic.[9] Thus, on the eve of the Famine, many Dubliners were living in overcrowded, multi-occupancy tenements with little or no sanitary provision, and residing under tenuous leases (usually by the week and sometimes by the day) for these overcrowded spaces, commonly termed 'fever nests' in the language of nineteenth-century social surveys.[10]

Contemporaries were aware of how the urban experience of the Famine was not known about to the same extent as that of rural Ireland. In December 1846, in the immediate aftermath of the second successive failure of the potato crop, the Catholic parish priest of St Michael's and St John's parish, Revd Andrew O'Connell, urged the readers of the *Freeman's Journal* that while public attention was focused on the national scale of the ensuing crisis,

> we should not lose sight of the sufferings of those more immediately the objects of our sympathy – I mean the destitute poor of this city, who at this moment are suffering grievously for want of food or fuel, and what is horrible to imagine, want of a night shelter from the inclemency of the present season.[11]

Four weeks later, a letter writer to the same paper, calling himself 'A FRIEND TO THE POOR', contrasted the survival strategies open to the rural and urban poor, concluding that the latter were at a disadvantage:

> The poor of Dublin alone are all but forgotten. Numbers of hard-working poor tradesmen have been thrown out of employment in consequence of the distressed state of the country. They have no "public works", and only a fraction of them can find shelter in the poorhouses and mendicity. They must inevitably die if some well devised scheme of relief be not immediately set on foot.[12]

In the same issue, the *Freeman's Journal* editorialised that

> citizens of Dublin have a more intimate knowledge of want, and misery, and suffering of the cottier population of Skibbereen, of Mayo, and Clare, than they have of the more appalling destitution of the hundreds of human beings who are huddled together in the lodging houses of Dublin.[13]

Such evidence suggests that, firstly, as early as the first week of January 1847 Skibbereen had entered the lexicon of Famine Ireland as synonymous with its severity, and secondly, contrary to Patrick Lynch and John Vaizey's findings that Dublin city and other 'maritime' economies were relatively isolated from the horrors of the Famine,[14] the populations of large urban centres were indeed impacted by the wider national crisis.[15]

Unlike the Poor Law Union workhouses, where admission registers allow us to glimpse the lives and actions of paupers who used the system – their name, age, home place, family members, and the dates on which they entered, left and oftentimes re-entered the workhouse – the records of Dublin's charities do not provide such a snapshot of individual recipients' experiences. The sources determine that attention is limited to the words and actions of the charities' managers and supporters, which illuminate other aspects of Famine Dublin previously unexplored by historians. This absence of source material from the perspective of the poor themselves means that we do not know how the poor experienced their encounters with charities but it is reasonable to assume that the giving of assistance (in the form of cash, food, fuel and clothing) evoked mixed feelings in the recipients: the acceptance of necessities undoubtedly brought relief for the penurious and destitute, but the social disparities of the parties, and the givers' expectations as to the moral behaviour of their beneficiaries, may have bred suspicion, resentment and tension. The poor, though, possessed agency in this exchange. Officers of charities in this period were known to complain of poor persons applying to, and oftentimes receiving alms from, multiple charities simultaneously, reflecting the poor's knowledge of Dublin's welfare landscape, as well as the insufficient co-ordination between the city's charities catering for the same, or similar, class of paupers.[16]

Before considering the impact of the Famine on Dublin's charities, it is fruitful to consider quantitively the capacity of some of the larger and more prominent societies and to contrast this capacity with the city's two Poor Law workhouses. In the early-1840s, the Strangers' Friend Society (SFS) – a Methodist charity established in 1790 that catered for the temporal wants of non-Methodists, favouring unemployed artisans and the typically industrious poor – relieved on average 5,798 persons annually, while in 1844 and 1845, the Sick and Indigent Roomkeepers' Society (SIRS) – a non-denominational charity, also established in 1790, aimed at relieving the 'respectable' poor – assisted on average 26,982 persons annually. In the cases of the SFS and the SIRS assistance to successful applicants came in the form of cash or in kind (for example, food, fuel, clothing or blankets), and was provided to the poor person/family in their own dwelling. On the other hand, the non-denominational Dublin Mendicity Association (DMA), which was founded in 1818, provided its paupers with food and assistance at its premises on Usher's Island, requiring paupers to enter the poorhouse in the morning, work throughout the day and leave in the early evening. The DMA, the city's most prominent charity focused on the relief of poverty, was greatly affected by the introduction of the Poor Law and the opening of the poor rates-funded workhouses; the numbers it was relieving on a *daily* basis fell from around 2,500 in 1838 to 340 in 1845.[17] There is evidence of a significant crossover between the clients of the DMA and another welfare organisation, the Bow Street Night Asylum.[18] Established in 1838 in the north inner city, the night asylum provided shelter, and no food, for the houseless poor, many of whom were non-locals; in 1844, the asylum catered for 34,579 persons during the year, sheltering on average ninety-five people every night.[19] It is important to note that despite the various capacities of the aforementioned charities – certainly not representing the totality of voluntary societies relieving poverty – Dublin's two workhouses loomed large over the city's welfare landscape. The North and South Dublin Union workhouses – both of which were subsumed into the physical buildings of eighteenth-century institutions – could each accommodate an estimated 2,000 paupers; at the height of the Famine, these capacities were exceeded considerably.[20]

IMPACT ON CHARITABLE SOCIETIES

The most obvious impact that the Famine exerted on Dublin's charities was in the increased number of applications for assistance; inevitably, demand for relief far outweighed the voluntary bodies' limited supplies. In its annual report for 1846 the Sick and Indigent Roomkeepers' Society expressed regret that the 27 per cent increase in the number of persons relieved during the year (rising from *c.*24,000 to more than 30,000)[21] 'fell infinitely short of the applications, in consequence of the want of means to administer relief'.[22] Two years later, the same society appealed to the public to continue supporting the institution, owing to its particular focus on relieving unemployed artisans – a category widely regarded as being industrious and 'deserving' of assistance. At a time when 'the workhouses are full to overflowing' and 'the trade of Dublin … is almost paralysed, if not entirely annihilated', assisting the habitually independent members of the labouring classes would restore pride to such persons and, crucially, keep them out of the workhouses.[23] In 1852 the society, while facing small numbers applying for relief, was still expressing regret that not all applicants received alms (either in cash or food, fuel or clothes), owing to insufficient resources.[24]

As well as the increasing number of applicants, charities saw their income levels fluctuating as well, reflecting the impact of the Famine and wider economic downturn on the charity's supporters, most of whom were from the city's merchant and trading classes. Broadly, charities benefitted from an increase in income from donations and bequests in 1847, reflecting public sympathy for the destitute during and following the onslaught of the winter of 1846–7. However, income peaked in 1847 and fell in subsequent years, owing to the diminished state of the economy and its effects on the income of the middle classes, who constituted the source of charities' voluntary income, but also perhaps owing to a localised version of the 'compassion fatigue' identified by Peter Gray as having marked the British public's benevolence to Irish Famine relief projects from late-1847 onwards.[25] This is best captured in the income levels recorded by the Mendicity Association. The society, among the most prominent on Dublin's welfare landscape, saw its income increase by 16 per cent in the first year of crisis (1845–6), from £1,983 to £2,308, before rising another 55 per cent in 1847, from £2,308 to £3,584. However, income dropped significantly the following year, by 53 per cent, falling from £3,584 to £1,685 during 1848 (see Table 1 below).

Table 1. Subscriptions and other casual income received by the Dublin Mendicity Association, 1838–48[27]

Year	Annual subscriptions (£)	Casual income (such as fines, legacies and donations) (£)	Total income (£)
1838	4,793	3,877	8,670
1839	6,366	4,815	11,181
1840	1,892	2,915	4,807
1841	661	1,330	1,991[26]
1842	564	1,336	1,900
1843	592	974	1,566
1844	717	1,209	1,927
1845	662	1,321	1,983
1846	1,143	1,165	2,308
1847	1,569	2,015	3,584
1848	708	977	1,685

In times of straitened circumstances charities continued with previous fundraising initiatives, such as charity sermons,[28] while continuing to receive, and benefit from, bequests.[29] A particularly novel fundraiser was the performance in December 1848 by 'Professor' John Henry Anderson, the world-renowned Scottish 'Wizard of the North', of his travelling show of music, magic and clairvoyance, in aid of the St Michan's conference of the Society of St Vincent de Paul.[30] Just four months later the same conference was the beneficiary of a charitable 'monster panorama and moving model of the revolution in Paris, June, 1848', hosted in the Rotunda concert room. The panorama was 'painted on upwards of Thirty Thousand feet of Canvas' and tickets to the attraction were priced between 6*d.* and 1*s.*[31]

Elsewhere in this volume Joe Curran outlines Dublin's charity landscape on the eve of the Famine. While Dublin boasted scores of charities – Curran provides the figure of 132 charitable and philanthropic entities, drawing on contemporary directories and almanacs – a number of organisations came into existence throughout the late-1840s in direct response to the Famine crisis.[32] The city's welfare landscape altered considerably with the arrival of the Society of St Vincent de Paul (SVP) in 1845, arguably the most active charities throughout the city, who modelled their approach to social activism on the founding conference in Paris, established in 1833. The SVP 'conferences' were parish-based associations of Catholic lay men who embraced the Vincentian approach of seeing the suffering Christ in the poor person, thus imbuing the poor with holy and 'deserving' qualities, and who exhibited the zeal to attend to the spiritual wants of the poor through home-visiting and catechesis.[33] Between 1845 and 1850 seven conferences of the Society of St Vincent de Paul were established within the city, whose activities included the distribution of food, clothing, cash and fuel, as well as related endeavours focused on moral and social improvement, fostered through home visiting.[34] In the spring of 1847 the St Michan's parish conference decided to concentrate its efforts on clothing the destitute poor, establishing a clothes depot for 'cast-off clothing' and urging donations from persons of all classes. Meanwhile, the social activism of the St Kevin's conference ranged from whitewashing the homes of up to seventy poor families to employing poor girls in bonnet-making; these were practical measures which, respectively, stymied the spread of infection among the lower classes and trained girls in 'habits of industry', equipping them with skills to increase their opportunities for independence.[35] The society's impact on the welfare landscape of Dublin city was immediate, and this can be attributed to the zeal of its members and the importance of home-visiting to its *caritas*. As early as 1846, a North Dublin Union Board of Guardians' member was urging as many of the union's inhabitants as possible to join the SVP, given 'the vast amount of good already achieved by that meritorious body'; such high praise suggests it is highly likely this guardian was himself an SVP member.[36] In a public letter published in December 1846, the society was one of three charities specifically named and championed by Catholic priest Revd Andrew O'Connell as providing relief to 'the sufferings of one's fellow-creatures ... in our own neighbourhood, at our own doors', in instances where the Poor Law union workhouses fell short.[37] The SVP conferences were, in their early months and years, already playing a crucial role in the city's welfare realm as one of numerous voluntary organisations plugging the hole left by the overwhelmed Poor Law workhouse system.

In framing its charitable work and the recipients of its assistance the SVP maintained distinctions between the 'deserving' and 'undeserving' poor, assuring the public that its efforts focused on the former. Like most charities the Society of St Vincent de Paul reflected the social perspectives, biases and expectations of its founders, who privileged respectability, industriousness, independence and restraint. For example, one charitable fundraiser in December 1848 on behalf of the St Michan's conference, based in the city's north-west, was advertised as being for 'the relief of the unemployed and starving artizans of the most wretched district in this city'.[38] The unemployed artisan was seen as someone whose distress was caused not by self-indulgence but through factors outside of one's control; the provision of temporary assistance would assist the recipient of charity to return to habits of industry, and did not threaten to pauperise the typically-independent artisan.[39] The centrality of respectability, morality and industry to the workings of the society was inherent to its ethos and was instilled into its lay members. In a spring 1847 circular to all Irish conferences from the society's national council, members were reminded to always bear in mind

> that Christian charity which binds every member of our Society in love and affection to the poor, sweetly constrains us, at all times, to embrace and to use with meakness [sic], with kindness, with patience, with perseverance, every opportunity of relieving the distressed, of consoling the afflicted, of instructing the ignorant, of upraising the dejected, and of guiding all into the paths of religion and virtue, of morality and industry.[40]

Another Vincentian newcomer to the city's welfare landscape, which had as its object 'the temporal and spiritual relief of the sick poor', was the Ladies' Association of Charity of St Vincent de Paul (LAC). The first branch was established in the southern suburb of Kingstown (Dun Laoghaire) in 1843, with a city (Metropolitan) branch formed in 1851.

As with the Society of St Vincent de Paul, the LAC was parish-based: home-visiting, sick calls, attendance on the dying and the provision of clothing were carried out by the lay women of the LAC, led by Margaret Aylward, later the foundress of the Sisters of the Holy Faith.[41] Run by a managing committee of women, the association had a special concern for relieving the 'spiritual wants of the poor in their sickness', and combined the relief of poverty with catechesis, instruction in parenting and household management.[42] In its first year of work the LAC members made almost 4,000 visits to the sick poor and relieved 217 families of their material wants.[43] The LAC was praised in Archbishop of Dublin Paul Cullen's pastoral of August 1852 for its services rendered to the poor, as well as being a model of zeal and edification which served as inspiration for other socially-active lay Catholics within his archdiocese.[44]

Early on, the association devoted considerable energies to 'the instruction of the ignorant' as a means of combatting proselytism in the evangelical Protestant schools so prevalent in Dublin's slums.[45] In this, the LAC's primary rival was the Society for Irish Church Missions, a Protestant missionary society (founded in 1847) that established and ran poor schools and residential homes in direct competition with Aylward's association. The early activities of the LAC and the IMC, both founded during the Famine years, anticipated the bitter struggles between Catholics and Protestant school managers in the city's slums in the 1850s and 1860s in an atmosphere of heightened sectarian suspicion and enmity.[46] As in the years before and during the demographic crisis of the 1840s, post-Famine philanthropy would continue to be marked by denominational rivalries.

Dublin's Protestants were also active in founding new charitable societies in the Famine years. In March 1847 the Dublin Parochial Association commenced its work in 'the relief of the poor of all denominations through the medium of the Parochial Clergy' of the Established Church.[47] The Church of Ireland clergy were held to be 'the most fitting channel of relief' and best placed for 'ascertaining those who are deserving of assistance, and detecting imposture'.[48] International networks within Freemasonry were also drawn upon in the raising and distribution of money for the poor: for example, Freemasons in India subscribed £5,000 for the Irish 'suffering poor' and, interestingly, this figure was 'exclusive of large sums from wealthy Hindoes of high caste, who have latterly been admitted into the order, by authority of the Grand Lodges [sic] of England'.[49] The Grand Lodge of England also granted the sum of £1,000 'to the famishing poor of Ireland and Scotland'.[50] As well as their own in-house initiatives, Irish Freemasons (mostly, but not exclusively, Protestants) contributed to external funds, such as the General Central Relief Committee.[51]

CHARITIES AND FAMINE-ERA MIGRANTS

Among the most pressing challenges faced by Dublin's charities in the 1840s was responding to the influx of rural migrants into the city centre. The percentage of Dubliners born outside of Dublin rose significantly between 1841 and 1851, rising from 27 to 39 per cent, 'largely the result of the Great Famine', according to Ó Gráda.[52] Large towns and cities throughout Ireland had always acted as magnets for the rural poor at times of acute distress.[53] As an urban centre with a large supply of casual labour, as well as being a port town and a hub for welfare provision, Dublin had long attracted rural migrants, a trend which multiplied during periods of scarcity. For instance, the impact of the famine and typhus fever epidemic of 1816-19 on the city and its population was aggravated by the arrival of countless numbers of rural poor, who settled in slums in the city's north-western quarter, from where the contagious typhus spread throughout the urban population.[54] In the late-1840s also, many rural migrants came in search of employment, poor relief or passage out of Ireland. Of those who arrived into the city large numbers stayed and settled into Dublin's growing slum quarters, particularly in the north-western hub around Church Street and Barrack Street. For those coming into the city from the north (from Counties Meath and Louth, for example) and the west (from central Leinster), the north-west of the city was a natural location in which to find accommodation and settle, whether temporarily or permanently. As Timothy Guinnane and Cormac Ó Gráda have noted, the North Dublin Poor Law Union was considerably exposed to the financial and logistical fall-out of the huge refugee inflow, owing to its geographic location in relation to surrounding counties, its proximity to the North Wall docks (where passengers coming from Britain disembarked) and the presence in the North Dublin union area of the Bow Street Night Asylum.[55]

Welfare organisations in the city experienced significant pressures in these distressed times and the importance played particularly by the Bow Street night asylum in assisting the new migrants was noted by the North Dublin Union Board of Guardians in April 1847:

> All flocking to the metropolis in vain hope of relief, impressed with the belief that where the seat of Government is, the noble and the wealthy will be found, but alas, on their arrival sad disappointment is their lot, they find nothing but distress and destitution and see around them, as it were, a making of their wants in the deserted mansions of the noble and untenanted dwellings of the once opulent Merchants, and then in the bitterness of despair hide themselves in this [Bow Street] asylum until hunger drives them to seek the shelter of the poor-house.[56]

Other institutions experienced influxes of migrants. At the Westmoreland Lock Hospital, which was by this stage catering largely for prostitutes suffering from venereal disease, admissions rose significantly during the late 1840s, and 70 per cent per cent of applicants during the Famine years were from outside Dublin.[57] Maurice Craig's description of Dublin at this time as a 'gigantic refugee camp' appears most apt.[58]

Many of Dublin's new inhabitants who applied for admission to the city's workhouses were refused, for a variety of reasons. Either they were not entitled to admission, or the workhouse was simply full and not accepting in any more inmates: for example, in the spring of 1847 there were around 2,900 inmates at the North Dublin Union, nearly 50 per cent more than the workhouse's capacity of 2,000.[59] In such circumstances, the migrant poor had little option but to fall back on the city's charitable societies. Some charities had novel ways of dealing with this influx. The Strangers' Friend Society (SFS) continued its work in relieving the non-local poor, who had no support networks in Dublin from which to draw assistance. Among the cases in 1846 dealt with by the SFS was that of a 'man of colour, who arrived from American a day or two ago', and who solicited assistance and advice from a police office on how best to travel to England.[60]

In December 1848, owing to a substantial increase in applications for admissions and increased pressure on finite resources, the Mendicity Association voted to restrict relief to only those in the greatest distress – thus, for the first time in its thirty-year history, the charity was resolving not to give relief to every eligible person who applied. As recently as its 1845 annual meeting, the association's pride in the fact that its doors remained open at all times for the receipt of destitute persons was evident. As the meeting heard, it was

> the only institution in Dublin, where a poor man might walk in at any moment he chose, sit down and get a wholesome meal free of charge. Let him come when he chose, he was welcome. No one was ever turned from the door.[61]

In explaining its Famine-era readjustment the society blamed the inadequacies of the city's union workhouses for this state of affairs, noting, for example, that the South Dublin Union did not readmit persons until one month after they last left the workhouse.[62] Paupers were thus forced to fall back on their own resources or the city's charities. Throughout Dublin's welfare landscape, organisations came under unprecedented pressure and relief, by necessity, could not reach all 'deserving' applicants, a fact that much aggrieved the charities' managers.[63]

The pressures experienced by the city's charities were stressed in numerous public appeals throughout this period. In 1846, one newspaper noted in respect of the SFS, which focused its resources on the non-local poor and also on industrious Dubliners who had fallen on hard times:

> For cases of distress comprehended in the design of the Strangers' Friend Society, no provision has been contemplated, or is, in fact, afforded by the Poor Law system, now in operation in this City.[64]

The SFS envisaged its beneficiaries as constituting the 'deserving', typically industrious poor, whose destitution was owing to no cause on their own part, and who would rather suffer in silence than seek alms on the public streets or submit oneself to the immoral atmosphere of the workhouse. In the eyes of the SFS, the 'respectable poor' saw the Poor Law workhouse as an unfathomable last resort. The charity, and its middle-class volunteers, feared for the poor's moral debasement, and that of their children, through exposure to the harsh regime and the immoral inmates, such as prostitutes and habitual criminals. The charities who catered for this 'honest' class of poor stressed in their public and private records the imperative to keep such persons away from the morally debilitating environment of the workhouse.[65] In a public appeal for funds in October 1846 the Benevolent Strangers' Friend Society (BSFS), which split from the SFS in 1816,[66] specified that its funds were limited to 'the destitute stranger … and in assisting the industrious poor to provide for their families when they have been reduced to need it through sickness or other casualties'. The BSFS aided 1,500 persons in 1845–6 – persons who, it stated, had been 'saved from being a burthen on their fellow-citizens in the poorhouses'.[67] The Sick and Indigent Roomkeepers' Society (SIRS) also reminded the public that its charity especially assisted the silent, suffering poor – 'a class of persons … the most likely to be neglected, because least disposed to make known their wants and necessities … [who live] where unobtrusive want conceals her wretchedness – where those who have known better days …' Such persons, the SIRS continued in its public appeal, 'are enabled to resume their customary occupations, and are saved from dropping down to the class of utter mendicancy, and to becoming a permanent burden on the community'.[68]

This 'mop-up' role of the charities was reflected in a November 1847 invitation to the lord lieutenant, the 4th earl of Clarendon, to serve as the Mendicity Association's patron:

> It has been found necessary to continue this voluntary institution in Dublin altho Union poorhouses have been established by law … During the last winter it was of essential service to the poor as more than 2,000 were daily fed in the months of March and April until out door relief was afforded. At present there are about 500 fed and particular attention is paid to the casual poor who have not an immediate claim on the union poorhouses.[69]

In December 1848, at a time when the Mendicity Association alerted the public to its rapidly dwindling finances and increasing inability to provide relief, it more assuredly addressed the failings of the Poor Law system:

> In the union poor houses, there is only one admission day each week; we ask where is the pauper to be relieved should the doors of our institution be closed. Again it is a rule of the South Union not to admit paupers unless a month has elapsed since they left the workhouse. Where is the pauper to meet with support in the interval, except in our institution or by begging for alms in the streets?[70]

THE VAGRANCY ACT, 1847

The circumstances of the Famine also led to Dublin's most prominent charity for the direct material relief of the poor – the Mendicity Association – publicly criticising perceived legislative pitfalls and the need for a more robust implementation of legal enactments. In this respect, the challenges of the Famine years drove the association to adopt a new role, that of public advocacy for social change on a national level, evident in the Mendicity Association's public criticism of the lax implementation of the 1847 Vagrancy Act, a statute addressing the central focus of the association's existence. This stood in stark contrast to the same organisation's reluctance – and the reluctance of other charities, such as the Sick and Indigent Roomkeepers' Society – to involve itself too publicly in the heated Poor Law debates of the mid- to late-1830s.[71]

The 1847 Vagrancy Act arose from the fact that the 1838 Irish Poor Law Act was devoid of any specific mention of, or provision for, mendicancy and measures to curtail beggars. The omission of vagrancy clauses arose from the Whig government's belief that in the absence of a legal entitlement to relief – a pivotal tenet of the Irish legislation, and a key distinction between the 1834 English New Poor Law and the system passed for Ireland four years later – the criminalisation of the soliciting of assistance would be an unjust cruelty.[72] However, long anticipated by social commentators who addressed the question of Irish poverty,[73] the omission of vagrancy clauses represented, for many, a weakness in the Poor Law legislation and was subject to criticism.[74] The urgency felt by Boards of Guardians for the enactment of a vagrancy law was driven by the fear that ratepayers would be subjected to double taxation – namely, the assessed poor rates, as well as alms to beggars, who were regularly paid-off merely as a way of getting rid of this nuisance.[75] A Vagrancy Act would, the argument went, act as an adjunct to the workhouse-based Poor Law system. Side-by-side with the Poor Law, such an act would complete the state's two-pronged approach to managing the destitute poor: those willing to submit to the institutional regime of the workhouse would be catered for within its walls, while recalcitrant mendicants who preferred to wander the roads could be detained and imprisoned. However, without the legislation and the policing powers to suppress vagrant mendicancy, efforts to effect the 'improvement' of the social and moral conditions of the Irish poor would be negated.

In the months prior to the passing of the Vagrancy Act of July 1847, public meetings across Ireland called on the government to insert vagrancy clauses into any poor law legislation that was under consideration.[76] The annual meeting of the Mendicity Association, held on 22 March 1847, saw an uncharacteristically blunt motion being passed, asserting that the organisation

> cannot, in justice to themselves, and their fellow citizens, and in due regard for the health and morals of the community in its present awful and critical position, refrain from deeply deploring, and at the same time calling the earnest attention of Government to the extensive and pernicious prevalence of mendicancy in the Metropolis, notwithstanding the existence therein of Two capacious Workhouses, and of this Mendicity Institution, aided by parochial exertions of unprecedented benevolence.[77]

When enacted four months later, the Vagrancy Act widened the range of powers open to the police for apprehension and, upon conviction, confinement for petty offences. A man's desertion of his wife and children, thus reducing them to paupers upon the workhouse doorstep at the expense of local ratepayers, was liable to three months' imprisonment with hard labour. The acts of begging 'in any public Place, Street, Highway, Court or Passage', of facilitating mendicancy among children, and wandering from one Poor Law union to another were all criminalised under this act, and these offences were to be punished with one month's imprisonment with hard labour.[78]

At its annual meeting in February 1848 the Mendicity Association expressed its 'deep regret' that in the seven months since the passing of the Vagrancy Act, 'the evil of mendicancy is but little abated' in the city.[79] The association's resolution, passed at a public meeting and subsequently reported in the Dublin papers, reflected a growing disquiet among the city's charities at the inadequate enforcement of the new vagrancy laws by the city's police. A driving influence of this anger were the wealthy merchant classes who founded and managed the city's charities, especially the Mendicity Association, a society whose early reports carried on their title pages the assertion "Of all men living we Merchants, who live by buying and selling, ought never to encourage Beggars".[80] The prominence given to this quote captured the reality that the commercial classes were the leading economic cohort running the organisation and also that they perceived their economic interests to be acutely vulnerable to beggars' solicitations. In urban centres throughout the island, shopkeepers were amongst the most vocal cohort calling for strict measures to prevent begging, owing to their shop doors being frequently 'swamped' by mendicants, thus inconveniencing them and their customers.[81] It appears that the Association's lobbying, complemented by a proclamation by the Lord Mayor 'against the vagrants and beggars who still so perseveringly molest our streets rather than seek refuge in the workhouses or employment in the Mendicity Institution',[82] applied pressure on the Dublin police, who set upon a vigorous enforcement of the Vagrancy Act throughout 1848 and into 1849, resulting in the removal of 3,000

> male and female vagrants, the great majority of whom consisted of strangers from even the

> remotest districts of the country without any legitimate claim on the Metropolis, and without which vigilant watchfulness the state of this city would be utterly insufferable.[83]

The Vagrancy Act had the impact of tripling the prison population throughout Ireland between 1847 and 1850, with new prisons being established to incorporate this increase, including Mountjoy Prison in Dublin, which was opened in 1850.[84] As Brian Crowley demonstrates elsewhere in this volume, in Dublin, as in towns and cities throughout Ireland, large numbers of those convicted under the statute were non-locals, who migrated from rural parts in search of relief or employment.[85] For example, the Dublin County Grand Jury attributed the substantial rise in committals to Kilmainham Gaol in 1848 to the implementation of the Vagrancy Act;[86] in 1849, of the 7,698 beggars imprisoned in Dublin, more than 6,000 (*c.*78 per cent) came from other parts of Ireland.[87] The authorities' use of the Vagrancy Act did not always include a custodial element and in many cases the act was used to remove 'strange' vagrants from the locality, through persuasion and the threat of arrest.[88]

CONCLUSION

Considering solely the work of charitable societies, it is possible to discern a vibrant and expanding charitable landscape in Dublin city during the Great Famine, albeit one coming under unprecedented pressure. The years immediately preceding the Famine saw welfare provision in Ireland in a state of flux, as the traditional role of parish vestries in administering poor relief declined in response to the nascent workhouse-centred Poor Law system. Welfare provided through the former channel was grounded in communal aspirations to relieve the temporal wants of the known, local and 'deserving' poor; relief provided through the latter was centred on the stigmatising pauperisation of the destitute and was institutionally based. Yet, when catastrophe struck in the mid to late 1840s, there was in Dublin an extensive and thriving philanthropic scene. During the Famine, the city's charities catered for countless numbers of poor persons who refused to apply to the two city workhouses, whose application had been refused or who were awaiting admission to a Poor Law institution. The fact that numerous new charities were established in the city during the crisis reflected the demand for their services, arising from the sheer failure of the centralised Poor Law system. These new charities were, perhaps invariably, denominationally based, reflecting the sectarian character of the Irish welfare landscape in the nineteenth century, wherein social reformers and philanthropists battled for both the souls and bodies of the poor. While noting the importance of corporate provision for the poor, through charitable societies, workhouses and parish vestries, it is important to acknowledge the 'known unknown' of welfare history – namely, the private, informal acts of charity that occurred between individuals, whether they be relatives, friends, neighbours or strangers. Evidence presented to the parliamentary Poor Inquiry of 1833–6 reveals the extent of private alms-giving and assistance on the eve of the Famine, particularly among the lower classes of Irish society. Multiple witnesses to the inquiry asserted that it was largely the poor who supported the poor and this assistance was provided through exchanges that did not necessitate the creation of any written record. The absence of source material prevents fruitful research on this particular topic but does not prevent the mere acknowledgement of this universal form of relief. Yet, the role of other corporate bodies, such as trade guilds, would further shine a light on the city's vast and disparate welfare landscape, while a study of newspaper notices appealing for assistance for those who had 'fallen' from comfortable circumstances, through bereavement or the failure of business, would reward further research and enrichen our understanding of the complexities of poverty and charity in mid-nineteenth-century Dublin.

Quakers and the Famine in Dublin

ROB GOODBODY

INTRODUCTION

At the outbreak of the Great Famine there were about 3,000 Quakers in Ireland. Quakerism had been in existence for nearly 200 years and the numbers of adherents in Ireland had probably peaked at about 5,000 at the end of the eighteenth century. This small Christian sect had survived persecution in the seventeenth century and had kept their heads down in the eighteenth, getting on with life as shopkeepers, artisans, farmers and millers.[1] A defining belief of Quakerism from its emergence in the north of England *c.*1650 was, and is, the inner light: that there is that of God in everyone.[2] This led to its distinctive form of worship, which was based on silent prayer and contemplation, without the need for clergy. It also led to a strong empathy with fellow human beings, since everyone was believed to have that of God in them, everyone was equally important and deserving of attention. This in turn led to a strong abhorrence of war, capital punishment, slavery and other maltreatment of people and also fostered a sense of social justice. For instance, George Fox, the founder of Quakerism, and William Edmondson, who brought Quakerism to Ireland, both spoke out against slavery in the seventeenth century, an official policy against slavery was adopted in the eighteenth century, and in the early nineteenth century Quakers from Ireland, Britain and the United States were to the forefront in the move to have slavery abolished in the British colonies and in the United States.[3] The Society of Friends – the more correct title, Quakerism being originally a term of abuse – was self-regulating and expected its members to adhere to the standards set by these beliefs, from which also sprung truth, honesty and fair dealing.[4]

These latter traits, in particular, were good for business, particularly when added to other Quaker tenets such as simplicity and a lack of ostentation. Quakers in business were trusted by others, which helped them to establish strong and successful enterprises, while their abhorrence of conspicuous consumption made it more likely that the profits of a business would be reinvested, in turn helping the firm to grow.[5] It was as a result of these factors that many Quaker businesses expanded in the early decades of the nineteenth century, particularly in trade and industry. In the Dublin area members of the Pim family were particularly prominent as merchants, manufacturers and railway pioneers. Other prominent names amongst Dublin Quakers were the families of Allen, Alexander, Barrington, Bewley, Doyle, Harvey, Hogg, Malone, Perry, Robinson, Todhunter and Woods. A number of Quaker families in other parts of the country were successful in the milling business, including the Grubb, Haughton, Malcolmson, Pim, Goodbody and

Fennell families. This essay examines how the Quaker community in Dublin reacted to the Famine, both on a local level and through the establishment of a relief organisation to operate throughout Ireland.

The impetus for Quakers to become involved in Famine relief stemmed from the belief in the inner light and the strong sense of social justice. This, however, could not in itself have resulted in relief operations being organised by a group with only about 3,000 members in a country with nearly 9,000,000 inhabitants. A further impediment was the distribution of Quakers around the country. In 1794 Quakers prepared a map of their meeting houses in Ireland and this had changed little by the 1840s.[6] This showed that there was only one meeting house in Connaught – though, in fact, this closed in the 1840s, so that, in effect, there were none in that province. There were also no Quaker meeting houses in Derry, Donegal, Fermanagh, Clare, Kerry, or north and west Cork. In fact, if an almost straight line were to be drawn connecting Coleraine, through Moate and Parsonstown (Birr), to Cork city, the only Quaker meeting west of the line in the 1840s was Limerick city.

As this essay will explore, what enabled Quakers to establish a sophisticated relief operation across Ireland was down to two factors. Firstly, there was a significant number of successful merchants amongst the Quaker community in Dublin, with their organisational skills and their ability to move goods over long distances. Secondly, the lack of a clergy or priesthood meant that the running of the Society of Friends was carried out by an elaborate network of committees with membership throughout the Irish Quaker community and with strong links to Quakers in other countries. This meant that Quakers throughout the country were known to each other, either through the committee structure or through family bonds and, usually through both, while the system of committees was easily adapted to the Famine relief organisation. The links with Quakers in other countries, particularly Britain and the United States, was crucial.[7]

INDIVIDUAL INVOLVEMENT

The Society of Friends, as an entity, did not get involved in Famine relief. The work was carried out by individuals, rather than under the auspices of the society, though this is a moot point, as Quakers would not have drawn a distinction between collective involvement of Quakers as individuals and official decisions by the Society of Friends. The only place where the distinction is relevant is in the records kept by the Society of Friends. Going back to the early days of Quakerism in Ireland there is an extremely good and relatively comprehensive collection of records, including minute books that record the decisions of the various committees as well as records of births, marriages and burials.[8] The minutes record meetings that were named for the frequency that they met; at national level there was the Half-Year Meeting, at regional level there was the Quarterly Meeting, while the Monthly Meetings looked after the more localised groups of meeting houses.

Some records also survive from individual meeting houses, including Monkstown, County Dublin. There were three meeting houses in Dublin city and county at the time of the Famine: Sycamore Alley/Eustace Street and Meath Place in the city, and Monkstown in south county Dublin. The two in the city dated back to the seventeenth century, though they had been enlarged since, while the Monkstown meeting house was established in 1832 in response to the large number of Quaker merchants who had moved to live in that area.

There is no mention of the Famine in any of the surviving minute books.[9] This may seem surprising, but it merely reflected the focus of these meetings on running the affairs of the Society of Friends, while it was individuals, on their own or collectively, who ran the Famine relief. This lack of minuted records means that little or no information survives to show how individuals responded to the Famine in their own areas, in contrast with the well-documented work of the Central Relief Committee (as noted below).[10] Tradition handed down over time has it that a soup kitchen was set up at Monkstown meeting house during the Famine and a plaque on the wall, erected in the late twentieth century, records this.

One item in the minutes of Monkstown Meeting indirectly relates to the Famine. Jonathan Pim was clerk of that meeting during the 1840s, this being roughly equivalent to the chairman of a committee, though in reality somewhere between chairman and minutes secretary. During the Famine he was one of the secretaries of the Central Relief Committee, as well as continuing to run his business, and as a result of the enormous pressures of time and energy he asked Monkstown Meeting to permit him to be released from his position as clerk. A committee was appointed to select a successor but reported back that it recommended no change![11]

CENTRAL RELIEF COMMITTEE

With the catastrophic failure of the potato crop in 1846 Quakers began to ask themselves whether there was anything that they could do to reduce the anticipated level of suffering. One Dublin Quaker, Joseph Bewley, wrote to Quakers throughout Ireland suggesting that members of the Society of Friends might wish to consider establishing a committee to organise some form of relief. This led to a decision to hold a meeting of members of the society to discuss the issue and this took place in the meeting house in Eustace Street, Dublin, on 13 November.[12]

The outcome of the meeting was a decision to establish a committee to be known as the Central Relief Committee of the Society of Friends (henceforth referred to as the CRC). The committee was to have two main aims: the raising of funds for distribution and the gathering of information in relation to the extent of the problem in different parts of the country, so as to prioritise the giving of relief where it was most needed. Twenty-one Quakers were appointed to this committee: all were men, as the experience in business was important and all were Dublin-based because of the difficulties of travel from further afield for the anticipated frequent meetings. In addition, corresponding members, twenty-one in total, were appointed from Quaker communities outside Dublin so that they could report to the CRC, though not actually members of that committee.

At the same time that Irish Quakers met in Dublin, British Quakers met in London to consider whether they would have a role to play and they also set up a relief committee.[13] The two committees coordinated their approaches, with the London committee responsible for raising funds, informing the British public and lobbying government. Letters were sent out from the two committees seeking support from Quakers elsewhere, with particular emphasis on the United States.

Once a committee had been established it needed somewhere to meet that would facilitate dealing with correspondence and the administration of relief efforts. The first meetings were held in the offices of the Mining Company of Ireland on Ormond Quay – probably because many of the committee members were significant shareholders in the company – and they met daily.[14] It soon became evident that the workload would be significant and they should rent office premises for a period of ten to twelve months and engage a clerk to keep the accounts and act as assistant secretary. Premises were found at 57 William Street South, Dublin, where they occupied two rooms from December 1846.[15] With the further escalation of the Famine and the workload of the CRC, they outgrew the two rooms and in April 1847 arranged with the committee for winding up the Agricultural and Commercial Bank to use part of the former bank premises at 43 Fleet Street.[16] The committee operated from that address until it came to winding down the operations at the end of the Famine, at which stage the office was moved to rooms at the top of premises owned by Pim Brothers at 22 William Street South.

The principal work carried out by the CRC during the Famine was the administration of food relief, though there were other activities in addition, and these are discussed below. During 1847 Quakers in Munster established subcommittees to run the relief operations through most of that province and a small part of south Galway. The rest of the country, including Dublin, was administered by the CRC. Part of the operations involved the receipt of food donations from abroad, storing it pending dispersal and allocating donations of food to those who would carry out the distribution to the needy in their own districts. Food ships, chiefly from America and Britain, entered various ports around the country, including Dublin. One example was the *Malabar*, which arrived at Dublin port on 15 June 1847 with a donation from the General Committee in New York for the Relief for the Famishing Poor in Ireland of 4,045 barrels of corn meal and 411 bags of rice, the latter equivalent to more than 21 tonnes.[17] In addition, there were 210 barrels and 208 bags of various foods, including corn meal, rye flour and corn, as well as several cases of clothing sent by a number of donors in New York. A third batch of goods on board was a donation of 223 barrels of food and 8 cases of clothing from Albany, New York. As was the arrangement, the food was transferred to the army commissariat for safe-keeping and it could be drawn down from any army depot in the country for distribution. In effect, the army acted as the equivalent of bankers to the CRC for holding and moving food donations. This facility had been proposed to the Treasury by Joseph Bewley of the CRC in March 1847 and agreed, following which Sir Charles Trevelyan, Assistant Secretary to the Treasury, instructed Sir Randolph Routh, Commissary-General to make the commissariat stores available for this purpose.[18]

The distribution of food to those who needed it by the CRC was a high-level operation, equivalent to wholesalers in business, as the numbers and distribution of Quakers was not sufficient to provide much assistance on the ground, as this needed the equivalent of the retailer. Instead, people applied for bulk food allocations to assist them in running soup kitchens or other appropriate means of distributing food within their own home areas. Many of these applicants were landed gentry, professionals or clergy, and they had often opened up soup kitchens but found that their own limited funds were inadequate to the scale of the problem.

While the bulk of the food was distributed to the poorer and worst hit parts of the country, a small but significant amount went to help the needy in Dublin. Out of a total of 7,724 tonnes of food and 294 soup boilers given as grants nationwide during the relief operations, 60 tonnes and one boiler went to Dublin.[19] This figure does not include the food distributed through the CRC's own soup kitchen at Charles Street Great, which is described below. Nonetheless, the fact was that some 60 tonnes of food relief was necessary in Dublin, which was less dependent on the potato than many other counties and which was also the home of some of the wealthiest people in Ireland, with the resources to give assistance locally.

Care is needed in reading the accounts of the CRC as some landowners applied for relief from their Dublin address, though it may have been destined for the poor of their home territory. For instance, Charlotte Johnston of Prospect Terrace, Kingstown, was granted a ton of Indian meal in May 1847, though this was to be sent to Donegal.[20] Catherine Plunket of Old Connaught was given a monetary grant in January 1847 and her mother, Louisa Plunket, also of Old Connaught, received donations later in the year.[21] Louisa Plunket's husband, Catherine's father, was the Church of Ireland bishop of Tuam, Killala and Achonry and it seems possible that the donations may have been intended for that area, though the CRC minutes record that delivery was to be to Old Connaught.[22]

There were, of course, donations that were clearly intended for the poor of Dublin. Indirect evidence for the soup kitchen run by Quakers at their meeting house in Monkstown is suggested by a series of food donations to Mary Greenwood Pim of Monkstown, typically of half a ton of Indian meal and 5 cwt of rice. Other recipients of bulk food donations include Sigismund S. Moss, of Golden Ball, Kilternan, Fanny Courtney of Tibradden, Rathfarnham, Martha Wright of Aungier Street and institutions such as the Mendicity Association on Usher's Quay, the Ladies' Relief Association on Upper Sackville Street, the Liberty Infant School and Kingstown Lying-in Hospital.[23]

Given the prolonged nature of the Famine, it became clear fairly quickly that those who had no money for food would also be unable to replace clothing that wore out. With the assistance of English Quakers, a system for collecting donations of clothing was established and a clothing subcommittee was appointed to receive these donations, sort them and pack them in bales for distribution. This committee met in premises in Back Lane, off Cornmarket, and had a warehouse at 17 Merchant's Quay. As with the food donations, recipients of clothing were generally local landed gentry, professionals or clergy, who distributed the clothing to the needy in their own district. In the Dublin area grants of clothing to be distributed locally were made to a variety of recipients, including John McHugh of St Doulough's, William Armstrong Hayes of Harold's Cross, Mary Mooney of Palmerstown and Mary Knott of Charlemont Street. A wide variety of items were on offer and this is illustrated by the donation to Nathaniel Williams of Cole Alley in December 1848, when he was sent fustian, flannel, calico, leather, 20 garments, 6 shirts, 2 chemises, 1¾ yards of cloth, 2 women's gowns, 6 flannel waistcoats, 6 mess coats, 1 pair of trousers, 20 rugs and 5 pairs of sheets.[24]

Some donations were intended to assist with schemes to provide employment and it is probable that the fabrics donated to Nathaniel Williams would have been used for this purpose in Dublin's Liberties, which had been the traditional centre of the textile trade in Dublin. The donation to Mary Knott was for 10 yards of flannel, probably also for giving employment. Other donations to organisations such as the Kingstown Industrial Society are also likely to have been for this purpose.[25]

CHARLES STREET SOUP COMMITTEE

While there was distress in rural areas of Dublin, the city had its own specific problems. As Ciarán McCabe's chapter in this volume discusses, even in normal times there was a significant level of poverty in the city due to the decline in traditional industries and the influx of people from rural areas. Charitable organisations were set up to provide assistance to the poor, most notably the Association for the Suppression of Mendicity in Dublin, while the parishes were also given some responsibilities and, from the late 1830s, the North Dublin Union and the South Dublin Union workhouses formed the official response.[26] The advent of the Famine resulted in an increase in the numbers of people living in poverty in Dublin, though, and required new approaches to poor relief. As so often happens during major crises, whether war, natural disaster or famine, refugees fled the countryside that had failed to feed them and moved to the cities in large numbers. Part of this was a move to the ports with a view to emigration, but some of it would have been in the hopes of finding work. Amongst the English Quakers who visited Ireland to help in the relief efforts was William Bennett, who arrived in Dublin in March 1847 with a sum of money donated by English Quakers and with which he intended to purchase seeds that he could distribute to the needy to help them to grow crops other than potatoes. He obtained his supply of seeds from Drummond's in Dawson Street and set off by coach for the western counties. In his account of his experiences, he wrote that

> We met along the road multitudes of emigrants, mostly on foot, with their bundles on their backs, proceeding to Dublin. A few had more than they could thus carry; and it was an affecting sight to observe numerous whole families, with their worldly all packed up on a donkey-cart … We met several hundreds in the course of this morning only, and the guard assured me that it was the same every day, and thicker at the week's commencement.[27]

One of the early considerations of the CRC, in November 1846, was 'encouraging the establishment of a soup kitchen in this city', firstly to provide relief for the poor and secondly to provide a model on which other soup kitchens could be based.[28] A subcommittee was set up to manage this and it met on the premises of Samuel Bewley & Co., tea and coffee dealers. After examining a number of potential premises, the subcommittee arranged to take a yard and premises at 2 Charles Street West, off Ormond Quay, in December 1846.[29] Over the next few weeks, the committee arranged for the fit out of the premises, including the provision of 'a steam boiler with three large vessels for making soup in and also a metal boiler for occasional use if required'. William Wright and his wife were employed to live on the premises and to manage the soup kitchen, while nine other men were appointed to assist.[30] On 20 January 1847 work commenced on the preparation of the first batch of soup, ready to be dispensed the next day. They calculated that they could produce 700 quarts of soup per day, equivalent to almost 800 litres, and that this would cost 6½*d.* per gallon, including the management, or labour, costs. The fit-out had cost £80 and a request was made to the CRC for £150 to cover expenses.[31]

While the Charles Street Soup Committee was comprised of about ten members, these were all busy people – mainly merchants, with one doctor – and it would not be possible for them to dispense the soup on a daily basis. Instead, a larger body of Quakers was appointed to the task, consisting of 12 men and 23 women. These were to attend at

Charles Street on a rota, with morning and afternoon shifts, six days per week; Sunday as a day of rest remained sacrosanct, even in a crisis. The rota also included the purchase of ingredients, consisting of peas, barley, oatmeal, pepper, onions, meat, bread and salt. Once the distribution of soup began it quickly became apparent that this system was imperfect and the system was reorganised into two committees: the first, with 12 members, would look after the overall management and the purchase of ingredients, while the second was to be made up of 12 managers, each of which would attend on a rota basis, receive money, issue tickets and open and close the premises. These were to work with an assistant manager who would ensure that a sufficient supply of soup and bread was ready, to cut the bread, see that order was maintained and to receive all visitors. These were all members of the Dublin Quaker community and served on a voluntary basis. A detailed set of rules was set down for the running of the soup kitchen and members of the committees were to be fined if they neglected their duties.[32]

Soup was to be dispensed a quart at a time at a charge of 1*d.* per quart, or 1½*d.* if bread were included. The purpose in the payment was to avoid pauperising the recipients, though it was a low price for the soup, at almost 40 per cent below the cost of producing it, at 6½*d.* per gallon. Soon a new policy was introduced to allow anyone to purchase up to two gallons at cost price for gratuitous distribution. Initially soup was to be dispensed twice a day, between 7.30 a.m. and 9 a.m. and between 12 midday and 3 p.m. The morning shift was later altered to open at 8 a.m.[33]

For the benefit of local people, the committee decided that tickets would be provided to the parishes of Michael and Johns', Bride's, Nicholas's and Audoen's at cost price (1*s.* 7½*d.* for a dozen tickets for soup only, or 2*s.* 1*d.* for soup and bread). This would allow the parish authorities to distribute the tickets among those they considered to be in need within their parishes. As those who presented themselves at the soup kitchen received sustenance at below cost price, it could be inferred that the committee felt that the parishes should take some responsibility for their own poor and should not be given the benefit of the discount. Shortly after this it was decided to add Paul's parish to the list. There are two points to note here. Firstly, Quakers did not use the title 'Saint'. Second, the minutes of the committee are silent on the basis for this choice of parishes; the initial list included only parishes on the far side of the River Liffey and even then Bride's parish was at a greater distance than Werburgh's or Andrew's from Charles Street although those parishes were not included. Even the addition of Paul's parish seems less than logical, as the soup kitchen lay within Michan's parish, and closer to Mary's than to Paul's. While the excluded parishes may have been wealthier, they must have included a certain level of poverty, particularly among refugees.[34] It seems likely, then, that those parishes that were excluded may already have had some form of local relief system established.

In early March 1847, after more than a month of operation, the Charles Street Soup Committee reported to the Central Relief Committee that they were now capable of making 2,400 quarts a day, using three vats of 200 gallons each and an iron boiler holding 80 gallons. In the first month they had distributed about 12,500 quarts directly to the needy, in addition to the amount provided to others for gratuitous distribution. The average distribution had been about 1,000 quarts a day and on some days it had reached 1,500 quarts.[35]

Each batch of soup was made with 150 pounds of beef, 70 pounds of peas, 42 pounds of oatmeal, 42 pounds of Scotch barley together with pepper, allspice and salt. It was acknowledged that the soup could be made at a lesser expense, but this would not be advisable, as the recipients needed the nutrition provided by this recipe. Various attempts were made to devise a less expensive recipe but were abandoned when it was found that the quality would suffer. The possibility of providing boiled rice on some days was also considered and was introduced on three days a week from March, as it was believed to reduce the incidence of gastric ailments. The committee was always conscious of the costs, particularly as the Famine was a time of rising food prices, such as the increase in the price of beef from 3¾*d.* to 4¼*d.* two months after the soup kitchen opened and two months later to 4¾*d.*[36]

The Charles Street soup shop remained in operation until July 1847, dispensing food twice a day, six days a week. The Temporary Relief Act, passed in early June, allowed the poor law unions to provide relief without the recipients entering the workhouse and eased the burden on the soup distribution by the voluntary sector. However, the Quaker soup kitchens were kept open for a time, in recognition of the time delay that would inevitably occur before outdoor relief became a reality.[37] Over the ensuing weeks, the demand for soup from the Charles Street facility gradually decreased.[38] On 6 July the committee discussed whether it was time to close the operation and unanimously agreed to seek the views of the Central Relief Committee. A week later it was reported that the CRC was also of this opinion and the decision was taken to close the soup kitchen at the end of that week. There was concern that there might be a need for the distribution of soup again and to this end it was decided to keep on the premises and to retain Mr and Mrs Wright as caretakers. In February 1848, the decision was taken that the soup kitchen would not reopen, and the premises were relinquished.[39]

During the six months that the Charles Street soup shop was in operation it dispensed 103,237 quarts of soup, a little more than half of which were sold at 1*d.* per quart, while the balance was dispensed through the gratuitous distribution of tickets. The total cost of the operation had been £917, of which £300 came from the Central Relief Committee of the Society of Friends by way of subsidy and £35 came from donations. Most of the balance came from the payments for soup or for soup tickets.[40] The emphasis on quality of the recipe is notable and bears comparison with the well-known recipe prepared for the government by the chef Alexis Soyer, which contained only one sixth of the quantity of meat.[41]

CONCLUSION

While it is acknowledged that the effects of the Famine were not as bad in Dublin as they were in many parts of the country, it is all too easy to dismiss Dublin as being unaffected. Clearly there were those in the city of Dublin and in the rural areas of the surrounding county who were deeply affected by the Famine and their suffering cannot be ignored merely because there were greater numbers suffering elsewhere. The system established by the Central Relief Committee of the Society of Friends to provide food, clothing and other relief throughout the country did not ignore those that suffered in smaller numbers in and around the city. The operation that was specific to Dublin was the Charles Street soup kitchen, and the conclusion of the CRC was that it 'accomplished, to a great degree, both the objects which were contemplated at its formation; for it not only afforded considerable relief to a large number of the poor of Dublin, but it was visited by many persons who were connected with similar establishments throughout the country.[42] The inference in the latter point is that others were able to draw on the experience of the Charles Street soup kitchen in organising soup kitchens in other locations and in devising an efficient and effective recipe for the soup.

SECTION III: INSTITUTIONS, HEALTHCARE AND MORTALITY

Childbirth and Maternity in Dublin, 1831–56

PHILOMENA GOREY

INTRODUCTION

Lombe Atthill, who was appointed Master to the Rotunda Lying-In Hospital, Dublin in 1875, began his medical career at the General Dispensary in Fleet Street in 1847. He described attending patients in 'low-lying slums contiguous to the river Liffey' with typhus and small-pox in overcrowded tenement rooms and damp, dark cellars without a window, a candle or a fireplace, the air foul.[1] He witnessed widespread distress, starvation, 'famine fever' and a failure to supply sufficient accommodation for 'the famine-stricken multitude of sick'.[2] Atthill was well placed to observe life during the Famine years in Ireland. He described a journey to Dublin with his father from his home in County Fermanagh in late 1846:

> Driving, say, for half a mile or more through smiling meadow or pasture lands, you would suddenly perceive an offensive stench, borne on the wind; then into view would come a field, often of large size, one mass of blackened stalks, a clear indication that the tubers were already rotting. But no one yet realized the full extent of the awful calamity which had befallen the country.[3]

As the Fleet Street facility was a charitable institution, funds did not extend to remunerate Atthill. This compelled him to accept a post as medical officer to Geashill dispensary district in King's County where he remained until 1851. The dispensary 'was situated in such a poor and uninviting district that no medical man would remain there a day longer than he could help'.[4]

Maternity services for the Irish poor first emerged as part of a more general provision for poor relief by charities and the state. The 1805 Dispensaries Act provided for the establishment of dispensaries for the poor who lived at such a distance from county infirmaries that they were unable to avail of the medical assistance at these infirmaries.[5] Dispensaries were entirely dependent on voluntary, charitable sources of funding and could, therefore, be located wherever financial support was raised.[6] The act demanded that according as subscriptions were raised, grand juries sanctioned a similar amount of money from taxation. There was no obligation on dispensaries to appoint midwives to attend the poor. Any extension of services to include midwifery was entirely at the discretion of local committees who regulated the affairs of the establishment. Maternity fell into three categories. The first were those women who could afford the attendance of an accoucheur at delivery.[7] They usually belonged to the larger tenant farmer class and the gentry in the countryside, or the prosperous artisan and trade classes in towns. This group would also have engaged the dispensary doctor, who might run a private practice alongside his dispensary commitments. Patients could expect to pay up to a guinea for the services of the doctor.[8] Women in the second category were either not entitled to dispensary relief or lived in a district where the rules of the dispensary excluded a maternity service.[9] They were delivered in small lying-in facilities, which depended on benevolence and gratuitous care from local medical men. Many larger towns had such facilities accommodating between four to 12 beds. They were Newry, Sligo, Ennis, Limerick, Tralee, Cork, Clonmel, Waterford, Kilkenny and New Ross.[10] In the third category, which included most births, were those women who were attended by a midwife, at a cost of between 2*s*. 6*d*. and 5*s*. Pre-Famine maternity relied heavily on the so-called 'ceremony of childbirth', where the mother was supported throughout her labour and confinement by female family members and neighbours, with a midwife in attendance.[11]

Dublin was different. While the histories of the Rotunda, the Coombe Lying-In Hospital and the National Maternity Hospitals have been well documented, little is known of the smaller lying-in facilities that were established in the city in the early nineteenth century.[12] Among them was the Anglesey Lying-In Hospital, located in Bishop Street, an extension of the Peter Street Medical School. It was opened in 1829 by Charles Davis and George Hayden, surgeons at the hospital.[13] The South-Eastern Lying-In Hospital was opened in 1834 in Cumberland Street by Thomas Beatty, lecturer in midwifery at the Park Street Medical School.[14] It contained 25 beds and was attached to a dispensary catering for mothers in the vicinity of the Grand Canal and Denzille Street area. The Wellesley Dispensary opened in 1827 in Mercer Street, where Samuel Cusack and Henry Maunsell were the attending accoucheurs. Women could attend three mornings a week for the relief of 'diseases of females. Patients too ill to attend were visited in their own homes.[15] The Western Lying-In Hospital was opened in 1835 and located in Arran Quay. This was established by clergymen from the surrounding Church of Ireland parishes to the west of the city, in conjunction with several laymen and a committee of ladies. It extended as far as Chapelizod to the west of the city. R. D. Speedy, surgeon and lecturer in midwifery at the Apothecaries' Hall, and Fleetwood Churchill, lecturer in midwifery at Digges Street Medical School, attended there.[16] Finally, the Kingstown Lying-In Hospital opened in York Street, Kingstown in 1842, serving the poor of the town and surrounding locality. It was deemed necessary because of its distance from Dublin.[17]

At this time the Coombe, which opened in 1828, could accommodate 31 beds, but due to a lack of funds C. J. O'Hara, the resident accoucheur, relied on 21 being available.[18] The Rotunda had accommodation for 140 beds at this time. It was the only lying-in hospital to have been granted a charter and the only one in receipt of parliamentary grants. Robert Shekleton was master from 1847 to 1853. Similar to other voluntary hospitals the principal motive for their foundation was the welfare of patients. An important function of these hospitals was the provision of clinical teaching, as well as practical obstetric training and experience for students which was a feature of medical education at the time. They all depended on charity for funding, in the form of voluntary contributions, an annual charity sermon and subscriptions of one guinea a year, which entitled the subscriber to become a governor of the institution and recommend patients. A penny-a-week subscription was gratefully received as well as old linen and clothes.[19] The accoucheurs who attended these institutions did so without payment.

Pregnancy, labour and lying-in continued throughout the years of the Great Famine. This chapter will analyse how medical men in Dublin negotiated safer childbirth against a background of poverty, overcrowding and disease. As the chapter concentrates on maternity, the emphasis will be on provisions for the care of poor women at the time of their confinement and not on the broader issues of welfare. While charitable societies and voluntary associations for the poor flourished in the city, the sick poor relied on medical charities for treatment. In the case of maternity, the seven institutions that operated are an important barometer for maternal care in the city. While there are no clinical reports for the years 1845–9 the facilities remained open until the early 1850s. Extant reports from 1832–42 allow an insight into the circumstances of poor mothers in the pre-Famine period. For the Famine years, one must look to the Rotunda for clinical analysis of the consequence of poverty and starvation.[20] The chapter will examine evidence for the numbers seeking relief at these institutions and consider the causes of maternal and infant mortality. Government initiatives in the years after the Great Famine will be discussed. The 1851 Medical Charities Act, although limited to dispensaries, was significant for the development of maternal welfare in dispensary districts in the later nineteenth century. The Dublin Hospitals Regulation Act, which established the Board of Superintendence of Dublin Hospitals in 1856, drew up general rules for the governance of hospitals demanding accountability for the clinical and administrative management of the hospitals in receipt of parliamentary grants.[21] This marked the end of the charitable lying-in institutions, since they could not compete in an environment which required annual reports, rules for clinical and administrative management, and a commitment to medical education.

Cormac Ó Gráda's article on the demography of Dublin in the early nineteenth century examines the admission records of the Rotunda Lying-In Hospital between the Act of Union of 1801 and the Great Famine in the 1840s.[22] The city's population rose by about one-third during these years, despite economic crises and industrial decline. It analyses the socio-economic circumstance of patients who attended the hospital, highlighting maternal and infant mortality and fertility trends in the period immediately prior to the Famine. This is a valuable precursor to Edward Sinclair and George Johnston's analysis of deliveries during the mastership of Shekleton and the years of distress.[23] Peter Gray traces the various campaigns for a poor law and examines the political and ideological debates preceding and surrounding the 1838 act.[24] Laurence Geary's social history of medicine and charity in Ireland illustrates how illness and poverty were negotiated through medical charities, particularly medical dispensaries, in the early nineteenth century. Geary describes developments in policymaking and legislation culminating in the 1851 Medical Charities Act.[25] Many of the women who attended the lying-in institutions under discussion lived in poverty or were forced into prostitution. These are the women who likely were the subjects of rescue work and rehabilitation. Maria Luddy's examination of the role of women in nineteenth-century philanthropy investigates both benevolent and reformist motivations at play. Virginia Crossman has highlighted how unmarried mothers and prostitutes continued to be marginalised in the later nineteenth century with the workhouse their only resort.[26] Julia Ann Bergin discusses how the Rotunda and Coombe lying-in hospitals fared in the post-Famine period, when the smaller charitable institutions closed, providing evidence of the complexities of measuring maternal mortality and morbidity in the later nineteenth century.[27]

MATERNAL WELFARE: EARLY NINETEENTH-CENTURY OBSERVATIONS

In 1830, the Clonmel surgeon-apothecary Denis Phelan was appointed by the Lord Lieutenant to carry out an inquiry into the state of medical charities.[28] The inclusion of the existing care of women during childbirth in the inquiry was one of the earliest indicators of a pressing need to introduce guidelines for maternal welfare. Phelan proposed a scheme for reducing maternal mortality whereby women could be trained as midwives in lying-in facilities in larger towns, similar to the provisions for teaching already in place at the Rotunda.[29] In 1833 a Royal Commission was established to conduct an inquiry into the widespread poverty in the country.[30] The inquiry drew attention to the conditions in which poor mothers gave birth in the pre-Famine period. It examined the circumstances in which women were confined in rural localities, in dispensary districts and in towns without a facility for assisting mothers during childbirth.[31] Evidence from the inquiry revealed that the custom among the poor was to depend on women who habitually acted as midwives. Although they may have been skilled, few had been formally instructed in midwifery.[32] The Rotunda ran a six-month course of training for female pupil midwives and medical students. In some cases, a local dispensary or landlord paid for the tuition of midwives. The numbers were wholly inadequate to provide a countrywide maternity service. Four hundred and sixty-one women attended the training course between 1833 and 1861.[33] Most medical men did not regard midwifery as a qualification they would choose to follow, yet were obliged to undertake the practice when settled in remote rural districts. While dispensary appointments did not demand a qualification in midwifery of the medical officer, the usefulness of the dispensary was undermined if it could not support women in difficult labour.[34] Childbirth and midwifery were not alluded to in the third and final report of the Poor Inquiry. The oral and testimonial evidence provided by the inquiry was marginalised in the complex policy discussions and public debate that followed, and its recommendations did not feature in the Poor Law Act.[35]

When the British Poor Law Commissioner George Nicholls came to Ireland in 1838 to implement the Poor Law Act, he set about dividing the country into 130 Poor Law Unions, each with a workhouse at its centre. Each union was administered by a board of guardians. Denis Phelan, now in his capacity as an Assistant Poor Law Commissioner, was instructed to conduct an inspection of medical institutions. Since dispensaries constituted the principal means of providing relief to the sick poor, the services they engaged were included. The report supplied further evidence of the deficiencies in respect of midwifery. Dangerous lying-in cases were attended by medical officers only when a fee of 5*s*. to 10*s*. was secured by a subscriber or provided by dispensary funds. Similar to the 1833–6 inquiry, the fact that many did not practice midwifery although dispensary districts may be a distance from the nearest practicing accoucheur was underlined.[36] A further 1843 report on medical charities highlighted the advantage of employing midwives to dispensary districts citing the desire that they should be trained at the Rotunda.[37] It was widely recognised by the 1840s that midwifery services for the poor were inadequate. The means of providing care to lying-in women, the appointment of midwives to dispensary districts, and the instruction of medical officers and midwives were all discussed in these reports.

WHO WERE THE MOTHERS?

The mothers who availed of the lying-in facilities in Dublin were of mixed backgrounds and varied circumstances. Ó Gráda's detailed analysis of the registry and ward books of the Rotunda in the early nineteenth century illustrate that between 20 to 25 per cent of all births in the city took place in the hospital. Information in the registry included the mother's age, the parish from which she came, the gender of the infant and her length of stay in the hospital. Husbands' occupations were concentrated in the labourer, semi-skilled and artisan classes. Maternal mortality was noted as well as stillbirths.[38] The mothers who attended the Coombe were usually the wives of servants from the Liberties. About 50 stillbirths a year were as a result of venereal disease, which prevailed extensively among poor females. With accommodation limited, when the hospital was full, all applicants were relieved as external patients, attended by medical students in their homes. Approximately 60 to 70 mothers were attended in the hospital each month and 90 to 100 were treated at home.[39] There was a dispensary attached to the hospital, which focused on diseases of women and children brought about chiefly as a result of poor diet and nourishment. Those who attended were from the environs of the Coombe with an average of 100 women and children seen every day.[40] The parishes around the Western Lying-In Hospital in Arran Quay included St Michans, which by the 1830s was the most overcrowded space in the city, with a population of 25,000.[41] Four families, up to 20 people, might live in one room measuring ten by twelve foot.[42] Nearly 50 per cent of women in the parish were born outside Dublin.[43] At the other side of the city, in the more affluent setting of Cumberland Street-Merrion Square, the South-Eastern Lying-In Hospital, had accommodation for 25 lying-in cases and accommodated private wards for patients paying £1 each.[44] Giving evidence at an inquiry into Dublin hospitals in 1854 William Wilde stated that the 1841 census returns record approximately one-quarter of patients who died in all hospitals in the city as being from the country, but argued that over the preceding ten years it was 'a great deal more'.[45] In the same report, Robert Shekleton, the incumbent master of the Rotunda, gave evidence that his patients were 'chiefly from the city', but that those figures were augmented by 90 to 100 annually with the wives of soldiers who were garrisoned in Dublin.[46] These figures were a reduction from those in the years 1849–51 when women from outside Dublin accounted for 156, 142 and 132 mothers respectively giving birth in the hospital.[47]

THE DUBLIN PRACTICE OF MIDWIFERY

Since Bartholomew Mosse relocated his lying-in facility, the Rotunda, to Great Britain Street in 1757, Dublin was regarded as a centre of obstetric excellence. Clinicians practicing in the city were to the forefront in the teaching of midwifery, the fight against puerperal fever and, from the 1860s, the introduction of asepsis in midwifery.[48] In the competitive medical market, practitioners, among them Fleetwood Churchill, Henry Maunsell, Thomas Beatty and R. D. Speedy, wrote midwifery texts and submitted clinical reports to journals such as the *Dublin Journal of Medical Science* and the *Edinburgh Medical and Surgical Journal.*

They read papers on new initiatives and findings in obstetrics at meetings of the Dublin Obstetrical Society and the Surgical Society of Ireland.[49] Publications by Rotunda masters and assistants on the practice in the hospital provide a vivid picture of early to mid-nineteenth century obstetrics.[50] Midwifery certificates from the private medical schools were recognised by universities, colleges, the army, maternity institutions and medical boards abroad.[51] The detailed clinical reports and case studies outlined by the authors of these texts illustrate the emerging techniques and instruments in the delivery of safer childbirth, such as turning the foetus, the skill of dealing with abnormal presentations, the use of the midwifery forceps which succeeded in reducing maternal mortality in obstructed labour, the first steps in the cautious use of chloroform and auscultation of the foetal heart during labour.[52] The texts include statistics for the age of the mother, duration of labour, and the interval between rupture of the membranes and the birth of the child.

There are accounts of various presentations, the turning of the infant in utero, haemorrhage, placenta praevia, the use of forceps, perforators and crochets if the foetus had died in utero and puerperal fever. Notwithstanding this, there was little new in the pharmacopiae of preparations available to medical men who still relied on little more than bleeding, purgatives, leeches and stupes (poultices) to medicate and treat their patients.[53] Calomel, comprising a mixture of mercury, jalap, a purgative drug from the root of a Mexican climbing plant and Dover's powder (another purgative), was used to purge the body of fever or inflammation. Stupes of very hot water, sometimes with turpentine added, were placed on the abdomen to blister the skin in order to expel fever. Leeches were commonly placed on the abdomen for the same purpose.

The Rotunda accommodated 140 beds in 1846 but only 103 were in use owing to lack of funding.[54] About 2,000 deliveries took place each year in the hospital. During a crisis of overcrowding and persistent epidemics of puerperal fever in the 1820s the parliamentary grant was threatened. The incumbent master, Robert Collins, committed to keeping the numbers admitted at 2,000.[55] Three hundred deliveries took place annually in the Coombe, with about 500 mothers attended in their own homes.[56] Minute books date from 1864. There are three extant clinical reports from the Wellesley Female Institution from 1832 and 1833. Approximately 450 women were seen at the dispensary each year. Two reports were recorded for the South-Eastern Lying-In Hospital from 1834 to 1837 and three from the Western Lying-In Hospital, dating from 1838 to 1842. There are no extant reports for the Kingstown and Anglesey Lying-In facilities – just a note in the 1835 *Dublin Almanac* to state that 26,105 women were attended from the Anglesey since it opened. The reports account for the numbers of women attended as both intern and extern patients at each of the facilities. Four hundred and forty-two women were seen at the Wellesley dispensary in 1832. Of that number, 70 are recorded as having had previous abortions, a ratio of almost 1 in 6.[57] Maunsell considered that this figure belied a higher rate of abortion among the lower classes in the city. He believed that the incidence of many abortions could be accounted for by the 'dissolute habits' of the poor and the 'privations and hardships to which they were subjected'.[58] There was a remarkably high incidence of infant mortality. Forty-three, or one in ten, babies died. A considerable number of these children were premature, either delivered of mothers who had syphilis or were 'manifestly syphilitic' themselves.[59] Ó Gráda has shown that this was a phenomenon in pre-Famine maternity as well.[60] Women in poverty were more vulnerable than men. Lack of employment, poor pay and the need to look after children made it difficult for women on their own to survive economically. Hence, many found themselves engaged in prostitution.[61] Sinclair and Johnston also equated abortion in the Rotunda with hardship – syphilis, hard work, general delicacy, ill treatment, mental affliction and a history of previous abortions.[62]

PRE-FAMINE CLINICAL REPORTS

Extant clinical reports reveal how the poor could avail of the maternity services. In the 1832 clinical report of the Wellesley Female Institution four mothers were listed as having died out of a total of 423 labours – of obstructed labour, haemorrhage due to placenta praevia, apoplexy (the description appears that this was a brain aneurysm) and cholera.[63] The 1833 clinical report records that 428 cases were presented at the facility for obstetric care. There were 12 abortions and 416 labours. One in ten of these mothers had suffered previous abortions. Four hundred and twenty-one infants were born, with 35 stillborn, a ratio of 1 in 12.[64] Two maternal deaths were recorded due to obstructed labour and eclampsia respectively.[65]

Thomas Beatty's report on the South-Eastern Lying-In Hospital for 1834 recorded that 310 mothers were delivered in the hospital and 100 were attended in labour at their own homes, with 410 infants born.[66] Twenty-six babies were stillborn or a mortality rate of 1 in 15.[67] There were seven cases of maternal mortality, three due to puerperal fever, two due to ovarian abscess, one from inflammation of the uterus and one case of pneumonia.[68] This latter case was a woman who was found by a pupil, lying on a clay floor in a damp cellar. She was removed to the hospital in labour but died two days after delivering her baby. Over 3,500 women and children were seen at the dispensary attached to the institution since it opened and 220 children were vaccinated against smallpox. By combining the internal and external departments of the institution Beatty could identify women whose pregnancies posed the greatest risk. He described four cases of placenta praevia where all of the women were transferred to hospital if they haemorrhaged or as soon as labour commenced. All of the mothers did well, whereas all of the infants were stillborn.[69] When a mother had a difficult labour, due to an arm presentation, Beatty 'had her moved in a jaunting car to the hospital'.[70] An epidemic of puerperal fever occurred in the hospital in late October of that year. At this time a similar epidemic prevailed at the Rotunda. Three of Beatty's patients presented with symptoms of puerperal fever: a high temperature, rapid pulse, tenderness and pain in the abdomen and cold, clammy skin. Treatments included 'leeches to the belly and constant stuping, with the occasional application of flannel wet with turpentine; calomel and opium given in frequent doses; and the free inunction of mercurial ointment'.[71] Three mothers died within three to five days of being stricken with fever. Beatty was convinced that six other patients who presented with similar but milder symptoms had also contracted the disease. These women recovered. Beatty observed:

> The co-existence of puerperal fever with erysipelas was very remarkable at this time and during the whole summer. It is well known that the latter disease committed terrible ravages in hospital and in private practice during the greater part of the year; and whether the diseases are identical or not, the experience then afforded gives strong ground to suppose that the same influence is favourable to the production of both.[72]

A similar observation with regard to the possibility of contagion and a link between puerperal fever and erysipelas was made by Samuel Labatt, master of the Rotunda at the height of an epidemic in that hospital in February 1820, but no conclusions were drawn from these theories at this time.[73]

When the Western Lying-In Hospital and Dispensary in Arran Quay opened in 1835, the governing committee hoped that it would be in a position to relieve about 300 women annually.[74] That figure increased year on year, from 374 in 1838 to 1506 by December 1842.[75] In their report, Churchill and Speedy stated that owing to the irregularity of entering case histories into the statistical register the report would be limited to 1,206 women. Forty-three cases of abortion were recorded, leaving a total of 1,163 cases of labour at full term. One thousand one hundred and seventy-five infants were born of which 63 died, over half that number due to the poverty of the mothers; 12 were premature, 15 were stillborn and four were syphilitic.[76] The extreme poverty of the poor in the parishes in the western district of the city – among them St Paul's, St Catherine's, St Audeon's and St Michan's – left families with barely sufficient food and clothing, overcrowded living quarters, 'frequently with nothing but a little straw for a bed and some articles of dress for the bed-clothes, their wretchedness presses on them with peculiar aggravation, at a time when more care, warmer clothing and better food are required'.[77]

THE FAMINE YEARS

Masters at the Rotunda had little choice but to maintain occupancy at approximately 2,000 cases annually. With space for 103 women and with 30 of these appropriated for 'chronic cases', 73 remained for labouring patients.[78] Rules for admission to the hospital were unchanged throughout the years of distress – women applied for a letter of recommendation to a clergyman in their parish, a governor of the hospital or any 'respectable citizen'.[79] This entitled mothers to be seen at the out-patient dispensary for an assessment of their general health and appropriate treatment prior to confinement. Although this was the established rule of the hospital, during these years Shekleton never refused admission to destitute women in labour; therefore, overcrowding was a regular feature.

While about one-third of the cases were first pregnancies, multiparous women accounted for the greatest number, with women returning to have fifth or sixth confinements at the hospital.[80] The clinical records throughout Shackleton's term of office chart the abnormalities of labour such as malpresentations, tedious and obstructed labour and the use of instruments. Obstetric emergencies – prolapsed cord, eclampsia and haemorrhage form part of the records. Case histories demonstrate clinical practice in the case of emergencies and prolonged labour, but none are more conspicuous than puerperal fever. The disease formed the highest single cause of maternal mortality. As Table 1 illustrates, 35 women died in 1845. Ten of that figure were ascribed to an epidemic of the disease occurring in March of that year.[81] Just one woman, the first to contract illness, was in poor health prior to labour. 1848–49 saw 72 women contract puerperal fever with a death rate of 42 women or 58.3 per cent.[82] In the absence of asepsis in contemporary treatment, it is more likely that women succumbed to fever due to cross-contamination. Lombe Atthill, Master from 1875–82, was the first incumbent to introduce carbolic soap and solution as a disinfectant at the hospital.[83]

Table 1. Birth and Death at the Rotunda Lying-In Hospital 1841–50

Year ending 31st December	Deliveries	Number of children born	Children died	Stillborn	Women died
1841	2,050	2,025	10	108	23
1842	2,237	2,171	25	128	21
1843	2,327	2,186	14	173	22
1844	2,176	2,114	28	137	14
1845	1,411	1,429	14	82	35
1846	2,025	2,047	31	123	17
1847	1,703	1,732	32	112	47
1848	1,816	1,831	27	143	35
1849	2,063	2,105	23	137	37
1850	1,982	2,013	22	150	17

Source: Figures compiled from *Public Works and Building Estimates, etc. Civil Services for the Year Ending 21 March 1850*, pp 295, 315, 347, 417, 455, 499, H.C. 1849 (268-i-vii), xxxi., Class VI, Gratuities for Charitable and Other Purposes, p. 27; Edward Sinclair and George Johnston, *Practical, Midwifery*, p. 16; *Census of Ireland for the Year 1851. Part V. Tables of Death. Vol. II. Containing the Tables and Index*, pp 52–3, H.C. 1856 [Cd 2087-I], xxix, 56–7.

Throughout the period of distress, the most obvious signs of poor maternal health were the numbers of women who came to the hospital with underlying chest conditions – tuberculosis, pleurisy, pneumonia, bronchitis and asthma account for the higher mortality rates in the years 1847–9. Eleven of these cases proved fatal when they developed respiratory distress following natural labour.[84] Epidemics of dysentery were prevalent in the years 1846–8.[85] Pregnant women were particularly vulnerable as diarrhoea and dehydration induced premature labour. While nursing mothers who contracted the disease could continue to breast-feed without fear of infecting their babies, there was usually a complete suppression of breast milk during the course of the disease.[86] Poverty, poor nutrition, cold and exposure caused poor maternal health and as Table 2 suggests was a consequence of premature labour.

Three hundred and twenty-five infants died in the hospital during Shekleton's term, a blend of prematurity, 'tedious labour' and foetal abnormality. Two hundred and twenty-eight of the babies who died, a mortality rate of approximately 70 per cent, were described as being 'puny', likely due to undernourishment in mothers. This figure underlines overwhelming poverty and destitution during pregnancy. Among the others, 28 died due to prolonged labour and 24 of the infants, described as 'overlain', were suspected cases of infanticide.[87] Sinclair and Johnston classified 'premature labour' into six groupings beginning with abortion at six weeks to 'simple' and 'complicated' viable premature labours at the later stages of gestation. Simple viable births were those after seven months gestation where the infant had a prospect of surviving. Complicated viable births were those with abnormal foetal presentation, accompanied by a complication or disease. They sought causes for the onset of premature labour. Their methodology was to deal with causes of prematurity, rather than delineate the numbers of cases per year. Evidence suggests that labour could be hazardous when the mother's health was compromised. Among 239 cases of simple viable premature births, one in five babies and all mothers survived. Of the 120 complicated viable premature births, one in eight infants survived and 13 mothers died of a combination of exhaustion (3), fever (2), dysentery (1), tuberculosis (1), chronic bronchitis (1), phlebitis (2) convulsions (2) and nephritis (1).[88] It could be argued that phlebitis, convulsions and nephritis were related to pregnancy. All of the other deaths were due to poverty and hardship.

Table 2. Causes of Premature Births at the Rotunda 1847–53

Period of Pregnancy					
Cause		**6 months**	**7 months**	**8 months**	**Total**
Unaccounted for		80	135	50	265
Previous Premature		9	19	3	31
Confinement					
Syphilis		11	16	1	28
Hard Work	over exertion				
	severe jolting in a car	9	19	8	36
	crushing in a crowd				
Hardship	cold & exposure				
	delivered in street	2	8	6	16
	sea sickness				
Fright	fall or blow				
	beating or quarrel	15	32	23	70
	fretting or anxiety				
	unmarried				
General Delicacy	bronchitis				
	diarrhoea/dysentery	6	7	4	17
	fever				
	phthisis (tuberculosis)				
Placenta Praevia		0	9	7	16
Convulsions		1	5	2	8
Deformity (in mother)		1	3	1	5

Source: Edward Sinclair and George Johnston, *Practical Midwifery*, p. 460.

Evidence suggests that poverty continued to cast a long shadow after the Famine years. Three cases of typhus occurred after the period of distress in 1852.[89] One case of destitution in a

23-year-old who was admitted to the hospital in a dying state, barely conscious and 'almost pulseless' occurred in 1852 also.[90] No satisfactory account of her circumstance could be given from those who brought her in to the hospital. She gave birth to a 'putrid' baby girl and died soon after. In 1853 a 22-year-old prostitute died after her first confinement. She developed erysipelas and died 24 days after delivery.[91] Scarlet fever occurred in a 25-year-old who gave birth to a healthy baby girl in 1854 following a short labour. The mother died after 12 days.[92] The period produced a significant drop in fertility rates. Through estimating age-specific mortality trends occurring during the period and analysing fertility trends in the 25 years before the Famine, Boyle and Ó Gráda calculated that there was a 25 per cent drop in fertility or 315,000 births that did not take place during the period.[93]

In the immediate aftermath of the Great Famine, the absence of any reference to maternal welfare in the Medical Charities Act of 1851, which reorganised the dispensary system, signifies the low priority given to childbearing.[94] This situation was reversed in 1852, when, under the direction of the Poor Law Commissioners, the governors of a small number of poor law unions and local dispensary committees appointed midwives in an effort to implement a state-subsidised maternity service for poor women who could expect to be attended by a trained midwife.[95] In 1853, 11 midwives were appointed to dispensaries in the Dundrum and Glencullen, Kingstown, Bray and Rathmichael districts of the Rathmichael Union, in County Dublin.[96] In the annual report for 1854–5, the Poor Law Commissioners outlined the changes that had been made to the original organisation of the dispensary districts, noting that a small number of midwives had been appointed 'to take charge of cases of natural labour' in the aforementioned dispensary districts.[97] This was a tacit understanding that the implementation of maternal welfare was underway in dispensary districts. Although the appointment of midwives was haphazard and uneven, dependent largely on the financial affairs of local facilities, the midwife was a recognised dispensary officer from this time.

CONCLUSION

The most significant distinction between childbirth in Dublin and other cities and towns in Ireland during the period was access to maternity services in the Dublin region. Evidence from the pre-Famine clinical reports illustrate the range of care available during pregnancy in dispensary facilities attached to the lying-in hospitals. At the time of confinement, care could be assured to mothers in the limited space of the accommodation or in their own homes or places of refuge. Evidence from the reports also point to poverty and overcrowded conditions as the population swelled from the mid-1830s and greater numbers sought assistance. The wives of the labourer and artisan classes continued to avail of the facilities of the Rotunda during the period, but there was also a parallel class of destitute mothers who presented to the hospital without the prescribed letter of recommendation or antenatal care. I would argue that these were the women who may have been undernourished, living in hardship in overcrowded conditions who gave birth prematurely, accounting for the high rate of infant mortality.

The smaller lying-in institutions in Dublin remained open throughout the years of the Great Famine. Unfortunately, no clinical records survive. The Lord Lieutenant commissioned an inquiry into the conditions and management of medical institutions in the city, with reference to applications for grants from public funds. It was completed in 1856.[98] The inquiry sought to establish the sources of funding of the institutions, the extent and management of their accommodation, and the possibility of advantageously consolidating a number of them. Significantly, the report recommended that all hospitals in receipt of parliamentary grants ought to offer medical instruction 'to the advancement of medical science'.[99] The Coombe, the Anglesey and the Rotunda were the only lying-in institutions to apply for parliamentary funding. The commissioners looked favourably on the Coombe because of its important location on the south side of the city. Further consideration was given to the scope of its extern department not just in relieving lying-in women but also in awarding medical students practical experience. One hundred and thirty-nine medical students attended the hospital in 1851, 1852 and 1853, affording it the status of a teaching facility. On that account, it was recommended that the facility should be awarded a parliamentary grant.[100] The Anglesey did not receive a favourable report. One of the Poor Law Medical Inspectors, Dr Hill, described the institution as not having

> the least pretension to be called a public hospital, it is simply a house, consisting of a number of very dirty rooms, some only of which have beds and of which the other furniture is very scanty and unfitting. For this so-called accommodation the women received into the house pay a sum of *five shillings* to the proprietor-master.[101]

The report led to the Dublin Hospitals Regulation Act.[102] The Board of Superintendence of Dublin Hospitals was established under the act to draw up rules for the governance of the hospitals and the clinical and administrative management in receipt of parliamentary grants. From this time the Coombe received a parliamentary grant of £200 per annum.[103] The authorities in the Coombe continued to focus on the hospital's extern service because of the limited accommodation in the building until the hospital was refurbished and extended in 1877.[104] Hospitals without grand jury presentments or other means of public funding were obliged to account for their clinical practice and to submit statistical returns annually to the newly-established board. This heralded the demise of the smaller institutions which were dependent on benevolence and the gratis attendance by accoucheurs.[105] The Kingstown Lying-In Hospital was the only facility to remain open after this time. The hospital had steadily declined although the population of the town increased to 16,000.[106] It eventually closed in 1871. Private medical schools in Dublin amalgamated towards the end of the nineteenth century, becoming part of the Royal College of Surgeons of Ireland and the Catholic University.[107]

'Items in the Sum of that Great Calamity': Suicide in Dublin During the Great Famine

GEORGINA LARAGY

Since the early days of historical studies of suicide, Emile Durkheim's sociological work, published in 1893, has dominated the field.[1] Social and cultural contexts such as urbanisation and religion have been used to explain national rates of suicide.[2] While Durkheim dealt with the relationship between national crises, including war and suicide, he contended that self-inflicted death decreased during such times because social cohesion brought people together.[3] However, Durkheim did not include discussions of famine in his work despite the fact that he was writing at the end of a century in which calamitous famines had affected countries throughout Europe.[4] Indeed the relationship between suicide and famine has yet to be explored in any depth. The national catastrophe that was the Great Irish Famine has been described by Cormac Ó'Gráda as 'uneven and divisive', yet it affords us an opportunity to examine Durkheim's ideas about national crises, social cohesion and suicide.[5]

In the ten years between 1841 and 1851, 869 people were recorded as having died by suicide across Ireland. This amounts to less than 1 per cent of all deaths during what was a catastrophic decade. In the city and county of Dublin 93 people ended their own lives.[6] According to William Wilde, 'the number of suicides ... presented a manifest increase [in 1846] ... and continued so until 1851'.[7]

The well-established link between trauma and suicide in contemporary medical literature is creating a framework enabling historians to ask new questions about historic cases of suicide. This has been particularly evident in studies of suicide during and after times of war.[8] This article contends that there is some value in considering the relationship between suicide, trauma and witnessing famine. As Ó Gráda says, 'nobody doubts the psychic scars inflicted ... on those who had to live through [Famine]'.[9] We read much about the impact of the Famine on workhouse admissions and mortality therein, and can conclude that being separated from family was traumatic.[10] Simon Gallaher, Melinda Grimsley-Smith and Stuart McLean examine different manifestations of that trauma through studies of orphaned and abandoned children, rates of insanity, as well as through historiographic studies and commemorative practices.[11] As Vincent Comerford notes, it is more difficult to reconstruct the 'fate of individual victims – in disease, dispossession, flight or death'.[12] References to doctors treating the sick and clergymen ministering to feverish flocks attest to the physical consequences of interacting with those facing starvation and death, but what of the psychological ramifications of witnessing that which elicited only silence from subsequent generations? Famine memories were 'not autobiographical even a few generations back'.[13] In two nineteenth-century historical studies of the Famine, Canon

John O'Rourke (1809–87) and W. B. O'Brien provided 'scarcely a scintilla of personal recollection' of the event itself despite the former being 'a student at Maynooth College' and the latter 'a Poor Law inspector'.[14]

This chapter explores the relationship between the Famine, trauma and suicide by looking closely at a single individual, Patrick Bardin, and assessing the ways in which his death by suicide in January 1847 helps contextualise the levels of poverty within the city of Dublin and the responses to such poverty at an individual and community level. The theoretical and historical relationship between suicide and social cohesion during times of national crises are examined and evidence of the collapse of social bonds during the Famine period created a context for an increase in suicide. Statistical analysis and individual case studies help us position Bardin within the broader experience of suicide during the crisis. Evidence suggests that the real incidence of suicide during the period was likely higher than that officially recorded by Wilde and his census commissioners. Finally, the remainder of the article reconstructs the life of Bardin, a water-bailiff from Dublin city until his death in the winter of Black '47.[15] This micro-historical approach allows us to explore the ways in which suicide can be used to ask questions about the impact of famine on individuals not traditionally considered its victims, and illuminate an example of what Ó Gráda has referred to as 'hierarchies of suffering' during the catastrophe.[16] Bardin's involvement in parochial relief, and his history of philanthropic and political activity contextualise the extent of the poverty that emerged in Dublin in early 1847 and which was surpassed by the summer of that year. His suicide was used by the press to construct a 'humanitarian narrative' that attempted to remake the social body in the wake of his death but also in the wider context of the Famine.[17]

THEORETICAL AND HISTORICAL RELATIONSHIP BETWEEN SUICIDE AND NATIONAL CRISES

In his study of suicide in eighteenth-century Ireland, James Kelly has noted no increase in its occurrence in the Famine of 1740–1.[18] Therefore, it is difficult to propose any correlation between that time of crisis and that of the 1840s. Nevertheless, there was a lack of statistical evidence to work with, and not all suicides were likely reported in the newspapers, which was the source of Kelly's dataset. Studies for seventeenth-century Sweden suggest a direct link between suicide and famine, and this chapter seeks to include Ireland in this recent historiographic development.[19] So, while there are no clear comparative timeframes in which to examine a direct link between famine and suicide, there are other ways to approach the question of a link between national catastrophe and self-inflicted death.

Writing at the end of the nineteenth century, Durkheim suggested that suicide increased at times of financial crisis or 'crises of prosperity … wherever serious adjustments take place in the social order, whether or not due to a sudden growth or to an unexpected catastrophe, men are more inclined to self-destruction'.[20] According to Durkheim, society and conscience both functioned to moderate the passions, 'for it is the only moral power superior to the individual, the authority of which he accepts'.[21] In accepting this authority and consenting to be curtailed, people accepted a 'bond … [that] is not physical but more; it is social … when society is disturbed by some painful crisis … it is momentarily incapable of exercising this influence; thence come the sudden rises in the curve of suicide.'[22] This explanation for higher numbers of suicides might have been applied to Ireland during the Famine, but Durkheim, ignoring the published reports by the census commission on deaths and disease, did not include any discussion of Ireland prior to 1864 when the official registration of deaths began. It is unfortunate, because, as shown below, the increase in suicides during a time of sharp population decline proves his point clearly. Durkheim's theories of suicide have become seminal, but his ideas were not entirely original in the 1890s.[23] In 1846 the *Freeman's Journal* noted an increase in suicide in England, linking it to a breakdown of 'social bonds [that] told of the absence of moral restraint and religious influence'. They claimed that 'instances in Ireland are uncommonly rare'.[24] This certainly appears to have been true, if we consider only the official figures. In 1846 76 people killed themselves, amounting to a rate of less than 1 per 100,000.[25] Nevertheless, the figures increased by almost 60% between 1846 and 1848 (from 76 to 120), which suggests a rupture in social cohesion, for which there is other compelling evidence.

As Daniel Donovan, a dispensary doctor from Cork, reported

> the most singular effect produced by the horrors of the Famine now raging is the severance of the ties of consanguinity which it has caused, and the destruction which it has induced, of the ardent domestic affections that has formed, perhaps the strongest trait in the character of the Irish peasant.[26]

Ó Gráda refers to a decline in hospitality and charity, an increase in crime, child abandonment and infanticide.[27] Challenges to the social and familial bonds were evident everywhere a hungry person turned – parents decided whether to feed themselves or their children; on entering a workhouse and after the Poor Law Amendment Act (1847) families were wrenched not only from their small-holdings, but also from each other by the workhouse policy of familial separation. Parents made decisions about who might survive an Atlantic voyage and who might not, leaving more vulnerable family members at home.[28] Enforced disruption of social and familial connections prevailed with increased emigration and workhouse admission. It is perhaps unsurprising then that those who felt themselves connected to family or community in normal circumstances and did not face starvation themselves also began to feel untethered amidst the chaos and uncertainty of famine conditions.

Not all suicides were detailed in the press though, and the information given does not always afford an in-depth social analysis. However, where such details exist it appears that suicide was a problem that cut across all walks and classes of life and suicide was not confined to those facing starvation. Mr James Scott of Dominick Street in Dublin, for example, killed himself by cutting his abdomen while in 'a state of mental derangement'.[29] Professor James McCullagh, an eminent mathematician from Trinity College Dublin who killed himself in October 1847, was reported to be suffering from 'suicidal mania'.[30] A 20-year-old 'remarkably handsome' woman, Sarah Callaghan, poisoned herself using arsenic in June 1848 owing to temporary insanity.[31] Newspaper comment on inquests of suicides occasionally connected such deaths to the Famine. For example, *The Pilot* reported that 'an unfortunate young woman' drowned herself in Eden Quay in April 1847. In a short paragraph the newspaper detailed her jump into the River Liffey and the rescue attempts made by a sailor on a nearby vessel, and concluded by attributing her suicide to 'hunger' and 'temporary insanity'.[32] There was no further examination of the context in which she had died. While 'unfortunate' could imply that she was a prostitute, she was described as 'a fine young woman, neatly dressed'.[33] Those who may have killed themselves for reasons linked to destitution and starvation in Dublin appear to have been few in number or at least their deaths did not attract the attention of the press or were not selected for publication.

STATISTICS

In William Wilde's report on deaths and disease published in 1856 to accompany the census taken in 1851, suicide was discussed briefly at different points throughout the report. At one point Wilde refers to it as 'items in the sum of that great calamity', suggesting that such deaths were small in number and, perhaps, not worthy of much analysis. Certainly, within the context of approximately 1,000,000 deaths between 1841 and 1851, 869 suicides in the country as a whole seem rather paltry. Nevertheless, there are two aspects of these figures that are worth unpicking because they provide us with some tentative evidence around how the Famine affected the investigation of sudden or violent death, and how the crisis impacted society more generally. Firstly, the accuracy of Wilde's figures is problematic and certainly the true number was likely to have been higher; and secondly, although suicide was likely to have been under-reported, a significant increase remains evident during the later years of the 1840s. Indeed, the number reported for 1848 (123) was not reached again until 1883 when the Registrar General recorded 124 persons as having killed themselves.[34]

Accuracy of the official figures was compromised for two reasons. Firstly, the figures were self-reported by families, and it is possible that some families may have failed to return or report a family death as suicide. Shame and negative attitudes towards suicide were evident during this period; it was less than 30 years since Westminster had passed a law forbidding ignominious burial at the crossroads, which had been a popular method of punishing the dead. Since 1823 the bodies of suicides had to be buried in recognised graveyards or churchyards, though the clergy decided whether or not prayers would be said at the burial.[35] The second issue impacting family reporting of causes of deaths is the fact that the numbers of families and entire households wiped out due to either death or emigration meant that the numbers left to report to the census commissioners in 1851 was significantly less, by almost one quarter. For both these reasons it is not unreasonable to conclude that the real numbers of suicide during the decade of the Famine were likely to have been greater than that reported.

Wilde himself was aware of the problem facing the commissioners and so he secured another source of information on violent deaths – namely, returns of inquests held on the dead. Since medieval times it was the duty of the coroner to investigate 'all who be found dead or suddenly slain', and by the nineteenth century there were coroners in districts and counties across Ireland, including two city coroners for Dublin and one for the county.[36] Each quarter, in order to receive payment and recoup their expenses, coroners made returns to the clerks of the crown who then forwarded the requests to the grand jury. Wilde requested the clerks also return these figures to the census commissioners to establish a corrective to possible errors in the family returns. However, the context of excess mortality in the late 1840s in particular meant that death investigations were far more numerous than they had been, and some districts did not have a coroner at different times during the decade.[37] In addition to the problems with the coronial system, the Irish Constabulary was also overstretched. At the time, the police were not only involved in general law and order duties, but were also taking agricultural statistics each year, reporting on the status of the crops in their respective districts. They also distributed relief and participated in the increasing number of evictions.[38] Although the duties and responsibilities of the constabulary likely impacted their ability to perform their normal duties, they reported greater numbers of deaths in need of investigation to the local coroners. Nevertheless, the combination of pressure on both the coronial and constabulary systems meant that inquests could not be considered entirely accurate either and Wilde, recognising this, requested that the constabulary provide returns of violent deaths on which no inquests were held for whatever reason.[39]

In Dublin, however, there were 2,250 inquests held between 1841–51, of which 73 were instances of suicide. Of the 73 who died in the city, 57 were men and 16 were women, which is a typical gender pattern. The majority (19) were men who cut their throat or stabbed themselves. The second highest mode of suicide was gunshot wound, no doubt inflated by the large military garrison present in Dublin.[40] Finally, poisoning and hanging were the third and fourth most popular means of killing oneself, with drowning being the most popular method for women. Dublin, along with Cork city, Waterford city, county Down and Carrickfergus town had the highest numbers of suicides during this period.

In Dublin city, 146 inquests listed the cause of death as uncertain (including found drowned, found dead, cause unknown and no verdict returned). It is possible that a number of those had intended suicide though it is impossible to say for certain. The discussion at the inquest of William Arthur Niblett held at 11 Sackville Street in October 1847 reveals the ways in which a death by suicide might have been suppressed and in a surprisingly public manner. Niblett was seen by witness Michael Guilfoyle taking 'a kind of a side run, and plunge into the [Royal] canal'. Guilfoyle did 'not think that the deceased did slip into the water, or miss his footing jumping into the canal', though this testimony was later questioned by a jury member and Guilfoyle admitted that if a person were to slip at that part of the canal bank they would not be able to stop falling. Another witness, Jane Colligan, saw Niblett take 'a slight run and threw himself into the canal on his side; he threw his umbrella away and his hat fell off ... she believe[d] he threw himself in purposely, but she was so dreadfully situated that she cannot give an opinion, the place is very slippery and dangerous'.[41] A witness who had taken dinner with Niblett and 'his lady' the previous Sunday remarked that the 'deceased appeared at first very much depressed in spirits ... He used often to complain of nervous headache.' Medical testimony at the inquest became key when Dr McVeigh, the dead man's personal physician, referred to Niblett's history of vertigo and how that might have contributed to his fall; also, '[the] deceased had an attack of nervous fever some time ago; and his nervous system suffered more or less'.[42] However, it seemed that a key piece of evidence was the fact that 'there was nothing in the state of the deceased's affairs which could cause any disturbance of mind. He was happy in his domestic circle and had nothing to affect him.' Appearing as counsel on behalf of the widow and family of Niblett, Mr Barry gave an impassioned speech at the close of evidence in which he called 'on the jury to return a verdict such as the evidence warranted, and to relieve the bereaved family of the deceased from the additional sorrow of a stigma being cast on his memory'. Coroner Kirwan, one of the two city coroners, disagreed:

> he was impressed with the belief that the deceased was accessory to his own death ... considered the evidence of ... Colligan very conclusive ... he would, however, leave the matter to the jury, who, he was sure, would return a conscientious verdict.

The combination of medical evidence, uncertainty on the part of the eye witnesses to the drowning and the coroner's 'able assistance in enabling us to come to a proper conclusion' lead to a verdict that disputed the headline of 'alleged suicide': 'We find that Arthur William Niblett met his death from drowning in the Royal Canal, and from the evidence before us we are of opinion that he fell into the water while under the influence of an attack of vertigo.'[43] This contradicted the popular and publicised conclusion that the deceased had in fact committed suicide; for example, the *Dublin Evening Packet* reported the death as a 'melancholy suicide' on 5 October 1847, a day before the inquest.

A similar case occurred in August 1845 when Frederick Howard, 'a gentleman of property', shot himself at his home in Rathmines, county Dublin. The dead man had 'very extraordinary impressions on his mind for the last fortnight that a conspiracy existed against him ... he did not think any man safe in society from a system of *espionage*.'[44] Further evidence of an 'aberration of mind' emerged at the inquest, alongside information that 'his brother and sister died in a madhouse'. Yet the position of the gun, which lay some distance from the body under a table, confused the witnesses, jury and coroner enough that the verdict did not declare the case a suicide: 'his death was caused by leaden shot, No. 5, fired from a gun or pistol, but whether said shot was fired by deceased in an unsound state of mind or by the hand of another person said jury could not say'.[45]

The two gentlemen discussed above were men of property, respectability and social connection. This is significant because at this time it was permissible for the Crown to confiscate the property of those found *felo de se* and, being men of property, this would most certainly have impacted their families. However, the alternate and much more common verdict of 'suicide whilst temporarily insane' was possible because clear evidence of insanity was offered in the cases of both Niblett and Howard.[46] In a period during which suicide was legally proscribed and financial penalties existed, the temporary insanity verdict would have ensured a suicide verdict but not punished the families in any practical way. It is likely then that social stigma drove these verdicts, which was made possible by the ambiguity of the evidence in both cases. Misclassification of deaths has been linked to class dynamics, but Victor Bailey has suggested that 'families, even those of respectability, were too shocked ... to think immediately of concealment' and these cases do bear this out.[47] Once a suicide had become public knowledge, it was difficult to attempt concealment, no matter the class.[48]

THE SUICIDE OF A RELIEVING OFFICER

On 17 January 1847 Patrick Bardin walked to the 'stable at the rere of his house, [and] cut ... his throat with one of his razors'.[49] The details of the inquest were carried in multiple newspapers, and an editorial and some correspondence appeared for a couple of days after the initial reports in the pages of the *Freeman's Journal*. Bardin was a public official, with responsibility for ensuring that coal and potatoes coming off ships along Dublin's quays were being accurately weighed.[50] The Lord Mayor had praised Bardin's work a year before his death observing: 'no person [had] taken more pains to put an end to the disgraceful frauds committed on the citizens of the poor than the water bailiff (Mr Bardin)'.[51] The Catholic parish priest of St Nicholas, Revd Flanagan, had similarly noted that he was 'foremost in every work of charity'.[52]

A week before his death by suicide Bardin had been appointed secretary and visiting officer to the relief committee of St Nicholas Without.[53] Although a Church of Ireland parish, the committee reflected the cross-denominational activities of the vestries in nineteenth-century Dublin, who had responsibility for poor relief, burial of the poor and fire engines.[54] The parish of St Nicholas Without was (and is) near St Patrick's Cathedral, south of the River Liffey.[55] In the week ending 19 January, during which Bardin had visited the poor, the committee had provided relief to 2,691 individuals, distributed more than one thousand pounds of bread and 687 quarts of soup, and expended £15 5*s*. 6*d*.[56] In order to evaluate who was entitled to or deserving relief Bardin had visited 'the inhabitants of Walker's-alley'. In the mid-nineteenth century, 'housing surrounding Walker's Alley, Goodman's Lane and Myler's Alley was one of the worst slums in the … city'.[57] Walker's Alley began three doors north and across the street from Bardin's home at 30 Patrick Street.[58] The people he had visited, 'were without food, fuel, clothing or anything … they were walking corpses … [it was] … a disgrace to a civilised country to witness such scenes'.[59] A man heavily engaged in 'the emerging associational culture of middle-class life' in Dublin, Bardin had worked privately and professionally 'protecting the poor' since least 1842.[60] As Ciarán McCabe relates, 'local paupers were known and more trustworthy than unknown, "strange" beggars'.[61] It is likely that he knew by sight, if not personally, some of the people he visited in that alley; those 'walking corpses' were his neighbours.[62]

In an effort to comprehend the difficulty of Bardin's job, the account of American visitor Asenath Nicholson, who visited Ireland in 1847, provides a useful perspective. She worked during that year in Cook Street, which was approximately one kilometre from Walker's Alley. She made this street 'the field of … [her] … winter's labour … chosen for its extreme poverty'.[63] Her reckoning of the choices she faced as a charity worker must have been akin to those of Bardin: 'ten pounds divided among a hundred, would not keep one from starvation many days'. Instead, Nicholson endeavoured to help a smaller number, hoping to keep them alive until further and 'more efficient' means of relief would emerge.[64] This arithmetic of hunger and relief and his intimate knowledge of the condition of Dublin's poor must have overwhelmed Bardin.

Dublin at the start of 1847 was a city on the precipice of disaster. Although the infestation that had been destroying the potato crop for three years in a row had first been detected in Dublin, the city itself had remained relatively free of the true impact of the catastrophe until the bitter winter of 1846–7 when the 'rapid deterioration of the urban environment … [resulted in] heaps of mud … for a mile and a half …' in the old city, as vast numbers of country beggars mingled with the traffic'.[65] Dublin 'became a vast refugee camp exacerbating the already overcrowded conditions of the poor'.[66] The winter of 1846–7 was particularly harsh across the country and relief works began closing in March 1847.[67] At its initial meeting the relief committee of St Nicholas Without declared that 'this season of suffering … [is] … we fear but commencing, and may be prolonged'.[68] On the day before Bardin killed himself, a meeting of 'peers, commoners and landed proprietors' had taken place in the Rotunda in Dublin to address the state of the country. Proposing to present their memorial to the Queen, various resolutions at the meeting noted the country as being in a state of 'ruin'; 'the people of Ireland... must perish in multitudes unless supplied with food'.[69] At a special meeting of Dublin Corporation in January 1847 a petition to both houses of parliament reported 'that so rapid is the progress of the terrible scourge ... that many hundreds of thousands must shortly perish'.[70]

Bardin had witnessed only the beginning of Dublin's famine and 'tendered his resignation' after one day of completing his duties, saying that 'from the scenes of misery he had witnessed he could not act'.[71] A neighbour, Edward Reynolds, who knew the dead man for 20 years, said he 'did not observe any despondency of mind in [the] deceased until he came in contact with the scenes of misery which he encountered in the parish'. Revd Mr Smyth stated that he had spoken to the deceased man in the days before his death, and he was despondent. Bardin's business had 'totally failed' it seemed, but 'he had capital remaining'.[72] There was no domestic reason for this his suicide either, according to numerous witnesses. The jury found that:

> Patrick Barden's death was caused by wounds inflicted by himself on his throat, with his own hand and razor in his stable ... while labouring under temporary aberration of intellect, and the jury find, after a most protracted and careful investigation that this temporary derangement of mind did not arise either from any embarrassment in his worldly affairs, nor the slightest want of domestic comforts and happiness, but solely and entirely from the painful impression made on a sensitive and humane person, but by his witnessing such melancholy scenes of starvation, destitution, and extreme distress, [in] the zealous discharge of his duties, as secretary to the relief committee of the parish, he necessarily had to inspect.[73]

The verdict at the inquest revealed the immediate emotional and psychological cost of witnessing starvation and locates Bardin within Ó Gráda's 'hierarchies of suffering' during this time.[74] The anonymous poor are the archetypal victims of famine, but middle-class professionals engaged in philanthropy who were not starving also died as a result of famine conditions and such deaths can tell us something important about trauma and famine. Ó Gráda detailed 'medical personnel ... workhouse officials and clergymen of all denominations [who] succumbed, mainly from typhoid fever'.[75] Breandán Mac Suibhne notes that in 1847 alone, '131 Irish medical men succumbed to "epidemic and contagious disease", with the vast majority (123) dying of fever'.[76] Exposure to disease and fear of contagion were very physical threats in the pre-antiseptic age.[77] Yet such considerations tend to privilege physical over mental suffering, largely because 'it is more difficult to document psychic trauma or post-traumatic stress effects than it is to count numbers of dead or wounded.'[78] New work by MacSuibhne demonstrates the emotional impact of the Famine, quite clearly stating that Bardin's contemporaries were aware of the psychological consequences of starvation; 'there was a sharp understanding in the 1840s that the effects of extreme want are not simply physical'.[79] What Patrick Bardin's case makes clear is that those who were in 'extreme want' were not the only ones who suffered mentally and emotionally: those who witnessed it also suffered.

Bardin's suicide garnered more than just the usual inquest report: an editorial also appeared in the *Freeman's Journal* which drew attention to conditions both visible and invisible then prevailing in the city. The editor was clearly attempting to elicit both compassion and action from his readers – typically middle-class, reform-minded Dubliners,

3.1. 'Skerries Hooker'. Engraving reproduced in Wallop Brabazon, *The Deep And Coast Fisheries of Ireland with suggestions for the working of a fishing company* (Dublin: James McGlashan, 1848), p. i.

3.2. 'Claddagh whale boat'. Engraving reproduced in Wallop Brabazon, *The Deep And Coast Fisheries of Ireland with suggestions for the working of a fishing company* (Dublin: James McGlashan, 1848), p. 21.

4.1. J. & J. Johnstone, 'George Heriot's Hospital, South Front', Edinburgh. Engraving reproduced in James Johnstone, *Historical and descriptive account of George Heriot's Hospital, including a memoir of the founder* (Edinburgh: Walker & Greig for J. Cunningham, etc., 1827), unpaginated. Public Domain Mark. Wellcome Collection.

4.2. Former Heriot's Foundation School, now Salvation Army Hostel, 323 Cowgate, Edinburgh. Photograph RCAHMS 2008. Courtesy of Crown Copyright: HES.

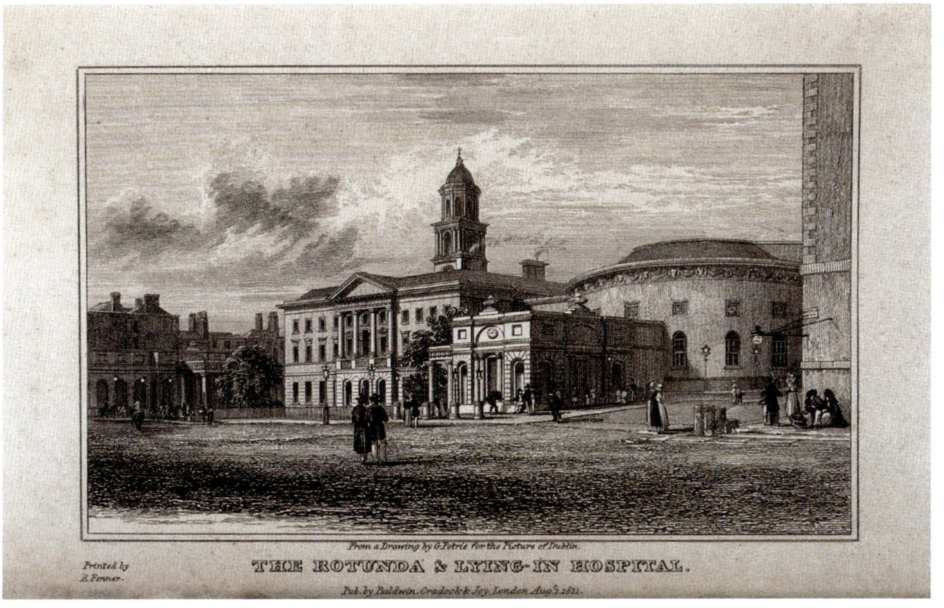

4.3. The Rotunda & Lying-in Hospital, Dublin, Ireland. Etching, 1821, after George Petrie. London: Baldwin, Cradock & Joy, 1 August 1821 (R. Fenner). Public Domain Mark. Wellcome Collection.

4.4. Mater Misericordiæ Hospital, Dublin. Photograph Robert French [between 1880-1900], Lawrence Collection. Courtesy of the National Library of Ireland.

9.1. 'Entrance to Kilmainham Gaol', *c.*1960s. Courtesy of Kilmainham Gaol Museum, KMGLM.21PC-1A26-18.

9.2. 'Kilmainham Gaol, Dublin'. Engraving, *Illustrated London News*, 6 March 1848. Courtesy of Kilmainham Gaol Museum, KMGLM.2020.0027.

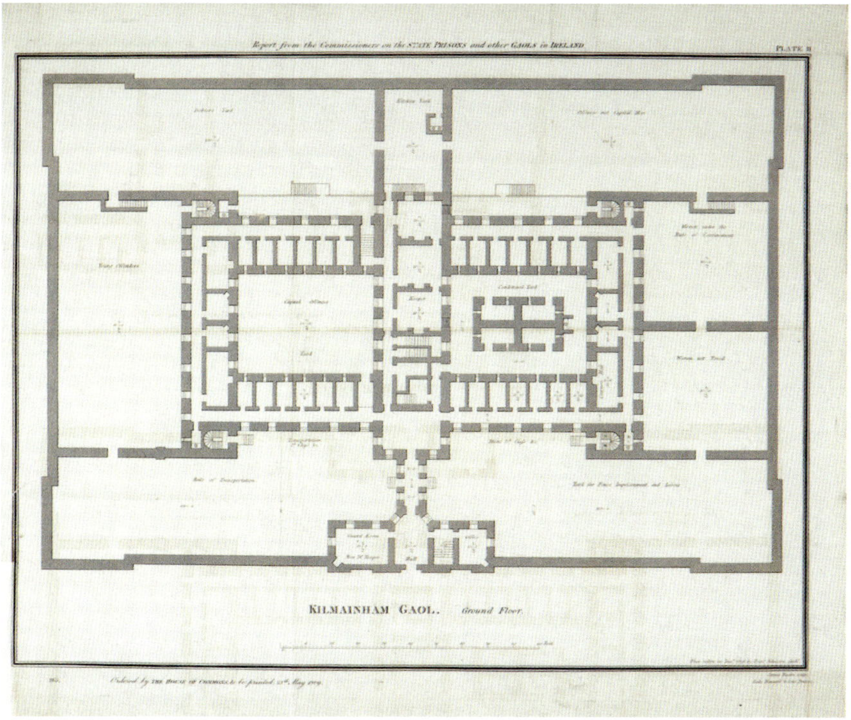

9.3. Francis Johnston. 'Ground floor plan' (taken in Dec. 1808), from *Report from the Commissioners on the State Prisons and other Gaols in Ireland*, 25 May 1809. Courtesy of Kilmainham Gaol Museum, KMGLM.03BK-1J53-04.

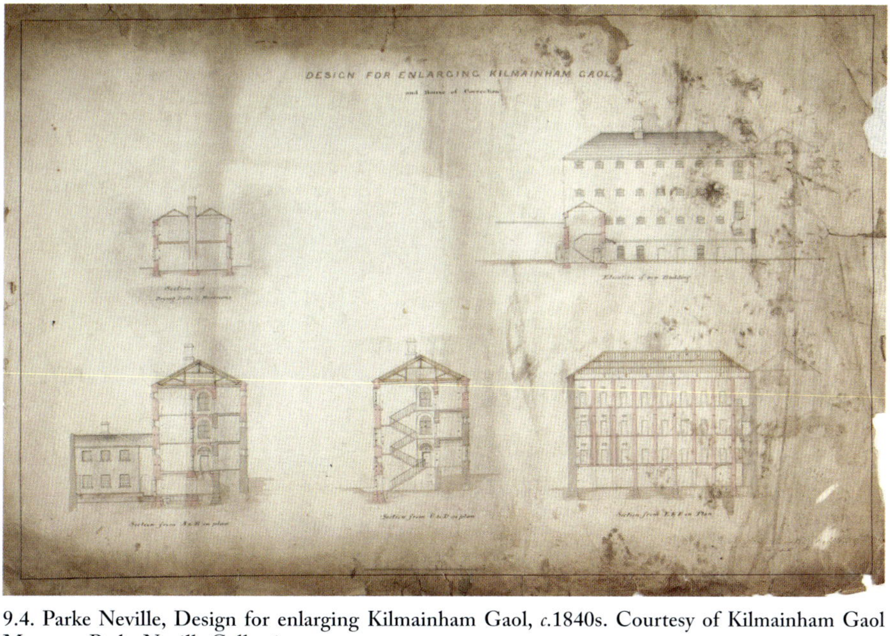

9.4. Parke Neville, Design for enlarging Kilmainham Gaol, *c.*1840s. Courtesy of Kilmainham Gaol Museum, Parke Neville Collection.

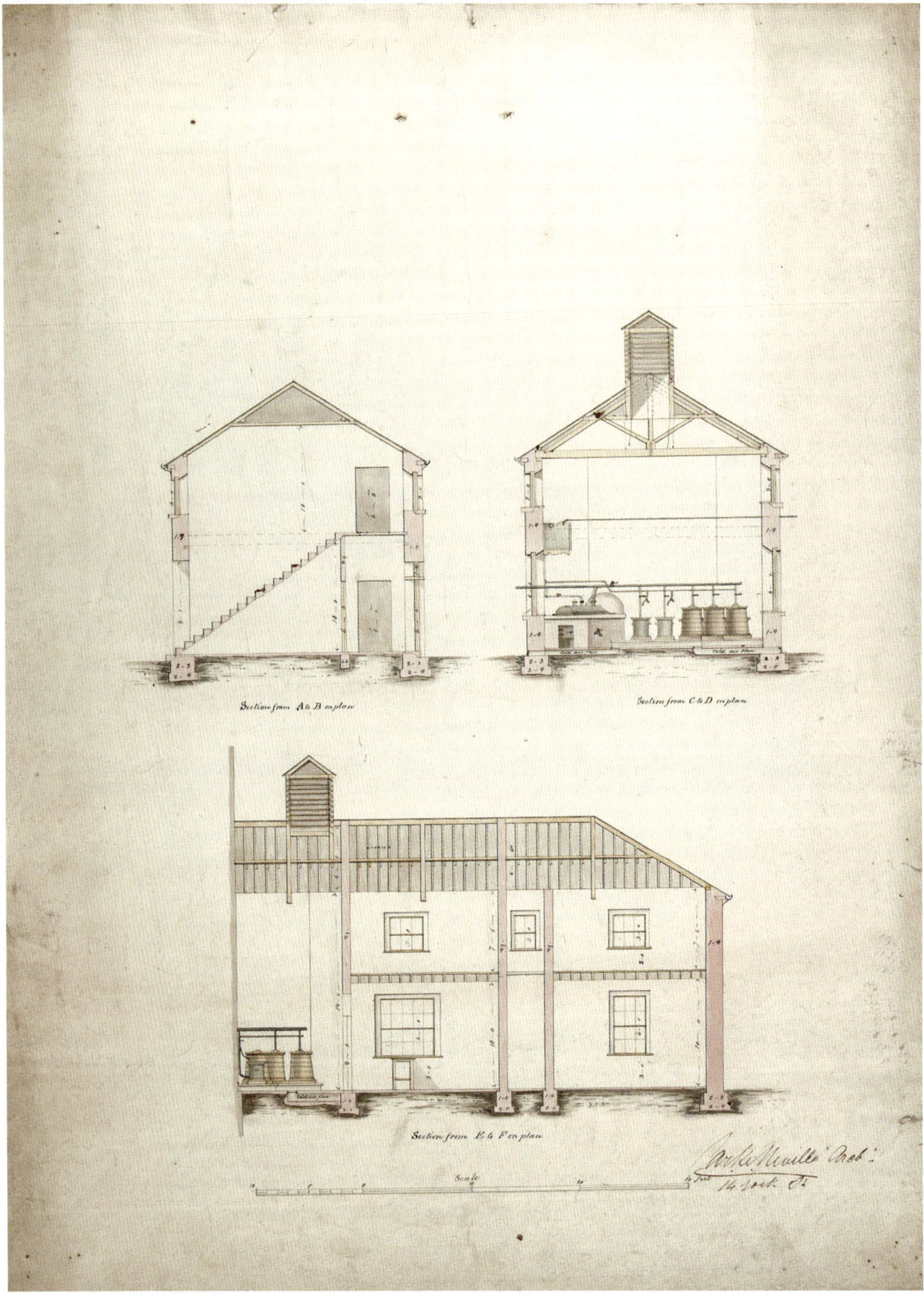

9.5. Parke Neville, Plan, Elevation and Section of an economical steam cooking apparatus planned to be fixed at Kilmainham Gaol, *c.*1840s. Courtesy of Kilmainham Gaol Museum, Parke Neville Collection.

ROYAL IRISH ART UNION, DISTRIBUTION OF PRIZES 1843;

As given by the London Illustrated News, immediately after the Occurrence.—(See page 12.)

11.1. 'Royal Irish Art Union, Distribution of Prizes 1843; As given by the London *Illustrated London News*, immediately after the Occurrence', from the *Report of the Committee of Selection of the Royal Irish Art Union*, 1843. Courtesy of UCD Special Collections.

11.2. Franz Xaver Winterhalter, *The Royal Family in 1846*, oil on canvas, RCIN 405413, Royal Collection Trust, © Her Majesty Queen Elizabeth II 2022.

11.3. Samuel Cousins, after Franz Xaver Winterhalter, *Queen Victoria, the Prince Consort and Family*, mixed method engraving, republished 15 February 1853 (originally published 20 March 1850 after a painting of 1846), NPG D48098, © National Portrait Gallery, London.

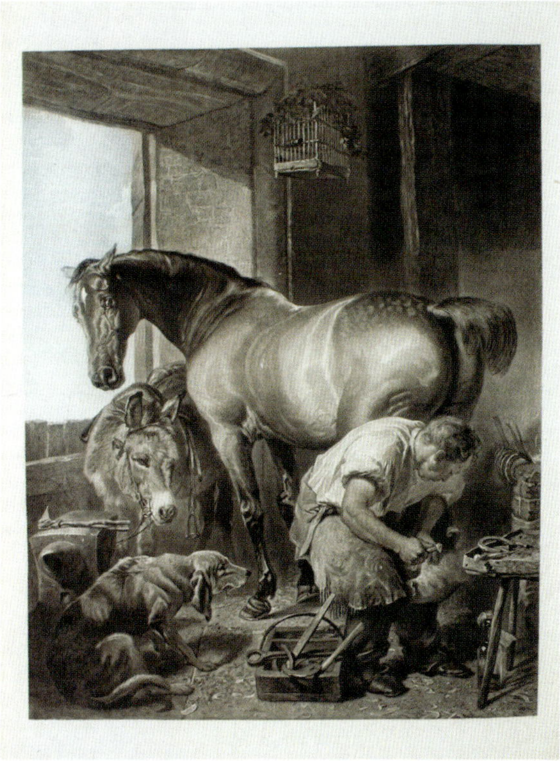

11.4. Charles George Lewis, after Edwin Landseer, *Shoeing the Horse*, *c.*1844, mixed mezzotint on paper, E.266-1970, © Victoria and Albert Museum, London.

11.5. Horace Vernet, Detail from *Prise de la Smala (Smalah) d'Abd-el-Kader par le Duc d'Aumale à Taguin, le 16 Mai 1843*, oil on canvas, MV2027. Courtesy of RMN-Grand Palais (Château de Versailles) / Gérard Blot / Hervé Lewandowski.

11.6. Alfred Decaen after Horace Vernet, *Prise de la Smalah d'Abd El-Kader, Copie commandée par Lord Hertford d'après un tableau commandé par Louis-Philippe pour la galerie des batailles du Musée de Versailles*, oil on canvas, PE629. Courtesy of RMN-Grand Palais (Domaine de Chantilly) /Jean-Gilles Berizzi.

11.7. Ferdinand Bol, *David's Dying Charge to Solomon*, 1643, oil on canvas, NGI. 47. Photo © National Gallery of Ireland.

12.1. Attributed to W. Holland Furlong, *St Mary's Pro-Cathedral, Dublin*. Salt print, mid-1840s. Talbot Photo 2(413), Fox Talbot Collection. By permission of the British Library.

12.2. Attributed to Calvert Richard Jones, *The Four Courts, Dublin*. Waxed paper negative (here shown as a digitally reversed positive), mid-1840s. Talbot Photo 1(299), Fox Talbot Collection. By permission of the British Library.

12.3. Attributed to Calvert Richard Jones, *Conciliation Hall, Dublin*. Waxed paper negative (here shown as a digitally reversed positive), mid-1840s. Talbot Photo 1(306), Fox Talbot Collection. By permission of the British Library.

12.4. Attributed to Calvert Richard Jones, *Customs House, Dublin*. Salt print, mid-1840s. Talbot Photo 2(611), Fox Talbot Collection. By permission of the British Library.

12.5. H. Harrison (engraver); James Mahony (artist). 'The funeral procession in Westmoreland Street, Dublin'. Engraving, *Illustrated London News*, 14 August 1847. Courtesy of the National Library of Ireland.

12.6. Edward Delaney, *Famine*, St Stephen's Green, Dublin, 1967. Photograph: Emily Mark-FitzGerald.

12.7. Rowan Gillespie, *Famine*, Custom House Quays, Dublin, 1997. Photograph: Emily Mark-FitzGerald.

12.8. *An Gorta Mór monument*, unveiled Glasnevin Cemetery, 11 September 2016. Photograph: Rachel M. Bewley-Bateman, Religious Society of Friends in Ireland.

12.9. Citizens of Poznań, Irish Polish Society, the Irish Culture Foundation (Poznan), and Dublin City Council. *Commemorative Plaque to Count Pawel Edmund Strzelecki*, Sackville Place, Dublin, 2015. Photograph: Emily Mark-FitzGerald.

'We see much, but what strikes our eyes bears only a very small proportion to the boundless wretchedness which swarms where only the beneficent steps of such men as Mr Barden have entered.'[80] In advancing this idea about a gap between what the average Dubliner might detect and the real conditions then prevailing, the *Freeman's Journal* reflected contemporary ideas about 'honourable poverty … the silent suffering of the honest poor, resigned to their wretched abodes, out of site'.[81] However, there were downsides to this 'silent suffering': the extent of hunger and deprivation would not be known except to those philanthropic men and women who entered the homes of the poor. Using Bardin's death, the editorial drew attention to not only the 'sensitive mind' of Bardin, but also the skeletal bodies of those 'walking corpses' in the alleys of the south Dublin parish. In order to have a greater impact on the reading public, the suffering of the hungry was merged with Bardin's mental torment on witnessing them; as McLean has suggested 'the spectacle of death … alters the spectator by impugning the physical separation of observer and observed'.[82] This attempt to bridge the gap between the reader, the relieving officer and the starving poor had a purpose. The *Freeman's Journal*:

> … call[ed] upon all whom God has blessed with the capacity to be charitable … on the tender and humane, of every class, to come in aid of their poor brethren, and remove that stigma on humanity – a fellow-being perishing of want in the midst of affluence … Let men read the evidence on the inquest, and then lay their hands on their hearts, satisfied that they have done their duty to humanity.[83]

In keeping with the repeal and reform politics of the paper, the editor deployed what Thomas Laqueur has called a 'humanitarian narrative' in order to build a case for further assistance from the more affluent members of Dublin society. We can see in the paper's appeal to its readers a reliance on the body, 'not only as the locus of pain but also the common bond between those who suffer and those who would help'.[84] Unlike the autopsy in Laqueur's account, however, the body (or bodies) being deployed here were not those of the dead man and subject of the inquest, but rather the bodies of those whom he had endeavoured to help.

What impact, if any, did the newspaper account of Bardin's suicide have on the contributions given to the parochial relief fund? At their first meeting in early January the St Nicholas Without relief committee had received approximately £106 and, although grateful, they noted that 'local contributions … [were]… utterly inadequate to preserve the Destitute Poor … from actual starvation'.[85] By the middle of February, after Bardin's suicide, the committee reported that they had received over £202 from subscribers, including a large grant from the Metropolitan Relief Committee.[86] It is possible that the publicity surrounding Bardin's death may have prompted those with the means to contribute further to the committee of which he was a part. However, conditions in the city were also worsening during this time, and between 19 and 30 January the numbers relieved by the committee had risen from 2,691 to 3,570. This was more than one quarter of the parish's population.[87] In early February the vestry minute books for St Nicholas Without parish recorded that the parochial authorities needed 'to make a reapplotment for coffins for the poor of the Parish' since the amount levied at the Easter vestry the previous year was now spent.[88] The amount had arisen by more than a quarter, and was similar to what it had been at the height of the cholera epidemic in 1832.[89] In March the number of individuals being relieved in Bardin's parish had risen to 4,188 and the committee were 'anxiously … draw[ing] attention to the exhausted state of their funds'.[90] The situation worsened until the summer of 1847 when conditions became truly apocalyptic.

CONCLUSION

Bardin's professional activities, his involvement in his local community via charitable work, and his political engagement in the repeal movement all demonstrate the extent to which he was bound intellectually, geographically and socially to his fellow man. The fraudulent weighing of food and fuel that he detected in 1846 while working as water-bailiff, the inability or unwillingness of fellow parishioners to contribute enough to alleviate starvation on their doorsteps, and the failure of Whitehall to acknowledge the petitions and memorials of Dublin elites demonstrate, at this distance, the rupture of the social bonds that had helped tether Bardin to his family and his community.[91] In this respect Bardin exemplifies Durkheim's theories about national crisis and suicide, and suggests a causative link between witnessing starvation and individual trauma. However, the response to Bardin's death also exemplifies the 'remaking of the social body' in the aftermath of individual tragedy. This is unexpected given the social stigma that attached to suicide during this period and was suggested by the open verdict in the case of Niblett. Bardin was not excluded from consecrated ground; on the contrary, he was buried in Glasnevin Cemetery in one of the first plots bought after it opened in 1832.[92] His burial reunited him with his parents and young son, ensured his inclusion in the religious community of the afterlife, and reflected his engagement with the political community of Repealers and O'Connellites in 1840s Dublin.[93] There was no 'breach in the social fabric' reflected in the posthumous treatment of his body.[94] His suicide did not result in punishment of his corpse or vicariously through his family; further, Peter Slevin, who succeeded him as water bailiff, promised 'to make a yearly allowance of forty pounds' to Bardin's widow and children.[95] Dublin Corporation made good on this promise in March 1847.[96] At a social level, the *Freeman's Journal*'s attempt to elicit sympathy and subscriptions from its readers also underlines the ways in which Bardin's death, when framed within a 'humanitarian narrative', was enlisted to remake the wider social body.

What does it tell us about contemporary attitudes towards the Famine if suicide, once an abhorrent crime thought to elicit further suicides, was viewed as explicable and used to draw attention to the horrific conditions of the starving?[97] This essay does not suggest that the Irish Famine transformed attitudes to suicide; a longer period of change had been underway since the eighteenth century when Kelly detected the beginnings of 'a more tolerable, but by no means tolerant' attitude to such deaths.[98] What it does reveal is the utility of suicidal death in communicating to the reading public the horrific conditions of Dublin city in early 1847. In this instance, suicide became a proxy to help express the inexpressible.[99]

Bardin's death, therefore, helps us reposition Famine-related suffering; it was not confined to starving bodies, workhouse sheds and roadside ditches. It was the lived experience of one who worked alongside municipal authorities and parish officers to alleviate others' suffering; it was the gesture of a man who went home to his wife and children after a day visiting the poor, but who could not forget the horror facing his neighbours across the street. By seeking out Famine victims in the streets of Dublin, it is possible to detect a psychological impact beyond the more familiar categories of victim – the orphaned children and lonely emigrants. In understanding what drove Bardin to kill himself we begin to understand the levels of trauma witnessed and experienced by those who survived the Famine.[100]

'That They Might Obtain the Shelter of a Prison': Kilmainham Gaol and the Great Famine

BRIAN CROWLEY

One of the few decorative features on the original façade of Kilmainham Gaol was a carved tympanum above the main entrance comprising five writhing serpents, bound and tethered by the chains of justice (Figure 9.1). For nearly half a century prior to the Famine of the 1840s, Kilmainham Gaol had acted not only as a place of punishment, but also a powerful deterrent to any member of the populace of Dublin who were considering a life of crime (Figure 9.2). Amidst the destabilising and disruptive years of the Famine and its aftermath, this role underwent a peculiar inversion as Kilmainham reluctantly became a place of shelter and a source of meagre relief for the poor and destitute who crowded into the city and its hinterland at that time. This article will examine why this unexpected change in the gaol's function came about, and how the overwhelming and catastrophic effects of the Famine derailed the Irish penal reform movement in the mid nineteenth century, exposing many of its inherent failings. It will also consider the longer-term consequences of the Famine on Kilmainham Gaol which continued long after the initial crisis had officially passed.

The early to mid nineteenth century saw an unparalleled period of prison building in Great Britain and Ireland. This building frenzy was underpinned by an evangelical belief in the power of prison architecture and systems of discipline to reform and remake those who had fallen into a life of crime and sin. The modern concept of the prison was relatively new as, prior to the late eighteenth century, the main purpose of prisons and gaols was to detain those awaiting punishment. These punishments were usually physical and publicly administered, and frequently involved the death penalty. However, as the eighteenth century progressed, the widespread use of capital and corporal punishment was increasingly seen as incompatible with the more humane values of the Enlightenment. Penal transportation to the American colonies was initially used as an alternative punishment, but when Britain lost those colonies in the 1770s this was no longer an option. Reformers turned instead to prisons and advocated for their development as places in which wrongdoers would not only be punished, but also undergo a programme of reform which would offer them the chance of moral redemption.

This new vision for prisons and punishment necessitated a fundamental reformation of the existing penal system. Eighteenth-century prisons were almost uniformly chaotic, dirty and squalid. The complete lack of discipline and the poor physical conditions in which prisoners were kept also made them breeding grounds for disease; as such, they became a significant threat to the health of the wider communities in which they were located. John Howard, a former Sheriff of Bedford, became one of the most vocal advocates for the reform of prisons.[1] He visited gaols and prisons across Great Britain, Ireland and continental Europe, reported on the conditions he found, and made recommendations to those responsible for running prisons on how they might be improved. Howard visited the original gaol in Kilmainham, which was located about a kilometre from the current Kilmainham Gaol Museum in what is now Old Kilmainham, on a number of occasions in the 1780s. In his description of his tour of Irish prisons in 1787–8 Howard wrote that he found it dirty, dangerous and disorganised. The windows were level with the ground 'and looked towards the street; in consequence of which spirits are easily conveyed to the prisoners'. In addition to finding many of the debtor prisoners drunk at eleven o'clock in the morning, Howard himself put out a fire which had started in the straw on which the prisoners lay. However, he noted that a new prison was being built 'in a fine situation'.[2]

Gaols were managed and funded locally, so responsibility for building the new Kilmainham Gaol lay with the grand jury for the county of Dublin. It was intended to house prisoners convicted of committing crimes within the county of Dublin; the city was a separate jurisdiction with its own prisons run by Dublin Corporation. The decision to build a state-of-the-art gaol can be seen as a reflection of the county authority's desire to be seen as a modern and forward-looking body at the forefront of the new prison reform crusade. The new gaol opened in 1796 and the earliest surviving architectural plans show a building built to reflect the latest ideas on prison reform (Figure 9.3).[3] The gaol was divided into two separate quadrangles with long corridors containing a series of individual cells designed to house one prisoner each. Male and female prisoners were kept in entirely separate parts of the complex, with female staff to care for the women. In addition, the building was designed to allow for the classification of prisoners into different types such as juveniles, convicts, petty criminals, untried prisoners and debtors. Each classification of prisoner had their own dedicated corridors and the design allowed them to pass to and from their designated exercise yard without seeing or interacting with the other classes of prisoners.

Despite its promise, the initial enthusiasm for prison reform amongst the members of the Dublin grand jury appears to have waned in the years that followed the gaol's opening. Both the building and its management were found wanting when the next wave of prison reform came in the 1820s. Under the Prisons (Ireland) Act of 1821[4] two inspectors-general were appointed to physically inspect every prison, gaol and bridewell in Ireland on an annual basis, and write a report on each one.[5] The first two inspectors-general were former military men: Major James Palmer and Major B. B. Woodward. In their report for 1824 on Kilmainham they wrote that the gaol:

> aims at nothing more than to be a receptacle for the safe custody of prisoners, and as such it is tolerably well regulated; but it is wholly devoid of any thing like a system which can improve the habits of the prisoners, or render confinement salutary or productive through the medium of their labour ...[6]

There was also an ongoing issue with overcrowding which prevented the introduction of proper prison discipline and, in the opinion of the inspectors-general, prevented it from having any rehabilitative effect. This problem was exacerbated by the use of part of the building by the government as a depot for convicts from north-eastern counties of Ireland awaiting transportation to penal colonies in Australia and elsewhere. Convicts were guilty of what would previously have been considered capital crimes and were treated as a separate class of prisoner. As such, they were the responsibility of the central government and not the grand jury of Dublin, and the government was responsible for the costs associated with housing them while they were in Kilmainham.[7]

For nearly two decades Majors Palmer and Woodward zealously promoted the latest ideas on prison reform and advocated for the construction of new, purpose-built, modern prisons. Their efforts were given legislative support in the form of the Irish Prisons Act, 1826,[8] which consolidated and reaffirmed existing legislation, while also strengthening local prison governance and promoting an extensive programme of prison building and modernisation. The Kilmainham Gaol building was found to be particularly deficient at this time. In contrast to the square, quadrangle design of Kilmainham, the inspectors-general advocated for the adoption of a radial plan for prisons which would allow for the maximum observation and inspection of prisoners and a more efficient, segregated and defined use of space. Along with overcrowding, the old-fashioned architectural design of Kilmainham Gaol was regularly cited in their reports as the main obstacle to it affecting change in the moral character of its inmates:

> The want of a power of inspection in Kilmainham, owing to the badness of the plan of the gaol (as of all old gaols) may render it expedient to take this subject into consideration in the erection of any additional building, in which the work-rooms or working-yards may be so contrived as to come under one view from an inspection-room or gallery. Until some work of this kind is effected, we fear that the objects of prison discipline will be confined to the safe-keeping, order, and cleanliness of the prison, which is a standard falling very short indeed of the intentions of the Legislature, or of the advantages to be found in the best county gaols.[9]

After many years of criticism and cajoling by the inspectors-general, funds were finally made available by the Dublin grand jury for the improvement of Kilmainham Gaol in the early 1840s. The Dublin-born architect Parke Neville was engaged to design and oversee a major extension to the women's section of the prison (Figure 9.4). The board of superintendence, a sub-committee of the Dublin County grand jury responsible for the gaol, made £1,595 available for the alterations.[10] Ironically, Kilmainham's sluggish progress in relation to the modernisation of the building worked to its advantage, as recent developments in the English prison system had led the inspectors-general advocating for a yet more advanced prison system and architecture. The new 'separate system' had been largely developed in Eastern State Penitentiary in Philadelphia. It involved isolating a prisoner in their cell for most of the day in the belief that this would not only prevent their corruption by other prisoners, but would also allow the prisoner the opportunity to 'commune with his conscience' and contemplate the improving lessons provided by the prison chaplain. On those occasions when prisoners did congregate together for religious services, exercise or outdoor work, no communication was permitted.[11] This new separate system necessitated a very particular and sophisticated architectural infrastructure. The design of the new model prison in Pentonville, London, which opened in 1842, was based completely on the requirements of the separate system. It became the model for practically every prison in Great Britain and Ireland for the rest of the century.

Pentonville Prison was designed by Major Joshua Jebb (a military engineer) and Neville was in close contact with him in respect of the developments in Pentonville when planning the additions to Kilmainham. In 1843 the inspectors-general noted that:

> Mr Neville states in his report 'that the additions and alterations comprised in this contract consist of 27 new cells, 13 feet long by 7 feet wide, and 11 feet high, which are arranged with the view of being warmed and ventilated according to the plan recommended by Major Jebb; also, a large laundry, store-room, two work-rooms, a large drying apartment, together with a kitchen and a work-shed, which are to be erected in the hard-labour yard, &e'.[12]

As prisoners had to spend so much time isolated in their cells, technological advances in central heating and ventilation systems were essential to the development of the separate system. Other improvements, such as the installation of new kitchens and cooking facilities, allowed for a significant change in the prison diet (Figure 9.5). Bread was largely replaced with potatoes, reducing the daily cost of feeding the prisoners to 2½*d.* per head, a reduction of 1*d.* Issues around the health of the prison and the prevention of outbreaks of disease were an ever-present concern and a further £345 was to be spent in improvements to the sewage system and the erection of a large tank which would:

> be supplied with water from a well within the walls of the gaol, by means of a powerful pump, to be worked by the prisoners. The old cess-pools, which were a source of great annoyance from the filth and foul air which were generated, are to be done away with; and the sewers are to be kept clean by the use of water, which is contrived to pass constantly through them from the tank.[13]

While arrangements in the gaol were still not perfect, and the works on the west wing needed to be replicated in the rest of the building, the inspectors now frequently praised Kilmainham Gaol and its personnel. The following year, when the works were finally completed, they reported that there was a total of 94 cells available. The new improvements, combined with space freed up as a result of the removal of many of the convict prisoners to the new convict depot in Smithfield, meant that the gaol was nearly able to provide a separate cell to each prisoner, the average occupancy of the gaol being 101⅓ prisoners in 1844.[14] The majority of these prisoners were there for relatively minor crimes, mostly petty larcenies, assaults and instances of drunkenness, and their sentences were short, often just a few days or weeks.

The story of the determined campaign to upgrade the accommodation in Kilmainham Gaol is representative of the wider efforts of the Inspectors-General in encouraging grand juries across the country to improve prison conditions. In the 1844 report they reflected on the achievements of their office since the publication of their first report in 1823. The inspectors felt it was permissible to:

> rejoice, not only in the gradual improvement made, but at the total absence of discreditable abuses and the growing interest taken by Grand Juries and Boards as well as the public in general, in the cause of prison discipline ...[15]

This somewhat reflective and congratulatory tone continued in the report for 1845, and this may have been partly due to the fact that this was the final report submitted by James

Palmer and Francis White (who replaced B. B. Woodward in 1841) before their retirement. Palmer had been in position since the post was established, and the report begins by saying

> We cannot, however, avoid stating that the gaols of Ireland, as a whole, are in a high state of good order and regularity, and that after much labour for years to obtain the co-operation of the local authorities, and to secure a succession of qualified officers, we may report that no absolute abuse exists, nor could exist without being rapidly known and investigated.[16]

They go on to note that

> Every county gaol in Ireland has, within the last 20 years, either erected new prisons or added materially to their accommodation, so that in most cases there is a cell for every prisoner at night, and as much classification of crime in day-rooms and work by day, as the law requires, and the Act permitting total separation of each prisoner is in progress in some gaols, and under consideration in all of them …[17]

The 1845 report is not without its criticisms and identifies many areas still in need of much improvement. In addition to calling for a centralised system for the selection and payment of prison officers, they also criticise the lack of proper and specific provision for young offenders and lunatics, and advocate for the removal of debtors from the prison population. Interestingly, the 1845 Report, which was published in January 1846, contains no reference to the first signs of the failure of the potato crop which had occurred some months earlier and which would ultimately lead to the Great Famine. It is clear that they had no idea that the events of the coming years would severely challenge, and at times overwhelm, the Irish prison system which they had laboured so long to develop.

Two new inspectors-general, Clement Johnson and Edward Corrigan, wrote the report for 1846 and were primarily preoccupied in asserting their *bona fides* as true believers in the prison reform mission. They advocated for the introduction of the separate system into Irish prisons, as they believed that

> the lower classes of Ireland [were] peculiarly fitted to profit by a system, which at once removes their ignorance, and convinces them that an interest is taken in their fate, a conviction which we hold to be of the highest importance to establish amongst an impressionable and imaginative people.[18]

However, in this report we see the first recognition that the Famine was having an effect on Irish prisons. Towards the end of their 'General Observations', the inspectors note that

> It is impossible for us to avoid some notice of the enormous increase of prisoners committed to the various gaols, which has taken place within the last few months. Great as that increase has been, in some instances amounting to 100 per cent, upon the average numbers, we think it our duty to state, that we do not consider such increase to have its origin in any evil disposition among the poorer classes, but to have been produced *in a great degree* by the heavy pressure of distress, and that in a *very great number* of instances small crimes have been committed for the purpose of obtaining that support in prison which could not be procured elsewhere.[19]

This largely sympathetic attitude is somewhat qualified in a later postscript to these remarks where they state that:

> Since writing the above, facts have come to our knowledge which compel us to modify, to a certain extent, the favourable opinion we have expressed with regard to the origin of crime. We are now obliged to state that many offences have been committed by evil disposed persons, not in want, but calculating on impunity, in the disturbed state of society occasioned by the general prevalence of distress. The latter part of the statement is, nevertheless, correct with regard to a great proportion of the minor offences.[20]

Despite the dramatic increase in criminality in areas of the country, Kilmainham was, for the time being, largely untouched by the growing distress in the country. The inspector-general with responsibility for Dublin that year, Edward Cottingham, was a former member of the Kilmainham board of superintendence and in his report on Kilmainham he referenced how that experience has given him 'the most useful instruction in the management of prison affairs'. He was at pains to mention that 'experience gained, not by books and theories, but by personal observation in other places, has impressed upon my mind the utility of the suggestions I have here offered'.[21] Ironically it would seem that overall numbers went down in Kilmainham in 1846, and numbers only began to really increase in 1847, reaching an historic high in 1850 (see Table 1).

Table 1: Prisoner Committals to Kilmainham Gaol, 1844–60[22]

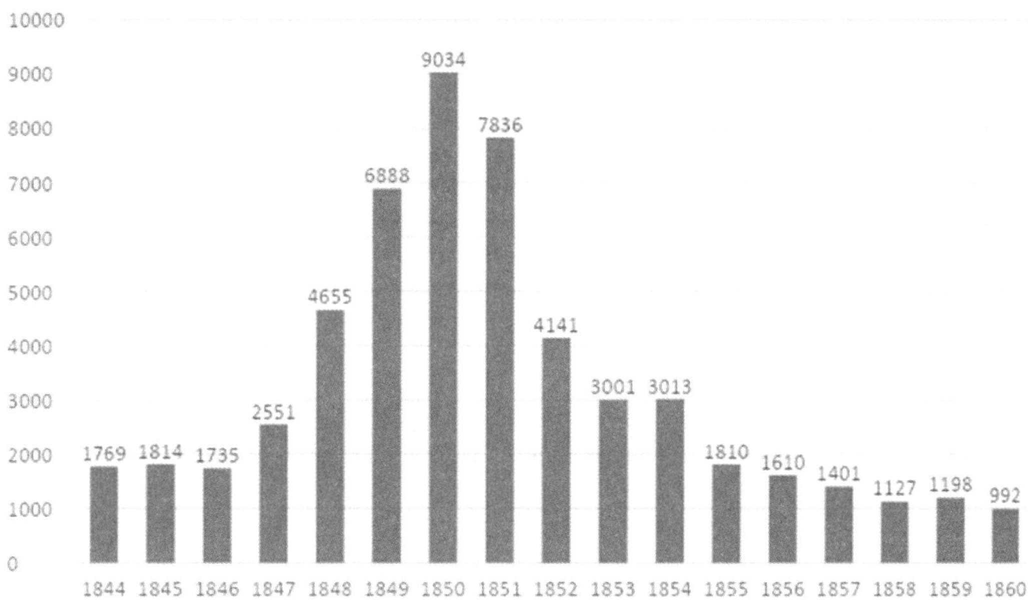

In contrast with 1846, the 1847 report saw no equivocation about the calamitous impact of the Famine on Irish prisons. The report opened with what can almost be described as a lamentation:

> No task can well be more discouraging and, indeed, melancholy, than that of attempting to detail the history of the Irish prisons for the year 1847 … The terrible catastrophe, which

> has disorganized the whole framework of society in Ireland, fell with full force upon the establishments under our charge; and instead of having a pleasing statement of improved discipline, enlarged prison accommodation, and advanced instruction, we can only describe industrial works given up, classification destroyed, separation unattempted, and disease and death increasing to a degree that could never have been contemplated by those acquainted with the usual orderly and healthy state of our gaols.[23]

The inspectors-generals identified three main causes which they felt were to blame for the huge numbers crowding into Irish prisons on what amounted to a perfect storm for the Irish prisons, namely:

> the occurrence in the same year, 1st, of distress amounting to famine; 2nd, the sudden cessation of transportation; and, 3rdly, the passing of the Vagrant Act – the effect of the first having been to quadruple the evils occasioned by the two last.[24]

Prison registers record an inevitable increase in crime as starving people began to steal in order to survive. In addition, free settlers in Van Diemen's Land (now Tasmania) had petitioned the imperial government to end convict transportation to the colony. This resulted in a two-year suspension of convict transportation, which began towards the end of 1846.[25] The result was an increase of convicts within the Irish penal system. As the Famine progressed, the inspectors-general came to believe that many desperate people were deliberately committing capital offences in the hopes of securing passage to Australia. The introduction to their 1849 report included a section entitled 'Cases of Convicts Who Committed Crime For The Purpose of Being Transported', citing examples of crimes purposely committed to secure transportation.[26] Kilmainham was particularly badly hit by the almost total cessation in penal transportation for male prisoners from 1846.[27] With a four-fold increase in capital crimes, and almost no penal colonies to transport prisoners to, Kilmainham was once again used as a male convict depot. Thus, Kilmainham found itself with a significant reduction in the number of cells at its disposal at a time when it was trying to cope with an unprecedented level of prisoners. However, the principal cause in this rise in prisoner numbers in Kilmainham and other Dublin prisons was the 1847 Vagrancy Act[28] which effectively saw the criminalisation of poverty. The poor and destitute were now liable for, and sometimes desirous of, incarceration if they had no other means of support and shelter. While the act may have grown out of a moral panic over a huge and growing rootless population wandering the country in search of relief, it also allowed the authorities to access and utilise the prison infrastructure in which so much public money had been invested in the previous two decades. Increasingly the prison system also found itself compensating for the deficiencies of the existing welfare system. Particular mention is made in the 1847 inspectors-general report of teenage boys committing crimes in the workhouse to take advantage of better rations in local prisons.[29] The influx of young people into overcrowded prisons was a source of particular concern as it was often no longer possible to protect them from the corrupting influence of older, more dissolute and hardened criminals.

Large numbers of sick and diseased paupers entering the prison system as a result of the Vagrancy Act led to a public health crisis in many prisons. Overall prison deaths in Irish prisons rose from 81 in 1845, to 131 in 1846, and to 1,315 deaths in 1847. In 1847 alone, 351 prisoners died in Cork County Gaol, the highest number that year.[30] This was largely attributed to a 'recent epidemic' of typhoid in the county.[31] The following year, Galway overtook Cork with 485 deaths in the county gaol. Although nowhere near the Cork or Galway numbers, Kilmainham also had a dramatic increase in prisoner mortalities going from one death in 1845, to three in 1846 and, its highest number, 29 in 1847. The inspectors-general described Kilmainham in 1847 as being as orderly and well-arranged as it could be, given the 'difficulties under which it, in common with all other prisons, labours at present', but the inspectors added that discipline was badly affected by the presence of vagrants. They also noted that the older, unglazed areas of the building appeared to be healthier, and described the gaol as being 'altogether airy and wholesome'.[32]

As the Famine progressed and prison numbers continued to rise, the inspectors-general sought to emphasise the extraordinary and unprecedented environment in which the prison system was now operating. The norms and certainties on which the entire prison reform movement was based upon simply no longer pertained. In 1848, they stated that, in ordinary circumstances, the cumulative improvements to the prison system in Ireland would have resulted in positive improvements to Irish society and a steady reduction in crime. However,

> the calamitous visitation of the few last years operating with no exclusive pressure affecting the most opulent and humblest poor alike, suspending employment and staying the hand of charity, has solely tried the integrity of our people: Larcenies have multiplied, because ordinarily, men will steal food rather than die ...

Witnessing the distress of the population at first hand, the inspectors urged parliament to look with empathy and understanding at the appalling circumstance of the

> vast numbers who, without means of earning subsistence, and unable to procure charitable aid, notoriously appropriated articles of trifling value that they might obtain the shelter of a prison under the guise of commitment for a criminal offence.

They hoped their detailed eye-witness reports would '... induce reflecting minds to pause before they pronounce unmeasured invective upon Irish people'.[33]

The crisis also posed an existential threat for the entire prison reform movement which the inspectors had been championing for more than twenty years. Despite the very substantial investment of public money in modern prisons and new forms of prison discipline, crime was increasing exponentially. Critics of the prison reform movement had begun to emerge, and in 1849 the inspectors-general were perturbed by those who were not only criticising the system, but were also seeking a return to the physical punishments of earlier times. They 'viewed with alarm the attempts that have been made to shake the confidence of the government and the public in what we believe to be the only course capable of producing a deterring, if not reformatory, effect.'[34] In order to defend the system, the inspectors-general had to make a distinction between regular criminals and those driven to acts of criminality by the extraordinary circumstances of the Famine. If the prison system was failing to reduce crime in Ireland, that was because it was designed to reform criminals who committed crimes due to their moral failings, not a desperate and starving populace who were doing whatever they could to survive. As far as the inspectors-general were concerned, the solution to this problem lay outside the prison system, with those responsible for provision of poor relief.

The reports of this period often contain overt criticism of the failure of other state organs to provide sufficient poor relief. They many of the problems being faced by the prison system to the fact that it had to compensate for the failures of the Poor Law system. Describing the overcrowding in Cork in 1847, they noted that, in common with gaols around the country, Cork County Gaol was 'sought after by the destitute classes as a comfortable refuge and security from the poorhouse'.[35] The food available in the gaols was more substantial and consistent than in the workhouses, and they also had a lower disease and mortality rate. It was also possible to access a prison without surrendering their property rights,[36] which was a requirement for those entering the workhouse. Thus, rather than being a deterrent, prison often became the preferred option of those driven to destitution. The overcrowding of prisons caused by the introduction of the 1847 Vagrancy Act was interpreted by the inspectors-general as a retrograde attempt by the government to use the prison system as a form of poor relief. In 1849 they wrote that

> It would not become us to make any remarks upon, the policy of the Vagrant Act, but we must observe, that while there does not seem to be any perceptible diminution in the number of mendicants since the passing of that measure, its influence in adding to the difficulties under which the gaols are now suffering, by filling them with paupers, is indisputable. Squalid, naked, and diseased, these miserable beings, who are often discharged in the morning only to be readmitted at night, interfere most seriously with the discipline and management of these establishments.[37]

The Inspectors were very clear that prisons were not welfare organisations and using them as such was not only inappropriate, but it also prevented them from fulfilling their proper purpose. These poor prisoners were usually in the prison for just 24 hours, 'so all advantage to be derived from instruction in schooling or handicraft is totally out of the question'.[38] In the 1850 report they also attribute a substantial increase in the number of vagrants in Irish prisons to the decision to reduce those in receipt of state-sponsored outdoor relief from 95,468 in 1849 to 2,780 in 1850.[39] The inspectors-general were fiercely protective of the prison infrastructure which had been painstakingly built up over the previous decades and resisted attempts to turn it into an adjunct to the workhouse system. They even suggested the establishment of a separate 'intermediate class of house of detention, between pauper asylums and criminal prisons, which latter ought to be exclusively restricted to those who have committed moral offences'.[40]

While they may have avoided the worst effects of the Famine, Kilmainham and the other Dublin prisons were most definitely at the forefront in terms of its after-effects. In 1849 the inspectors-general made reference to the 'shoals of vagrants [who] have been attracted from the pauperised districts to more favoured localities in the hope of obtaining relief'.[41] These vagrants also incited a degree of moral panic, and in 1850 they made reference to a

> wandering population [that] has been turned to account by professional thieves and divided into gangs who prowl throughout the country reconnoitring, or, to use their own phrase, 'setting' such houses and premises as appear to offer easy entrance, and then rifling them at a favourable opportunity.[42]

With a quarter of the prison taken up with convicts awaiting transportation, Kilmainham struggled to deal with the influx of vagrants and by 1849 housing up to five prisoners in cells designed for one became commonplace.[43] To discourage the poor from using the prison system as a source of relief rather than the workhouse, in 1849 the food allowance for prisoners serving a sentence of under a month was decreased throughout the prison system. In the introduction to their 1849 report, the inspector-generals first set out the 'Previous Dietary' which consisted of :

> Breakfast: 8 oz. of meal .made into stirabout, with 1 pint of new-milk or buttermilk.
> Dinner: 1 lb of good-bread, and 1 pint of new-milk.
> *(I. G. twenty-eight report, 1849 p. ix)*

The new, reduced dietary (see Table 2), devised three separate classes for men, women and children under 10, each of whom were to receive different daily food rations.

Table 2: Reduced Irish Prison Diet

PRESENT DIETARY.

	Class 1.	Class 2.	Class 3.
	Males	Females	Males and Females under 10 Years
Breakfast	8 oz. meal in stirabout, ½ pint of new-milk,	7 oz. meal in stirabout, ½ pint of new-milk,	5 oz. meal in stirabout, ½ pint of new-milk,
Dinner	14 oz. bread, 1 pint of new-milk,	12 oz. bread, ¾ pint of new-milk,	10 oz. bread, ½ pint of new-milk,
Supper	————	————	4 oz. bread, 1½ naggin of new-milk

Source: *I. G. Twenty-Eighth Report, 1849*, p. ix.

Male prisoners with sentences of less than two months, could be allowed extra rations in cold weather if they were engaged in 'exhausting labour' and approval was given by the gaol medical officer. On the other hand, it would seem that women's rations were significantly decreased, and in the specific report on Kilmainham Gaol the inspectors mention that 'no complaints have been made of its insufficiency except by some of the females' (*I. G. twenty-eight report,* 1849 p.19). Although it was possible to replace the daily bread allowance with potatoes, they were not served again in Kilmainham until 1855. Provision was also made in 1850 to replace milk with gruel, but this was only permitted two times a week, and not for both meals *(I. G. twenty-ninth report,* 1850 p. xii).

As the effects of the Famine began to ease, the inspectors-general expressed the hope in their report for 1850 that the growing agricultural industry in the country would provide work for 'the able-bodied who are willing to work'.[44] However, despite a decrease in many counties, the overall numbers of prisoners confined in Irish prisons increased by 3,393 between 1849 to 1850, rising from 112,478 to 115,871.[45] This was largely due to a rise in prisoner numbers in some metropolitan areas, but specifically in Dublin, where the combined numbers for the county gaol at Kilmainham, the city gaol for men (Richmond Bridewell) and the women's city gaol (Grangegorman Penitentiary) reached 35,037 in 1850, an increase of 5,400 on the year before.[46] As a result, the situation in Dublin gaols was the primary focus of the introduction to the 1850 report with particular attention being paid to Richmond Bridewell, as this institution had the highest rate of inmates convicted of vagrancy in the country. Of the 14,245 committals, 7,702 (54.1 per cent) were for vagrancy and of these, only 786 prisoners came from Dublin city and county.[47] While increased job opportunities were a source of relief for the able-bodied 'willing to work', the inspectors-general believed that the 'indolent and refractory' could be dissuaded from idleness by the stringent imposition of punishments for vagrancy in the form of 'what is most distasteful to them: low diet, hard labour, and compulsory cleanliness'.[48] They quoted extensively and approvingly from a letter from Mr Marques, the governor of Richmond Bridewell, in which he outlined his attempts to deal with the challenge of dealing with the influx of vagrants. Initially they contrived, with the co-operation of the magistrates, to limit the sentences of those charged with vagrancy to 24 hours 'in order to avoid feeding them', unless they were in actual want. However, this policy was suspended on 1 January 1851 due to doubts about the legality of not feeding prisoners, even for a short one-day sentence. Once they began feeding prisoners dinner, it seems that the gaol was being used by the poor as a source of board and lodgings, with around 100 prisoners arriving every day to receive their dinner only to be released the following morning. To counteract this development, a new procedure was introduced for vagrants: they were now to be imprisoned for a minimum of 48 hours, and their sentence was to include mandatory hard labour, walking on the treadmill for the able-bodied or stone-breaking for the young, elderly or infirm. Those who did not carry out their tasks satisfactorily had their dinner rations cut in half. A cold bath and mandatory hair-cutting also formed part of the sentence.[49]

The system for dealing with vagrants pioneered in Richmond seem to have been subsequently adopted in Kilmainham. In 1851 the Governor of Kilmainham attributed a decrease in the number of vagrants coming to the Gaol to an order of the Board of Superintendence that on arrival in Kilmainham vagrants were to have their

> hair cut close, plunged into a cold bath, and there well-scrubbed with a brush; on the next morning they are put to a task of stone-breaking or oakum picking, and do not get dinner till the task has been performed.[50]

As shown in Table 3 (in respect of 1851), while general crime figures remained high, vagrants constituted by far the largest group in Kilmainham, 5,474 (69.9 per cent) out of a total of 7,836 committals.

Table 3: Monthly Returns for Kilmainham Gaol, 1851[51]

Class of Prisoners	January	February	March	April	May	June	July	August	September	October	November	December	Total
Criminals, &c.,	143	146	129	129	173	220	220	213	149	182	133	127	1,964
Drunkards, &c.,	26	25	14	18	24	29	30	49	32	27	37	35	346
Debtors, . .	5	2	1	5	13	3	8	9	2	1	2	1	52
Vagrants, . .	643	880	1074	493	346	404	386	227	180	254	284	303	5,474
Total, .	817	1,053	1,218	645	556	656	644	498	363	464	456	466	7,836

R. Allison, Governor.

One of the many concerns about the number of people entering the prison system was the danger of creating a substantial and permanent criminal class for whom prison was no longer a deterrent:

> the evil that is produced is so enormous as to threaten the total demoralisation of the lower orders; slowing itself in the abolition of all distinctions between right and wrong, and generating a habit of committing crimes either for the sake of obtaining board and lodging in a gaol, where comfort with a moderate degree of labour tend to make the loss of liberty of comparative little consequence.[52]

Dublin prisons in particular were too overcrowded to employ many of their usual disciplinary measures and provide adequate separation of prisoners. This must have been a source of considerable concern, particularly given the increased numbers of young and first time-offenders entering the prison system who were in danger of 'contamination' through associating with experienced criminals. Indeed, while the inspectors-general noted with approval the recommendations issued the previous year by a parliamentary select committee that 'that entire separation, except during the hours of labour and religious worship and instruction, is absolutely necessary for preventing contamination, and for securing a proper system of prison discipline' they also acknowledged that in the case of Irish prisons, 'the space now available is wholly inadequate' to carry out these measures.[53] Not only were overcrowded prisons like Kilmainham failing to reduce levels of crime in the county, they may also inadvertently have been facilitating the creation of criminal gangs and relationships in the prison.

While the numbers of inmates in Kilmainham and other Dublin prisons in 1850 and 1851 were alarming, as the worst effects of the Famine began to ease and the Dublin economy began to recover, they did begin to fall. However, prison numbers in Kilmainham for the first half of the 1850s still remained much higher than they had been in the pre-Famine era. While the overall population of the country had fallen dramatically, the number of people living in Dublin were growing and the city expanded well beyond its borders into what was then still County Dublin and, therefore, the gaol's catchment area. The pressure on Kilmainham was eased with the opening of Mountjoy Prison in 1850, which resulted in the permanent removal of all convicts from the gaol. Convictions under the Vagrancy Act also fell dramatically as Famine-era distress receded. In their report for 1853 the inspectors-general predicted that the numbers of adult male prisoners would continue to fall due to improved employment opportunities, increased emigration and enlistment in the army as a result of the outbreak of the Crimean War.[54] With the worst of the crisis over, they returned to pre-Famine role of advocating for the improvement in prison buildings and systems of discipline. The inspectors-general believed that Irish prisons needed to make up for the lost years of the Famine by upgrading their buildings and introducing the necessary infrastructure to enable them to properly implement the separate system.

While they could point to a significant reduction in the overall numbers of prisoners, two worrying legacies of the Famine remained for Kilmainham Gaol. Irish prisons in the 1850s continued to house high levels of juvenile and female prisoners. Indeed, at the same time that they highlighted the reduction in male prisoners due to the outbreak of war, in 1853 the Inspectors-General also predicted that the women and children who depended on them for economic support would be 'exposed … for a time at least, to greater trials and temptations' and many of them would find themselves caught up in the penal system and be added to the already large population of underage and female prisoners.[55] While the challenge of what to do with juvenile prisoners would be addressed as part of a larger, UK-wide approach to underage crime in the 1850s, the issue of the high number of women in Irish gaols proved to be a uniquely Irish problem which proved stubbornly unresponsive to the efforts of the Irish penal establishment to improve it. The experiences of female prisoners in the Irish convict system are explored in Elaine Farrell's most recent work, *Women, Crime and Punishment in Ireland: Life in the Nineteenth Century Prison*. Convict prisons such as Mountjoy replaced penal transportation as the punishment for those convicted of more serious crimes. Unlike prisoners in local gaols like Kilmainham, convict prisoners served longer sentences. During their time in prison they progressed though different 'classes', and earned privileges and remission of their sentences through good behaviour. As a result, their prison experiences were often meticulously documented and files were maintained containing details of their behaviour, their state of health and often correspondence they sent and received. While similar levels of documentation was not carried out for prisoners in local gaols, many of the women who Farrell writes about would have served time in both the local and convict systems.[56]

Kilmainham and the other Dublin gaols were the most affected by the rise in juvenile crime in the post-Famine period. In 1850, 25 per cent of larcenies in Dublin were committed by youths, the majority of whom were originally from outside the city and county. In a depiction reminiscent of Charles Dickens's *Oliver Twist*, the inspectors described the process by which children fell into a life of crime:

> [they] have become pickpockets and thieves from falling into the company of old offenders in the streets and in the wretched lodging cellars which are the hotbeds of vice and scenes of

> hardened iniquity. Many of these boys have the strongest claim on the public care, being the destitute and friendless orphans of those who fell victim to the famine ...[57]

An increase in juvenile crime was also a concern in England and Wales, and the 1852 report noted with approval that the Westminster parliament had launched an inquiry into this issue. However, they were at pains to emphasise that the surge in juvenile crime had a different root cause in Ireland. In contrast with England, in Ireland 'the temptations to crime, such as penny theatres, and similar low places of amusement, are fewer'. However, the

> other stimulants to infraction of the laws are yet more numerous and powerful, namely, the total inadequacy of accommodation to secure the ordinary decencies of life in the houses of the lower classes, &c., &c., and the want of any recognised means of education and industrial training. If these grave defects are found to operate injuriously in England, how much more severely must they be felt in Ireland, where the wretchedness and filth of the habitations of the poor almost furnish an apology for turning the children into the streets, and where the low wages and scanty employment of the town population reduce the daily food to a minimum which elsewhere would be considered incompatible with the maintenance of mere existence.[58]

By 1853, 5,225 (42.7 per cent) out of 12,238 juvenile prisoners were without parental care, 2,000 of them being 'absolute' orphans.[59] The reports for the first half of the 1850s focussed particular attention on the issue of juvenile crime and the inspectors-general assembled masses of statistical data about the number of juvenile prisoners, the crimes for which they were charged and/or convicted, and their parental situation. This information undoubtedly fed into the legislation which was being drafted at the time in Westminster to address juvenile crime in Ireland, as well as England and Wales. An act of parliament to set up juvenile reformatories in England and Wales was passed in 1854.[60] Similar legislation for Ireland was introduced in 1858[61] when the first Irish reformatory school opened in a former military barracks in Glencree, County Wicklow. Kilmainham and other gaols continued to play a relatively minor role in the punishment of young people, as the act allowed for juveniles to be sent to a reform school provided that they had previously served at least 14 days in prison.[62] Some young offenders continued to be sentenced to prison sentences only, without any reference to time in a reformatory. By the early 1860s the falling levels of juvenile convictions, combined with the setting up of dedicated reformatory schools, meant that in official circles at least the issue of juvenile crime was seen as being under control and no longer seems to have been a significant issue for the authorities in Kilmainham.

In the same way that the disquiet of the inspectors-generals in respect of juvenile crime predated the Famine, they had long been concerned about the disparity between levels in female criminality in Ireland in contrast to England and Wales. Significantly, Grangegorman Female Penitentiary in Dublin city was the first female-only prison in Great Britain and Ireland.[63] However, as was the case with juveniles, the effects of the Famine intensified and exacerbated this pre-existing problem. Less than 25 per cent of the prison population in England was female,[64] while in Ireland it was 43.4 per cent in 1854.[65] The situation was worse in Leinster where women made up over 51 per cent of the prison population, mostly due to committals to Dublin prisons.

Table 4: Male and Female Prisoner Numbers by Province, 1853 and 1854[66]

Abstract showing the Distribution into Provinces

	1853		1854	
	Males.	Females.	Males.	Females
Ulster	5,626	3,135	5,531	2,966
Munster	15,601	8,091	12,041	7,055
Leinster*	17,694	17,477	14,270	15,063
Connaught	3,571	1,824	2,350	1,169
Total,	42,492	30, 527	34,192	26,253
Gross Total,	73,019		60,445	

*The large preponderance if numbers in Leinster is produced by the committals to the City of Dublin Prisons:-

Richmond Bridewell, Males,	7,287	17,775
Grangegorman, Females	10,488	

While the overall figures for men and women prisoners were falling, the proportional increase in female prisoners nationally between 1853 and 1854 from 41.8 per cent to 43.4 per cent was concerning.[67] The inspectors-general noted that the improving economy was not offering the same level of employment opportunities to women. As can be seen in the table in Table 5, the percentage of female prisoners held in Kilmainham increased significantly after the Famine, and remained consistently high throughout the 1850s and into the 1860s. This would suggest that a significant number of the poor and destitute women who fled to the capital as a result of the Famine found themselves trapped in the penal system in the years that followed.

Lack of industrialisation, even in the larger cities, meant there were limited job opportunities for working-class women even in more prosperous times. The main forms of employment for women were domestic service and agriculture, but as Maria Luddy notes, the number of women in paid employment dropped from 29 per cent in 1861 to 19.5 per cent in 1911.[68] Given the lack of alternative economic opportunities available to them, many poor women turned to prostitution and petty crime. As Luddy points out, prostitution itself was not outlawed, so police needed other grounds to arrest them.[69] Thus, in the case of the prison registers for Kilmainham Gaol, the charges laid against women engaged in prostitution centre on the fact that they are a source of disorder and public annoyance, though it is interesting to note the frequency with which these women were identified in the prison register as prostitutes. For example, Eliza Kenny, who appears to have served around 80 different sentences in Kilmainham between 1840 and 1849, was charged on a number of occasions with being a prostitute 'annoying the public' and being a 'disorderly prostitute'.[70] Margaret Cardiff was originally from The Coombe in Dublin city, but seems to have been settled in Kingstown (Dun Laoghaire). On 27 June 1848, aged approximately sixteen-years-old, she served her first sentence in Kilmainham Gaol when she was sentenced to one months' imprisonment for 'loitering about Kingstown for the purposes of prostitution'.[71] Over the next twenty years she appears to have served approximately 70 different sentences, most of which centred on identifying her as a prostitute and, therefore, a threat to public order.

Table 5: Breakdown of prison numbers in Kilmainham Gaol by gender, 1846–65

Year	Male prisoners committed	Female prisoners committed	Total prisoners committed	Male prisoners %	Female prisoners %
1846	1,120	615	1,735	66.5	35.5
1847	1,730	821	2,551	67.8	31.2
1848[72]	-	-	4,665	-	-
1849	-	-	6,888	-	-
1850[73]	5,583	3,050	8,633	64.7	35.3
1851	4,510	3,162	7,672	58.8	41.2
1852[74]	2,185	1,888	4,073	53.6	46.4
1853	1,663	1,327	2,960	55.0	45.0
1854	1,459	1,489	2,948	49.5	50.5
1855	910	900	1,810	50.3	49.7
1856	799	811	1,610	49.6	50.4
1857	775	626	1,401	55.3	44.7
1858	576	551	1,127	51.1	48.9
1859	577	621	1,198	48.2	51.8
1860	502	490	992	50.6	49.4
1861	605	493	1,098	55.0	45.0
1862	743	435	1,178	63.1	36.9
1863	727	475	1,202	60.5	39.5
1864	703	474	1,177	59.7	40.3
1865	732	575	1,307	56.0	44.0

Both before and after the Famine, these women would also have found it much harder than their male equivalents to escape the cycle of criminality and repeated imprisonment. One of the most significant differences between male and female prisoners was in their respective rates of recidivism. In 1852, on the day the inspector-general made his inspection, ten male prisoners held in Kilmainham had served two prison sentences, as opposed to 22 females. Only two men had served three sentences but ten women had. While 25 women had served four sentences or more, not one man in the gaol at that time had done so. In 1853, 108 males accounted for 172 committals, whereas 130 females accounted for 330.[75] These women generally served short sentences (i.e. usually less than a month) for relatively minor crimes such as stealing, vagrancy, assault, drunkenness and prostitution. Unlike women who committed more serious crimes and were given relatively long sentences of penal servitude in the newly-established convict prison system, the prison experiences of female petty criminals housed in county gaols like Kilmainham were largely unrecorded beyond the prison registers. However, because of the volume of convictions accrued by individual women, it is sometimes possible to get a crude sense of the trajectory of their lives over a period of years from tracing their entries in the prison registers. Between 1848 and 1868, Margaret Cardiff is recorded as being anywhere from 5'1" to 5'5", suggesting that she may have still been growing at this time and possibly much younger than 16 when first arrested. Her eyes are alternatively described as being grey or blue, though occasionally they are given as hazel. Similarly, depending on the entry her hair colour is anything from fair to dark brown. While some prison officials describe her complexion as 'fresh', there are a number of others that say she had pock marks or pitted skin, perhaps a legacy of a serious illness. There is also considerable variation in the ages recorded for her in different prison entries. Her position on the margins of society seems to have resulted in a chaotic existence; in addition to convictions related to her work as a prostitute, she also served several sentences for drunkenness, breaches of the peace and destruction of property.[76] Margaret was also arrested for attempting suicide on two occasions.[77] The number of her convictions in which the consumption of alcohol was a factor seems to have been a common feature for many women prisoners in the 1850s. In 1852, 206 women were committed to Kilmainham Gaol for drunkenness as opposed to 184 men.[78]

Women like Margaret Cardiff would have faced a much more extreme degree of economic and social exclusion on their release than their male counterparts. Serving a prison sentence carried a particular stigma for women, particularly if they were involved in prostitution. Gaols and workhouses often tried to segregate prostitutes away from other female prisoners; in 1855 Kilmainham was criticised for having only two separate classes of female prisoner, 'one for vagrants and persons of abandoned character, and the second for all *other offenders without distinction*'.[79] Regardless of these institutional distinctions, on the outside women would have been considered morally tainted by any potential employer as a result of their association with the penal system, regardless of the nature of their crime. Even women who simply lived in areas or streets associated with prostitution found themselves unable to secure positions as domestic servants.[80] Street prostitutes in particular were considered pariahs: Maria Luddy quotes from a Scottish missionary, William Logan, who visited Ireland in 1845 and noted that women who engaged in street prostitution were even excluded from work in the better class of brothel.[81] Elaine Farrell has also asserted that the criminal justice system itself was, ironically, a significant factor in Irish female recidivism in the nineteenth century: 'while social and economic circumstances rendered further criminal activity almost inevitable for some, nineteenth-century legislation and practices were stacked in favour of recommittal.'[82] The stigma of having been identified as being prostitutes by the legal and police system made women like Eliza Kenny and Margaret Cardiff vulnerable to arrest as soon as they entered a public space. Their very existence was deemed a source of disorder and legitimate grounds for incarceration. Kilmainham had, proportionally, one of the largest female populations of any county gaol in the country. As can be seen in Table 5, in 1854, 1856 and 1859 women actually outnumbered men. Faced with this unprecedented situation, the inspectors-general doubled down on their belief that the solution to female criminality lay in the provision of well-designed and well-run prisons, and attributed the high level of recidivism among women prisoners in Kilmainham to the physical inadequacies of the building, and the women's wing in particular. While it may have been the most modern area of the prison, the proportional increase in women prisoners was not reflected in the amount of space allotted to them in the building. Better provision for female prisoners was seen as essential. In 1853 the inspectors-general concluded that the root cause of the disparity between male and female recidivism was 'the inadequate accommodation of their [female] department, and to the consequent imperfection of restrictive and deterrent discipline'.[83]

The inspectors-general intensified their advocacy of the new 'separate' system which they believed would be particularly effective with female prisoners. Faced with a prison population made up of increasing numbers of women in the aftermath of the Famine, in 1851 the inspectors urged a stricter imposition of prison discipline for female prisoners in the belief that:

> separation ... as an instrument of reformation is indispensable for women of the class and character from which the inmates of prisons are usually supplied ... those who in association are the loudest and boldest, are, when isolated, completely broken into submission, and if not softened into repentance, as is so often the case, are at least subdued to a wholesome fear of the recurrence of such penal seclusion.[84]

The ongoing failure of the penal system to prevent recidivism amongst many female prisoners offered an uncomfortable challenge to the accepted dogma that the primary means to reduce crime and reform prisoners and lay in the provision of modern and well-run prisons. There is even a suggestion, perhaps for the first time, that not all types of prisoners were capable of experiencing moral reformation as a result of undergoing a period under the separate system. Instead, they emphasise that it was particularly effective in controlling and subduing women prisoners. Table 5 also demonstrates that in the decade or more after end of the Famine, they did not seem to be able to reverse the proportional rise in female prisoners in Kilmainham which it had brought about. In 1860, after a decade of high levels of female incarceration, the cause of female recidivism was still largely being blamed on the 'the inferior means of accommodation, and consequently of corrective accommodation which are provided for them in our prisons'. However, there was also at least some acknowledgement that women faced greater, and often insurmountable, barriers when attempting to escape a life of criminality following their release from prison:

> Among males, a large portion of our criminals is derived from offences arising out political and sectarian feud, faction fights and quarrels at fairs and markets, under the excitement of intoxication. Such offences do not argue a very low degree of moral depravity; nor are the perpetrators, when discharged from gaol, debarred from the restoration of their ordinary station within the community, and from the resumption of their usual occupations. But females who have once fallen into habits of drunkenness or unchastity, are driven to desperation, by finding the almost insuperable difficulties, which prevent their retrieving their former position, and thus sink lower and lower in the social scale, till they become thoroughly unsexed and brutalized, and callous to the imperfect machinery of deterrent and reformatory discipline, which is brought to bear upon them.[85]

Despite its sympathetic tone towards the plight of female prisoners, this assessment also betrays a more disturbing attitude towards women in the prison system. While they admit that men might not always follow the correct moral path, they were still seen as capable of redemption and rehabilitation. The 'typical' male crimes of faction fighting and quarrelling at fairs were seen to be the result of their failure to control their natural masculine instincts, often due to the influence of alcohol. When women entered a life of crime, on the other hand, it was an unnatural and irredeemable fall. These female prisoners had strayed so far from the Victorian feminine ideal that they had become 'unsexed' and could no longer be classed as women.[86] Ultimately, the inspectors-general's primary instinct was always to defend the penal reform system. They could not accept that Irish prisons had been incapable of addressing the long-term consequences of so many women entering the penal system as a result of the Famine. The truth was, if anything, the penal system trapped these women in a cycle of repeated incarceration. Rather than admit their failure to bring about positive change in the lives of women prisoners, they attributed the problem of female recidivism to an inherent disorder within the women themselves. To support their theory, the inspectors portrayed these women as being so morally depraved and brutalised by their experiences that they were beyond the hope of any kind of moral reformation. For this class of (supposedly) irredeemable female prisoner, the function of their incarceration was no longer rehabilitation, but simply control.

Interestingly, although the female quarter was described in the 1855 report as 'inferior to that of any county gaol in Ireland',[87] work began the following year to replace the eastern section of Kilmainham Gaol with a new modern wing which would exclusively house male prisoners. Designed by architect John McCurdy, the new east wing was in many ways the apotheosis of prison reform architecture. Each cell met the size requirements laid out in the regulations, thus enabling the proper introduction of the separate system. To prevent communication by tapping on water pipes, the cells were heated by hot air vents which formed part of a sophisticated central-heating system. The cells opened out into a large hall which was lit from above by a vast glass canopy. Its curved, panoptic design allowed the prison guards to easily observe all the cells at the same time. When the first prisoners occupied the new wing in 1862 it was in many ways the culmination of a project to modernise the building which had begun in the 1840s, only to be postponed for a more than a decade by the Famine. Ironically, by the time it was complete, belief in the power of prison to bring about a moral transformation in prisoners was already beginning to wane. The influence of prison reformers had declined and prison administrators and bureaucrats were now in the ascendant. This did not mark the end of the separate system however, although it had been 'advanced as a method for securing the reformation of offenders, it imposed such rigorous severity that it was easily embraced by those whose main interest was in punishing criminals and producing deterrence'.[88]

Prison numbers were already declining when the new east wing opened and this continued for the rest of the century, largely due to the long-term demographic change brought about by the Famine. As the general population continued to fall in the post-Famine years, so too did the prison population. The high level of emigration among young men, who normally constitute the biggest part of the prison population, further accelerated the decrease in numbers. In 1878 control of all Irish convict and local prisons was centralised under the General Prisons Board (GPB). They initiated a survey the following year which revealed that Ireland had twice the number of prisons for its population in comparison with England, with a much lower rate of imprisonment.[89] The GPB were anxious to reduce costs and, finding themselves with a large number of buildings which were surplus to requirement, they began to close prisons around the country. With the number of committals continuing to fall, Kilmainham ceased to be a civil prison in February 1910 and was eventually handed over for use by the British military.

SECTION IV:
THE FAMINE IN CULTURAL HISTORY

Dublin Fictions and the Economics of Famine Memory

CHRISTOPHER CUSACK

Even though Dublin City was seriously affected by the Great Famine, the Irish capital rarely features as an important topos in the cultural memory of the crisis. This includes literary representations of the event: while many authors writing about the Famine have been Dublin denizens, the city appears only infrequently in works of Famine fiction published from the 1840s onwards. If mentioned at all, it is mostly off-stage, and associated not with the starving poor but with the upper-middle and upper classes – the place where the sons of the gentry attend Trinity College or prepare for the bar exam, where the heads of landed families go to arrange financial and legal matters, or where the wealthy consult physicians when they consider the expertise of local doctors insufficient.[1] Alternatively, the city – or even more specifically, 'Dublin Castle' – functions as a metonym for the institution of British power in Ireland. Despite the grinding poverty of a large part of the city's native population, the influx of starving migrants from other parts of the country, and the 1849 cholera epidemic, Dublin is rarely part of the Famine imaginary.[2]

The Famine has familiar literary referents that typically vary little from rendering to rendering. Conventional narratives tend to focus on Ireland's rural areas and the direct, local effects of the crop failures and rampant disease on the peasantry as well as, frequently, the inhabitants of the Big Houses.[3] When Irish market towns and cities feature, they are usually either associated with the middle and upper classes, or are mentioned as way-stations for emigrants setting out for England or North America. For the most part, texts draw on the same store of plots, character types, locations, images, and rhetorical modes, and Dublin in particular is not an intrinsic part of that repertoire.

Yet the fact that Dublin rarely has a significant presence in Famine fiction in itself provides insight into the construction of Famine memory. This essay explores the representation of Dublin in a number of Famine narratives from the twentieth and twenty-first centuries to argue that an important reason why the city rarely features in such fiction is the economic dimensions of the Famine's iconography. As the date range of these texts suggests, this iconography has remained remarkably uniform since the crisis and extensive representations of Dublin really are quite rare. In 'Attie and His Father' by the pseudonymous 'Slieve Foy' (1912), James Stephens's *Hunger* (1918), and Colum McCann's *TransAtlantic* (2013), there is an irresolvable friction between different economic systems that mostly plays out at character level as tension between the city, avatar of modernity, and the country, locus of history and tradition. Economics and subjectivity are intertwined, and authenticity is constructed by representing victimhood – an expression of what Giorgio

Agamben has termed 'bare life'[4] – as existing outside the disciplining progress of capital. Within this differential mode of remembrance, Dublin cannot signify Famine suffering.

DUBLIN, CAPITAL AND HOMO ECONOMICUS

While suffering was rife in Dublin as well as the countryside, even during the Famine commentators based in the capital seldom reflected on the way the crisis affected the city. As an editorial in the *Freeman's Journal* stated in January 1847:

> the citizens of Dublin have a more intimate knowledge of the want, and misery, and suffering of the cottier population of Skibbereen, of Mayo, and of Clare, than they have of the appalling destitution of the hundreds of human beings who are huddled together in the lodging houses of Dublin.[5]

In the public imagination, then as now, the Famine was an agricultural crisis that laid waste to the countryside. As Cormac Ó Gráda has shown, however, the erroneous belief that Dublin was largely spared the crisis is premised on the idea that the capital, unlike most of Ireland, was part of a British maritime economy and thus integrated more deeply with major British cities such as Liverpool and London than with the rest of Ireland, which supposedly mitigated the impact of the crisis.

Yet, the Famine did in fact seriously affect the capital, firstly because, as Ó Gráda argues, Dublin's commercial economy and the rural subsistence economy outside the capital were in fact more interdependent than has been claimed. Markets were indeed affected by the decline in purchasing power outside the capital, though this development did not concern the poor as much as the other classes. Secondly, as is common during famines, destitute people migrated to the city, which led to overcrowding in certain areas and boosted the incidence of epidemic disease. As in other poor law unions around the country, the workhouses in Dublin were overtaxed and the city did experience excess mortality, if not to the same extent as rural areas in the south and the west of the country.[6] All the same, Famine memory, as manifested in literary representation, by and large ignores these aspects of Dublin's history.

The contours of Famine representation have changed little since the 1840s and 1850s[7], and even novels published in the past few years, such as Paul Lynch's *Grace* (2017) or Marita Conlon-McKenna's *The Hungry Road* (2020), adhere largely to conventions first popularised by authors such as William Carleton and Anthony Trollope. Common referents make it easier to share a story, which often becomes standardised in the process. As the memory of the Famine was often instrumentalised for political ends across the spectrum, it was particularly important that the story was unambiguous, with familiar depictions of suffering and easily identifiable villains and heroes. Such homogenisation was often also a marketing choice, as the received narrative of the crisis tended to sell well.[8] Given this genealogy, it is not surprising that Dublin did not gain a prominent position in the literary tradition. Another tradition of conceptualising the Famine also comes into play when considering the representation of Dublin in Famine writing. As Peter Gray has shown, while the polemical nationalist account of the Famine has prevailed, there is also a 'political-economic "memory" of the Famine [that] was shaped by the policy debates and interpretative polemics produced during the catastrophe itself'.[9] Most Famine fiction – including, in fact, overtly nationalist narratives – engages with this discourse, regardless of ideological position.

In the years leading up to the Famine, many commentators considered Ireland to be 'completely outside the system of market value'[10], having instead an obsolete economic structure that failed to conform to the tenets of England's rapidly modernising agricultural and industrial economy. As David Lloyd writes, in traditional Irish peasant life, and particularly the *clachan* system, 'labor and what the modern subject considers to be recreation were integrated in ways inimical to capitalist modes of production'.[11] Commentators such as Charles Trevelyan and Thomas Carlyle believed that the potato supplied 'an abundance of nutrition that obviate[d] the need to enter the developing wage-labor market'.[12] As they believed that 'material conditions, social forms and moral character unfolded together',[13] the advocates of political economy considered its adoption 'a fundamental precondition for Irish social and moral advancement'.[14]

This view, advocated by people such as Richard Whately, Church of Ireland archbishop of Dublin and before that Drummond Professor of Political Economy at Oxford, produced a 'scientific blueprint for Irish regeneration'[15] that focused particularly on the rationalisation of agriculture and the consolidation of farms, which would include clearing the land and ending cottierism. This would facilitate the assimilation of the Irish rural poor into the labour force, or alternatively cause them to emigrate. Such changes would reform the (Catholic) 'Irish character', and turn the peasantry from backwards and indolent farmers who 'murder the good soil', as a land agent in William Barry's *The Wizard's Knot* (1901) claims,[16] into industrious labourers.

Whately, Trevelyan and others believed strongly that the Famine would allow the stratifying and moralising force of economic rationalisation to bring the Irish into the fold of capitalist modernity. According to their theories, the full adoption of political economy and its governing principle, free-trade liberalism, would be the only way to save Ireland – and the Irish – from the abyss. In this sense, economic and social reform – 'progress' – was fundamentally also about moulding the individual to meet the demands of capital.

Conversely, most nationalist commentators believed that the Famine was fatally aggravated by the ideological premise of the British government's response to the crisis. As Alice Stopford Green stated, 'Englishmen could not understand Irish conditions. The political economy they advocated for their own country had no relation to Ireland.'[17] Moreover, *laissez-faire* and the sanctity of property were also seen as key causes of the eventual magnitude of the crisis. '[A]ll except a few men', James Connolly caustically remarked, 'had elevated landlord property and capitalist political economy to a fetish to be worshipped, and upon the altar of that fetish Ireland perished.'[18]

Many works of Famine fiction from the crisis onwards engage explicitly with this economic discourse.[19] Indeed, novels such as Justin McCarthy's *Mononia* (1900), William Barry's *The Wizard's Knot* (1901) and Louis J. Walsh's polemical *The Next Time* (1919) contain entire chapters that are little more than political treatises presented as dialogue – the title of Walsh's chapter, as unimaginative as the rest of his novel, is 'Damn their economics!'.[20] Regardless of political affiliation, in fiction too the Famine is almost invariably conceptualised in relation to the discursive framework of political economy.

Nineteenth-century economic theory tried to construct a *homo economicus*, a model subject who was 'resolutely rational' and self-interested.[21] As John Stuart Mill argued, political economy 'is concerned with [the subject] solely as a being who desires to possess wealth, and who is capable of judging of the comparative efficacy of means for obtaining that end'.[22] This quintessential figure of capitalist modernity represented the conviction that political economy was inherently rational and objective, and the most effective – and desirable – agents within the system mirrored these qualities. In Sarah Comyn's view, '[t]he divergent forces of economic secularity and Christian morality that converge on the conceptions of *homo economicus* [...] characterise the maelstrom of Victorian modernity'.[23]

Comyn argues that nineteenth-century fiction engaged in various ways with this figure, but given the extent to which this particular brand of economic discourse has shaped the memory of the Famine, it is hardly surprising that representations of the poor are often diametrically opposed to this model of *homo economicus*. In the same way that the mid nineteenth-century Irish economy is recalcitrant to political economy, in fiction the Irish peasant exists outside the system, even if their lives are inevitably shaped by its forces. Representations of Dublin as *locus economicus*, fully structured by the forces of capital, cannot accommodate conventional depictions of the 'bare life' produced by the Famine, 'whose abundance of lack haunts the promise of abundance that capitalism holds out'.[24] In this regard, the starving subject is the 'unincorporated point of differentiation' of the political and economic construct that is Dublin in the Famine imaginary.[25] The way the capital features in the memory of the crisis thus rules out, almost by definition, the typical representations of poverty and the poor that define most Famine fiction.

'Dublin's a long way aff': 'Slieve Foy's' 'Attie and his father' (1912)

The contrast between such economic modalities and the individual's inability to transition between the two is a key plot point in the short story 'Attie and his father: A tale of the Irish poor' by the pseudonymous 'Slieve Foy'.[26] Set in Co. Kerry in May 1847, the story is largely a characteristic example of sentimental Famine fiction, with its stereotypical depiction of Irish rural life, use of brogue, strong sense of Catholic morality, and central deathbed scene.[27] Although Dublin is not depicted in recognisable detail – no streets, areas, or landmarks are named – it plays a pivotal role. Its representation exemplifies the notion that there are two types of poverty, only one of which can feature naturally in the story of the Famine.

Realising he can no longer support his children and elderly mother due to the crisis, even though they have been on 'starvation allowance' for weeks (presumably outdoor relief), 'peasant farmer' John Sullivan decides to take them to the workhouse so he can travel to Dublin to find paid work. This is a last resort, as 'Dublin's a long way aff'[28] – not just geographically, but metaphorically as well, as the only way to make this plan work is to abandon his family and become a wage labourer rather than subsistence farmer.

The moment Sullivan arrives in Dublin is also the moment concrete, specific references to money are introduced: 'At length, Sullivan reached Dublin – hungry, penniless, and foot-sore.'[29] While 'penniless' still indicates that Sullivan is destitute, the use of a numismatic adjective rather than the much less differentiated epithet 'poor' used earlier in the story marks his passing from a rural into an urban setting and signals his imminent transformation into a new kind of economic subject. The positioning of 'penniless' between two words that indicate physical discomfort moreover suggests that impecuniosity – from Latin *pecunia*, 'money' – in itself, and not just its ramifications, can register as a somatic affliction, as much part of the bodily experience of poverty as physiological symptoms such as starvation.[30]

The depiction of the city is a marked contrast with the cosy domestic scene in the family's cottage at the beginning of the story and the description of the Kerry mountainside they have abandoned. Sullivan's arrival is described with blatant pathetic fallacy: 'Rain was falling in torrents as he entered the city. The timid stranger fancied that most of the poor people he met had a bold, vicious look, and this impression increased his despondency.'[31] Urban poverty seems markedly different from the more gentle and humane poverty that characterised his life as a subsistence farmer. Although he does encounter charitable people in Dublin, it becomes clear that urban poverty is unnatural, removed from the ostensible simplicity of the land. As a subsistence farmer, the precondition for food was its production; here, labour has to be converted into a wage, which must then be used to procure the means to survive. There is no longer a direct link between labour and nourishment, or the body and the land.

Sullivan's conversion as an economic subject the moment he arrives in Dublin initially suggests that salvation lies in the subject's subsumption into the wage-labour market. From this point onwards, most transactions are presented in exact pecuniary terms (though not Sullivan's wage, which is only described as 'small'). Sullivan finds lodgings for 'a shilling a week'. Yet when he leaves to find his family after a strange presentiment of disaster, it turns out that wage labour too is not the way to save his family. His wages barely cover his expenses, and he leaves Dublin with 'exactly threepence in his pocket' – one measly penny saved per week of labour (though he also had to buy new shoes).[32] All the same, he remembers his promise to his young son Attie to buy him toys. On the way to the workhouse, he purchases a whistle at 'one halfpenny' and 'a penny whip'.[33]

Once there, Sullivan finds his mother dead and his son Attie dying from scarlet fever. Here, the story becomes a standard Christian deathbed narrative: Attie is 'beautiful as an angel, his cheeks aglow, his gold curls on the pillow'.[34] Having spent his few pennies on toys for his son, Sullivan has to depend on charity even for Attie's 'small, rude coffin'.[35]

Sullivan's effort to battle poverty by venturing into Dublin has been in vain. Obviously, he cannot transform at will into *homo economicus*. Not only does he fail to make enough money to save his family, but he fully exhausts his meagre funds by buying gifts – hardly the decision of the rational, dispassionate, self-interested economic agent projected by political economy. Sullivan is no less poor than before he left his family at the workhouse. The transition from subsistence farming to wage labour, from beautiful Kerry to dreary Dublin, has been counter-productive. If they had stayed at home, they would likely have met a similar fate, but at least they would have suffered together.

Although the story does not subscribe to the moralism of political economy, it is a didactic tale all the same. While Attie's death is considered tragic for his father – and arguably for this Irish type more generally – the narrator emphasises that Attie, who now 'looked the embodiment of a holy prayer', has moved on to 'that life in which there were no poor'.[36] The story concludes with a description of Sullivan's grief: while Attie has moved on to a better place, Sullivan is left 'more dead than alive'.[37] The story's subtitle, 'A story of the poor', suggests that the Sullivans actually represent an entire class. The narrative implies that the advent of the type of economic modernity represented by Dublin has a detrimental effect on the Irish peasantry, and that the culture of the rural poor – and indeed their faith – is much more authentic, as it is unsullied by money and materialism, and instead marked by a gentle simplicity.

Representative of an Irish type that is inherently recalcitrant to modernity, Sullivan could either be *pater familias* or *homo economicus*, but not both. The moment he endeavours to integrate into the wage-labour market by travelling to Dublin, the *locus economicus* of Famine memory, he precipitates the family's doom and finds himself markedly worse off than before.[38]

'THEY ENTERED WILD COUNTRY': COLUM MCCANN'S *TRANSATLANTIC* (2013)

While 'Attie and his father' demonstrates the economic contrasts between city and country by transporting a Kerry *homo non-economicus* to Dublin, Colum McCann's well-received *TransAtlantic*, one of the most high-profile Irish historical novels of recent years, contrasts the rural and urban poor by means of a differential representation focalised through the eyes of a visitor, the formerly enslaved abolitionist Frederick Douglass. The story by 'Slieve Foy' positions the urban environment as alien and hostile, but McCann's novel, conversely, depicts the world outside the city as anachronistic and foreign. By depicting Douglass's 1845 journey from Dublin to Cork through rural Ireland just after it has suffered its first cataclysmic loss of the potato crop, the novel's Famine chapter, 'Freeman', is able to set up an opposition between different versions of poverty, highlighting the idea that reality in Dublin is defined by money, which inflects the format of urban destitution and excludes it from the Famine imaginary.

McCann's novel covers several periods in Irish and Irish diasporic history, and imagines familial through-lines connecting them all. Chronologically (though not structurally), the narrative begins with Frederick Douglass's sojourn to Ireland in 1845. Douglass stays at the home of his Irish publisher, the Quaker Richard Webb, who also accompanies him to Cork. At the Webb residence, he meets Lily, a domestic servant who later emigrates to the United States and whose descendants are key characters in the novel's other narrative strands. Technically, Lily is a Famine emigrant, though her experiences are atypical, as she consciously decides to give up a position as a domestic servant in an affluent Quaker household in Dublin to emigrate. In this sense, she does not match the typical profile of the Irish Famine migrant, who usually left not because they chose to, but because of necessity. However, while Lily remains significant throughout the novel, the representation of the Famine does not actually focus on her.

Rather, the crisis features as an emerging context for Douglass's observations about Ireland. His interior monologue often consists of exposition about Irish conditions, compared with Douglass's own experience of slavery and knowledge of conditions in the United States. The state of Dublin shocks Douglass, much as he is accustomed to dire want:

> The filth was staggering. Douglass had never seen anything quite like it, even in Boston. Piles of human waste slushed down the gutter. It sloshed its way into fetid puddles. Men lay collapsed

> by the railings of rooming houses. Women walked in rags, less than rags: as rags. Children ran barefoot. The carcass of a donkey was left bloated in the courtyard of a tenement. Dogs went forth, lean-shouldered.[39]

Unlike 'Slieve Foy', which idealises Irish poverty to a certain extent, McCann focuses on its grim material reality. His descriptions of urban squalor hark back to Henry Mayhew and Charles Dickens, though the imagery also mirrors familiar representations of the Famine, including the references to animals, which also feature in the later descriptions of Famine victims, such as a man with 'a long, loping, simian stride'.[40]

Despite poverty and its concomitant ills, however, Dublin is a bustling town. Its urchins in particular seem to conform to the stereotype of the garrulous and energetic Irish. They chase the coach, try to jump on board and engage Douglass in conversation. Though they look frightful, they behave like normal children, running around and playing:

> The youngest amongst them was no more than three years old. His chest was bony. Leaves were tangled in his filthy hair. A fresh wound underneath his eye.
> – Come and jump with us, mister!
> The rope twisted and twirled in the air, slapped in a puddle, rose again, kicked up water drops as it twirled.[41]

Once they start travelling south, Douglass and Webb encounter people suffering from the effects of the crop failure. This episode is somewhat anachronistic, as there was no excess mortality yet when Douglass travelled through the south of Ireland and McCann's depiction of famine suffering is obviously rooted in representations of later stages of the crisis, including James Mahony's famous engravings published in the *Illustrated London News* in 1847. While the physical and material descriptions are similar to those of the urban poor, rural poverty is qualitatively different. Whereas the Dublin poor are boisterous and loquacious, the rural poor are lethargic and largely voiceless:

> On the muddy paths, they glimpsed moving rags. The rags seemed more animate than the bodies within. As they passed, the families regarded them. The children appeared marooned by hunger.
> [...] In the fields, near stunted trees, men started balefully into the distance. One man's mouth was smeared with brown paste: perhaps he had been eating bark. The man watched impassively as the carriage went by [...].[42]

The people seem caught in a dissociative state, stuck outside modernity, as the behaviour of one woman they encounter suggests: 'She repeated a phrase in Irish: it sounded like a form of prayer.'[43]

Indeed, this wasteland seems literally beyond the Pale, and they only come across this suffering because they take a wrong turn and end up in 'wild country'.[44] Dublin is a filthy place and, in many ways, new to Douglass, but at least he can make sense of its denizens. Even if the poor look otherworldly, 'almost lunar'[45], they are communicative and world-wise. The famine-stricken countryside, on the other hand, is a post-apocalyptic wasteland with '[b]roken fences. Ruined castles. [...] stunted trees'.[46] Despite his own traumatic past, Douglass has no frame of reference to make sense of the type of ostensibly anachronistic suffering he encounters and when they arrive in Cork he is relieved 'to be back to privilege again'.[47] Urban poverty is marked by squalor and misery but at least it is comprehensible. The terrible enormity of famine suffering, however, transcends Douglass's ability to make sense of it – as indeed does the landscape itself, which is delineated somewhere between the sublime romanticism of Caspar David Friedrich and the bleak absurdity of Samuel Beckett.[48]

References to money are legion in the 'Freeman' episode, but precise amounts are only given for very big sums – the donations for the abolitionist movement collected through Douglass's lectures – or very small sums, not the type of expenses that a middle-class citizen would consider normal, such as the purchase of a new garment. As Webb is giving his guest a tour of Dublin, he commands Douglass not to give any money to beggars. Douglass is quick to succumb, however, which draws more beggars to the coach. Small sums are specified: a ha'penny, a 'small copper coin' (a penny); and the poor have a clear sense of the value of money, sometimes asking for precise sums: 'Give us sixpence, will ya?'.[49] Money animates the urban poor and brings them flocking, as it is their main preoccupation.

The most poignant scene in this episode also revolves around money but it is the rejection of money that is significant here. The scene capitalises on the affective power of the image of a mother and her dead child, a common trope in the iconography of famine.[50] In the 'wild country', Douglass and Webb encounter a famished woman dragging a baby along on an improvised sled. The woman is so disturbed by grief and hunger that she refuses to countenance that her baby is in fact long dead. She tries to give the infant to Webb in the hope that he will take care of it: '"For the love of God, the child's hungry", she said.'[51] Webb does not know how to deal with this confrontation with deep suffering and tries to buy his way out. He offers her 'a coin' but she does not accept it, and he increases his offer in the hope that she will take it and leave them alone:

> Webb fumbled in his small leather purse again and held out a six-penny piece. Still, the woman did not take it. The baby was clutched to her chest. The men stood rooted to the spot. A paralysis had swept over them.[52]

This is of course the paralysis with which Joyce and other twentieth-century writers, such as Beckett, had diagnosed Ireland. In their inability to deal with this scene of pre-modern horror, the men become part of the barren landscape, 'rooted to the spot': 'Douglass felt himself become the dark of the road.'[53]

The woman continues to insist that the men take her baby. Even though the body is already decomposing – not even 'bare life' anymore – she maintains that it is alive. As she will not accept the money he offers her, Webb drops the coin in front of the woman, 'his hands shaking' as he turns to leave. Before they go on, Douglass picks up 'the muddy coin' and presses it into the woman's hand: 'She did not look at it. It slipped through her fingers. Her lips moved but she did not say a thing.'[54] Douglass and Webb, too, are shocked into muteness; when they travel onwards, they do not mention the encounter. What they have experienced is an example of what David Lloyd has termed the 'indigent sublime':

> a moment that uncannily resembles the moment of identification, but that at one and the same time appears as a moment of *non*-recognition of a subject in the other and antithetically dissolves the distance on which the integrity of the observing subject depends, leading to panic and dread.[55]

One of the reasons Douglass and Webb fail to come to terms with the scene they encounter is the fact that they cannot structure it by turning it into a financial transaction. In *TransAtlantic*, as in 'Attie and his father', money is indexical. It marks the distinction between city and country, conceptualised as a tension between modernity and the pre-modern. Yet, while 'Slieve Foy's' idealised representation of traditional Irish life presents the monetary turn in the narrative as an allegory for the disintegration of the traditional Irish peasantry, in *TransAtlantic* money highlights the tragedy of famine. It draws attention to the idea that the famine-stricken peasantry inhabit a pre-modern world in which there is a fatal disconnect between the use value central to subsistence farming and the exchange value of money. It also highlights the structural inequity of the system, which creates the conditions in which famine can strike. The Dublin-based Webb, more interested in the cause of American abolitionism than in addressing domestic issues, ultimately shrugs this off as 'a law of the land, unwritten, inevitable, awful'.[56]

In *TransAtlantic*, Dublin poverty is part of a familiar and intelligible system. It is quantifiable and can be alleviated with money – or at least the cognitive dissonance of affluent citizens can. The hunger-stricken land outside of the capital, however, confounds the logic of political economy. An infusion of capital cannot instantly mitigate Famine suffering, which is, after all, sublime – not transactional, but metaphysical.

'HUNGRY PEOPLE IN DUBLIN WERE NUMEROUS': JAMES STEPHENS'S *HUNGER* (1918)

Seventy years after the *Freeman's Journal* complained about the obliviousness of Dublin's more affluent citizens to endemic poverty in their own city, the Irish Revivalist James Stephens, writing under the pseudonym James Esse, used the iconography of the Famine to depict urban poverty in contemporary Dublin. *Hunger* (1918) is an anomaly in Stephens's oeuvre, and it has been largely neglected in the scholarship. Only a few critics have remarked on its connections with the literature of the Great Famine. In her study of Stephens's oeuvre, Patricia McFate remarks that it is 'a relentless portrait of misery comparable to that presented in the nineteenth century by William Carleton's *The Black Prophet: A Tale of the Famine* [*sic*] [1847].' However, McFate stops short of reading the text as a self-conscious Famine story, even though her analysis points in this direction.[57] Joseph Lennon mentions the story as a rare example of early twentieth-century Irish fiction which deals head-on rather than 'elliptically' with the memory of the Famine,[58] and Kevin Whelan links the story with the privations of Stephens's childhood.[59] Given the imagery and language used, however, it is evident that the story writes back to the memory of the Famine.

Unlike the other examples discussed in this essay, *Hunger* is not premised on the dichotomy between Dublin city and rural Ireland. Instead, it is fully set in the capital and mediates the memory of the Great Famine to provide a framework for its representation of destitution in wartime Dublin.[60] Unlike the other two texts discussed here, the characters in *Hunger* are fully dependent on wage labour. The nameless protagonists' suffering is framed in monetary terms, and the story is full of references to precise sums of money and their provenance. In fact, money is so central to the narrative that the main character is almost divested of an individual identity. Yet while *homo economicus* yields his individuality to gain agency in a modern economic system, the characters in *Hunger* lose their identity because they have no agency whatsoever. Their life, like that of the poor in mid nineteenth-century Ireland, is fully controlled by systemic forces outside their control. The story's single reference to the countryside only highlights this powerlessness, as the protagonists' relatives too seemingly lack the ability to manage their own situation.

The story is focalised through a poor young mother of three whose husband is not a tenant farmer or landless labourer but rather a housepainter. However, like agricultural labour, his job is seasonal, and like Irish subsistence farmers relying on potatoes the family suffer a number of hungry or 'lean months' every year when work is scarce.[61] A few months' wages have to be made to cover the entire year, supplemented with whatever money the children can collect through begging. As a result, hunger is

> a condition which was normal for them all, and into which the children had been born. They could scarcely die of hunger for they were native to it: they were hunger, and there was no other hunger but them: and they only made a noise about food when they saw food.[62]

The use of repetition, parataxis, and asyndeton betray a biblical influence on Stephens's style (and prefigure McCann's descriptions of poverty), giving the story a more universal resonance while also emphasising the relentlessness of the hunger they have to endure.

The family's fortunes continue to deteriorate. First, the husband sustains an injury and is unable to work for three weeks. The year after, war breaks out, there is no more work and food prices skyrocket. Then they lose a child to 'a disease which, whatever it was at the top, was hunger at the bottom'.[63] The husband and wife decide that the former should go to Scotland to find work in the munition factories but once he leaves nothing more is heard from him. As soon as the father departs, the rest of the family become fully dependent on mendicancy. From this point onwards, their life literally becomes measured out in pennies: begging on the streets of Dublin, the mother 'got a penny here, a penny there; and bought bread; sometimes even she got a twist of tea: she could manage until the end of the week, until her man sent the money' – which, however, never arrives.[64]

Throughout the story, the characters remain nameless, but having to beg further strips the woman and her children of their humanity, as the people they approach refuse to see them as human. The children 'unearthed [pennies] from strangers as though they dug in those loath souls for coin'.[65] The mother fares little better, meeting all sorts of rejection and disapproval, and only occasionally success: 'At times someone, without glancing at her, stuck a hand in a pocket without halting in their stride. One day she got twopence, one day she got sixpence, one day she got nothing.'[66] All the mother can think of is money and the food it could buy, and like the starving people Douglass and Webb encounter in *TransAtlantic*, she becomes increasingly apathetic, stuck 'in an immobile maze of attention'.[67] Ultimately, she is forced to apply for relief, as she can no longer feed her children and herself, and they are about to be evicted.

As in 'Attie and His Father', applying for relief means surrendering the integrity of the family home. On her way to 'the house of the gentleman who could give her the ticket which would get her food to bring home to the children', the mother keeps thinking of her home and family: 'Her mind was back in the rooms looking at the children [...] telling them that in a little while she would be back and she would bring them something.'[68] But as she returns home, she finds another child dead of starvation.

The morning after, the relief officer comes to inspect her house and is 'introduced to a room swept almost as clean of furniture as a dog kennel is', with the dead infant – 'a quiet morsel of death' – still in its cot.[69] *Hunger* uses zoomorphism to accentuate the dehumanising effect of poverty, like *TransAtlantic* and numerous other representations of the Great Famine, which often show 'a marked struggle to find adequate language, sometimes bordering on animalistic terms and labouring to retain a humanizing perspective'.[70] The children are compared to 'a famished crow' and 'little dogs that yap and whine and cannot be made to stop', and the mother's distress is described as 'the dumb agony of an animal'.[71] Yet Stephens's use of such language is a strategy to emphasise the ways in which structural poverty affects subjectivity. A life barely sustained by grudgingly relinquished pennies is hardly a life at all.

While the representative of the charity pays the arrears and ensures that the mother and her only remaining child can at least stay in their home, he also finally receives an update about the husband, who 'was found dead in a laneway' in Scotland: 'He had no lodgings in the city, and at the post-mortem examination it was found that he had died of hunger and exposure.'[72] The image of a corpse by the roadside is ubiquitous in representations of the Great Famine, for instance in Patrick Sheehan's *Glenanaar* (1905): 'Here and there by the wayside a corpse stares at the passers-by, as it lies against the hedge where it had sought shelter. The pallor of its face is darkened by lines of green around the mouth, the dried juice of grass and nettles.'[73] Even in death, Stephens's character remains nameless, his identity fully eradicated by the economics of poverty. He leaves home to earn money, yet the very lack of money that necessitated this step ultimately results in his death.

These lives take place in the space between transactions, and descriptions of money function in lieu of character development. Poverty reifies the poor: they are no longer individuals, but functions defined by their positions vis-à-vis a system that is inimical to non-normative economic modalities. For Stephens, poverty is palimpsestic: although the context is different, its effects are the same in Dublin in 1918 as they were in rural Ireland in 1847. As Emily Mark-FitzGerald writes, the memory of the Famine 'holds the capacity to include variation and divergence of symbol and meaning, whilst retaining common narrative forms that grant it cultural currency across geographies and communities'.[74] Stephens uses the Famine as a readily recognisable frame of reference with a unique cultural resonance to draw attention to the plight of Dublin's poor, but the relentlessness of his story suggests that the city's position as emblem of capitalist modernity again precludes the resolution of hunger – and, by extension, of Famine memory.

CONCLUSION

In 1848–9, as many as 60,000 people were dependent on outdoor relief in Dublin.[75] In the North Dublin Union, a large proportion of those who died were lone children who had travelled to Dublin from the south and west of Ireland hoping to find relief. By any measure, Dublin had its fair share of famine suffering, and as the *Freeman's Journal* angrily suggested to its readers, they need not look outside Dublin to discover victims of the ruthless brand of progress dictated by political economy. 'Bare life' and the indigent sublime were not confined to the farther reaches of the country.

Yet Famine memory, regardless of political hue, is often premised on a metaphysical opposition between those whose lives are structured productively by hegemonic economic formations, and those whose poverty represents 'an ethos that escapes the logic of property and economic reason'[76] – *homo economicus* and his opposite. The homogenising calculus of capitalist modernity as promoted by Whately, Trevelyan and others is contingent on the exclusion of particular Irish subjectivities that cannot be assimilated. My analyses of 'Attie and his father', *TransAtlantic* and *Hunger* demonstrate that as crucibles of such modes of signification, representations of Dublin cannot converge organically with the conventions of Famine memory. The streets of Dublin may be haunted by poverty but they are no Famine roads.

'A Very Ready Sale': Exhibiting, Viewing and Selling Art in Dublin, 1845–49

KATHRYN MILLIGAN

In April 1847, the Irish novelist and travel writer Anna Maria Hall (Mrs S. C. Hall) appealed to the readers of the London-based *Art-Union Monthly Journal* to make contributions to her private fund for Famine relief.[1] Acknowledging the discrepancy between a journal 'devoted to Art and all its branches ... which creates necessities and fosters the luxury which feeds thousands', Hall entreated the reader to act on their 'sufficient confidence in me to devote small sums – too small for public subscriptions – to my almonry, knowing that I could bestow them where they would be properly applied.'[2] Over the next three months, Hall contributed further articles that detailed the Famine conditions in Ireland, detailing the efforts made to provide relief through private charities and cottage industries. These articles placed the issue of the Famine in the hands of readers across Ireland and Britain, alongside auction, art union and exhibition reports, engravings of fine art and sculpture, and general news relating to cultural matters. Aimed at subscribers to various art unions active in the period, the *Art-Union Monthly Juornal* regularly included Ireland in its round-up of exhibitions and other notable artistic events, a feature which continued through the period of the Famine. The direct plea for philanthropic assistance from Hall is unusual and diverges from her other contributions to the journal which tended to discuss on notable artistic or architectural sites.

Focusing on Dublin, the institutional centre of Ireland's artistic life, this chapter will examine the exhibition of fine art in the city during the period of the Famine, outlining the main venues where the public could access fine art and the types of works that were displayed there. This, of course, is set against a background of economic decline, an urban population in flux, and ongoing political tensions over the management of the crisis. As will be seen however, aside from straightened economic circumstances, the ongoing Famine appears to have little impact on Dublin's exhibition culture. This approach draws on Catherine Roach's recent exploration of exhibitions in nineteenth-century London, which outlines how the range of exhibitions occurring in an urban environment can be considered as an 'ecosystem', allowing for a 'consideration of both the broader conditions of display and the actions of individual figures who navigated these conditions.'[3] As Roach notes, in 1820s London, several distinctive venues for the display of visual art had emerged, including formal institutions for artists, such as the Royal Academy, the British Institution, and the Society of Painters in Watercolours; single artist exhibitions in rented spaces; and domestic galleries in large town houses, usually showing aristocratic collections.

Throughout the first half of the nineteenth century, the exhibition 'ecosystem' of 1840s Dublin mirrored, overlapped, and intersected with that of London, with the latter category being a notable exception, with only a small number of private homes offering notable art collections.[4] However, when applied to a city such as Dublin, Roach's ecosystem model must also take into account the wider imperial context, and network of influence and exchange that characterised its relationship to London and Britain, in both institutional and commercial settings.

By 1845, the Dublin's exhibition ecosystem was characterised by three types of fine art display. The institutional centre of this was the Royal Hibernian Academy (RHA) which, from its foundation in 1823, provided a sort of domestic equivalent to its London counterpart. It was established with the 'principal object … being to afford the best opportunities for cultivating the fine arts in Ireland', including a school 'for the instruction of such persons in those arts as shall evince such a position of talent as may afford a fair prospect of their future success', and an annual exhibition as 'a means of diffusing among the public a taste for the fine arts'.[5] John Turpin has recently outlined the (usually short-lived) societies and exhibition groups prior to the foundation of the RHA: without repeating this in detail here, it is worth noting in relation to Roach's concept of the ecosystem that in 1814 the Royal Irish Institution (RII) began its own exhibiting activities, mirroring the British Institution. Furthermore, when the RHA received the warrant for its charter from George IV, it lacked the funds to officially register it: in a clear act of solidarity, the RII stepped in and provided the money, replicating what Roach has termed a 'mutually sustaining environment'.[6] The nature of the Academy's inception and funding aligned it with the politics of the British crown and parliament, as well as the British administration in Dublin, a fact which (as will be seen) hampered its efforts to encourage a strictly 'national' school.

In addition to these formal institutions for supporting art and artists, the Dublin art world also contained numerous commercial spaces for the viewing and purchasing of art, art supplies, and other luxury paper goods: these were known as 'repositories' in contemporary parlance and several Dublin firms specialised in one-painting exhibitions to supplement their sales of prints, stationary, collectibles, and books. Two of these businesses in the 1840s were run by their eponymous owners, Thomas Cranfield and Adolphus Lesage. The latter's premises were located at 40 Lower Sackville Street, close to the RHA on Abbey Street Lower, while across the city, Cranfield operated his services from 23 Westmoreland Street, before moving to 115 Grafton Street in 1849. A final component in this system is a small number of exhibition venues which were available to hire for temporary exhibitions, such as the rooms of the RII on College Street; those of the Royal Dublin Society (RDS) in Leinster House, Kildare Street; and the Rotunda Assembly Rooms at the junction of Sackville Street and Parnell Square. These venues were also often used to display panoramas: painted, and often moving screens, showing historical and contemporary events; hired by independent operators who toured Britain and Ireland with their works. While lying beyond the remit of this article, the display of panoramas in nineteenth-century Dublin formed an important aspect of the city's visual and social culture, and often attracted a wider audience than displays of fine art.[7] With the opening of the RHA, RII and RDS premises in the 1820s, three new spaces for exhibition and display contributed to a growing culture of middle-class sociability and entertainment in the city.

NATIONAL TENSION: THE ROYAL HIBERNIAN ACADEMY AND THE ROYAL IRISH ART UNION

As outlined above, at its foundation the RHA sought to provide a means to encourage the fine arts in Ireland through education and exhibitions, as well as through providing professional recognition through full and associate membership. Its early years were characterised by financial and other difficulties: the first annual exhibition took place in 1826 at the new Academy House, designed and gifted by the Academy's first president, Francis Johnston. Almost from the inception of its annual exhibition, the RHA invited non-resident, usually British artists, to contribute canvases to the display; for example, in 1834 Martin Cregan wrote to John Constable, asking if he might send works across for the exhibition.[8] This, as Philip McEvansoneya notes, was 'in order to make up the numbers, to increase the interest in the exhibitions and, unmistakably, to elevate the general standard of what was on display.'[9] Despite this intervention, through the 1830s the annual exhibition was disparaged in the Irish press as mediocre, and in many ways, reflecting poorly on the state of the visual arts in Ireland. Exhibitors and sales dwindled, and by the 1840s, a stimulus for the institution was badly needed.

In 1839, this inducement came in the form of the Royal Irish Art Union (RIAU) promoted and managed by Stewart Blacker (1813–81), with a committee of noblemen, including the marquess of Ormond and the earl of Charlemont. The chief purpose of the RIAU was to stimulate the production of fine art by artists in Ireland and contribute to a national school of art through the purchase of works directly from contemporary exhibitions. This was funded through the sale of tickets to subscribers: artworks were selected for purchase by the Union's committee and then a lottery was held to disburse the works to ticket holders. The decision to have a selection committee was unusual: as Turpin notes, similar organisations in England offered their subscribers a voucher with which they could select their own works, a practice more in keeping with 'the Victorian spirit of freedom and choice', indicating that a rather patrician attitude towards the arts still reigned in Ireland.[10] Further funds were raised for the RIAU though the commissioning and sale of engravings and through an annual exhibition of the selected works. With each of these activities, the Union hoped to encourage artists in Ireland to produce work, as well as encourage Irish people to become patrons.

Through the early years of the 1840s, the RIAU amassed several thousand subscribers and purchased works from the RHA totalling £6,649 between 1840 and 1843.[11] In 1843, the *Illustrated London News* produced an engraving of the prize-giving in the rooms of the Royal Dublin Society: it shows the selected paintings stacked high against the back wall, and a crowd of eager subscribers waiting to see if their number will be called, capturing a sense of busy activity and anticipation (Figure 11.1). The scene was reproduced in the annual report of the RIAU, along with extracts from newspapers, one of which stated that during the exhibition, 'a vast concourse of all classes attended during the period it remained open (a fortnight), and yet not a single instance of irregularity or injury occurred.'[12] The promotion of art beyond the aristocracy and gentry was a central tenet of the art-union movement, but this quote shows some of the scepticism still attached to this idea in 1840s Ireland. The economic benefit of the RIAU (to both the RHA and its artists) was short-lived, however: in 1844 the organisation was declared illegal, and only officially reinstated in 1846 under new regulation by the Board of Trade.[13] The RIAU did continue to operate from that date, albeit to a lesser extent, and through the Famine period commissioned and sold engravings by Irish artists such as Michael Angelo Hayes, David Wilkie, Frederick Goodall, and Joseph Patrick Haverty.[14] These were largely idealised views of Irish rural life, which promoted the idea of developing and nurturing a national school of distinctively Irish art, but did not evidence any engagement with contemporary rural distress or Famine conditions.[15]

However, the most crucial debate within the RHA and the RIAU in this period concerned the extent to which the aspiration of a 'national' school of Irish art was pursued, particularly due to their encouragement and purchase of works by non-resident British artists. In addition to the works directly sought by the RHA from their British peers, the early success of the RIAU had encouraged additional non-resident artists to send works to the annual exhibition, and these were among those selected by the union's committee for the ballot. In 1842, a group of artists (which included RHA members) had founded another group, the Society of Irish Artists, who stated that they would only exhibit and support work by Irish artists. Further discontent was expressed, as Turpin outlines, by RHA exhibitors who complained that English painters were hung in more prominent positions on the Academy's walls, an accusation that is both 'impossible to assess without more evidence but is reasonable to assume'.[16] As the crisis of the Famine approached in the mid 1840s, the nationalist press fanned the flames of this dissatisfaction, for example, in the pages of the *Freeman's Journal* or *The Nation*.[17] With a stated aim to support and encourage 'native' talent, the RHA struggled through the 1840s to navigate the competing challenges of financial hardship, nationalist politics, and difficulties of attracting an engaged audience, which had been an issue since its foundation. By 1847, the Academy was weakened by 'the shrinkage of cross-channel exhibits, and to the non-appearance of regular Irish contributors', which Turpin argues was undoubtedly influenced by the conditions of the Famine and ongoing economic stress, although this is difficult to assess in any great detail.[18] This is a necessarily brief account of some of the key developments at the heart of the artistic establishment in Ireland but provides an important context for which other modes and locations of display need to be considered. If a key constituent part of the ecosystem of exhibition and display network struggled, how did the other constituent parts react, share, or avoid the same issues?

THE SINGLE-PAINTING EXHIBITION: CRANFIELD AND LESAGE

In August 1849, Queen Victoria, Prince Albert and their children paid a visit to Ireland, arriving in Cork before travelling to Dublin and Belfast. The response to the visit was mixed to say the least: as Margarita Cappock has noted, the organisers were keen to ensure that the visitors were 'spared having to witness the unpalatable horrors', yet the ongoing economic and social devastation could not be ignored.[19] In Dublin, the visit was celebrated with lavish street decorations, including illuminations and other light shows, funded by general subscription. This decision, made by Dublin Corporation, was strongly opposed from some quarters, with one commentator declaring in the *Freeman's Journal* that 'Dublin throws herself not upon her knees to Majesty, but on her face. She spreads, not her cloak, on the floor for her Majesty to walk over, but gives *herself* [*sic*] to be the gangway. Proud be the step of Majesty as she tramples on her … so will she best fulfil the wishes of her liege subjects of Dublin.'[20] For the visit of the royal family, the two repositories mentioned at the outset of this chapter – Cranfield and Lesage – also found the means to capitalise on the festivities, chiefly by displaying prints and paintings of royal portraits and subjects.

Prior to the arrival of the Queen and her family in the city, the *Dublin Evening Post* reported that in 'every emporium and print shop for the sale of art in Dublin, portraits of the Queen and Prince Albert are exhibited ... and we are assured they command a very ready sale'.[21] Going a step further than souvenir portraits, the *Post* also noted that 'Alderman Moon, of the City of London, in compliance with the request of Mr Thomas Cranfield, the eminent publisher and print seller of this city, has lent Winterhalter's celebrated painting of the Royal family in domestic life, which he will exhibit in his spacious gallery in Grafton-street, during the Queen's visit'.[22] Here, 'Alderman Moon' refers to Sir Francis Graham Moon (1797–1871), a printseller and stationer in London. Franz Xaver Winterhalter's (1805-73) *The Royal Family in 1846* (oil on canvas, 1846, Royal Collections Trust) had previously been exhibited in St James's Palace, London (Figure 11.2). Moon, seizing a commercial opportunity, purchased the copyright of the painting from the artist and was entrusted to publish an engraving of the picture. This was carried out by Samuel Cousins (1801–87) and advertised for sale in 1849 (Figure 11.3). Likewise, Lesage advertised that his store would display Edwin Landseer's 'Windsor in the Present Times' being an 'admirable painting, containing portraits of her Majesty, Prince Albert, and the young Princesses &c., ... This painting is considered one of the best works of this eminent artist'.[23]

It remains unclear whether the works exhibited in the rooms of Cranfield and Lesage were the original works that are now part of the Royal Collection, autograph replicas, or indeed copies by another artist in oil, watercolour, or engraving. The practice of creating and exhibiting autograph replicas or variations by the original artist, or copies by another hand, was well-established, as was the creation and sale of prints (usually engravings) of well-received works.[24] In the case of the Winterhalter portrait, it seems likely that the painting exhibited was a copy by another artist, as it was not the first time that Cranfield had exhibited this portrait of the young royal family. In March 1848, *The Pilot* reported that Cranfield had exhibited on his premises a 'beautiful copy by Cunningham of this world-famed Picture'.[25] A year previous, the *Freeman's Journal* and several other English papers reported that 'Mr H. F. Cunningham had the honour of submitting to the Queen and Prince Albert his water-colour drawing, taken by command of her Majesty from Winterhalter's picture of the royal family.'[26] It is therefore more probable that Cunningham's water-colour, and not the original oil, is what Dublin viewers encountered in Cranfield's gallery. This copy toured through several cities through 1848 and 1849, including York, Leeds, Birmingham, Glasgow, and Aberdeen. Several newspaper accounts stated that Cunningham's copy was on the same scale as the engraving to be produced by Cousins for Moon. Although the whereabouts of Cunningham's copy is now unknown, it could be speculated that the version by an anonymous artist now in the Royal Collections Trust (watercolour and body colour on paper, after 1846, RC913334): the measurements are also in line with Cousin's engraving, finally published in 1850. Following the exhibition of the painting in Dublin in 1849, it travelled across the country, and the public could also view the royal family portrait in Cork, at Fletcher's on Patrick Street and at Hodgson's on the High Street, Belfast: unfortunately, no further details of the scale or medium of the exhibited work are given in the press reports.

Whether through copies or engravings, the fact remains that for the duration of this royal visit the citizens of Dublin could immerse themselves in the visual world of the British monarchy, and if their pocket extended to it, could then purchase a souvenir print of commemorative collection to furnish their own home with the memories of the visit.[27] These special displays of single notable artworks did not first emerge in 1840s: the American painter John Singleton-Copley had introduced the format to London in 1781, building on the success of the one-artist show as pioneered by Nathaniel Hone in 1775.[28] From at least the 1820s single paintings had been exhibited in Dublin, ranging from Théodore Géricault's imposing *Raft of the Medusa* (1819, oil on canvas, Louvre, Paris) in 1821 to Thomas Jones Barker's *The Secret of England's Greatness* (*c.* 1862–3, oil on canvas, National Portrait Gallery, London) in 1864), which was also exhibited in Belfast.[29] As the selection of royal paintings in 1849 suggests, the displays at the Cranfield and Lesage galleries tended towards the imperial rather than the national, a trend present throughout their one- or two-painting exhibitions during the 1840s. It also suggests how Dublin was connected to a network of cities which hosted these single painting displays, spanning England, Scotland, and Ireland, and on some occasions, Wales. The cost associated with visiting these exhibitions underscored that they were spaces of middle- and upper-class sociability, a fashionable pastime for the city's cultural elite: for example, in August 1849, Lesage offered free entry to subscribers or one shilling for non-subscribers, and Cranfield advertised that admission was 'by ticket on application'.[30] That scenes of the royal family's domestic life by British artists appeared with no apparent protest in August 1849 points to the perceived differences between two of the city's spaces of display: in the same period the RHA, as a national academy, was chastised for displaying the works of non-native artists, while, elsewhere, imported and imperial works became part of the city's spectacle and celebration. This commercial and fashionable interest is also reflected elsewhere in the artistic works that both Lesage and Cranfield selected for display.

Both Lesage and Cranfield exhibited works by Edwin Henry Landseer (1803–73) during the 1840s, bringing several of the artist's depictions of domestic and wild animals to their premises as part of an effort to produce and sell engravings. The foremost animal painter of his day, Landseer had achieved considerable social and financial success through his paintings of sporting, highland, and domestic animal subjects. Lesage was the forerunner in bringing the artist's work to Dublin: in October 1845, his horse painting *Shoeing* (oil on canvas, exhibited 1844, Tate) as displayed in Sackville Street for about a week, advertised as 'the original painting that created such a sensation at the exhibition of the Royal Academy last year' (Figure 11.4).[31] Admission to see the painting was by ticket, for which patrons had to apply directly to Lesage; however the *Dublin Evening Mail* assured their readers that he was 'very liberal in the distribution'.[32] After its sojourn in Dublin, *Shoeing* travelled to the repository of J. Ling in Norwich, where an advertisement stated that 'The picture when exhibited in Dublin, had at least 30,000 people to see it'.[33] While this figure is undoubtedly inflated, the painting was likely popular, as it was the first time that an original painting by the artist was exhibited in Dublin. Its success was swiftly followed by two further displays in 1846, when Lesage presented 'A Companion to Shoeing', and Cranfield, *Horses Drinking in the Courtyard of an Ancient Mansion.* The latter of these, most likely the painting now in the collection of the Lake District National Trust under the title of *Horses Taken in to Bait* (oil on canvas, 1840, National Trust) as exhibited alongside a finished proof of the engraving which had taken the engraver, J. H. Watt, six years to complete.[34] A connection to London, and the Royal Academy, was an important marketing tool for businesses like Cranfield and Lesage, as was the patronage of the vice-regal court. Visits by the Lord Lieutenant, or his family, were announced in the press, along with others from the nobility: for example, when Landseer's dog painting *Alexander and Diogenes* (1848, oil on canvas, Tate, London) was exhibited in December 1848, a roll call including the Duke of Leinster, Lord and Lady Dufferin, and others was published in several of the daily papers.

While paintings by British (and occasionally Irish) artists made up most of the single-painting exhibitions at these repositories, Lesage made efforts to bring French artworks to the Irish capital. While this reached its zenith in the two decades after the Famine, in the 1840s the seemingly most ambitious of these loans was an exhibition of Horace Vernet's (1789–1863) spectacular *Taking of the Smahla of Abd-el-Kader* (oil on canvas, 1844, Musée National du Château, Versailles) in September 1848. Measuring 489x2139cm, this large painting is panoramic in scale and conception, having been commissioned by King Louis-Philippe for the Museum of French History at the Palace of Versailles. The *Smahla* depicts the battle of the 16 May 1843, when the French army raided the camp of the Algerian resistance leader Emir Adbelkader al-Jazairi (1808–83) while he was absent on an expedition.[35] Successful in their mission, the force captured around 3,000 people and many of Abd-el-Kader's possessions, including his war chest and library. An article published to coincide with the exhibition of Vernet's battle scene in Dublin stated that 'On the occasion of Mr. Le Sage's [*sic*] visit to Paris, from which city he has just returned, he was struck by the magnificence and splendour of one of Horace Vernet's finest battle pieces' and that as few people in Ireland 'had the pleasure of visiting the Louvre Gallery or the princely collection of paintings at Versailles', they 'would feel deeply and heartily gratified at hearing that one of the noblest works of an artist ... is now on view in our city.'[36] The painting was described at length in the newspapers, and Lesage's enterprise in bringing it to Ireland richly applauded. Several of the reports focused on Vernet's depiction of the women of the camp, described as 'fair odalisques', whose clothing has been thrown 'into such breeching abandonment'.[37] Even to those readers who could not visit the painting in Dublin, the *Freeman's Journal*'s description of 'the old, the young, the swarthy negro, and the beautiful female slave ... endeavouring to fly in a confused mass before the terrific approach of the cavalry which comes on them like an avalanche', would evoke a mental picture of the exotic spectacle (Figure 11.5).[38] The admission fee to see the painting was one shilling and was available to the Dublin public from 'nine until dusk'.[39]

Its presence in Dublin seemed to be a coup for Lesage: although its exhibition in the Louvre in 1845 was widely publicised in the English press, the painting does not seem to have been exhibited there, making its display at Lesage's unique to this island. However, a note of caution should be sounded. In the first instance, the months preceding the painting's exhibition in Dublin marked an intense period of change in France in general, and Paris in particular, with the fall of the July Monarchy, the subsequent calling of the Second Republic, and the June Days revolution. Considering these events, could Lesage have negotiated and coordinated a loan of this large painting at this time? Furthermore, the Dublin press described the canvas exhibited at the Dublin repository as measuring '22 feet long by 4 feet 9 inches long', equating roughly to 670x149.5cm. While still large in scale, this measurement does not tally with that of the original created for Versailles, suggesting instead that the version shown in Dublin may have been either a smaller autograph replica or variation by Vernet or perhaps a copy by another artist. Although a copy with these measurements has not been traced to date, the practice of making or commissioning copies of artworks was not unusual, as seen with the Winterhalter copy by Cunningham. In this instance, for example, a copy of the *Smahla* was produced in 1865 by Alfred Decaen (1820–1902), commissioned by Richard Seymour-Conway, fourth marquess of Hertford, for his private collection, measuring 140x450cm – a fraction of Vernet's original (Figure 11.6).[40] The practice of circulating and exhibiting autograph replicas or copies may seem strange to a twenty-first century reader, but was a common feature of nineteenth-century visual culture. It is likely that audiences were aware that the artwork they were viewing was potentially by a different hand, or not the first iteration of a composition: however, it was the image, and the opportunity to see the design of an artist or the representation of a particular person, family, or event, that was prized.

Like Vernet's battle scene, military themed paintings were a consistent feature of the works shown in commercial spaces. In the summer of 1849 Lesage included Hippolyte Paul Delaroche's (1797–1856) study for the head of Napoleon (from the larger *Napoleon Contemplating His Abdication at Fontainebleau*, 1840) borrowed from the collection of the Marquis of Titchfield, in his line-up.[41] This was surely a timely choice: in 1848 Queen Victoria had purchased a small-scale version of Delaroche's painting (other larger autograph versions are in the Leipzig Museum der Bildenden Künst and the Musée de l'Armée, Paris) as a gift for Prince Albert, and thus Lesage forged a further connection to the royal visitors. The printseller closed out the year with a further military painting: Francis Grant's depiction of *Viscount Hardinge, Governor-General of India accompanied by his two sons and Colonel Wood on the Battle Field of Ferozeshah* (oil on canvas, *c.* 1849, private collection) recording a scene from the First Anglo-Sikh War, 1845–6.[42] The response of the press to the exhibition of this painting was limited, however an article reproduced in both the *Freeman's Journal* and the *Dublin Weekly Register* drew attention to its merits as one of Hardinge's 'most glorious Indian victories'. 'We have seen few pictures,' the author continued, 'which combine the value of portraiture with general historic effect more successfully than this fine work of Mr. Grant's.'[43] It was not the first time that a scene from this imperial war had been shown in Dublin: in November 1846, the noted panoramist, Marshall, had brought his entertainment 'illustrative of the recent campaigns … and triumphant defeat of the Sikh Army 'and measuring 20,000 square feet to a specially refitted building on Abbey Street.[44] With six showings a day, and tickets ranging from sixpence to two shillings, the panorama offered a popular and more affordable opportunity for Dubliners to engage with the spectacle of empire.

THE STAND-ALONE EXHIBITION: RELIGIOUS SPECTACLE AND OLD MASTERS

Turning to the third category of fine art exhibition seen in nineteenth-century Dublin, the final section of this chapter will consider the stand-alone, temporary exhibition. Although they occurred less frequently, this type of display was staged in a hired space – more akin to the presentation of a panorama – with similar ticketing structures to those used in the fine art repositories. Notable among these exhibitions is the display of two large-scale religious paintings which were exhibited twice in this decade, appearing for the first time from October 1839 to March 1840, and then again in January to May 1846. Claude-Marie Dubufe (1790–1864) had been a student of the noted history painter Jacques-Louis David and began exhibiting works at the Paris Salon in 1810. The two canvases exhibited in Dublin, *Adam and Eve* and *Paradise Lost* (1827, oil on canvas, Musée d'Arts de Nantes), made their debut at the Salon in 1827 and were also shown at the Royal Academy, London in 1829. Over the course of the 1830s the pendant works toured several American cities, where some concerns were raised over the propriety of the large, nude figures. There did not seem to have been any such qualms in Dublin: in January 1840 the *Freeman's Journal* reported that 'few exhibitions have ever been opened in Dublin which afford more attraction for a repetition of visits'.[45] In 1839–40, admission to see the paintings was priced at one shilling for a single admittance, or two shillings and sixpence for a season ticket; six years later, it was one shilling, with children and schools half price. At the close of the exhibition, in both 1840 and 1846, James Creighton (the owner of the paintings and organiser of the tour) invited children from the city's Sunday and charity schools to attend the exhibition gratis, so long as they were accompanied by their teacher.[46] By 1846, the newspaper could claim that they had been exhibited 'to the universal admiration of one million two hundred thousand persons'.[47] As with the description of Vernet's 'odalisques', written reports on the two paintings frequently focused on the figure of Eve, the accuracy of the depiction of skin and flesh; or the representation of innocence and guilt, suggesting that there was a more prurient appeal to viewing the works.[48]

Whether animal, military, or religious, the examples of fine art display discussed so far offer little sense of how the ongoing social and economic distress caused by the famine impacted or involved itself with the activity of viewing, exhibiting and selling art in 1840s Dublin, except by its absence. There is, however, one notable exception to this situation. In 1847, the RIAU (led by Blacker) organised an exhibition of old master paintings which would serve the dual purpose of reinvigorating the practice of showing old masters in the city and raising money for famine relief, as the proceeds of the ticket sales would be donated 'for relief of the present very urgent distress'.[49] In the RIUA's report for 1846, précised in the *Art-Union Monthly* in March 1847, noted that the union had 'long anticipated being able to revive the Exhibitions of the 'Old Masters' which gave in former years so much satisfaction to the people, and spread so much taste and knowledge on the subject of Art'. Furthermore, the report noted, it 'will be doubly gratifying to those who give themselves the great mental treat of viewing a really good collection of Art to feel assured and to know that every farthing of what they pay to enjoy it goes to relieve and support the famishing and the destitute'.[50] In mid-January, Blacker advertised the exhibition in the national papers, calling on collectors to consider loaning their art treasures: a provisional committee was formed, and within a day of the exhibition being announced, he could report 'several letters from gentlemen anxious to co-operate'. Further to this, the committee also drafted a 'list of the principal noblemen and gentlemen in Ireland possessed of valuable and desirable works of art and directed a form of application requesting their kind assistance and co-operation'.[51]

The speed with which Blacker and the committee were able to assemble the exhibition is notable: having been announced in mid-January, the exhibition opened at the RII for a private view on 4 March, and to subscribers on the following day. In fact, Blacker advertised on following day that the exhibition was open to 'Subscribers of Family Tickets (Price, One Pound each), admitting the Holders and their immediate Families for Three

Days, reserved for the Court Circle, and for the whole season afterwards'.[52] After this time, individual tickets could be purchased for one shilling, a season ticket for half-a-crown, or further family tickets for one pound.[53] Shortly after the opening, provision was made for art students to have access to the exhibition before the general public was admitted, enabling them to 'have access in the mornings to study from such works as the proprietors have given permission to be studied from'. The sessions of this were overseen by a 'leading artist, and a member of the committee ... one to give every suggestion as to art that might be required, and the other to see that every facility and accommodation are afforded'.[54] Furthermore, the committee also produced an extensive catalogue which in addition to listing the works on display, also included short introductions to the artists, and gestured towards their significance in an art historical narrative – offering a beginner's guide to new visitors. The arrangements made for access to the exhibition, whether for the more exclusive 'court circle' or the city's art students, spoke to the careful balancing of the committee's interest. On the one hand, the financial success (meaning the amount raised for relief) depended on patronage from the city's wealthiest inhabitants, and the opportunity for 'private' or 'exclusive' access was surely enticing for those who wished to see and be seen. Additionally, by encouraging students to come and copy from the works exhibited and through the descriptive catalogue, the RIAU continued in its mission to stimulate and encourage the fine arts.

A comprehensive report of the exhibition was carried in the May issue of the *Art-Union Monthly Journal*. The author of the report found much to praise in the exhibition, which was described as 'one of the most remarkable and gratifying exhibitions ever opened in Ireland'.[55] Paintings came, for example, from the Viceregal Lodge in the Phoenix Park, the Mansion House, and Trinity College collections. Further works from private collections came from the Marquis of Drogheda, the Earls of Charlemont, Milltown and Arran, Viscounts Harberton and Gort, and Lord Talbot de Malahide. Legal and clerical families were also among the donors, for example, the Honourable and Revered Dean Maud and the Right Honourable Judge Ball, amongst others. Changes in ownership and attribution for many of the 228 works included in the exhibition make it difficult for their whereabouts to be traced now, although there are some notable exceptions. For example, a Rembrandt loaned by the Earl of Charlemont, *Judas Returning the Thirty Pieces of Silver* (oil on panel, 1629) is now in the collection of Mulgrave Castle, Yorkshire, having passed through the hands of Lord Iveagh and Lord Moyne in the interim.[56] Two works were loaned from the collection of the Viceregal Lodge by the then Lord Lieutenant, the Earl of Bessborough: Ferdinand Bol's *David's Dying Charge to Solomon* (oil on canvas, 1643, National Gallery of Ireland) (Figure 11.7) and a work listed as being by Melchior de Hondecoeter and Jan Weenix, titled *The Entry into the Ark*. The former of these was deposited with the RII for the nascent national collection in 1854 by the Earl of St Germans with its attribution unchanged; the latter, which shares this later provenance, is Pieter Boel's, *Noah's Ark* (oil on canvas, *c.*1650–74, National Gallery of Ireland). Many, if not all, of the works lent by the Earl of Milltown are now in the National Gallery of Ireland's collection, having been part of the 1902 Milltown Gift, one of the most notable donations in the institution's history. This includes, for example, Nicolas Poussin's *Holy Family* (oil on canvas, 1649) and Peter Paul Rubens, *The Calydonian Boar Hunt* (oil on panel, after 1640), listed in the 1847 catalogue as 'Meleager and Atlanta'. A full examination of the contents of this exhibition lies beyond the scope of this chapter, however an extended study of the collections and collectors who contributed (particularly those from outside of the titled donors), and how the attributions of the paintings have altered over time, could be revealing of trends in middle- and upper-middle class collecting in nineteenth-century Ireland. The RIAU was successful in its aim to raise money for famine relief, with over £500 donated to the General Relief Fund at its close.[57]

CONCLUSION: EXHIBITING AND VIEWING ART IN HARD TIMES

Returning to Roach's idea of the exhibition ecosystem, and the idea that this enables a 'consideration of both the broader conditions of display and the actions of individual figures who navigated these conditions', it can be seen from this brief study of fine art displays in 1840s Dublin that this approach can be enlightening, while also leaving some frustrating challenges. Examining the fine art displays proffered by the RHA and commercial exhibition venues – whether printsellers or hired spaces – the tension between national (or nationalist) ambition and the appeal of 'imported' artworks becomes more starkly apparent. The still-fledging RHA was caught between encouraging and stimulating Irish art training and production; heading calls for more nationalist subject matter to be displayed on the walls of Academy house and attracting the city's cultural elite to patronise the institution through admission tickets and picture sales. The support for the art union suggests that this was a preferred way for people to support the fine arts, perhaps because of the element of chance, but this system was also entangled in the cultural politics of 'native' versus 'British' art. As this conversation, broadly surmised as nationalist versus unionist, continued through the 1840s, the city's commercial venues (exemplified here by Cranfield and Lesage) capitalised on the expanding network of one-painting exhibitions that criss-crossed the cities of Britain, bringing together the worlds of fine art and spectacle for those who could afford to pay for it. It is worth considering, perhaps, that the encouragement of a 'national' school of art was something separate to a 'nationalist' one: the former encompassing a broad range of art production both from Ireland and further afield, the latter a narrower definition of artistic subjects and traits. The third type of display, exhibitions in hired venues such as Creighton's double-visit with the Dubufe paintings, which could also be marketed as a type of spectacle – whether religious or otherwise – offering a form of respectable entertainment, frilled with some charitable endeavour. The triple forces of entertainment, education, and charity merged with the fine arts in the RIAU's 'Works of the Ancient Masters' exhibition, offering a clearer (if more singular) example of how the Dublin artworld engaged with the ongoing Famine. This engagement was, however, enacted through the medium and social performance of philanthropy and charitable giving, with the visible spectre of hunger and poverty removed to an abstract space firmly outside of the exhibition rooms.

Thus, an examination of fine art exhibitions in Dublin during the period of the Famine suggests that the conditions of display were driven by commercial need, presumably in turn facilitated by public support, with an ongoing and unresolved discussion about the development of a national school of 'Irish' painting. Individual figures do emerge, for example, Thomas Cranfield, Adolphus Lesage, and Stewart Blacker. Further investigations of these figures, however, is frustrated by a lack of surviving archival material: we know little of their backgrounds, their art world connections, or the annual records of their sales or profits. The most notable absence is the voice of those people who attended these exhibitions, who purchased season or single-admission tickets, or placed their name on a subscriber's list. While we can list and look at the works that could be viewed in shops and rooms across the city, little can be gleaned about the first-hand experience of walking into a warm, gaslit room to see Dubufe's imposing nude figures, or how an aspiring artist responded to the work of Bol or Rubens, removed from the walls of country house and relocated to College Street. From what evidence does remain for this crucial period in Ireland's history, when one shilling could transport a well-to-do Dubliner to the battlefields of Algeria or India, the devastated countryside of Ireland could easily be put out of sight, and the impact of the Famine on their own city, out of mind.

Epilogue: Famine Memory and the City

EMILY MARK-FITZGERALD

The oldest extant photographs of Dublin coincide with the Famine, and depict around twenty sites in the city, with an additional six taken in wider county Dublin and Wicklow (Figures 12.1-4). Given that no direct photographs of the Famine have yet been identified, this is an extraordinary set of images, dating from the mid-1840s, less than a decade after photography itself had been invented in 1839.

Not much is known about them: they are very early calotypes – delicate paper negatives and their corresponding salted paper prints[1] – most of which found their way to William Fox Talbot (inventor of the calotype) and his photographic studio in Lacock Abbey, England. They have been variably attributed to Talbot himself, his associate Revd Calvert Richard Jones, William Holland Furlong, or unidentified Irish photographers who may have sent their negatives to Fox Talbot for printing.[2] Negatives and prints from this period are difficult to date precisely, but the presence of watermarks from 1842 and 1846 on several prints suggests a reliable dating of the mid 1840s. As paper negatives directly contact-printed onto textured paper, calotypes have a diffuse and blurred quality, often mottled in tone and with strong contrasts of light and dark, and the Dublin images share these characteristics.

The long exposure times required of the calotype process precluded the capture of motion or dynamic scenes. As is typical for calotypes of the period, the photographs of the city are nearly exclusively of its architecture. The camera's lens is primed on Dublin's proudest built achievements: St Mary's Pro-Cathedral (Figure 12.1); Amiens St Railway Station; Christ Church Cathedral; the Bank of Ireland. In abundance are the symbols of colonial rule and power: Dublin Castle; the statue of William III on College Green; and the Four Courts (Figure 12.2). For the most part, the Dublin calotypes are curiously devoid of life and people: one assumes the photographer(s) must have selected early, bright mornings in order to encounter such empty streets and suitably still subjects. We catch only glimpses of human figures in these scenes, usually rigidly posed to enable their capture: a group of well-dressed men, a woman and a child are framed against St George's Church in Hardwicke Place; soldiers stand at ease in a group in the upper yard of Dublin Castle; two men recline on a slab in the graveyard of St Patrick's Cathedral. In one of the more distinctive images, two groups of men assemble outside of Conciliation Hall on Burgh Quay, headquarters of Daniel O'Connell's Repeal Association (Figure 12.3). One comprises three well-dressed men from the photographic expedition, carefully posed and standing slightly apart from one another, their gaze locked on the lens (these same individuals can be identified in several other photographs, including Figure 12.2. A second group is huddled off to the side and are less distinct, more informally attired – very possibly members of the Repeal Association, as a number of them appear to wear the distinctive 'Repeal cap'.

The contrast between those aware and unaware of the camera's presence – between those early photographers in control of these Dublin views, clearly marked as elite in their posture and dress, and those who are merely their subjects – reproduces the class divides of the period. Yet despite the effort to produce desired depictions of civic grandeur and solemnity, the city resists. Shadows of Dublin's inhabitants creep into the edges of the frame: they appear as ghost-like figures on the pavements, or indistinct groupings at the base of a monument, or resting along the Custom House quayside crammed with ships (Figures 12.4). Their active conversations or perambulations render them illegible in photographic terms: they are the city in motion, and therefore invisible to a technology that records only stillness.

The Famine does not appear in these photographs – which may be a consequence of their chronology – but neither does the poverty and social subordination that made Ireland so vulnerable in the years leading to the cataclysm. Such subjects were not common in 1840s Irish photography.[3] In any event, the Dublin calotypes are records of a particular kind of seeing – capturing fragments of lived reality. They document the city in its formal arrangements, but remind us of the partiality of historical documents. Where and how we look – whether as historical or contemporary observers – determines what we may understand, and what can and cannot be revealed, about Dublin during the Famine decade.

Such photographs, in their faded materiality and dissolving forms, also recall the evanescence of Famine memory in the city, and perhaps also Dublin's reputation as a place relatively untouched by the catastrophe – a reputation countered by this volume. Famine 'silences' or 'absences' are well-worn post-memorial tropes that do not entirely withstand historical scrutiny; as with the city of Dublin itself, famine memory is sedimentary, palimpsestic, and shape-shifting.[4]

Although the abandonment of respectful interment of the dead in overwhelmed rural communities was one of the Famine's most abhorred characteristics, one of the largest funerals of nineteenth-century Ireland took place in Dublin in August 1847. It commemorated not the Famine dead, but Daniel O'Connell, who had died on 15 May 1847 in Genoa en route to Rome. Following a funerary oration in Rome (and the removal of O'Connell's heart for burial there) his remains were transported to Dublin, arriving at Custom House Quay on Monday 2 August 1847 aboard the *Duchess of Kent*, and processing to the Metropolitan Chapel on Marlborough Street, where his coffin lay in state until the funeral rites on Wednesday. The following day thousands of people thronged the streets as O'Connell's funeral cortege wound its way towards Glasnevin Cemetery, led by the ornate (now empty) gilded chariot which had borne him three years earlier in a triumphal procession upon his release from Richmond Bridewell Prison.

Irish and international newspapers recounted in text and image these elaborate scenes of public mourning enacted amidst Dublin's streets and buildings: on 14 August 1847 the *Illustrated London News* (*ILN*) featured a meticulously detailed account of every facet of the four-day funeral (Figures 12.5). Eight large engravings by its Cork-born artist James Mahony (perhaps best known for his sketches of the Famine published in the *ILN* from 1847–9) observed these scenes of mass mourning, and the paper commented on the unhappy coincidence of O'Connell's death with the onset of famine:

Alas! what mockery of the dead!
Before the hearse the triumph car!
Death smiles in triumph o'er the head
Of him, whose great heart sleeps afar
Broken, when fell his fiery star
From the ascendant, and the Land
Saw Pestilence and Famine war
Triumphantly on Erin's strand.[5]

It is tempting to speculate that such manifestations of public grief may have served as a proxy for the many thousands dying of hunger and disease at this same point in time. Yet references to the Famine dead amongst the orations and public accounts of O'Connell's funeral are uncommon and oblique. We do catch glimpses of disruption of the steady and solemn obsequies of August 1847 – the *ILN* notes how as the hearse passed Redmond's Hill 'a vast crowd of women set up the death wail, peculiar to the Irish'[6] – but it is otherwise difficult to ascertain if or how public crowds drew lines of connection between the death of O'Connell and the despondency of the Famine. It is perhaps more plausible, as Patrick Geoghegan has argued, that O'Connell's death galvanised a sense of national sorrow over the failed national ambitions which O'Connell's late decline represented.[7]

In the decades after the Famine the capital's attention was fixated on two further O'Connellite commemorations: the construction of the O'Connell memorial round tower and crypt in Glasnevin (completed in 1855, with his remains reinterred in 1869); and the erection of the great bronze statue on Sackville Street, conceived in 1866 by the acclaimed Dublin-born sculptor John Henry Foley, and finally completed by Thomas Brock (after Foley's death) in 1883. Each conformed (respectively) to popular artistic tastes of the mid-19th century, namely Gaelic revivalism and a French-inspired heroic realism – the latter elevating an ennobled bronze figure of 'The Liberator' supported by allegorical representations of four winged 'Victories' and a high-relief frieze of the 'people of Ireland' in procession encircling its drum.[8] No hint of the Famine's devastation directly informed such projects, though they did signal a new confidence in developing native commemorative forms distinct from the symbols of empire, and the continuing assertion of the constitutional nationalism that O'Connell had embodied.

For later generations, the turbulent revolutionary and civil war period saw little in the way of Famine commemorative interest in the capital or elsewhere. Likewise the centenary of the Famine in the 1940s, falling at the end of the second World War, occasioned little beyond de Valera's commissioning of R. Dudley Edwards and T. Desmond Williams' *The great famine: studies in Irish history, 1845–52* (not published until 1956) and the Irish Folklore Commission survey on the Famine undertaken from 1944–5. In the 1960s, however, a few years following the publication of Cecil Woodham-Smith's best-selling Famine history *The Great Hunger* in 1962, two new commemorations appeared in the city, both by the sculptor Edward Delaney. His *Famine* bronze sculptural group, located opposite his commissioned sculpture of Wolfe Tone at the northeast corner of St Stephen's Green, was unveiled in 1967 (Figures 12.6). The previous year, to mark the 50th anniversary of 1916, Delaney created the memorial to Thomas Davis which stands in College Green, and on his own initiative added Famine scenes to bronze plaques at the base of its fountain.[9]

Three decades later, Delaney's student John Behan, who had assisted with the St Stephen's Green monuments, would go on to sculpt Ireland's National Famine Memorial, his *Ghost Ship* located at the foot of Croagh Patrick in Co Mayo and unveiled in 1997.[10] The burst of commemorative activity around the 150th anniversary of the Famine left further deposits in Dublin: Rowan Gillespie's *Famine* (1997) (Figures 12.7) was originally a private commission by Norma Smurfit the was eventually located in the Dublin Docklands (though not designed specifically for that site) and gifted to the Irish State. Its central urban location and contemporary visual prominence have made it the highest-profile and most-photographed Famine monument in the country, eclipsing the more rural official 'national' monument in Mayo. Today it is flanked by the *Jeanie Johnston*, a replica Famine-era ship (now museum) which began life as a community project in the early 1990s in Co Kerry and was completed in 2002, finding its way to a permanent mooring alongside Gillespie's *Famine* group by the Liffey on Custom House Quay.[11] In September 2016, President Michael D. Higgins unveiled a new Famine monument in Glasnevin cemetery to coincide with the National Famine Commemoration (an annual event established in 2009), a mid-nineteenth-century high cross donated by the Glasnevin Trust (Figures 12.8).

Other recent additions to the city's Famine memorial landscape are most certainly the consequence of more recent migrant flows and demographic change. In 2015 a plaque commemorating the Polish count Paul Strzelecki was installed at the side of the former Clery's department store on O'Connell Street, marking his contribution to Famine relief while in the service of the British Relief Association in 1847–9 (Figures 12.9). The plaque was created with the support of the citizens of Poznán (Strzelecki's birthplace), the Irish Polish Society, the Irish Culture Foundation (Poznán), and Dublin City Council. Although Strzelecki's work was based initially in the west of Ireland, he later maintained an office in Dublin off Sackville Street, hence the location of the memorial on Sackville Place.[12] The Docklands' status as a site for emigrant memory was further amplified with the opening of the EPIC Emigration Museum in 2018 in the CHQ building, a privately funded museum focused on the Irish diaspora, emigration histories (including that of the Famine), and promoting genealogical tourism.

Perhaps unusually, none of the capital's commemorations, with the exception of the Glasnevin monument marking Famine-era burials, were designed to reflect the Famine's impacts on Dublin. They have been products of aspirant (O'Connell) or current (Strzelecki) political states; more generic commemorations of the Famine which reference death or emigration but are not specific to the city (Delaney and Gillespie's *Famine* works; the *Jeanie Johnston*[13]); or function as tourism sites with a mixed remit of public history and celebratory heritage (EPIC). Localised, place or event-based commemorations of Famine memory in Dublin city and county are more elusive. One of the few is a tiny plaque in Monkstown, Co Dublin (date unknown) in the wall of the Quaker Meeting House, which notes, 'At the time of the Famine in 1848 food prepared in a kitchen behind this wall was distributed to the needy through a window here'.

The physical remnants of the Famine period, omnipresent in the contemporary Irish countryside – abandoned stone cottages, lazy-bed fields and stone walls, famine roads – have no parallel in Dublin. Nevertheless, the remaining built legacy of the Famine period is arguably as extensive in Dublin as elsewhere, and its social and political ripples just as profound.[14] Following the passing of the Irish Poor Law in 1838, four Poor Law Unions in the greater Dublin area were established in 1839: Dublin South[15] and Dublin North[16] in the city; and Rathdown[17] and Balrothery[18] in south and north County Dublin.[19] In the case of Dublin South and North, the Unions absorbed large complexes of long-existing hospitals, asylums, and workhouse structures in the city; Rathdown and Balrothery comprised new sites and Poor Law districts. All four Unions had existing or new workhouses re-designed or built to George Wilkinson's specifications, and opened between 1840 and 1841.[20] This Poor Law infrastructure bore the brunt of the Famine's impacts, but unfortunately no substantive comparative analysis of their role during the 1840s has been undertaken.[21] Additional fever hospitals and sheds in Cork Street, Kilmainham, Glasnevin and Balbriggan were opened in 1846–7 to cope with rising levels of disease and overcrowding.[22]

In the post-Famine period, the four unions met mixed fates: Dublin South and North merged to form the southside-based Dublin Union in 1918, subsequently known as St Kevin's; Rathdown closed in 1920 and its inmates were transferred to Dublin South; and Balrothery closed in 1925.[23] Whilst neither Dublin North nor Balrothery workhouse buildings survive into the present, both Dublin South and Rathdown's workhouses were incorporated into St James's and St Colmcille's Hospitals, respectively. The new National Children's Hospital (currently under construction) is planned for part of the existing St James' workhouse site. The present invisibility of these Famine architectures in Dublin city and county obscures their sprawling grip on the lives of many thousands during the 1840s–50s.

Other parts of the Dublin South and North Unions' built fabric were adapted into other welfare institutions in the late nineteenth and early twentieth century. The former workhouse school for Dublin South in Pelletstown became a National School and orphanage for South Dublin Union (1910–1919/20), and later St Patrick's Mother and Baby Home (1919–85). The North Union's former workhouse school in Cabra (just a few hundred yards away on the Navan Road, also known as Cabra Auxiliary) lasted until 1925, when it became St Vincent's, a home for children with intellectual disabilities (1925–present). St Patrick's and St Vincent's were both ultimately run by the Sisters of Charity of St Vincent de Paul, and St Vincent's Centre is still in operation.[24] The fraught histories of these twentieth-century Dublin welfare institutions were subjected to investigation by the Commission of Investigation into Mother and Baby Homes (2015–21), whose Final Report detailed their inner workings and the often-harrowing testimonies of those who worked and lived in them.[25]

To date, no physical commemoration of the four Dublin Unions' role during the Famine exists.[26] Nor has the traumatic legacy of abuse of women and children within later twentieth-century institutions in the city received any permanent form of public memorialisation.[27] Kilmainham Gaol is unique in its depth of engagement with institutional histories of confinement in Dublin in the nineteenth and twentieth centuries, but the absence of a comprehensive city museum on par with other European capitals[28] leaves these deeply connected stories untold. Such histories especially warrant new cultural representations and interpretations as the city's accretions threaten their material remnants and visibility.

The physical separation, marginalisation, suffering and deaths of people in Irish society due to their poverty, or perceived (im)morality are entangled histories that cannot be simplistically bifurcated across pre- and post-independence Ireland. Nor should we ignore how the Famine's impacts, and social mechanisms of survival and resilience, as well as loss, took particular forms in urban spaces. By adopting a view of the city as an accumulative and non-linear phenomenon – what Walter Benjamin understood as a 'labyrinth' of violence, opportunity, destruction, and renewal[29] – we may begin to reconstitute Dublin and the Famine as a constellation of historical experiences, whose traces are manifest in its records, literatures, images, oralities, materialities, and architectures. The city still awaits more granular investigations to help us 'see the people [...] as more than shadows cold and wan, that is, to see them for who they were not who they became'[30] – to help us focus those blurred figures at the peripheries of the 1840s Dublin calotypes.

Notes

Dublin and the Great Irish Famine: Introduction

1. William J. Smyth, 'The province of Leinster and the Great Famine' in John Crowley, William J. Smyth and Mike Murphy (eds), *Atlas of the Great Irish Famine* (Cork, 2012), p. 332.
2. Exceptions include: Charles Read, 'The Irish Famine and unusual market behaviour in Cork' in *Irish Economic and Social History 44* (2017), pp 3–18; Christine Kinealy and Gerard MacAtasney, *The Hidden Famine: Hunger, Poverty and Sectarianism in Belfast* (London, 2000).
3. Mary E. Daly, 'An alien institution? Attitudes towards the city in nineteenth and twentieth-century Irish society' in *Études Irlandaises 10* (1985), pp 181–94, esp. pp 182–3, 192; 'Irish urban history: a survey' in *Urban History Yearbook*, vol. 13 (May 1986), pp 61–72. For more recent discussions of these themes, see David Dickson, 'Town and city' in Eugenio F. Biagini and Mary E. Daly (eds), *The Cambridge Social History of Modern Ireland* (Cambridge, 2017), pp 112–28; Dickson, 'What happened to modern Irish history?' in *Urban History* 46: 1 (2019), pp 10–20.
4. Ó Gráda, *Black '47*, pp 157–93; Timothy W. Guinnane and Cormac Ó Gráda, 'Mortality in the North Dublin Union during the Great Famine', in *Economic History Review* 55:3 (2002), pp 487–506; Cormac Ó Gráda, 'The market for potatoes in Dublin in the 1840s' in idem, *Ireland's Great Famine: Interdisciplinary Essays* (Dublin, 2005), pp 106–20.
5. David Dickson, *Dublin, the Making of a Capital City* (London, 2014), pp 308–09, 316–17.
6. Smyth, 'The province of Leinster and the Great Famine', pp 330–33.
7. Jacinta Prunty, *Dublin Slums, 1800–1925: A Study in Urban Geography* (Dublin, 1998), pp 227–31; Audrey Woods, *Dublin Outsiders: A History of the Mendicity Institution 1818–1998* (Dublin, 1998), pp 122–37; Deirdre Lindsay, *Dublin's Oldest Charity: The Sick and Indigent Roomkeepers' Society 1790–1990* (Dublin, 1990), pp 29–30.
8. Donal A. Kerr, *'A Nation of Beggars'? Priests, People, and Politics in Famine Ireland, 1846–1852* (Oxford, 1994), pp 32–4, 49–50; Christine Kinealy, *Charity and the Great Hunger in Ireland: The Kindness of Strangers* (London and New York, 2013), pp 125–35. For Liam Kennedy's comment, see his 'Ireland, Irish-America and the man who 'invented' genocide' in idem, *Unhappy the Land? The Most Oppressed People Ever, the Irish?* (Sallins, 2016), p. 115.
9. See for example *Women and Philanthropy in Nineteenth-Century Ireland* (Cambridge, 1995); *Prostitution and Irish society, 1800–1940* (Cambridge, 2007); *Children and Childhood in Irish Society, 1500 to the Present*, ed. with James M. Smith (Dublin, 2014).
10. Ciarán Reilly, 'Feasting in a time of Famine: Dublin Castle and the Great Hunger', in Niamh O'Sullivan (ed.), *Coming Home: Art and the Great Hunger* (Hamden, CT, 2018), pp 37–48.
11. Douglas Bennett, *The Encyclopaedia of Dublin: Revised and Expanded* (1991; reprint, Dublin, 2005); E. E. O'Donnell, *The Annals of Dublin: Fair City* (Dublin, 1987), p. 146; Tom Kennedy (ed.), *Victorian Dublin* (Dublin, 1980).
12. See also Mary Hatfield's comments on the perceived paradox of 'happiness' in nineteenth-century Ireland, in her 'Introduction', in Mary Hatfield (ed.), *Happiness in Nineteenth-Century Ireland* (Liverpool, 2021), pp 1–14.
13. Brian Griffin, '"The more sport the merrier, say we": sport in Ireland during the Great Famine', in *Irish Economic and Social History* 45 (2018), pp 90–114; Ciarán Reilly, *John Plunket Joly and the Great Famine in King's County* (Dublin, 2012).
14. Juliana Adelman, *Civilised by Beasts: Animals and Urban Change in Nineteenth-Century Dublin* (Manchester, 2020), pp 62–90.
15. Dickson, *Dublin, the Making of a Capital City*, p. 308.
16. Maurice Craig, *Dublin 1660–1860* (1952; reprint, Dublin, 1980), p. 309. See also Prunty, *Dublin Slums*, pp 227–31, 286–7.
17. Reilly, John Plunket Joly; Declan Curran, 'Articles of Practical Banking written by Practical Bankers': The Bankers' Magazine Reportage of the Great Irish Famine', in *Irish Economic and Social History* 43 (2016), pp 21–49.

18. https://www.rte.ie/history/the-great-irish-famine/

Dublin and the Great Famine: An Overview

1. Liam Kennedy and Peter M. Solar, 'The famine that wasn't? 1799–1801 in Ireland', Queen's University Centre for Economic History working paper 2019-06 (Oct. 2019).
2. David Dickson, *Dublin: The Making of a Capital City* (London, 2014), p. 317.
3. Joe Curran, below p. 42.
4. Fergus A. D'Arcy, *Raising Dublin, Raising Ireland: A Friar's Campaign* (Dublin, 2018), pp 201–23. The first six Irish branches ('conferences') of the Society of St Vincent de Paul were established in Dublin in 1844–6 (John Gerard Martin, 'The Society of St Vincent de Paul as an emerging social phenomenon in mid-nineteenth century Ireland', MA thesis, National College of Ireland, 1993, p. 187).
5. The workhouse was located outside the city bounds in the parish of Clondermot. It contained 731 inmates.
6. Maurice Craig, *Dublin, 1660-1860* (Dublin, 1980), p. 309.
7. Ó Gráda, *Black '47*, pp 168–9.
8. Ó Gráda, *Black '47*, p. 173; idem, 'The next world and the new world: relief, migration, and the Great Irish Famine', in *Journal of Economic History* 79:2 (2019), pp 319–55, at p. 337.
9. Ciarán Reilly, below p. 4.
10. Frank Neal, *Black '47: Britain and the Famine Irish* (London, 1998); John Belchem, *Irish, Catholic, and Scouse: The Story of the Liverpool-Irish, 1800–1939* (Liverpool, 2007); Lewis Darwen, Donald M. McRaild, Brian Gurrin, and Liam Kennedy, '"Irish fever" in Britain during the Great Famine: immigration, disease, and the legacy of 'Black '47', in *Irish Historical Studies* 44:166 (Nov. 2020), pp 270–94.
11. Brian Crowley, below p. 104.
12. Matthias Blum, Christopher L. Colvin and Eoin McLaughlin, 'Scarring and selection in the Great Irish Famine', Queen's University Centre for Economic History working paper, 2017–08 (2017).
13. Cormac Ó Gráda, 'The Rotunda and the people of Dublin, 1745–1995', in Alan Browne (ed.), *Masters, Midwives, and Ladies in Waiting: The Rotunda Hospital 1745–1995* (Dublin, 1995), pp 240–63, at pp 250–2.
14. See, for example, Christopher Morash, *Writing the Irish Famine* (Oxford, 1995); Melissa Fegan, *Literature and the Irish Famine, 1845–1919* (Oxford, 2002); George Cusack and Sarah Goss (eds), *Hungry Words: Images of Famine in the Irish Canon* (Dublin, 2006); Lindsay Janssen, 'From silence to plenty: the Famine in early twentieth-century periodical fiction', in *Éire-Ireland* 54:3–4 (2019), pp 121–41.
15. Letter from Frederick Douglass to William Lloyd Garrison, 1 Jan. 1846, in Philip Foner (ed.), *Life and Writings of Frederick Douglass* (New York, 1950), vol. i, p. 125.
16. Augustine Martin, 'The short stories of James Stephens', in *Colby Quarterly* 6:8 (Dec. 1963), pp 343–53, p. 351.
17. Christopher Cusack, below, p. 132.
18. Timothy W. Guinnane and Cormac Ó Gráda, 'Mortality in the North Dublin Union during the Great Famine', in *Economic History Review*, 55:3 (2002), pp 487–506; Frank Corrigan, 'Dublin Workhouses during the Great Famine', in *Dublin Historical Record*, 29:2 (1976), pp 59–65.
19. Deirdre Lindsay and David Fitzpatrick, *Records of the Irish Famine: A Guide to Local Archives, 1840–1855* (Dublin, 1993), p. 48; National Library of Ireland, 'Catholic parish registers at the NLI' (https://registers.nli.ie/); National Archives of Ireland, 'The List of Church of Ireland Parish registers (updated 2017) (https://www.nationalarchives.ie/wp-content/uploads/2018/02/PARISHREGISTERS.pdf).
20. Compare Andrés Eiríksson, '"Paupers and beggars' brats": Parsonstown Workhouse in the Famine', updated 29 Nov 2020 (available at: https://www.rte.ie/history/famine-ireland/2020/0825/1161218-paupers-and-beggars-brats-parsonstown-workhouse-in-the-famine/).
21. Guinnane and Ó Gráda, 'Mortality', p. 495; Dickson, *Dublin*, p. 317.
22. Compare Brian M. Walker, 'Politicians, elections, and catastrophe: the general election of 1847,' *Irish Political Studies* 22:1 (2007), pp 1–34.
23. My thanks to Breandán Mac Suibhne and Fionn Ó Gráda for useful comments on an earlier draft.

SECTION I: BUSINESS LIFE AND INDUSTRY

'A Little London, All Alive': Some Experiences of the World of Goods and Commodities in Famine Dublin

1. Diary of Elizabeth Smith, 13 July 1845 (in private possession).
2. Ibid., 31 July 1840.
3. Ibid., 15 Apr. 1841.
4. Diary of John Plunket Joly, 6 July 1847 (NLI, MS 17,035). Hereafter cited as Joly diary. For more on Joly, see Ciarán Reilly, *John Plunket Joly and the Great Famine in King's County* (Dublin, 2012).
5. Joly diary, 6 July 1847.
6. Ó Gráda, *Black '47*, p. 160.
7. Maurice Craig, *Dublin 1660–1860* (reprint, Dublin, 1980), p. 309.
8. *FJ*, 28 May 1849.
9. Frank Cullen, *Dublin 1847: City of the Ordnance Survey* (Dublin, 2015), pp 9–11.
10. I am grateful to Nicola Kelly, archivist at Office of Public Works/ Maynooth University Archive & Research Centre (OMARC) for sharing details of the Knight of Glin Trade Label collection.
11. See Christine Kinealy, *Charity and the Great Hunger: The Kindness of Strangers* (London, 2013).
12. Samuel Lewis, *A Topographical Dictionary of Ireland* (2 vols, London, 1837), vol. 1, p. 535.
13. Lewis, *Topographical Dictionary*, vol. 1, p. 536. See also *Dublin Weekly Mail*, 12 May 1849.
14. Diary of Elizabeth Smith, 21 Sept. 1845 (in private possession).
15. See Hession, below, pp 24–35.
16. *FJ*, 17 Mar. 1847.
17. *DEP*, 29 Apr. 1847.
18. *DMA*, 24 Dec. 1846.
19. *Kerry Examiner*, 2 Feb. 1847.
20. See for example *WDWM*, 12 May 1849.
21. Diary of Elizabeth Smith, 30 Nov. 1845 (in private possession).
22. Ibid., 30 Nov. 1845.
23. *DMA*, 27 Nov. 1846.
24. Diary of Elizabeth Smith, 8 Dec. 1845 (in private possession).
25. *FJ*, 26 Mar. 1847.
26. *Westmeath Independent*, 2 Dec. 1848.
27. See for example *DEM*, 5 May 1848.
28. *DMA*, 8 May 1846. See also *The Nation*, 14 Mar. 1846.
29. *DEPC*, 22 May 1847.
30. Diary of Elizabeth Smith, 24 June 1846 (in private possession).
31. See Ruth Delany, *The Grand Canal of Ireland* (Newtown Abbot, 1973), p. 71.
32. Bewley's advertisements regularly appeared in national and provincial papers. See for example, *FJ*, 1 Apr. 1845, 27 Mar. 1846.
33. Diary of Elizabeth Smith, 4 Dec. 1842 (in private possession).
34. See for example *DMR*, 14 Aug. 1840.
35. *DMA*, 6 Nov. 1846.
36. Ibid., 15 May 1846.
37. *FJ*, 8 Sept. 1846.
38. *DEPC*, 11 May 1847.
39. Diary of Elizabeth Smith, 29 Apr. 1846 (in private possession).
40. *DMA*, 2 Jan. 1846.
41. *DWR*, 24 Mar. 1849.
42. *DWN*, 13 Dec. 1845.
43. *Belfast Newsletter*, 9 Jan. 1849.
44. See *The Advocate: or, Irish Industrial Journal*, 1 Aug. 1849.
45. Diary of Elizabeth Smith, 6 Sept. 1849 (in private possession).
46. *DWN*, 16 Oct. 1847.
47. *Tipperary Vindicator*, 4 Dec. 1847.

48. Diary of Elizabeth Smith, 31 Jan. 1846 (in private possession).
49. *FJ*, 9 Jan. 1846.
50. Ibid., 20 Jan. 1848.
51. *DWR*, 15 Sept. 1849.
52. *DEPC*, 11 May 1847.
53. *DWR*, 19 May 1849.
54. *FJ*, 3 May 1849. See also *Armagh Guardian*, 26 Nov. 1849.
55. See for example *DEPC*, 28 Jan. 1847.
56. Kathryn Milligan, below, *passim*.
57. RDS, *The Report and Adjudication of the Judges on the Exhibition of Irish Manufacture, Produce and Invention* (Dublin, 1847), p. 3. See for example RDS, *Catalogue of Articles of Irish Manufacture, Produce and Invention, Exhibited at the Society's House, 30 June 1847* (Dublin, 1847).
58. *King's County Chronicle*, 6 Oct. 1847.
59. See, for example, *DEPC*, 28 Sept. 1847.
60. Joly diary, 19 July 1846.
61. Joly diary, 16 Nov. 1846.
62. Patrick Henchy, 'The Joly family: Jasper Robert Joly and the National Library', in *Irish University Review*, 7:2 (autumn, 1977), pp 184–98.
63. Joly diary, 28 Jan. 1848.
64. Diary of Elizabeth Smith, 25 June 1847 (in private possession).
65. Ibid., 21 July 1847.
66. Ibid., 23 Dec. 1847.
67. Ibid., 14 Feb. 1845.
68. *Ballyshannon Herald*, 15 Jan. 1847.
69. *Cork Examiner*, 15 Jan. 1847.
70. *DEP*, 9 Jan. 1847.
71. *FJ*, 13 Mar. 1847.
72. Ibid., 21 May 1847.
73. Diary of Elizabeth Smith, 30 Apr. 1848 (in private possession).
74. Ibid., 21 July 1847.
75. Ibid., 25 Nov. 1849.
76. Ibid., 9 Sept. 1849.
77. *FJ*, 15 Feb. 1848.
78. Ibid., 4 Dec. 1851.
79. Diary of Elizabeth Smith, 23 Mar. 1850.
80. Ibid., 28 Mar. 1851.
81. Ibid., 21 July 1851.
82. Ibid., 4 May 1848.
83. Ibid., 23 Mar. 1846.
84. Ibid., 26 June 1846.

'*Ad Libitum* Banking'?: Dublin's Role Within the Famine-Era Irish Banking System

1. The term 'joint-stock bank' refers to a bank which is owned and controlled by shareholders. For an overview of the emergence of joint-stock banking in Britain and Ireland in the nineteenth century, see: C.W. Munn, 'The emergence of joint-stock banking in the British Isles: a comparative approach', in *Business History* 30:1 (1988), pp 69–83.
2. For a more detailed treatment of Irish Famine-era savings banks and micro-credit, see: Ó Gráda, *Black '47*, pp 149–56; Eoin McLaughlin, '"Profligacy in the encouragement of thrift": Savings banks in Ireland, 1817–1914', in *Business History* 56:4 (2014), pp 569–91; Cormac Ó Gráda, 'Savings banks, famine, and financial contagion: Ireland in the 1840s and 1850s', in *Irish Economic and Social History* 36 (2009), pp 21–36.
3. The Famine-era annual reports of Irish joint-stock banks are discussed further in Declan Curran, 'Organizational narrative and memory in social context: representations of the Great Irish Famine in

official publications of Irish joint-stock banks', in Marguerite Corporaal and Peter Gray (eds), *The Great Irish Famine and Social Class: Conflicts, Responsibilities, Representations* (Oxford, 2019).
4. Commercial banks bought short-term bills of exchange at a discount from merchants as part of their routine banking business. In purchasing these bills, banks provided merchants with bank notes, coins, or a credit on their account. In return, banks recouped the full value of the bill when payment was made by the merchant's debtor, with the discount rate representing the fee charged by the bank for providing this service. See G. L. Barrow, *The Emergence of the Irish Banking System, 1820–1845* (Dublin, 1975), p. 36; Michael Collins, *Money and Banking in the UK: A History* (New York, 1988), p. 97.
5. Cormac Ó Gráda, *Ireland: A New Economic History, 1780–1939* (Oxford, 1994), p. 141.
6. F. G. Hall, *The Bank of Ireland, 1783–1946* (Dublin and Oxford, 1949), pp 216–19.
7. Barrow, *The Emergence of the Irish Banking System*, pp 215–19 (Appendix 3).
8. *Bankers' Magazine* 8 (June 1848), p. 390.
9. Institutions are defined in this chapter as per the institutional economist Douglass North: a set of humanly-devised constraints that structure political, economic and social interaction, consisting of both formal rules and informal constraints. See Douglass North, 'Institutions', in *Journal of Economic Perspectives* 5:1 (winter 1991), pp 97–112.
10. Ó Gráda, *Black '47*, pp 149–56.
11. *Second Report from the Select Committee on Commercial Distress; with the minutes of evidence*, p. 41, H.C. 1847–8 (584), viii, Pt I, 561 (Q. 6644). Advocates of the extension of this restrictive regulatory regime to Ireland sought to depict the Irish nineteenth-century development as one of perpetual banking crisis. During the 1848 inquiry of the Committee on Commercial Distress, Robert Peel, the British prime minister who introduced the 1844 and 1845 legislation, spoke of 'the ruin that has prevailed in former years through a great part of Ireland from the insolvency of different banks': ibid., (Q. 6645). However, the workings of the Irish banking system also featured in a wider contemporary debate regarding a 'want of capital' in Ireland. G. L. Smyth castigated Bank of Ireland for having been 'the vampire of the national prosperity', while Montgomery Martin argued that 'one of the chief grievances in Ireland is her banking system'. On the other hand, Neilson Hancock (professor of political economy in Dublin University) was critical of what he considered to be a conflation of the concepts of circulating medium and capital: G. L. Smith, *Banking in Ireland: Remarks on the Renewal of the Charter of Bank of Ireland* (London, 1840); R. Montgomery Martin, *Ireland before and after the Union with Great Britain* (3rd edn, London and Dublin, 1848), p. 248; W. Neilson Hancock, *Is there really a want of capital in Ireland?* (Dublin, 1851).
12. L. M. Cullen, 'Landlords, bankers and merchants: the early Irish banking world, 1700–1820', in A. E. Murphy (ed.), *Economists and the Irish Economy* (Dublin, 1984), pp 30–2; P. McGowan, *Money and Banking in Ireland: Origins, Development and Future* (Dublin, 1990), p. 9.
13. Cullen, 'Landlords, bankers and merchants', p. 36.
14. Ibid.
15. Geo. II, c. 16 (Ire).
16. Cullen, 'Landlords, bankers and merchants', p. 38; L. M. Cullen, *Anglo-Irish Trade, 1660–1800* (Manchester, 1968), p. 201.
17. Cullen, *Anglo-Irish Trade*, p.201. Among these merchant discount houses prominent in Dublin in the 1780s were the houses of Joshua & Joseph Pim and that of Robert Shaw. Shaw formed a private bank in 1797; it was later subsumed into the Royal Bank of Ireland when it was established as a joint-stock bank in 1836. Other Dublin banks active at that time included La Touche's (est. 1713), Newcommen's (est. 1722) and Finlay's (est. 1754): Barrow, *Emergence of the Irish Banking System*, pp 131, 203–07.
18. McGowan, *Money and Banking in Ireland*, p. 10.
19. McGowan describes eighteenth-century Irish banks as being 'primarily concerned with facilitating the transfer of agricultural output from the countryside to Dublin and abroad, and placing the proceeds of the sale of the output at the disposal of the landlords': ibid., p. 9.
20. Cullen, 'Landlords, bankers and merchants', pp 32, 39. Barrow describes La Touche's banking services for its landed clientele based in Dublin and London as '[operating] mainly by the clearance of drafts and bills against accounts, and [making] considerable loans against deposits of stock or on personal bonds with sureties': Barrow, *Emergence of the Irish Banking System*, p. 203.
21. Cullen, 'Landlords, bankers and merchants', p. 35.

22. Bank of Ireland's office was initially located in Mary's Abbey near Dublin's Four Courts. The bank relocated to College Green in 1808: Hall, *Bank of Ireland*, pp 47–9; McGowan, *Money and Banking in Ireland*, pp 12–13.
23. Barrow, *Emergence of the Irish Banking System*, p. 3.
24. Hall, *Bank of Ireland*, p. 41
25. A. M. Fraser, 'David Digges La Touche, banker, and a few of his descendants', in *Dublin Historical Record* 5: 2 (1943), p. 65.
26. Hall, *Bank of Ireland*, p. 43.
27. McGowan, *Money and Banking in Ireland*, p. 13; Oliver MacDonagh, 'The Victorian bank, 1824–1914', in F. S. L. Lyons (ed.), *Bicentenary Essays: Bank of Ireland, 1783–1983* (Dublin, 1983), p. 31.
28. Cullen, *Anglo-Irish Trade*, pp 204, 215.
29. Mary E. Daly, *Social and Economic History of Ireland since 1800* (Dublin, 1981), p. 13.
30. Mary E. Daly, *The Famine in Ireland* (Dundalk, 1986), pp 21–4.
31. Collins, *Money and Banking in the UK*, p. 12.
32. Barrow, *Emergence of the Irish Banking System*, pp 17–19; Collins, *Money and Banking in the UK*, p. 12.
33. Philip Ollerenshaw, *Banking in Nineteenth-Century Ireland. The Belfast Banks, 1825–1914* (Manchester, 1987), p. 9.
34. Cullen, 'Landlords, bankers and merchants', pp 40–43.
35. Ollerenshaw, *Banking in Nineteenth-Century Ireland*, p. 4.
36. Barrow, *Emergence of the Irish Banking System*, p. 64.
37. Ibid., p. 61.
38. Ibid., pp 68–70.
39. James William Gilbart, *History of Banking in Ireland* (2nd edn, London, 1836), p. 37.
40. Barrow, *Emergence of the Irish Banking System*, pp 72–8.
41. Ibid.
42. *Bankers' Magazine*, 5 (July 1846), pp 201–8.
43. As noted above, the north east of Ireland, particularly in industrialised Belfast, had also developed banking features distinct from those in Dublin. A number of joint-stock banks formed in Ulster in the 1820s and 1830s, which lay outside Bank of Ireland's 50-mile radius. Northern Banking Company (est. 1825 in Belfast) subsequently developed a set of 12 branches across Ulster by 1845), while the Belfast Banking Company (est. 1827) also established a branch presence (18) throughout the northern province by 1845 and Ulster Bank (est. 1836) went on to open 15 branches across Ulster by 1845. As well as the 16 branches that Provincial established in Ulster, Bank of Ireland also set up four branches in the province: Barrow, *Emergence of the Irish Banking System*, pp 129–31; Lyn Gallagher, The Ulster Bank Story (1998), pp 5–11.
44. Barrow, *Emergence of the Irish Banking System*, pp 215–20.
45. Ibid., p. 80.
46. Daniel O'Connell to P.V. Fitzpatrick, 8 July 1834, in Maurice R. O'Connell (ed.), *The Correspondence of Daniel O'Connell: vol. v, 1833–1836* (IMC, Dublin, 1977), p. 161.
47. *FJ*, 16 July 1834.
48. Daniel O'Connell to P. V. Fitzpatrick, 16 Aug. 1839, in Maurice R. O'Connell (ed.), *The Correspondence of Daniel O'Connell: vol. vi, 1837–1840* (IMC, Dublin, 1977), pp 271–2.
49. Barrow, *Emergence of the Irish Banking System*, p. 57.
50. *FJ*, 10 Dec. 1835; Barrow, *Emergence of the Irish Banking System*, p. 118; Kenneth Milne, *A History of the Royal Bank of Ireland* (Dublin, 1964), pp 25–43.
51. A further regional bank, Tipperary Bank, was formed in 1838 and entered into an agreement with Bank of Ireland to exclusively issue that bank's notes. From 1842 its office was located in Clonmel, County Tipperary and it had opened nine branches by 1845. Tipperary Bank collapsed in 1856 as a result of reckless investments in overseas railway speculation: see Cormac Ó Gráda, 'The last major Irish bank failure before 2008', in *Financial History Review* 19:2 (2012), pp 201–2.
52. Barrow, *Emergence of the Irish Banking System*, pp 215–20 (Appendix 3).
53. Ibid.
54. Ibid., p. 154.
55. Ibid., pp 118–19.
56. McGowan, *Money and Banking in Ireland*, p. 14.

57. Ibid., p. 35.
58. For further discussion based on minutes of meetings of Bank of Ireland court of directors, see: Declan Curran, '"A dreadful pressure for money": the Bank Charter Act 1844 and Bankers' (Ireland) Act 1845 in the context of the Great Irish Famine', in Andrew G. Newby (ed), '*The Enormous Failure of Nature': Famine and Society in the Nineteenth Century* (Helsinki, 2017), pp 21–46.
59. John Clapham *The Bank of England: A History. Volume 2, 1797–1914* (Cambridge, 1944), pp 179–83; Collins, *Money and Banking in the UK*, p. 30.
60. Clapham, *The Bank of England. Volume 2*, pp 169–72.
61. Ibid.
62. Clapham, *The Bank of England. Vol. II*, pp 179–83; Collins, *Money and Banking in the UK*, p. 73.
63. Critics of the Bank Charter Act 1844 pointed to the unwieldiness of a restrictive monetary regime in a time of crisis. Indeed, the financial crisis of 1825 was only ameliorated by the Bank of England being authorised by the British Treasury to dramatically increase its level of note issue in order to assuage panic amongst the general public. The Bank Charter Act 1844 removed the discretion of the Bank of England to increase the amount of currency in circulation in times of economic stress. The deficient potato harvest of 1845 would swiftly place the rigidity inherent in the Act under intense scrutiny, as famine conditions necessitated an importation of grain which would trigger an unanticipated outflow of gold from the British financial system. See, for example: *Bankers' Magazine* (Feb. 1847), p. 261. Indeed, in the face of British gold outflows, the Bank Charter Act was temporarily suspended in 1847, 1857 and 1866. However, the Act remained unchanged until 1928: F. W. Fetter and D. Gregory, *Monetary and Financial Policy in 19th-Century Britain* (Dublin, 1973), p. 25; Currency and Bank Notes Act, 1928 (18 & 19 Geo. V, c. 13).
64. Barrow, *Emergence of the Irish Banking System*, pp 99–101.
65. MacDonagh, 'The Victorian bank', p. 36.
66. McGowan, *Money and Banking in Ireland*, p. 38.
67. Hall, *Bank of Ireland*, pp 216–19.
68. *Bank for International Settlements. Issues in the Governance of Central Banks: A Report from the Central Bank Governance Group*, (Basel, 2009), pp 17–20.
69. Hall, *Bank of Ireland*, pp 193–214.
70. *Bankers' Magazine* 6 (Mar. 1847), p. 414.
71. *Bankers' Magazine* (Aug. 1847), p. 345.
72. Anon., 'Agriculture and commerce condition of Ireland: the bank returns', in *Dublin University Magazine* 102:34 (1849), p. 380.
73. *Bankers' Magazine* (Feb. 1847), p. 261.
74. Rudiger Dornbusch and Jacob A. Frenkel, 'The gold standard and the Bank of England in the crisis of 1847', in Michael D. Bordo and Anna J. Schwartz (eds), *A Retrospective on the Classic Gold Standard 1821–1931* (Chicago, 1984), p. 236; F. W. Fetter, *Development of British Monetary Orthodoxy, 1797–1875* (Cambridge, MA, 1965), p. 209.
75. *Second Report, SC on Commercial Distress; with the minutes of evidence*, Q. 6669.
76. Ibid., Q. 6672.
77. *Bankers' Magazine* 4–10 (1846–53).
78. *Second Report, SC on Commercial Distress; with the minutes of evidence*, Q. 6615 and 6616.
79. Ibid., Q. 6644.
80. Ibid., Q. 6649.
81. Ibid., Q. 6618.

Taming the Channel: Technology, Liberalism and the Irish Sea, c.1845–52

1. Thomas Carlyle, 'Repeal the Union', in *Examiner*, 29 Apr. 1848.
2. Thomas Carlyle to Charles Gavan Duffy, 26 Apr. 1851, in Charles Gavan Duffy, *Conversations with Carlyle* (New York, 1892), p. 173.
3. Thomas Carlyle, 'Signs of the times', in *Critical and Miscellaneous Essays*, vol. 2 (Boston, 1839), pp 142–56; idem, *Chartism* (London, 1840), p. 28; idem, 'Occasional discourse on the negro question', in *Fraser's Magazine* 40 (1849), p. 679.

4. Leo Marx, *The Machine in the Garden: Technology and the Pastoral Ideal in America* (London, 1964), pp 170–188, 373–4.
5. D. I. Jackson, *The Geology of the Irish Sea* (London, 1995), pp 1–3; T. W. Freeman, *Ireland: A General and Regional Geography* (London, 1965), pp 41–2.
6. Philip Sidney Bagwell, *The Transport Revolution from 1770* (London, 1974), p. 53.
7. K. T. Rowland, *Steam at Sea: A History of Steam Navigation* (Newton Abbot, 1970), p. 55.
8. H. S. Irvine, 'Some aspects of passenger traffic between Britain and Ireland 1820–1850', in *Journal of Transport History* 4:4 (1960), pp 225–7; Freda Harcourt, 'Charles Wye Williams and Irish steam shipping, 1820–50', in *Journal of Transport History* 8:2 (1992), p. 149.
9. Peter M. Solar, 'Shipping and economic development in nineteenth-century Ireland', in *Economic History Review* 59:4 (2006), p. 725; John Armstrong and David M. Williams, *The Impact of Technological Change: The Early Steamship in Britain* (St John's, Newfoundland, 2011), p. 44.
10. Oliver MacDonagh, 'Sea communications in the nineteenth century', in Kevin B. Nowlan (ed.), *Travel and Transport in Ireland* (Dublin, 1973), p. 124; *Return of Steam Vessels Registered in United Kingdom*, pp 1–16, H.C. 1845 (349), xvii; B. R. Mitchell, *International Historical Statistics: Europe 1750–1993* (London, 1998), pp 710–14; idem, *Historical Statistics: The Americas 1750–1988* (London, 1993), p. 560.
11. Antony Adler, *Neptune's Laboratory: Fantasy, Fear, and Science at Sea* (Cambridge, 2019), pp 19–21.
12. I borrow this suggestive concept from the fields of literary and museum studies. See: Mary Louise Pratt, *Imperial Eyes: Travel and Transculturation* (London, 1991), pp 6–7; James Clifford, *Routes: Travel and Translation in the Late Twentieth Century* (Cambridge, 1997), p. 192.
13. Alf Hornborg, J. R. McNeill and Juan Martínez Alier, 'Introduction: environment as political ecology', in Alf Hornborg, J. R. McNeill and Juan Martínez Alier (eds), *Rethinking Environmental History: World-System History and Global Environmental Change* (New York, 2007), p. 3.
14. The National Archives (TNA), HO/47/52/16, A. Chambre to H. Addington, 27 July 1813; 'Naval warfare of England and America', in *Chambers's Edinburgh Journal* 485 (15 May 1841), p. 135; 'The cruise of "The Willing Lass"', in *Bentley's Miscellany* 30 (July 1851), p. 605; Albert Bushnell Hart, *Formation of the Union, 1750–1829* (London, 1893), p. 212.
15. *Liverpool Advertiser*, 29 Feb. 1760; Anon., 'Thurot, the pirate', in *The Kaleidoscope* 10:522 (29 June 1830), p. 421; Anon., 'Fragments of voyages and travels', in *Quarterly Review* 47:93 (Mar. 1832), p. 148.
16. TNA, ADM/175/18, 'Irish coast guard nominations', 1827–48; William Webb, *Coastguard: An Official History of HM Coastguard* (London, 1976), p. 24.
17. David Anderson, *Modern Law of the Sea: Selected Essays* (Leiden, 2008), p. 184. For the implications of this shift on the regulation of commercial traffic, see: L. M. Cullen, 'The smuggling trade in Ireland in the eighteenth century', in *Proceedings of the Royal Irish Academy* 67 (1968–9), p. 161; Gavan Daly, 'English smugglers, the channel, and the Napoleonic wars, 1800–1814', in *Journal of British Studies* 46:1 (Jan. 2007), p. 46.
18. For the importance of expertise to the 'epistemological mastery of national territory', see: Michael Hannah, *Governmentality and the Mastery of Territory in Nineteenth-Century America* (Cambridge, 2000), p. 40. Traditional beliefs relating to the sea continued well into the nineteenth century. See: National University of Ireland, Galway, Hardiman Library, G22/1/1/1/58, Becker Collection, 'Sea monsters in Irish folklore', n. d.
19. Anon., 'The salmon and sea fisheries', in *Dublin University Magazine* 227:38 (Nov. 1851), p. 527; Philip E. Steinberg, *The Social Construction of the Ocean* (Cambridge, 2001), pp 37–8.
20. Richard Valpy, 'The resources of the Irish Sea fisheries', in *Journal of the Statistical Society of London* 11:1 (Mar. 1848), p. 55; James Ward, *How to Regenerate Ireland or Facts from the Fisheries* (London, 1850), p. 22; Anon., *The Salmon and Sea Fisheries Containing Comments upon the Existing and Proposed Legislation and a Practical Inquiry into the State of the Irish Fisheries* (Dublin, 1852), p. 38; William Temple, *The Works of Sir William Temple in Two Volumes*, vol. 1 (London, 1740), p. 119.
21. Thomas W. Fulton, *The Sovereignty of the Sea: An Historical Account of the Claims of England to the Dominion of the British Seas and of the Evolution of the Territorial Waters* (Edinburgh, 1911), p. 614; Renaud Morieux, *The Channel: England, France and the Construction of a Maritime Border in the Eighteenth Century* (Cambridge, 2016), pp 206–7.

22. Anna Gambles, 'Free trade and state formation: the political economy of fisheries policy in Britain and the United Kingdom circa 1780–1850', in *Journal of British Studies* 39:3 (July 2000), pp 292, 311–13.
23. James A. Blake, *The History and Position of the Sea Fisheries of Ireland, and How They May be Made to Afford Increased Food and Employment* (Waterford, 1868), p. 70.
24. Herbert Francis Hore, *An Inquiry into the Legislation, Control and Improvement of the Salmon and Sea Fisheries of Ireland* (Dublin, 1850), pp 19, 24, 47; Anon., *The Salmon and Sea Fisheries*, p. 41; *First Report of the Commissioners of Inquiry into the State of the Irish Fisheries:With the Minutes of Evidence and Appendix*, p. 2, H.C. 1837 (22), xxi.
25. Ibid.
26. *First Annual Report of the Commissioners of Fisheries, Ireland*, p. 2, H.C. 1843 (224), xxvii.
27. *The Third Annual Report of the Commissioners of Public Works, in re the Fisheries of Ireland*, pp 3–4, H.C. 1845 (320), xxvi; *The Fourth Annual Report of the Commissioners of Public Works, in re the Fisheries of Ireland*, p. 11, H.C. 1846 (713), xxii.
28. Peter Jones, 'The long "lost" history of bottom trawling in England, *c.*1350–1650', in *International Journal of Maritime History* 30:2 (2018), pp 201–17.
29. Peter Jones, 'The spread of bottom trawling in the British Isles, *c.*1700–1860', in *International Journal of Maritime History* 30:4 (2018), p. 686; Jim Mac Laughlin, *Troubled Waters: A Social and Cultural History of Ireland's Sea Fisheries* (Dublin, 2010), p. 263.
30. *SN*, 20 Apr. 1774; *Hibernian Journal*, 25 Apr. 1774.
31. Edmond P. Symes, 'The Torbay fishermen in Ringsend', in *Dublin Historical Record* 53:2 (2000), pp 139–40, 144; Christopher Moriarty, 'Fish and fisheries', in John Wilson Foster (ed.), *Nature in Ireland:A Scientific and Cultural History* (Dublin 1997), pp 287–8.
32. George N. Whatley, *Hints for the Improvement of the Irish Fishery* (London, 1803); *SN*, 20 Nov. 1818; *DWR*, 19 Feb. 1820; *Southern Reporter*, 27 Sept. 1825; *Waterford Mail*, 28 Sept. 1825; *DMR*, 1 Apr. 1826; *DEP*, 15 Jan. 1828; *Southern Reporter*, 9 Feb. 1828; *Cork Constitution*, 12 Feb. 1828.
33. NLI, Ms. 3419, 'Minute book of the Dublin Fishery Company, 1818–1824', 28 Sept. 1822, 6. Dec. 1823; J. L. J. Hughes, 'The Dublin Fishery Company, 1818–1830', in *Dublin Historical Record* 12:2 (1951), pp 34–5.
34. David B. Thomson, *The Seine Net: Its Origin, Evolution and Use* (London, 1969), p. 1; Dietrich Sahrhage and Johannes Lundbeck, *A History of Fishing* (New York, 1992), pp 127–8; James J. Davin, 'The future of Ireland's inland fisheries', in *Studies: An Irish Quarterly Review* 42:165 (Mar. 1953), p. 44; Anon., *Observations Regarding the Salmon Fishery of Scotland Especially with Reference to The Stake-Net Mode of Fishing* (Edinburgh, 1824), p. 9; Anon., *An Inquiry Into the Present State and Means of Improving the Salmon Fisheries Including a Digest of the Evidence* (London, 1827), p. 103; William J. Ffennell, *Remarks on Past and Present Legislation for the Protection of the Salmon Fisheries of Ireland* (London, 1863), p. 5.
35. The penetration of this material and technological culture into popular practice and memory in the decades following the Famine can be seen in accounts of such fishing instruments. See: University College Dublin, National Folklore Collection, the Schools' Collection, vol. 295, p. 180; ibid., vol. 463, pp 21–2; Dan Graham, 'The Dingle fish trawling controversy 1849–1862', in *Kerry Magazine* 9 (1998), p. 18; John B. Roney, '[Mis-]managing fisheries on the west coast of Ireland in the nineteenth century', in *Humanities* 8:4 (2019), p. 6.
36. Hore, *An Inquiry into the Legislation*, p. 193; *The Third Annual Report of the Commissioners of Public Works, in re the Fisheries of Ireland*, pp 12–15, H.C. 1845 (320), xxvi.
37. Mac Laughlin, *Troubled Waters*, p. 284; *Report from Her Majesty's Commissioners of Inquiry into the State of the Law and Practice in Respect to the Occupation of Land in Ireland*, p. 159, H.C. 1845 (605), xix.
38. *Report of the Commissioners Appointed to Take the Census of Ireland, for the Year 1841*, pp 1–504, H.C. 1843 (504), xxiv; *The Third Annual Report of the Commissioners of Public Works, in re the Fisheries of Ireland*, pp 12–18, H.C. 1845 (320), xxvi.
39. *Evidence Taken Before Her Majesty's Commissioners of Inquiry into the State of the Law and Practice in Respect to the Occupation of Land in Ireland. Part II*, pp 479, 481, 917, H.C. 1845 (616), xx; *Evidence Taken Before Her Majesty's Commissioners of Inquiry into the State of the Law and Practice in Respect to the Occupation of Land in Ireland. Part III*, p. 506, H.C. 1845 (657), xxi.
40. *Poor Inquiry (Ireland). Appendix (C.) Parts I. and II. Part I. Reports on the State of the Poor, and on the Charitable Institutions in some of the Principal Towns*, p. 53d, H.C. 1836 (35), xxx.

41. *First Report of the Commissioners of Inquiry into the State of the Irish Fisheries: With the Minutes of Evidence and Appendix*, p. iv, H.C. 1837 (22), xxi.
42. *The Second Annual Report of the Commissioners of Fisheries, Ireland*, p. 4, H.C. 1844 (502), xxx.
43. Hore, *An Inquiry into the Legislation*, p. 131.
44. Ibid., p. 128. See also: Wallop Brabazon, *The Deep and Coast Fisheries of Ireland with Suggestions for the Working of a Fishing Company* (Dublin, 1848), p. 12.
45. Cecil Woodham Smith, *The Great Hunger: Ireland 1845–1849* (London, 1962), p. 165; Christine Kinealy, *A Death-Dealing Famine: The Great Hunger in Ireland* (London, 1997), p. 82; Ó Gráda, *Black '47*, p. 122; idem, *Famine: A Short History* (Princeton, 2009), p. 76.
46. Cathal Póirtéir, *The Great Irish Famine* (Dublin, 1995), p. 65; Christine Kinealy, *Charity and the Great Hunger in Ireland: The Kindness of Strangers* (Dublin, 2013), pp 6, 30; James S. Donnelly Jr., *The Great Irish Potato Famine* (Stroud, 2002), pp 148, 150; *Report from the Select Committee on Kilrush Union, Together with the Proceedings of the Committee, Minutes of Evidence, etc.*, p. 227, H.C. 1850 (613), xi.
47. Asenath Nicholson, *Annals of the Famine in Ireland, in 1847, 1848, and 1849* (New York, 1851), p. 236.
48. Ó Gráda, *Famine: A Short History*, p. 81.
49. Trevelyan, *The Irish Crisis*, pp 44, 69.
50. Ibid., p. 69.
51. Newcastle University (hereafter NU), Robinson Library Special Collections, Trevelyan Papers, CET/1/12, Charles Trevelyan to Stephen Spring Rice, 10 Feb. 1847.
52. University of Oxford, Bodleian Library, Clarendon papers, MS. Clar. dep. Irish box 60, Charles Trevelyan to Lord Clarendon, 12 July 1847.
53. NU, Robinson Library Special Collections, Trevelyan Papers, CET/1/12, Charles Trevelayn to William Mulvany, 6 Mar. 1847; TNA, T64/367A/2, George Whalley to Charles Trevelayn, 2 Aug. 1847; NLI, Monteagle papers, Ms. 13, 361 /1–2, Spring Rice to Trevelyan., n.d. [1847]; NAI, M. 1369, 'Patent of the Royal Irish Fisheries Co.', 8 June 1848.
54. NU, Robinson Library Special Collections, Trevelyan Papers, CET/1/18, Charles Trevelayn to M. Upsher, 6 Dec. 1847; CET/1/18, Charles Trevelyan to Lord Clarendon, 13, 23 Dec. 1847.
55. TNA, AO19/41/12, 'Audit of Fish Curing Establishments', 1846–7; NU, Robinson Library Special Collections, Trevelyan Papers, CET/1/13, Charles Trevelyan to John Burgoyne, 30 Mar. 1847. This was very much a two-way process, with lobbying by trawling companies playing a role. See: Public Records Office of Northern Ireland (hereafter PRONI), Irish Potato Famine papers, T3300/16/4, 'Petition of the Irish Deep Sea Fishing and Fishing Boat Company to the Lord Lieutenant', n.d. [1846].
56. Trevelyan, *The Irish Crisis*, p. 69.
57. Ibid.
58. NU, Robinson Library Special Collections, Trevelyan Papers, CET/1/16, Charles Trevelyan to Lord Clarendon, 10, 17 July 1847.
59. NAI, OPW 8/76/901, Robert MacNeale to H. R. Paine, 22 Dec. 1845. For a similar message from Co. Down, see: PRONI, Annesley Papers, D1854/6/3, JR Moore to Lt Col Harry Jones, 25 Jan. 1847; 25 May 1850.
60. *Correspondence Explanatory of the Measures Adopted by Her Majesty's Government for the Relief of Distress Arising from the Failure of the Potato Crop in Ireland*, p. 276, H.C. 1846 (735), xxxvii; *Correspondence from July, 1846, to January, 1847, Relating to the Measures Adopted for the Relief of the Distress in Ireland. Board of Works Series*, p. 74, H.C. 1847 (764), l.
61. NU, Robinson Library Special Collections, Trevelyan Papers, CET/1/16, Charles Trevelyan to Lord Clarendon, 10, 17 July 1847.
62. *Transactions of the Central Relief Committee of the Society of Friends During the Famine in Ireland in 1846 and 1847* (Dublin, 1852), pp 79, 391–3 407, 414. See also: TNA, Russell papers, PRO 30/22/8C/56, J. R. Barry to Lord Clarendon, 2 Jan. 1850.
63. Ibid., pp 190, 480–1.
64. Ibid., pp 80, 83–4, 395, 403–4, 406–8, 410–14; Cork City and County Archives, SM924, Cork Auxiliary Committee, 'Ballycotton Poor Relief Report', 1850.
65. Ibid., p. 414; Thomas Smith Harvey, *Facts from the Fisheries: Contained in Four Quarterly Reports from the Ring, County Waterford* (Waterford, 1848), pp 1–8; Tom O'Donoghue, 'The development of the Ring fishing industry, 1846–1864', in *Decies* 31 (1981), pp 3–14.

66. *Transactions of the Central Relief Committee*, p. 302.
67. *Newry Telegraph*, 16 Oct. 1851; *Downpatrick Recorder*, 18 Oct. 1851; *Galway Vindicator*, 26 May 1852; *Galway Mercury*, 26 June 1852; *King's County Chronicle*, 23 June 1852; *The Ulsterman*, 16 Apr. 1853; *Connaught Watchman*, 27 Apr. 1853. Conflict relating to the use of weirs, seine and draught nets intensified both inshore and at sea in this period. See also: PRONI, Listowel Papers, D585/90, J. Home to M. Hackett, 3 June 1847; University College Cork, Boole Library Special Collections, Bantry House Papers, BL/EP/B/2061, 'Fisheries Mouth of the Glengariff River', Mar. 1848; NLI, Lismore Papers, MS 43,450/ 11, Basil Orpin to Lord Devonshire, 3 Aug. 1850.
68. For inshore conflicts, see: Marilyn Silverman, 'How custom became a crime on the River Nore: cot fishing at Bennettsbridge, 1837–95', in *In the Shadow of the Steeple* 9 (2006), pp 66–85; idem, 'From fisher to poacher: public right and private property in the salmon fishery of the River Nore in the nineteenth century', in Marilyn Silverman and P. H. Gulliver (eds), *Approaching the Past: Historical Anthropology through Irish Case Studies* (New York, 1992), pp 99–141. For Luddites: Kevin Robins and Frank Webster, 'New technology: Luddism and the critique of political economy', in Les Levidow and B. Young (eds), *Science, Technology and the Labour Process*, vol. 2 (London, 1983), pp 9–48; Steven E. Jones, *Against Technology: From the Luddites to Neo-Luddism* (London, 2006), pp 7–8.
69. *The Fourth Annual Report of the Commissioners of Public Works, in re the Fisheries of Ireland*, pp iv–v, H.C. 1846 (713), xxii.
70. Brabazon, *The Deep and Coast Fisheries of Ireland*, p. ix. Complaints of over-fishing directed against trawlers became acute in the coast off Dublin from the 1830s. See for example: NLI, Ms. 13629/1, 'A statement of the fishermen of Baldoyle', Jan. 1833.
71. Robert Longfield, *The Fishery Laws of Ireland* (London, 1863), pp cc–ccv. This geography of Irish Sea technical dominance persisted for over a century up to the internationalisation of Irish fisheries following accession to the European Union's Common Fisheries Policy from 1973. See: D. A. Gilmor, 'Sea fishery expansion in the Republic of Ireland', in *Geography* 57:4 (1972), pp 344–5.
72. NAI, CSORP/1823/620, Henry Townsend to William Gregory, 10 Apr. 1823.
73. *First Report of the Commissioners of Inquiry into the State of the Irish Fisheries: With the Minutes of Evidence and Appendix*, p. 193, H.C. 1837 (22), xxi.
74. *FJ*, 4 July 1846; ibid., 5 July 1848; *Evening Freeman*, 22 July 1852.
75. *SN*, 28 May 1853.
76. *FJ*, 13 Nov. 1852.
77. *DEM*, 28 June 1847.
78. *DEPC*, 23 July 1850.
79. *The Advocate*, 20 Mar. 1850; *DEPC*, 23 July 1850.
80. *DEPC*, 23 July 1850.
81. George Bentinck, *Railways in Ireland: The Speech of the Rt. Hon. Lord George Bentinck* (London, 1847).
82. *Report by Registrar of Joint Stock Companies to Committee of Council for Trade, 1845*, pp 1–51, H.C. 1846 (694), xliii; *Report by Registrar of Joint Stock Companies to Committee of Council for Trade, 1846*, pp 1–20, H.C. 1847 (293), lix; *Report by Registrar of Joint Stock Companies to Committee of Council for Trade, 1847*, pp 1–12, H.C. 1847–48 (339), li; *Report by Registrar of Joint Stock Companies to Committee of Council for Trade, 1848*, pp 1–10, H.C. 1849 (128), l; *Report by Registrar of Joint Stock Companies to Committee of Council for Trade, 1849*, pp 1–10, H.C. 1850 (224), lii; *Report by Registrar of Joint Stock Companies to Committee of Council for Trade, 1850*, pp 1–12, H.C. 1851 (119), liii; *Report by Registrar of Joint Stock Companies to Committee of Council for Trade, 1851*, pp 1–12, H.C. 1852 (147), li; *Report by Registrar of Joint Stock Companies to Committee of Council for Trade, 1852*, pp 1–20, H.C. 1852–53 (216), xcix.
83. TNA, Board of Trade (hereafter BT) 41/323/1866, 'The Irish Fishing Boat Company', 9 Feb. 1846; BT 41/323/1863, 'The Irish Deep Sea Fishing and Irish Coast Fishing Piers and Harbour Association', 12. Feb. 1846; BT 41/323/1867, 'The Irish Fishing and Fishing Boat Company', 6 Nov. 1846; BT/41/155/878, 'The Coast of Ireland Fishing Company', 23 Dec. 1846.
84. George Preston White, *Three Suggestions for the Investment of Capital* (London, 1851), p. 28. For the same argument in similar contemporary publications, see: James Caird, *The Plantation Scheme: or, The West of Ireland as a Field of Investment* (London, 1850), pp 47–53, 157–60; George Ellis, *Irish Ethnology Socially and Politically Considered* (Dublin, 1852), pp 116–17; William Bullock Webster, *Ireland Considered as a Field for Investment or Residence* (Dublin, 1852), pp 55–6.

85. White, *Three Suggestions*, p. 29.
86. For early examples of harbour development through the Consolidated Loan Fund, see for the cases of Skerries and Dún Laoghaire: NAI, CSORP/1818/400, John Galloway to Hans Hamilton, 13 May 1818; CSORP/1819/399, Charles Grant to William Gregory, 23 June 1819.
87. Surrey History Centre, Goulburn papers, 304/A1/2/3/84, William Gregory to Henry Goulburn, 30 Mar. 1822; 304/A1/1/5/73, Arthur Wellesley to Henry Goulburn, 15 May 1823.
88. University of Southampton, Special Collections, Wellington Papers, WP1/195/76, Arthur Wellesley to Charles Lennox, 25 Mar. 1808; NAI, CSORP/1820/243, John Cossart to William Gregory, 30 May 1820; University of Southampton, Special Collections, Wellington Papers, WP1/930/6, Arthur Wellesley to Charles Grant, 5 Apr. 1828; WP1/1054/43, Arthur Wellesley to Henry Goulburn, 19 Oct. 1829.
89. Ibid., WP1/927/4, Charles Grant to Arthur Wellesley, 11 Apr. 1828.
90. *Coms. of Irish Fisheries, Eighth Report, 1826–27*, pp 11, 14, H.C. 1826–27 (487), xi; *First Report of the Commissioners of Inquiry into the State of the Irish Fisheries: With the Minutes of Evidence and Appendix*, p. 23, H.C. 1837 (22), xxi.
91. See the annual reports of the Commissioners of Public Works from: *Public Works, Ireland. The First Report of the Commissioners of Public Works in Ireland*, pp 1–4, H.C. 1831–32 (327), xxiii, to: *Public Works. Fourteenth Annual Report from the Board of Public Works in Ireland*, pp 1–48, H.C. 1847 (762), xvii, inclusive.
92. *An Act to Encourage the Sea Fisheries of Ireland, by Promoting and Aiding with Grants of Public Money, the Construction of Piers, Harbours and other Works* (1846), 9 & 10. Vict., c. 3; *An Act for the Further Improvement of the Fishery Piers and Harbours of Ireland* (1847), 10 & 11 Vict., c. 75.
93. *Fifteenth Annual Report from the Board of Public Works in Ireland 1847*, pp 9–11, H.C. 1847 (847), xvii; *Sixteenth Report from the Board of Public Works, Ireland*, p. 290, H.C. 1847–48 (983), xxxvii; *Seventeenth Report from the Board of Public Works, Ireland*, pp 270–80, H.C. 1849 (1098), xxiii; *Eighteenth Report from the Board of Public Works, Ireland*, pp 184–5, H.C. 1850 (1235), xxv; *Nineteenth Report from the Board of Public Works, Ireland*, pp 158–9, H.C. 1851 (1414), xxv.
94. Kevin O'Rourke and Jeffrey Williamson, *Globalization and History: The Evolution of a Nineteenth-Century Atlantic Economy* (Cambridge, 1999), p. 1.
95. *Shipping. Returns of Sailing Vessels Registered at Each Port of the United Kingdom, Including Isle of Man, &c. in 1845*, pp 1–12, H.C. 1846 (155), xlv; *Shipping ... in 1846*, pp 1–4, H.C. 1847 (308), lx; *Shipping ... in 1847*, pp 1–14, H.C. 1847–48 (241), lx; *Shipping ... in 1848*, pp 1–14, H.C. 1849 (181), li; *Shipping ... in 1849*, pp 1–14, H.C. 1850 (182), lii; *Shipping ... in 1850*, pp 1–14, H.C. 1851 (155), lii; *Shipping ... in 1851*, pp 1–14, H.C. 1852 (218), xlix.
96. *Select Committee on Causes of Shipwrecks. Report, Minutes of Evidence, Appendix, Index*, pp 323, 348, H.C. 1836 (567), xvii; *First Report from the Select Committee on Shipwrecks; Together with Minutes of Evidence, Appendix, and Index*, pp 51–3, H.C. 1843 (549), ix; *Memorial to Admiralty, March 1854, from Inhabitants of Drogheda, Praying for Government Survey of E. Coast of Ireland, for Harbour of Refuge*, p. 2, H.C. 1854–55 (322), xlvii.
97. *Select Committee on Emigrant Ships. First Report, Minutes of Evidence*, pp 1–3, H.C. 1854 (163), xiii; *Report of Investigation into Loss of* Annie Jane, *by Captain F.W. Beechy*, pp 1–85, H.C. 1854 (1724), lx; *Report of Investigation into Loss of* Olinda, *of Liverpool, by Captain W. H. Walker*, pp 1–19, H.C. 1854 (1726), lx; *Report of Investigation into Circumstances attending Loss of Steam-Ship* Erin's Queen, *of Belfast, by Collision with Steam-Ship* Sabrina, *of Cork, by Cmdr. Robertson*, pp 1–11, H.C. 1854–55 (1874), xlvi; *Report of Investigation into Loss of* Morna, *of Belfast, by Cmdr. Robertson*, pp 1–14, H.C. 1854–55 (1904), xlvi; Kevin Kenny, *The American Irish: A History* (London, 2000), p. 101.
98. Frank Neal, 'Liverpool, the Irish steamship companies and the Famine Irish', in *Immigrants and Minorities* 5:1 (1986), pp 28–61.
99. Valerie E. Chancellor, *The Political Life of Joseph Hume, 1777–1855: The Scot who was for over 30 Years a Radical Leader in the British House of Commons* (London, 1986), pp 9–10.
100. Anon., 'Aqueducts and canals: Duke of Bridgewater', in *Quarterly Review* 73 (Mar. 1844), p. 314; Anon., 'Filling up the Irish Channel', in *Hood's Magazine* 6:6 (Dec. 1846), p. 561.
101. For the classic debate on this topic, see: Ronald H. Coase, 'The Lighthouse in economics', in *Journal of Law and Economics* 17 (1974), pp 357–59; David E. van Zandt, 'The lessons of the lighthouse: "government" or "Private" provision of goods', in *Journal of Legal Studies* 22:1 (1993), pp 47–72; Lawrence W. C. Lai *et al.*, 'The political economy of Coase's lighthouse in history (part II):

lighthouse development along the coast of China', in *Town Planning Review* 79:5 (2008), pp 555–79; Laurent Carnis, 'The provision of lighthouses services: a political economy perspective', in *Public Choice* 157:1 (2013), pp 51–6.
102. Sharma Krauskopf, *Irish Lighthouses* (Guilford, 2001), p. 17; David Stevenson, *The World's Lighthouses Before 1820* (Oxford, 1959), p. 87.
103. TNA, PRO 30/9/139, Charles Abbot papers, Thomas Rogers, 'Statement of Irish coastal lighthouses', 7 Sept. 1801; *Report from the Select Committee on Lighthouses; with the Minutes of Evidence, and an Appendix and Index.*, p. lxxiii, H.C. 1834 (590), xii; United Kingdom Hydrographic Office Archive, LTR1/1/1–33, 'Record copies of published volumes of Lights List', 1856–99; *Royal Commission on Lighthouse Administration. Volume II. Minutes of Evidence Taken before the Royal Commission on Lighthouse Administration, with Appendices and Index. Appendix B.VI*, pp 332–36, H.C. 1908 [Cd. 3937], xlix.
104. St John's Point (1845); Roancarrigmore (1847); Dún Laoghaire East (1847); Broadhaven (1848); Ardnakinna Point (1850); Spit bank (1851); Mine Head (1851); Ballycotton (1851); Dún Laoghaire West (1852); Youghal (1852); Old Head of Kinsale (1853); Little Samphire Island (1854); Loophead (1854); Fastnet (1854).
105. *Report of the Commissioners Appointed to Inquire into the Condition and Management of Lights, Buoys, and Beacons*, p. 226, H.C. 1861 (2793), xxv.
106. Ibid.; James Taylor, 'Private property, public interest, and the role of the state in nineteenth-century Britain: the case of the lighthouses', in *Historical Journal* 44:3 (Sept. 2001), p. 767.
107. J. S. Mill, *Principles of Political Economy: With Some of Their Applications*, vol. 2 (London, 1848), p. 546.
108. Theresa Levitt, 'When lighthouses became public goods: the role of technological change', in *Technology and Culture* 61:1 (2020), pp 144–72.
109. Thomas Drummond, 'On the illumination of light-houses', in *Philosophical Transactions of the Royal Society of London* 120 (1830), pp 383–98; *Report from the Select Committee on Lighthouses; Together with the Minutes of Evidence, Appendix, and Index*, p. 332, H.C. 1845 (607), ix; Alexander Mitchell, *On Submarine Foundations, Particularly the Screw-pile and Moorings* (London, 1848), pp 5–61; John Tyndall, 'A story of our lighthouses', in *Nineteenth Century* 24 (1888), pp 61–80. For two scholarly case studies, see: Frank A. J. L. James, '"The civil engineer's talent": Michael Faraday, science, engineering and the English lighthouse service, 1836–1865', in *Transactions of the Newcomen Society* 70 (1998), pp 153–60; Roy MacLeod, 'Science and government in Victorian England: lighthouse illumination and the Board of Trade, 1866–1886', in *Isis* 60:1 (1969), pp 4–38.
110. As in the case of lighthouses, see: Lai, 'The political economy of Coase's lighthouse', p. 577; Carnis, 'The provision of lighthouses services', p. 55; Erik Lindberg, 'From private to public provision of public goods: English lighthouses between the seventeenth and nineteenth centuries', in *Journal of Policy History* 25:4 (2013), pp 553–4.
111. Although influenced by commercial and municipal figureheads, the board came under sustained criticism for its exclusion of certain mercantile and shipping interests. See: *Tidal Harbours Commission. Second Report of the Commissioners, with Minutes of Evidence, Appendices, Supplement and Index*, p. 43a, H.C. 1846 (692), l.
112. Harcourt, 'Charles Wye Williams', p. 152.
113. For lighthouses and shipping lanes, see: Eric Tagliacozzo, 'The Lit archipelago: coast lighting and the imperial optic in insular southeast Asia, 1860–1910', in *Technology and Culture* 46:2 (2005), p. 328.
114. Patrick N. Wyse Jackson, 'Alexander Nimmo's "On The Application of the Science of Geology to the Purposes of Practical Navigation" (1825): the first investigation of marine geology and its bearing on the geology of offshore south west British Isles', in *Earth Sciences History* 15:2 (1996), pp 167–71; Alexander Nimmo, *New Piloting Directions for St George's Channel and the Coast of Ireland* (London, 1832); *Navy Estimates for the Year 1846–47*, p. 17, H.C. 1846 (51), xxvi; *Index to Report on the Navy Estimates, from the Select Committee on Navy, Army, and Ordnance Estimates*, p. 764, H.C. 1846–48 (555), cdxxix.
115. *Tidal Harbours Commission. First Report of the Commissioners*, p. xvi, H.C. 1845 (665), xvi.
116. *Report from the Select Committee on the Harbours of Refuge with the Minutes of Evidence*, p. v, H.C. 1836 (334), xx. For similar emphasis but in relation to the English Channel, see: *Report of the Commissioners upon the Subject of Harbours of Refuge*, p. 13, H.C. 1845 (611), xvi.
117. *Report from Select Committee on London and Dublin Roads*, pp 1–4, H.C. 1836 (427), xxi; *Second Report of the Commissioners Appointed to Consider and Recommend a General System of Railways for*

Ireland, p. 223, H.C. 1837–38 (145), xxxv; *Select Committee on Post Office Communication with Ireland*, p. 6, H.C. 1842 (373), ix; *First Report of the Select Committee on Shipwrecks, 1843*, p. 48, H.C. 1843 (549), ix.
118. *Holyhead Harbour Commission. Copy of the Minutes of the Evidence Taken Before the Commissioners Appointed to Inquire into Mr. Rendel's Plan for the Proposed Harbour at Holyhead*, p. 10, H.C. 1847 (516), xvi; Mervyn Hughes, 'Telford, Parnell and the Great Irish Road', in *Journal Transport History* 4 (1963), pp 199–208.
119. *Treasury Minute, April 1846, Relative to Formation of Harbour at Holyhead, and Agreements with Chester and Holyhead Railway Company to Contribute Towards Harbour*, pp 2–3, H.C. 1847 (140), lxi; *Holyhead and Portdynllaen Harbours. Further Copies of all Reports not yet Laid Before Parliament, on the Comparative Merits of Holyhead and Portdynllaen as a Harbour of Refuge for the Channel Trade*, pp 3, 9, 14, H.C. 1846 (553), xlv; *Report of the Select Committee on Holyhead Harbour Bill; with Minutes of Evidence*, p. 61, H.C. 1847 (546), viii. For the relevant annual votes, see: *The Finance Accounts I.—VIII. of the United Kingdom of Great Britain and Ireland, for the Year 1845, Ended Fifth January 1845*, p. 125, H.C. (144), xxv; *The Finance Accounts I.—VIII. ... 1846*, p. 122, H.C. 1847 (220), xxxiv; *The Finance Accounts I.—VIII. ... 1847*, p. 120, H.C. 1847–48 (201), xxxix; *The Finance Accounts I.—VIII. ... 1848*, p. 116, H.C. 1849 (153), xxx; *The Finance Accounts I.—VIII. ... 1849*, p. 115, H.C. 1850 (169), xxx; *The Finance Accounts I.—VIII. ... 1851*, p. 114, H.C. 1851 (136), xxxi; *The Finance Accounts I.—VIII. ... 1852*, p. 103, H.C. 1852 (196), xxviii; *The Finance Accounts I.—VIII. ... 1852*, p. 102, H.C. 1852–53 (275), lvii.
120. Edward Parry, *Parry's Railway Companion from Chester to Holyhead* (London, 1848), p. 16; *Holyhead Harbour Commission. Explanation of Chart of Proposed Site for Harbour, Showing the Results of the Examination of the Bottom*, pp 32–3, H.C. 2847 (446), xvi.
121. Philip Lloyd, 'The Chester and Holyhead railway and its political impact on North Wales and British policy towards Ireland, 1835–1900' (unpublished Ph.D. thesis, University of York, 2017), pp 126–7.
122. Amos Shartle Hershey, *The Essentials of International Public Law* (London, 1915), p. 217; J. D. Davies, '"Great Neptunes of the main": myths, mangled histories and 'maritime monarchy' in the Stuart navy, 1603–1714', in J. D. Davies, Alan James and Gijs Rommelse (eds), *Ideologies of Western Naval Power,* c.*1500–1815* (London, 2019), p. 107.
123. Peter Hession, 'Imagining the railway revolution in pre-Famine Ireland: technology, governance and the Drummond Commission, 1832–39', in Richard Butler (ed.), *Dreams of the Future in Nineteenth-Century Ireland* (Liverpool, 2021), pp 258-82.
124. Chris Otter, 'Making liberalism durable: vision and civility in the late Victorian city', in *Social History* 27:1 (2002), p. 3.
125. Christopher Hamlin, 'Environment and disease in Ireland', in Virginia Berridge and Martin Gorsky (eds.) *Environment, Health, and History* (London, 2011), p. 46.
126. Kinealy, *Charity and the Great Hunger*, p. 9; eadem, *A Death-Dealing Famine: The Great Hunger in Ireland* (London, 1997), p. 149.
127. Paul Robbins, *Political Ecology: A Critical Introduction* (Oxford, 2020), p. vii.

SECTION II: CHARITY AND PHILANTHROPY

'The Metropolis of the Poor': Charity and Perceptions of Dublin on the Eve of the Great Famine

1. *Charitable Institutions (Dublin). Copy of a Letter From the Under Secretary to the Lord Lieutenant… to the Commissioners Appointed to Report on Certain Charitable Institutions in Dublin*, p. 5, H.C. 1842 (337), xxxviii, 11.
2. Richard Rodger, *Transformation of Edinburgh: Land, Property and Trust in the Nineteenth Century* (Cambridge, 2001), p. 21; Robert J. Morris, 'Philanthropy and poor relief in 19th-century Edinburgh: the example of a capital city without a national government', in *Mélanges de l'Ecole française de Rome. Italie et Méditerranée* 111:1 (1999), pp 367–79.

3. David Dickson, 'Death of a capital? Dublin and the consequences of Union', in *Proceedings of the British Academy* 107 (2001), p. 115; David Dickson, *Dublin: The Making of a Capital City* (London, 2014), chapters six and seven. Dickson's arguments heavily influenced this chapter.
4. For similar ideas about how events for scientific bodies affected towns' reputations, see Louise Miskell, 'Meeting places: the Scientific Congress and the host town in the south-west of England, 1836–1877', in *Urban History* 39:2 (2012), pp 246–62.
5. Graeme Morton, 'The boundaries of civil society in a stateless nation: governing of nineteenth-century Edinburgh. Civil society in the stateless nation', in *Mélanges de l'Ecole Français de Rome, Italie et Méditerranée* 111:2 (1999), pp 763–4. He specifically used 'stateless capital' in an abstract for his paper 'Scotland's disgrace: negotiating governance in the shadow of empire' at the 'Conflicted Cities Workshop/Conference' held at Trinity College Dublin on 7 June 2014: https://conflictedcities.wordpress.com/abstracts/ (accessed 26 Jan. 2020).
6. Rosemary Sweet, *The English Town 1680–1840: Government, Society and Culture* (Harlow, 1999), pp 220–28.
7. Helen M. Rapport, 'Edinburgh and Glasgow: civic identity and rivalry 1752–1842', unpublished PhD Thesis (University of Stirling, 2012), pp 10–12.
8. Simon Gunn, 'Ritual and civic culture in the English industrial city, *c.*1835–1914', in Robert J. Morris and Richard H. Trainor (eds), *Urban Governance: Britain and Beyond since 1750* (Aldershot, Hampshire and Burlington, VT, 2000), pp 226–41.
9. Richard J. Butler, '"The radicals in these Reform times": politics, grand juries, and Ireland's unbuilt assize courthouses, 1800–50', in *Architectural History* 58 (2015), pp 109–39.
10. Thomas Chalmers, *The Christian and Civic Economy of Large Towns: Volume I* (3 vols, Glasgow, 1821); see also chapter three in S. J. Brown, *Thomas Chalmers and the Godly Commonwealth in Scotland* (Oxford, 1983).
11. R. J. Morris, 'Civil society and the nature of urbanism: Britain 1750–1850', in *Urban History* 25:3 (1998), pp 297–9.
12. Robert J. Morris, 'Governance: two centuries of urban growth', in Morris and Trainor (eds), *Urban Governance*, pp 3–7, 12.
13. Maria Luddy, *Women and Philanthropy in Nineteenth-Century Ireland* (Cambridge, 1995).
14. For example, Martin Gorsky, 'Mutual aid and civil society in nineteenth-century Bristol', in *Urban History* 25:3 (1998), p. 314.
15. *The Scotsman*, 26 Dec. 1818; *The Witness*, 3 Mar. 1841; *Dublin Evening Mail*, 27 May 1840; *DMR*, 25 July 1842.
16. For example, John James McGregor, *The New Picture of Dublin: Comprehending a History of the City …* (Dublin, 1821); John Stark, *Picture of Edinburgh: Containing a Description of the City …* (3rd edn., Edinburgh, 1823); Thomas Oliver, *A New Picture of Newcastle Upon Tyne …* (Newcastle-upon-Tyne, 1831). See David Dickson, 'Town and city', in Eugenio F. Biagini and Mary E. Daly (eds), *The Cambridge Social History of Modern Ireland* (Cambridge, 2017), pp 112–28, at pp 112–13.
17. Graeme Morton, 'Civil society, municipal government and the state: enshrinement, empowerment and legitimacy. Scotland, 1800–1929', in *Urban History* 3:3 (1998), pp 348–67; Morris, 'Philanthropy and poor relief in 19th-century Edinburgh', pp 367–79.
18. Morris, 'Philanthropy and poor relief', *passim*.
19. Rapport, 'Edinburgh and Glasgow', pp 9–10.
20. Peter Gray, *The Making of the Irish Poor Law, 1815–1843* (Manchester and New York, 2009), pp 67–70.
21. Rapport, 'Edinburgh and Glasgow', pp 9–10; Rebecca Madgin and Richard Rodger, 'Inspiring capital? Deconstructing myths and reconstructing urban environments, Edinburgh, 1860–2010', in *Urban History*, 40:3 (2013), pp 507–8.
22. David Dickson, 'Second city syndrome: reflections on three Irish cases', in S. J. Connolly (ed.), *Kingdoms United? Great Britain and Ireland Since 1500: Integration and Diversity* (Dublin and Portland, OR, 1999), pp 95–6, 106–7.
23. Alice Johnson, *Middle-Class Life in Victorian Belfast* (Liverpool, 2020), pp 303–4.
24. Kildare-Place Society.
25. *Thom's Irish Almanac … for the Year 1845* (Dublin, 1845).
26. Compare praise by the ultra-Protestant *DEM* (9 Apr. 1824) and mocking descriptions in the liberal *FJ* (14 May 1835).

27. Jacinta Prunty, *Dublin Slums, 1800–1925: A Study in Urban Geography* (Dublin and Portland, OR, 1998), pp 33, 197–9; William J. Jackson, '"The Collector will call": controlling philanthropy through the annual reports of the Royal Infirmary of Edinburgh, 1837–1856', in *Accounting History Review* 22:1 (2012), p. 56.
28. For example, *Poor Inquiry (Ireland). Appendix (C.) – Part II. Report on the City of Dublin* ..., pp 28, 30, H.C. 1836 [Cd 35], xxx, 254, 256. In Edinburgh regional societies composed of natives of particular counties or regions living in Edinburgh were established. These often had the aim of supporting charities operating in the regions in order to prevent poor people from migrating from these areas to Edinburgh. See examples in *Oliver and Boyd's New Edinburgh Almanac ... for 1845* (Edinburgh, 1845). For a discussion of the aims of one of these societies, see the meeting of the Edinburgh Aberdeenshire Club in *The Scotsman*, 3 Mar. 1831.
29. Gray, *Making of the Irish Poor Law*, pp 188–91.
30. The authors were politician George Alexander Hamilton, and the bankers David Charles La Touche and John Barlow. The report was one of several commissioned during the nineteenth century to investigate why some Dublin charities received annual grants from parliament. See chapter five in Joseph Simon Curran, 'Civil society in the stateless capital: charity and authority in Dublin and Edinburgh *c.*1815–1845', unpublished PhD Thesis (University of Edinburgh, 2017).
31. Police Commissioners' minutes, 10 Aug. 1836 (Edinburgh City Archives, ED009/1/8, 1834–1838), pp 320–2.
32. Many Catholic charities in particular tended to be missing from Dublin's 'almanac' record': *1845 Thom's; 1845 Oliver and Boyd.*
33. *Oliver and Boyd.*
34. R. J. Morris, 'Urban associations in England and Scotland, 1750–1914: the formation of the middle class or the formation of a civil society', in Graeme Morton *et al.* (eds), *Civil Society, Associations and Urban Places: Class, Nation and Culture in Nineteenth-Century Europe* (Aldershot and Burlington, VT, 2006), pp 139–58.
35. Chapter Three in Curran, 'Civil society in the stateless capital'.
36. Martin Gorsky, *Patterns of Philanthropy: Charity and Society in Nineteenth-Century Bristol* (Suffolk and Rochester, New York, 1999), pp 39–47.
37. See, for example, criticisms in *The Scotsman*, 31 Jan. 1835.
38. Rodger, *Transformation*, pp 12, 111–14.
39. Morris, 'Philanthropy and poor relief', pp 377–8.
40. *Oliver and Boyd*, p. 509.
41. For a discussion of these processes, see Rodger, *Transformation*, pp 111–15.
42. Morris, 'Philanthropy and poor relief', pp 377–8. See also Frank Walker, 'National romanticism and the architecture of the city', in George Gordon (ed.), *Perspectives of the Scottish City* (Aberdeen, 1985), pp 126–33.
43. *Poor Inquiry (Ireland). Appendix (C.), Part II. Report on the City of Dublin*, pp 66–8, 75–6. Christine Casey and Newman Foundation (Dublin, Ireland) Library, *Dublin: The City within the Grand and Royal Canals and the Circular Road with the Phoenix Park* (London and New Haven. 2005), pp 565, 681–2, 684.
44. T. Moorhead, *A Short History of Sir Patrick Dun's Hospital* (Dublin, 1942), pp 55–7, 65.
45. T. Percy C. Kirkpatrick, *The History of Doctor Steevens' Hospital, Dublin, 1720–1920* (Dublin, 1924), pp 128–9.
46. Moorhead, *Dun's*, p. 57; Kirkpatrick, *Steevens'*, pp 225–6.
47. Casey and Newman Foundation, *Dublin: The City*, pp 162–6, 681–2, 684.
48. *FJ*, 9 May 1845.
49. *London to Dublin: With a Trip to the Irish Lakes and the Mountains of Connamara* [*sic*] ... (London and Dublin, [1853]), p. 162.
50. Casey and Newman Foundation, *Dublin: The City*, pp 565–6, 641.
51. Ibid., pp 252, 458–9, 552.
52. Dickson, 'Death of a capital?', pp 117–18.
53. Ibid., p. 125.
54. Mendicity Society minutes, quoted in Audrey Woods, *Dublin Outsiders: A History of Mendicity Institution 1818–1998* (Dublin, 1998), p. 46.
55. Maurice Craig, *Dublin 1660–1860* (London, 1952), p. 136.

56. Mary E. Daly, 'Catholic Dublin: the public expression in the age of Paul Cullen', in Dáire Keogh and Albert McDonell (eds), *Cardinal Paul Cullen and His World* (Dublin, 2011), pp 130–45.
57. Craig, *Dublin*, pp 291–4; Casey and Newman Foundation, *Dublin: The City*, pp 53–6; Niamh Nic Ghabhann, '"A development of practical Catholic Emancipation": the laying of the foundations for the Roman Catholic urban landscape, 1850–1900', in *Urban History* 46:1 (2019), pp 48–50.
58. *FJ*, 4 Aug. 1857.
59. https://www.buildingsofireland.ie/buildings-search/building/50060276/mater-hospital-dublin-city (accessed 26 Jan. 2020).
60. J. G. Kohl, 'Scotland', in idem, *Ireland, Scotland, and England* (London, 1844), p. 18; *Oliver and Boyd 1845*, p. 514.
61. Kohl, 'Scotland', pp 17–18.
62. See, for example, the *FJ*'s description (10 May 1837) of the annual bazaar for the House of Refuge held in the Rotunda. The newspaper noted that the previous day the 'attendance' had been 'fashionable in the extreme' and on the following day 'the Gardens are to thrown open for a promenade. A military band will attend. We anticipate a brilliant display of fashion.' See also: *The Scotsman*'s description of a 'Grand Dress Promenade' held for the benefit of several Edinburgh charities whose attendance included 'a liberal sprinkling of our local aristocracy': *The Scotsman*, 17 Mar. 1841. See also comments in *The Scotsman*, 6 Sept. 1834, 24 Sept. 1843.
63. Gorsky, *Patterns*, p. 205.
64. *A Short Account of the Institution for the Education of Deaf and Dumb Children of the Poor Established on the 25th June 1810 …* (Edinburgh, 1814); *The Scotsman*, 3 July 1839; *Third Report of the National Institution for the Education of the Deaf and Dumb. Established in Dublin, May 18, 1816 …* (Dublin, 1819); *FJ*, 21 Feb. 1820.
65. *Caledonian Mercury*, 6 June 1844.
66. For an example of the influence of a similar ceremony from slightly later in Dublin, see Nic Ghabhann, '"A development of practical Catholic Emancipation"', pp 54–5.
67. Lesley Whiteside, *A History of the King's Hospital* (2nd edn., Dublin, 1985), *passim*.
68. Rosa Mulholland Gilbert (ed.), *Calendar of Ancient Records of Dublin in the Possession of the Municipal Corporation of Dublin Volume XVIII* (Dublin, 1907), pp 548–9.
69. Gilbert (ed.), *Calendar of Ancient Records of Dublin … Volume XVIII*, pp 236–7, 548–9.
70. Rosa Mulholland Gilbert (ed.), *Calendar of Ancient Records of Dublin in the Possession of the Municipal Corporation of Dublin Volume XIX* (Dublin, 1944), pp 354, 360.
71. King's Hospital board minute book, 24 Apr. 1828, pp 242–3 (King's Hospital Archive, MS 11 K.H); ibid., 10 June 1829, p. 237.
72. *FJ*, 10 May 1828.
73. *FJ*, 5 May 1828.
74. Ciarán McCabe, *Begging, Charity and Religion in Pre-Famine Ireland* (Liverpool, 2018), pp 103–5.
75. Woods, *Dublin Outsiders*, pp 89–90.
76. Ibid., p. 116.
77. *FJ*, 22 Aug. 1839.
78. *FJ*, 16 July 1844. See also O'Connell's speeches at Dublin's Catholic orphan societies: *FJ*, 10 Jan. 1844, 27 Nov. 1838.
79. For contemporary press comment on this report, see *MR*, 15 July 1842; *FJ*, 15 July 1842; *DEM*, 18 July 1842.
80. For a detailed discussion of these grants, see: Joe Curran, 'Charity, finance, and legitimacy: exploring stateless-capital status in early nineteenth-century Dublin and Edinburgh', in *Journal of Urban History*, online edition 29 Sept. 2019.
81. *Charitable Institutions (Dublin)* (1842), p. 8.
82. Patrick Joyce, *The Rule of Freedom, Liberalism and the Modern City* (London and New York, 2003), pp 150–6.
83. Gray, *The Making of the Irish Poor Law*, pp 296–7, 300–301, 311, 314–315, 322–324.
84. Rosalind Mitchison, *The Old Poor Law in Scotland: The Experience of Poverty, 1574–1845* (Edinburgh, 2000), pp 214–15; Stephanie Blackden, 'The board of supervision and the Scottish Parochial Medical Service, 1845-95', in *Medical History* 30 (1986), pp 145–8.

The Impact of the Great Famine on Voluntary Charitable Societies in Dublin City

1. Frank Corrigan, 'Dublin workhouses during the Great Famine', in *Dublin Historical Record* 29 (1976), pp 59–65; Helen Burke, *The People and the Poor in Nineteenth-Century Ireland* (Dublin, 1987); Jacinta Prunty, *Dublin Slums, 1800–1925: A study in Urban Geography* (Dublin, 1998), pp 227–31; Timothy W. Guinnane and Cormac Ó Gráda, 'Mortality in the North Dublin Union during the Great Famine', in *Economic History Review* 55:3 (2002), pp 487–506; Sinéad Collins, *Balrothery Poor Law Union, County Dublin, 1839–1851* (Dublin, 2005).
2. This chapter focuses on charities that provided direct material assistance to the poor, thus excluding medical, educational and (expressly) missionary charities.
3. Timothy P. O'Neill, 'The charities and famine in mid-nineteenth-century Ireland', in Jacqueline Hill and Colm Lennon (eds), *Luxury and Austerity. Historical Studies XXI. Papers Read Before the 23rd Irish Conference of Historians, Held at St Patrick's College., Maynooth, 16–18 May 1997* (Dublin, 1999), pp 137–46.
4. Fergus D'Arcy, *Raising Dublin, Raising Ireland: A Friar's Campaigns. Father John Spratt, O. Carm. (1796–1871)* (Dublin, 2018), pp 201–23.
5. Deirdre Lindsay, *Dublin's Oldest Charity: The Sick and Indigent Roomkeepers' Society 1790–1990* (Dublin, 1990), pp 29–30; Audrey Woods, *Dublin Outsiders: A History of the Mendicity Institution 1818–1998* (Dublin, 1998), pp 122–31.
6. Cormac Ó Gráda, 'Famine in Dublin city', in idem, *Black '47*, pp 157–93.
7. W. E. Vaughan and A. J. Fitzpatrick (eds), *Irish Historical Statistics: Population, 1821–1971* (Dublin, 1978), p. 28.
8. Thomas Willis, *Facts Connected with the Social and Sanitary Condition of the Working Classes in the City of Dublin* (Dublin, 1845), p. 31.
9. Prunty, *Dublin Slums*, pp 17–61.
10. Ibid., pp 109–18.
11. *FJ*, 5 Dec. 1846.
12. *FJ*, 4 Jan. 1847. Here, the 'mendicity' refers to the Mendicity Association's premises on Usher's Island.
13. Ibid.
14. Patrick Lynch and John Vaizey, *Guinness's Brewery in the Irish Economy, 1759–1876* (Cambridge, 1960), pp 165–7.
15. See, for example, Christine Kinealy and Gerard MacAtasney, *The Hidden Famine: Poverty, Hunger, and Sectarianism in Belfast, 1840–50* (London, 2000).
16. See, for example, [Robert Perceval], *An Attempt Toward a Plan for Rendering the Charitable Institutions of Dublin More Effective by Cooperation* (Dublin, 1818).
17. For all of the aforementioned statistical data, see Ciarán McCabe, '"The Going out of the Voluntary and the Coming in of the Compulsory": the Impact of the 1838 Irish Poor Law on Voluntary Charitable Societies in Dublin City', in *Irish Economic and Social History* 45:1 (2018), pp 47–69, at p. 65.
18. *FJ*, 21 Feb. 1845.
19. *Waterford Mail*, 8 Aug. 1838; *Twenty-Seventh Annual Report of the Managing Committee of the Association for the Suppression of Mendicity in Dublin, for the Year 1844* (Dublin, 1845), pp 12–13.
20. *Appendices A to C. to the Tenth Report of the Poor Law Commissioners*, Appendix B, p. 313, H.C. 1844 [Cd 589], xix, 331; Guinnane and Ó Gráda, 'Mortality in the North Dublin Union', pp 487–506, esp. at p. 494.
21. The figures for 1845 and 1846 were 23,887 and 30,342 people, respectively. See *FJ*, 21 Jan. 1846 & 23 Jan. 1847.
22. *FJ*, 23 Jan. 1847.
23. Ibid., 19 Jan. 1849.
24. Ibid., 23 Jan. 1852.
25. Peter Gray, 'National humiliation and the Great Hunger: fast and famine in 1847', in *Irish Historical Studies* 32:126 (Nov. 2000), pp 193–216. See also Ó Gráda, 'Famine in Dublin city', p. 185.
26. The noticeable decline in income between 1839 and 1841 was a direct result of the introduction of the Poor Law, which was funded through compulsory rates on property holders, many of whom subsequently reduced or ceased their voluntary charitable donations. For a discussion of this issue in

the context of Dublin's charities, see: McCabe, '"The going out of the voluntary and the coming in of the compulsory"', *passim*.
27. *Thirty-First Annual Report of the Managing Committee of the Association for the Suppression of Mendicity in Dublin. For the year 1848* (Dublin, 1849), p. 21. Figures have been rounded to the nearest pound.
28. For a small sample, see: *SN*, 7 Nov. 1846 (Sick and Indigent Roomkeepers' Society); *The Pilot*, 13 Jan. 1847 (Sisters of Mercy's House of Mercy); *FJ*, 4 Apr. 1848 (St Kevin's conference of SVP).
29. Lindsay, *Dublin's Oldest Charity*, pp 34–5.
30. *FJ*, 11 Dec. 1848.
31. *FJ*, 24 Apr. 1849. For a more detailed description of the panorama, see *Dublin Evening Post*, 19 Apr. 1849.
32. See Curran, above, p. 32.
33. Máire Ní Chearbhaill, 'Charity, church and the Society of St Vincent de Paul', in Colm Lennon (ed.), *Confraternities and Sodalities in Ireland: Charity, Devotion and Sociability* (Dublin, 2012), pp 169–85.
34. *Report of the Proceedings of the Society of St. Vincent de Paul, in Ireland, During the Year 1848* (Dublin, n.d. [*c.*1848]), p. 14; *The Pilot*, 2 Jan. 1849.
35. *FJ*, 21 Apr. 1847.
36. Ibid., 15 Oct. 1846.
37. The other charities named were both nondenominational organisations that attracted the support of Catholic clergymen — the Mendicity Association and the Sick and Indigent Roomkeepers' Society. See: *FJ*, 5 Dec. 1846.
38. *FJ*, 11 Dec. 1848.
39. For a discussion of these themes, see: Ciarán McCabe, *Begging, Charity and Religion in Pre-Famine Ireland* (Liverpool, 2018), pp 6–10; Virginia Crossman, *Poverty and the Poor Law in Ireland, 1850–1914* (Liverpool, 2013), pp 12–32; Lindsey Earner-Byrne, *Letters of the Catholic Poor: Poverty in Independent Ireland, 1920–1940* (Cambridge, 2017), pp 18–19, 29–31.
40. *Society of St. Vincent de Paul. Council of Ireland. The Circular of the President General of the 21st November, 1846. To Which is Appended, the Letter of the President of the Council of Ireland, on 9th February, 1847* (Dublin, 1847), p. 23.
41. For Aylward, see Jacinta Prunty, *Margaret Aylward 1810–1889: Lady of Charity, Sister of Faith* (Dublin, 1999).
42. Ibid., p. 23.
43. *Ladies' Association of Charity of St. Vincent de Paul. Under the Patronage of His Grace the Lord Archbishop. The First Annual Report* (Dublin, 1852), p. 13.
44. *Weekly Freeman's Journal*, 7 Aug. 1852.
45. *Ladies' Association of Charity, of St Vincent de Paul. Under the Patronage of His Grace the Lord Archbishop. The First Annual Report* (Dublin, 1852), p. 20.
46. Prunty, *Margaret Aylward*, pp 40–55; eadem, 'Battle plans and battlegrounds: Protestant mission activity in the Dublin slums, 1840s–1880s', in Crawford Gribben and Andrew R. Holmes (eds), *Protestant Millennialism, Evangelicalism and Irish Society, 1790–2005* (Basingstoke, 2006), pp 119–43; Margaret H. Preston, *Charitable Words: Women, Philanthropy, and the Language of Charity in Nineteenth-Century Dublin* (Wesport, CT, 2004), pp 67–99; Miriam Moffitt, *The Society for Irish Church Missions to the Roman Catholics, 1849–1950* (Manchester, 2010).
47. Dublin Parochial Association minute book, n.d., f. 1v (R.C.B.L., Dublin Parochial Association papers, MS 129.1.1).
48. Dublin Parochial Association minute book, 29 Mar. 1847. See also Ó Grada, 'Famine in Dublin city', pp 185–7.
49. *Dublin Evening Post*, 16 Jan. 1847; *Southern Reporter and Cork Commercial Courier*, 21 Jan. 1847.
50. *Banner of Ulster*, 23 Mar. 1847.
51. *WDWM*, 3 July 1847.
52. Cormac Ó Gráda, 'Mass migration as disaster relief', in idem, *Ireland's Great Famine: Interdisciplinary Perspectives* (Dublin, 2006), p. 121. See also David Dickson, *Dublin: The Making of a Capital City* (London, 2014), pp 308, 317.
53. For migration into Famine-era Cork, see: *Dublin Evening Post*, 11 Feb. 1847. For Belfast, see: Jonathan Bardon, *Belfast: An Illustrated History* (Belfast, 1983), p. 97.

54. 'A table of the population of Church and Barrack Street', n.d. [*c*.1817] (NAI, Chief Secretary's Office Official Papers, OP 474/8); F. Barker and J. Cheyne, *An Account of the Rise, Progress, and Decline of the Fever Lately Epidemical in Ireland, Together with Communications from Physicians in the Provinces, and Various Official Documents* (2 vols, London, 1821), ii, pp 159–64.
55. Guinnane and Ó Gráda, 'Mortality in the North Dublin Union', pp 494–5.
56. North Dublin Union Board of Guardians minutes, 14 Apr. 1847, cited in Prunty, *Dublin Slums*, p. 287. See also *FJ*, 15 Apr. 1847. According to one North Dublin Union guardian, 'the night asylum in Bow-street, where infected people crowded together, and rambled about the city the next day, was calculated to spread disease': *FJ*, 6 May 1847.
57. Ó Gráda, 'Famine in Dublin city', p. 179; *Dublin Hospitals. Statements of the Number of Persons Relieved During each of the last Three Years Ending 31 December 1851, in each of the Dublin Hospitals …*, p. 4, H.C. 1852 (121), xlvii, 248. The hospital's average intake rose from 744 in 1842–7 to approximately 1,000 in 1848–52.
58. Maurice Craig, *Dublin 1660–1860* (reprint, Dublin, 1980), p. 309.
59. Prunty, *Dublin Slums*, p. 229; *Appendices B. to F. to the Eighth Annual Report of the Poor Law Commissioners*, Appendix E, p. 385, H.C. 1842 [Cd 399], xix, 397.
60. *SN*, 9 Mar. 1846.
61. *FJ*, 21 Feb. 1845.
62. Woods, *Dublin Outsiders*, pp 129–30.
63. D'Arcy, *Raising Dublin, Raising Ireland*, p. 205.
64. *SN*, 26 Oct. 1846.
65. McCabe, '"The going out of the voluntary and the coming in of the compulsory"', pp 50, 60–1.
66. For this society and the split, see Ciarán McCabe, 'The early years of the Strangers' Friend Society, Dublin: 1790–1845', in *Bulletin of the Methodist Historical Society of Ireland* 19 (2014), pp 65–93.
67. *SN*, 23 Oct. 1846.
68. *The Pilot*, 13 Jan. 1847.
69. Dublin Mendicity Association minute book, 23 Nov. 1847 (NLI, MS 32,599/6).
70. Ibid., 16 Dec. 1848. The Mendicity Association had raised concerns in its annual report for 1844 of the limitations on access to workhouse services, given that access was not granted every day of the week: *FJ*, 21 Feb. 1845.
71. Woods, *Dublin Outsiders*, pp 111–12. A motion to discuss the need for statutory anti-vagrancy measures was defeated at the Mendicity Association's 1845 annual meeting, owing to procedural objections: *FJ*, 21 Feb. 1845. For the Sick and Indigent Roomkeepers' Society, see: Lindsay, *Dublin's Oldest Charity*, p. 27.
72. *Hansard 3*, xlii, 695 (30 Apr. 1838) (Colonel Edward Conolly); ibid., 697 (Sir Edward Sugden); ibid., 714 (Lord Edward Stanley); Peter Gray, *The Making of the Irish Poor Law, 1815–43* (Manchester, 2009), pp 302–03, 327.
73. [Nassau Senior], 'Mendicancy in Ireland', in *Edinburgh Review* 77:156 (Apr. 1843), p. 392; *Report of the Select Committee on the State of the Poor in Ireland; Being a Summary of the First, Second and Third Reports of Evidence Taken Before that Committee: Together with an Appendix of Accounts and Papers*, p. 23, H.C. 1830 (667), vii, 23; *Third Report of the Commissioners for Inquiring into the Condition of the Poorer Classes in Ireland*, p. 27, H.C. 1836 [C 43], xxx, 27. In his second report on the proposed Irish Poor Bill, Nicholls advised as to the necessity of vagrancy clauses, either within the Poor Law itself or by way of a separate enactment, writing: 'To establish a Poor Law, without at the same time suppressing mendicancy, would be very imperfect legislation, especially with reference to the present condition of the Irish people': *Second Report of Geo. Nicholls, Esq., to Her Majesty's Principal Secretary of State for the Home Department, on Poor Laws, Ireland*, p. 28, H.C. 1837–38 [C 104], xxxviii, 684.
74. *Hansard 3*, xlii, 695 (30 Apr. 1838) (Colonel Edward Conolly).
75. *Mendicancy, Ireland. Resolutions Passed by Boards of Guardians in Ireland, Relative to the Suppression of Mendicancy and Vagrancy*, H.C. 1840 (168), xlviii, 357. See also Gray, *Making of the Irish Poor Law*, pp 302–03; McCabe, *Begging, Charity and Religion*, pp 57–8, 114–18.
76. *FJ*, 2, 4 Mar. 1847.
77. *The Pilot*, 1 Mar. 1847.
78. Vagrancy Act, 10 & 11 Vict., c. 84, s. 2, 3 (22 July 1847).
79. Mendicity Association minute book, 22 Feb. 1848 (NLI, MS 32,599/6).

80. This quote is from a 1711 edition of *The Spectator*: McCabe, *Begging, Charity and Religion*, p. 114. Also, ibid., pp 114–18.
81. McCabe, *Begging, Charity and Religion*, pp 85–92, 114–18.
82. Dublin Mendicity Association minute book, 10 July 1848 (NLI, MS 32,599/6).
83. Ibid., 20 Feb 1849. These 3,000 beggars comprised approximately 1,800 males and 1,200 females, and no further information is available as to the number of children among these totals: *FJ*, 20 Feb. 1849. See also Ó Gráda, 'Famine in Dublin city', pp 187–91.
84. Elizabeth Dooley, 'Sir Walter Crofton and the Irish or intermediate system of prison discipline', in Ian O'Donnell and Finbar McAuley (eds), *Criminal Justice History: Themes and Controversies from Pre-Independence Ireland* (Dublin, 2003), p. 198; Ó Gráda, 'Famine in Dublin city', p. 187. The new prisons opened during the Famine years were the bridewells in Ballina and Swinford (County Mayo), Ballybay and Clones (County Monaghan), Newtownards (County Down), Castletowndelvin (County Westmeath) and Tinahealy (County Wicklow): Cf. *Prisons of Ireland. Twenty-Fourth Report of the Inspectors-General on the General State of the Prisons of Ireland, 1845; With Appendices*, p. 92, H.C. 1846 [C 697], xx, 348 and *Prisons of Ireland. Twenty-Ninth Report of the Inspectors-General on the General State of the Prisons of Ireland, 1850; with Appendices*, p. 117, H.C. 1851 [C 1364], xxviii, 493. See also Richard J. Butler, *Building the Irish Courthouse and Prison: A Political History, 1750–1850* (Cork, 2020), pp 308–24.
85. See Crowley, above, p. 104.
86. *FJ*, 21 Apr. 1848.
87. *Thirty-Second Annual Report of the Managing Committee of the Association for the Suppression of Mendicity in Dublin. For the Year 1849* (Dublin, 1850), p. 12.
88. The Vagrancy Act remained the primary statute governing police powers in the curtailment of street begging until it was struck down by the High Court in 2007 as being unconstitutional; street begging is now regulated by the Criminal Justice (Public Order) Act 2011.

Quakers and the Famine in Dublin

1. For further reading on Quakers in Ireland see Maurice Wigham, *The Irish Quakers*, (Dublin, 1992).
2. Henry van Etten, *George Fox and the Quakers* (London, 1959), p. 32.
3. Wigham, *The Irish Quakers*, pp 61–62; Hannah Maria Wigham, *A Christian Philanthropist of Dublin – a memoir of Richard Allen* (Dublin, 1886), pp 20–37.
4. Isabel Grubb, *Irish Quakers* (Cork, 2018), p. 1.
5. Richard S. Harrison, 'Irish Quakers in flour milling', in Andy Bielenberg (ed.), *Irish Flour Milling – a history, 600-2000* (Dublin, 2003), pp 86–103.
6. *A Map of Friends Meetings in Ireland 1794*, no cartographer or printer given; author's collection. This map is also available in the Friends Historical Library, Dublin.
7. The work of the Quaker community during the Great Famine is documented in a number of works, notably Helen E. Hatton, *The Largest Amount of Good – Quaker Relief in Ireland 1654–1921* (Montreal, 1993); Christine Kinealy, *Charity and the Great Hunger in Ireland – the Kindness of Strangers* (London and New York, 2013) and Rob Goodbody, *A Suitable Channel: Quaker Relief in the Great Famine* (Bray, 1995).
8. Records of the Society of Friends are held in the Friends Historical Library, Stocking Lane, Dublin 16. Many of the records relating to Ulster are held in Lisburn Meeting House, Co. Antrim. The Religious Society of Friends in Ireland is an all-Ireland body.
9. Yearly Meetings Committee minute book (Friends Historical Library, Dublin (FHLD), YM D4); Leinster Quarterly Meeting minute book (FHLD, QM1/A5).
10. The records of the CRC and its various committees remained in the offices of Pim Brothers, where the committee was based at the end of the Famine. In the early twentieth century, the records were lodged in the Public Record Office and are now held in the National Archives of Ireland, Bishop Street, Dublin. Some other papers relating to the Famine, such as publications and family correspondence, are held in the Friends Historical Library, Dublin.
11. Monkstown Preparative Men's Meeting minutes, 9 May 1847 (FHLD, PM Dub II A1). There is no mention of the Famine in the Women's Meeting minutes.
12. For a fuller account of the Quaker relief efforts throughout Ireland, see Goodbody, *Suitable Channel*.

13. *Transactions of the Central Relief Committee of the Society of Friends during the Famine in Ireland* (Dublin, 1852), p. 34.
14. *The Anglo Celt*, 1 Jan. 1847.
15. Central Relief Committee (CRC) minute book no. 1, 24 Dec. 1846 (NAI, 2.506.2 (IA 42 139)).
16. Ibid., 22 Apr. 1847.
17. CRC accounts of freight (NAI, 507 4 (1A 42 38)).
18. *Transactions of the Central Relief Committee of the Society of Friends During the Famine in Ireland* (reprint, Dublin, 1996), appendix XIII, pp 370–1.
19. Ibid., appendix XXVIII, pp 472–3.
20. CRC, Ulster Subcommittee, 26 May 1847 (NAI, 2 505 25 (1A 42 118)).
21. CRC account book, Jan. 1847 (NAI, 2.205.22); ibid., 8 May and 24 Oct. 1848 (2.506.38).
22. J. B. Leslie and D. W. T. Crooks, *Clergy of Tuam, Killala and Achonry – Biographical Succession Lists* (Belfast, 2008), p. 589.
23. CRC Leinster subcommittee (NAI, 2.505.25).
24. Clothing delivery book no. 1 (NAI, 2.505.22).
25. Ibid.; CRC account book (NAI, 2.506.38).
26. Jacinta Prunty, *Dublin Slums 1800–1925: A Study in Urban Geography* (Dublin, 1999), pp 205–30.
27. William Bennett, *Narrative of a Recent Journey of Six Weeks in Ireland* (London and Dublin, 1847), p. 5.
28. CRC Committee book no. 1, 26 Nov. 1846 (NAI, 2.506.2 (1A 42 139)).
29. Ibid., 24 Dec. 1846; Griffith's Valuation.
30. Proceedings of Charles Street Soup Committee, 16, 20 Jan. 1847 (NAI, 2.506.5 (1A 42 162)).
31. Ibid.
32. Ibid., 22, 26 Jan., 2 Feb. 1847.
33. Ibid., 22, 26 Jan., 2, 23 Feb. 1847.
34. Ibid., 26 Jan., 2 Feb. 1847.
35. Ibid., 2 Mar. 1847.
36. Ibid., 2, 9, 17, 23 Mar., 11 May 1847.
37. Kinealy, *Charity and the Great Hunger in Ireland*, p. 66.
38. *Transactions*, p. 54.
39. Proceedings of Charles Street Soup Committee, 6, 13 July 1847, 15 Feb. 1848.
40. *Transactions*, p. 359.
41. Hatton, *The Largest Amount of Good*, p. 140.
42. *Transactions*, p. 54.

SECTION III: INSTITUTIONS, HEALTHCARE AND MORTALITY

Childbirth and Maternity in Dublin, 1831–56

1. Lombe Atthill, *Recollections of an Irish Doctor* (London, 1911), pp 133–4.
2. Ibid., p. 133.
3. Ibid., p. 128.
4. Ibid., p. 138.
5. An Act to Amend and Render More Effectual an Act Made in the Parliament of Ireland in the Fifth Year of His Present Majesty, entitled "An Act for Erecting and Establishing Public Infirmaries or Hospitals in this Kingdom", 1805 (45 Geo. III, c. 111).
6. Laurence M. Geary, *Medicine and Charity in Ireland 1718–1851* (Dublin, 2004), pp 45–69.
7. The term 'accoucheur' was replaced by the modern term 'obstetrician' around the 1860s.
8. Geary, *Medicine and Charity*, p. 136; Catherine Cox, 'Access and engagement: The medical dispensary service in post-famine Ireland', in Catherine Cox and Maria Luddy (eds), *Cultures of Care in Irish Medical History 1750-1970* (Basingstoke, 2010), pp 57–78.
9. For example, dispensaries in Thomastown, Co. Kilkenny, Dunmore and Loughrea, Co. Galway, Bantry and Aghada, Co. Cork and Naas, Co. Kildare were among dispensaries that did not entitle

mothers to obstetric care: *First Report from His Majesty's Commissioners for Inquiring into the Condition of the Poor Classes in Ireland. Appendix B*, pp, 4, 9, 24, H.C. 1835 (369), xxxii, 4, 9, 24.
10. *The Census of Ireland for the Year 1851. Part III. Report on the Status of Disease*, pp 94–5, H.C. 1854 [Cd 1765], lviii, 98–9.
11. Linda A. Pollock, 'Embarking on a rough passage: the experience of pregnancy in early modern society', in Valerie Fildes (ed.), *Women as Mothers in Pre-Industrial England* (London, 1990), pp 39–67; Patricia Crawford, 'The construction and experience of maternity in seventeenth-century England', in ibid., pp 3–38; Adrian Wilson, 'The ceremony of childbirth and its interpretation', in ibid., pp 68–107; Adrian Wilson, 'Participant or patient? Seventeenth-century childbirth from the mother's point of view', in Roy Porter (ed.), *Patients and Practitioners: Lay Perceptions of Medicine in Pre-Industrial Society* (Cambridge, 1986), pp 129–44; Clodagh Tait, 'Safely delivered: Childbirth, wet-nursing, gossip-feasts and churching in Ireland *c.*1530–1690', in *Irish Economic and Social History* 30 (2003), pp 1–23.
12. T. P. C. Kirkpatrick and H. Jellett, *The Book of the Rotunda Hospital* (London, 1913); O'Donel T. D. Browne, *The Rotunda Hospital, 1745-1947* (Edinburgh, 1947); Ian Campbell Ross, *Public Virtue, Public Love. The Early Years of the Dublin Lying-In Hospital* (Dublin, 1986); Alan Brown (ed.), *Masters, Midwives and Ladies-In-Waiting: The Rotunda Hospital 1745–1995* (Dublin, 1995); Gary A. Boyd, *Dublin 1745–1922. Hospitals, Spectacle & Vice* (Dublin, 2006); J. K. Feeney, *The Coombe Lying-In Hospital* (Dublin, 1980); Tony Farmar, *Holles Street, 1894–1994: The National Maternity Hospital: A Centenary History* (Dublin, 1994).
13. John Fleetwood, 'Dublin private medical schools in the nineteenth century', in *Dublin Historical Record* 36:1 (spring, 1993), pp 31–45; G. T. Hayden, *A Lecture, Introductory to a Course on Midwifery and the Diseases of Females and Children, Delivered at the Anglesey Lying-In Hospital* (Dublin, 1832); https://wellcomecollection.org, accessed 12 Nov. 2019; *The Dublin Almanac and General Registry of Ireland for the Year 1835* (Dublin, 1835), p. 299.
14. *Dublin Almanac, 1835*, p. 301
15. S. Cusack, 'Report of the Wellesley Female Institution', in *The Dublin Hospital Reports and Communications in Medicine and Surgery* 5 (Dublin, 1830), pp 494–524. Diseases of females included gynaecological and obstetric disorders.
16. *The Dublin Almanac and General Registry for Ireland* (Dublin, 1847), p. 346
17. John Fleetwood, 'The Kingstown Lying-In Hospital 1842–1871', in *Dun Laoghaire Journal* 6 (1997), pp 8–11.
18. *The Dublin Almanac for 1835*, p. 299
19. *The Dublin Almanac for 1835*, p. 299; *The Dublin Almanac for the Year 1847*, pp 346–8; *A Sermon Preached for the Benefit of the South-Eastern Lying-In Hospital in St. Peter's Church, Dublin, on Sunday, 27 October 1844* (Dublin, 1845); *An Appeal on Behalf of the Western Lying-in Hospital and Dispensary* (Dublin, 1845); *FJ*, 10 Oct. 1846.
20. Edward Sinclair and George Johnston, *Practical Midwifery Comprising an Account of 13,748 Deliveries which Occurred in the Dublin Lying-In Hospital during a Period of Seven Years Commencing 1847* (London, 1858).
21. An Act for the Better Regulation of the House of Industry Hospitals and other Hospitals in Dublin Supported Wholly or In Part by Parliamentary Grants, 1856 (19 & 20 Vict., c. 110).
22. Cormac Ó Gráda, 'Dublin's demography in the early nineteenth century: evidence from the Rotunda', in *Population Studies* 45:1 (Mar. 1991), pp 43–54.
23. Sinclair & Johnston, *Practical Midwifery.*
24. Peter Gray, *The Making of the Irish Poor Law, 1815–43* (Manchester, 2009).
25. Geary, *Medicine and Charity.*
26. Maria Luddy, *Women and Philanthropy in Nineteenth-Century Ireland* (Cambridge, 1995); Maria Luddy, *Prostitution and Irish Society, 1800–1940* (Cambridge, 2007); Virginia Crossman, *Poverty and the Poor Law in Ireland 1850-1914* (Liverpool, 2013), chapter six.
27. Julia Ann Bergin, 'Birth and death in Dublin's nineteenth-century lying-in hospitals', in Elaine Farrell (ed.), *'She Said She Was in the Family Way': Pregnancy and Infancy in Modern Ireland* (London, 2012), pp 91–114.
28. Denis Phelan, *A Statistical Inquiry into the Present State of the Medical Charities of Ireland; with Suggestions for a Medical Poor Law, by Which They May be Rendered Much More Extensively Efficient* (Dublin, 1835).
29. Ibid., p. 310

30. The Royal Commission for Inquiring into the Condition of the Poorer Classes in Ireland.
31. *First Report, Poor Inquiry, 1835 Appendix A*, pp 296, 313, 338, 346, H.C. 1835 (369), xxxii, 312, 329, 354, 362; *First Report, Poor Inquiry, 1835, Appendix B, Part I*, pp 2, 8, 54, 109, 202, 261.
32. *First Report, Poor Inquiry, 1835, Appendix B*, p. 46.
33. Rotunda Hospital Male and Female Pupil's Book, 1833–61 (NAI, Rotunda Archives, BR/DUB 22).
34. *First Report From His Majesty's Commissioners, Appendix (B), General Report*, p. 46. There was no guarantee that male practitioners had midwifery training. A diploma in midwifery was not compulsory for Poor Law medical officers until the second Medical Act which was passed in 1886.
35. Gray, *The Making of the Irish Poor Law*, pp 112–30; Niall Ó Ciosáin, 'The Poor Inquiry and Irish society – a consensus theory of truth', in *Transactions of the Royal Historical Society* 20 (Dec. 2010), pp 127–39; An Act for the More Effectual Relief for the Destitute Poor in Ireland, 1838 (37 & 38 Vict., c. 96).
36. *Report of the Poor Law Commissioners, on Medical Charities, Ireland, Pursuant to the 46th Section of the Act 1 & 2 Victoria, c. 56*, p. 5, H.C. 1841, session 1 [Cd 324], xi, 1; Cox, 'Access and Engagement', pp 66–70.
37. *Report from the Select Committee on Medical Charities, Ireland; together with the Minutes of Evidence, Appendix, and Index*, p. 183, H.C. 1843 (412), x, 197.
38. Ó Gráda, 'Dublin's demography', pp 44, 46.
39. *First Report from His Majesty's Commissioners, Appendix (C), Part II*, p. 73.
40. Ibid., p. 73.
41. 'The general and statistical report upon the principal charitable institutions in the city of Dublin not receiving parliamentary aid', *Poor Inquiry (Ireland). Appendix (C.)—Part II*, p. 101, H.C. 1836 [Cd 35], xxx, 327.
42. Ibid., p. 104.
43. Thomas Willis, *Facts Connected with the Social and Sanitary Condition of the Working Classes in the City of Dublin with Tables of Sickness, Medical Attendance, Deaths, Expectations of Life &c. &c. Together with Some Gleanings from the Census Returns of 1841* (Dublin, 1845), p. 14.
44. *The Dublin Almanac for 1847*, p. 348.
45. *Report from the Select Committee on Dublin Hospitals together with the Proceedings of the Committee, Minutes of Evidence, Appendix and Index*, pp 185–6, H.C. 1854 (338), xii, 203–04.
46. Ibid., p. 42.
47. *Statement of Numbers of Persons Relieved in Dublin Hospitals, 1849–51 viz: – The Richmond Surgical, The Hardwicke Fever, The Whitworth Medical, Stevens, The Meath, The Cork-Street Fever, The Westmorland Lock, The Lying-in and The Hospital for Incurables*, p. 5, H.C. 1852 (121), xlvii, 245.
48. Philomena Gorey, 'Managing midwifery in Dublin: practice and practitioners, 1700–1800', in Margaret H. Preston and Margaret Ó hÓgartaigh (eds.), *Gender and Medicine in Ireland 1700–1950* (Syracuse, NY, 2012), pp 123–37; eadem, 'Puerperal fever in Dublin: the case of the Rotunda Lying-In Hospital', in Lisa Marie Griffith and Ciarán Wallace (eds.), *Grave Matters. Death and Dying in Dublin, 1500 to the Present* (Dublin, 2016), pp 46–60; Lombe Atthill 'On Metria (so-called puerperal fever)', in *British Medical Journal* 2:1180 (Aug. 1883), p. 260; Arthur V. Macan, 'Report of the Rotunda Hospital for the year ending November 1883', in *The Dublin Journal of Medical Science* 70 (June 1884), pp 481–94.
49. Henry Maunsell, *The Dublin Practice of Midwifery* (London, 1834); Fleetwood Churchill, *On the Diseases of Women Including those of Pregnancy and Childbed* (London, 1843); Fleetwood Churchhill, *On the Theory and Practice of Midwifery* (6th edn, London, 1872).
50. Robert Collins, *A Practical Treatise of Midwifery Containing the Results of 16,654 Births, Occurring in the Dublin Lying-In Hospital, During a Period of Seven Years, Commencing November 1816*, (London, 1835); Alfred McClintock and Samuel Hardy, *Practical Observations on Midwifery and the Diseases Incident to the Puerperal State* (Dublin, 1848); Sinclair & Johnston, *Practical Midwifery*.
51. *The Dublin Almanac and General Registry of Ireland for the year 1849* (Dublin, 1849), p. 376.
52. For a survey on the introduction of anaesthesia into childbirth, see David Caton, *What a Blessing She Had Chloroform. The Medical and Social Response to the Pain of Childbirth from 1800 to the Present* (New Haven, CT, 1999); for auscultation, see McClintock and Harvey, *Practical Observations on Midwifery*, pp 85–6.
53. Churchill, *On the Theory and Practice of Midwifery*, pp 344–73, 424–64.

54. *Report from the Select Committee on Dublin Hospitals*, p. 40, H.C. 1854 (338), xii, 56.
55. *Charitable Institutions, Dublin. Reports of the Commissioners Appointed by the Lord Lieutenant of Ireland to Report on Certain Charitable Institutions in the City of Dublin: viz. 1. The Lying-in Hospital; 2. Dr. Steevens' Hospital; 3. Fever Hospital, Cork Street; 4. The Hospital of Incurables; 5. The Westmorland Lock Hospital; and 6. The House of Industry*, pp 5–6, H.C. 1830 (7), xxvi, 5–6.
56. *Dublin Almanac, 1835*, p. 299.
57. Henry Maunsell, 'Report of the obstetric practice of the Wellesley Female Institution During the Year 1832', in *Edinburgh and Surgical Journal* 40:117 (1833), pp 293–303.
58. Ibid., p. 297
59. Ibid.
60. Ó Gráda, 'Dublin's Demography', p. 49.
61. Luddy, *Prostitution and Irish Society*, pp 3–5, 41–54; Luddy, *Women and Philanthropy*, pp 3, 98–101.
62. Sinclair & Johnston, *Practical Midwifery*, p. 454.
63. Maunsell, 'Report of the Obstetric Practice of the Wellesley Female Institution', pp 298, 299, 301.
64. Henry Maunsell, 'Report of the Obstetric Practice at the Wellesley Female Institution during the Year 1833', in *Dublin Journal of Medical and Chemical Science* 5:8 (1834), pp 367–80.
65. Ibid., pp 372, 375.
66. Thomas Edward Beatty, 'First Report of the New Lying-in Hospital, Dublin, for the Year 1834', in *Dublin Journal of Medical and Chemical Science* 8:12 (1836), pp 66–96.
67. Ibid., p. 69.
68. Ibid., p. 70.
69. Ibid., pp 75–6.
70. Ibid., p. 72.
71. Ibid., p. 77.
72. Ibid., p. 78.
73. Both bacterial infections were caused by the Beta Haemolytic Streptococcus, Lancefield Group A. See Gorey, 'Puerperal fever in Dublin', pp 51–4. The germ theory of disease was not widely accepted until the 1850s. See Christopher Hamlin, 'Predisposing causes and public health in early nineteenth-century thought', in *The Society for the Social History of Medicine* 5:1 (1992), pp 43–70; Irvine Loudon, *The Tragedy of Childbed Fever: an International Study of Maternal Care and Maternal Mortality, 1800–1950* (Oxford, 2000), pp 111–24; Christine Hallett, 'The attempt to understand puerperal fever in the eighteenth and early nineteenth centuries; the influence of the inflammation theory, in *Medical History* 49:1 (Jan. 2005), pp 1–28.
74. *Report of the Western Lying-in Hospital and Dispensary, 25 Arran-Quay for the Year 1845* (Dublin, 1836), pp 1–11.
75. Fleetwood Churchill, 'The third medical report of the Western Lying-In Hospital and Dispensary, 31, Arran-Quay', in *The Dublin Journal of Medical Science* 15:1 (1838), pp 179–88; Fleetwood Churchill, 'The fourth medical report of the Western Lying-In Hospital and Dispensary, 31, Arran-Quay', in *Edinburgh Medical and Surgical Journal* 53:143 (Apr. 1840), pp 394–9; Fleetwood Churchill and R. D. Speedy, 'Medical report of the Western Lying-In Hospital and Dispensary, 25, Arran Quay, for the years 1841–42' in *Dublin Journal of Medical Science* 23 (July, 1843), pp 393–400.
76. Churchill and Speedy, 'Medical report of the Western Lying-In Hospital', p. 393.Medical Report Hospital and
77. 'Appeal on behalf of the Western Lying-In Hospital and Dispensary', in *Report of the Western Lying-In Hospital*, p. 8.
78. *Report, SC, Dublin Hospitals* (1854), p. 40. 'Chronic Cases' were those women who suffered from disorders of the reproductive system or mothers who were transferred to gynaecological wards on discharge. Bergin has argued that this was an attempt to conceal morbidity after delivery most likely caused by puerperal fever. See Bergin, 'Birth and death', p. 106.
79. Sinclair & Johnston, *Practical Midwifery*, p. 9.
80. Bergin, 'Birth and death', p. 39; Sinclair & Johnston, *Practical Midwifery*, p. 16.
81. Alfred McClintock, 'An account of the late epidemic of puerperal fever at the Dublin Lying-In Hospital', in *Dublin Journal of Medical Science* 27:2 (1845), pp 212–22.
82. Sinclair & Johnston, *Practical Midwifery*, p. 544.
83. Lombe Atthill, 'On Metria (so-called puerperal fever)', in *British Medical Journal*, 2:1180 (11 Aug. 1883), p. 260; Loudon, *Death in Childbirth*, pp 49–84.

84. Sinclair & Johnston, *Practical Midwifery*, pp 62–5.
85. R. Mayne, 'Observations of the late epidemic dysentery in Dublin', in *Dublin Quarterly Journal of Medical Science* 7:14 (May 1849), pp 294–308.
86. Ibid., p. 308.
87. Sinclair & Johnston, *Practical Midwifery*, p. 562.
88. Ibid., p. 456.
89. Ibid., p. 61.
90. Ibid., p. 69.
91. Ibid., p. 70. See also, Crossman, *Poverty and the Poor Law in Ireland,* pp 181–6.
92. Sinclair & Johnston, *Practical Midwifery*, p. 70.
93. Phelim Boyle and Cormac Ó Gráda, 'Fertility trends, excess mortality and the Great Irish Famine', in *Demography* 23:4 (Nov. 1986), pp 534–62.
94. An Act to Provide for the Better Distribution, Support and Management of Medical Charities in Ireland; and to Amend an Act of the Eleventh Year of Her Majesty, to Provide for the Execution of Laws for the Relief of the Poor in Ireland, 1851 (14 & 15 Vict., c. 68); Geary, *Medicine and Charity*, pp 210–16.
95. *Medical Charities Ireland. First annual report of the Commissioners for administering the laws for the relief of the poor in Ireland, under the Medical Charities Act, 14 & 15 Vic., c.68,* Appendix B, No. 1, pp 103, 109, 157, H.C. 1852–3 [Cd 1609], l, 325.
96. Ibid., p. 91
97. *Medical Charities Ireland. Third Annual Report of the Commissioners for Administering the Laws for the Relief of the Poor in Ireland, Under the Medical Charities Act, 14 & 15 Vic., c. 68*, p. xiii, H.C. 1854–5 [Cd 1908], xvi, 193.
98. *Report of the Commissioners Appointed to Inquire into the Hospitals of Dublin with Appendices*, H.C. 1856 [Cd 2063], xix, 115.
99. Ibid., pp 5, 18.
100. Ibid., p. 8.
101. Ibid., p. 23.
102. An Act for the Better Regulation of the House of Industry Hospitals and Other Hospitals in Dublin Supported Wholly or in Part by Parliamentary Grants, 1856 (19 & 20 Vict., c. 110).
103. *First Annual Report of the Board of Superintendence of Dublin Hospitals, with Appendices*, p. 11, H.C. 1857–8 [Cd 2353], xxiii, 533.
104. *Nineteenth Annual Report of the Board of Superintendence of Dublin hospitals, with Appendices*, pp 8–9, H.C.1878 [Cd 1936], xl, 499.
105. Bergin, 'Birth and death', p. 94.
106. Fleetwood, 'The Kingstown Lying-in Hospital'.
107. T. P. C. Kirkpatrick, 'The schools of medicine in Dublin in the nineteenth century', in *The British Medical Journal* 2:3784 (July 1933), pp 109–12; Fleetwood, 'Dublin private medical schools', pp 31–4.

'Items in the Sum of that Great Calamity': Suicide in Dublin During the Great Famine

1. Emile Durkheim, *Suicide: A Study in Sociology*, trans. John A. Spaulding and George Simpson (London, 2000); Olive Anderson, *Suicide in Victorian and Edwardian England* (Oxford, 1987); Victor Bailey, *'This Rash Act': Suicide in the Victorian City* (Stanford, 2000).
2. Bailey, '*This Rash Act*', pp 15–33.
3. Durkheim, *Suicide*, pp 138, 246.
4. Durkeim, *Suicide*, p. 138. Italy, Spain, Germany, Switzerland, Austria, the Low Countries, Ireland, northern Europe and Russia all experienced famine at some point during the nineteenth century: Guido Alfani and Cormac Ó Gráda (eds), *Famine in European History* (Cambridge, 2017), p. 10.
5. Cormac Ó Gráda, 'Famine, trauma and memory' in *Bealoideas* 69 (2001), p. 140.
6. *The Census of Ireland for the Year 1851. Part V. Tables of Deaths. Vol II. Containing the Tables and Index*, pp 209, 217, H.C. 1856 [Cd 2087-I], xxix, 213, 221 (20 of those occurring in the county and 74 in the city limits, i.e. between the Royal and Grand Canals on the north and south of the river Liffey).

7. *The Census of Ireland for the Year 1851. Part V. Tables of Deaths. Vol. I. Containing the Report, Tables of Pestilence, and Analysis of the Tables of Death*, p. 279, H.C. 1856 [Cd 2053], xxix, 543.
8. Diane Miller Sommerville, *Aberration of Mind: Suicide and Suffering in the Civil War-Era South* (Chapel Hill, NC, 2018) pp 17, 23–48.
9. Ó Gráda, 'Famine, trauma and memory', p. 141.
10. Timothy W. Guinnane and Cormac Ó Gráda, 'Mortality in the North Dublin Union during the Great Famine', in *Economic History Review* 55:3 (2002), pp 487–506.
11. Simon Gallaher, 'Grim scars of the Great Hunger: orphaned and abandoned children in the workhouses during the 1850s and 1860s', in Christine Kinealy, Jason King and Gerard Moran (eds), *Children and the Great Hunger in Ireland* (Hamden, CT, 2018), pp 51–73; Melinda Grimsley-Smith, 'Revisiting a 'demographic freak': Irish asylums and hidden hunger', in *Social History of Medicine* 25:2 (May 2012), pp 307–23; Stuart McLean, *The Event and Its Terrors: Ireland, Famine, Modernity* (Stanford, 2004).
12. R. V. Comerford, 'Grievance, scourge or shame? The complexity of attitudes to Ireland's Famine' in Christian Noack, Lindsay Janssen and R. V. Comerford (eds), *Holodomor and Gorta Mór: Histories, Memories and Representations of Famine in Ukraine and Ireland* (London, 2012), p. 52.
13. Ó Gráda, 'Famine, trauma and memory', p. 133.
14. Comerford, 'Grievance, scourge or shame?', pp 52–5.
15. *FJ*, 18 Jan. 1847.
16. Ó Grada, 'Famine, trauma and memory', p. 123. On microhistory, see Lindsey Earner-Byrne, 'The rape of Mary M.: a microhistory of sexual violence and moral redemption in 1920s Ireland', in *Journal of the History of Sexuality* 24:1 (2015), pp 75–98.
17. Thomas Laqueur, 'Bodies, details and the humanitarian narrative', in Lynn Hunt (ed.), *The New Cultural History* (Berkeley, 1989), pp 176–204. For more on how death and dead bodies can remake communities, see Thomas Laqueur, *The Work of the Dead: A Cultural History of Mortal Remains,* (Princeton, 2015), pp 1–28.
18. James Kelly, 'Suicide in eighteenth-century Ireland', in James Kelly and Mary Ann Lyons (eds), *Death and Dying in Ireland, Britain and Europe: Historical Perspectives* (Dublin, 2013), pp 95–142.
19. Riikka Miettinen, *Suicide, Law, and Community in Early Modern Sweden,* (Basingstoke, 2019), pp 119, 138.
20. Durkheim, *Suicide*, p. 246.
21. Ibid., pp 248–9.
22. Ibid., p. 251
23. David Lederer, 'Suicide statistics as moral statistics: suicide, sociology and the state' in Kelly and Lyons (eds), *Death and dying*, pp 232–4; idem, 'Sociology's "one law": moral statistics, modernity, religion, and German nationalism in the suicide studies of Adolf Wagner and Alexander von Oettingen', in *Journal of Social History* 46:3 (spring, 2013), pp 684–99.
24. *FJ*, 19 Mar. 1846.
25. The rate of suicide in 1845 was less than 1 per 100,000 (calculation based on 1841 population of 8,199,953).
26. Breandán Mac Suibhne, *Subjects Lacking Words: The Gray Zone of the Great Famine,* (Harmen, CT, 2017), p. 16.
27. Ó Grada, 'Famine, trauma and memory', p. 129.
28. Jason King, 'Finding a voice: Irish Famine orphan Robert Walsh's search for his younger sister', in Kinealy *et al.* (eds), *Children and the Great Hunger*, pp 123–38.
29. *FJ*, 7 Nov. 1846.
30. *Dublin Medical Press,* 10 Nov. 1847.
31. *FJ*, 17 June 1848.
32. Ibid., 2 Apr. 1847
33. *The Pilot,* 2 Apr. 1847. For more on 'unfortunate' as a moniker applied to prostitutes during the nineteenth century, see Maria Luddy, *Prostitution in Ireland, 1800–1925* (Cambridge, 2007), p. 17.
34. *Census of Ireland, 1851. Part V. Tables of Deaths. Vol. I.*, p. 314; *Twenty-First Annual Report of the Registrar General for Ireland, 1884* [Cd 4538], H.C. 1884-85, xvii, 887; Lisa Shortall, 'Instances of death in infancy and childhood in the inquest casebooks of James Dillon, King's County Coroner, 1836-1859', in *Offaly Heritage*, 10 (2018), pp 134–67.
35. Geo IV, c. 52 [U.K.] (*Felo de Se Act*) (1822).

36. Michael J. Clark, 'General practice and coroners' practice: medico-legal work and the Irish medical profession, *c.*1830–*c.*1890', in Catherine Cox and Maria Luddy (eds), *Cultures of Care in Irish Medical History, 1750–1970* (Basingstoke, 2010), pp 37–56.
37. In Longford there was no coroner from November 1842 until August 1847, and Meath was deficient until June 1842: *Census of Ireland, 1851. Part V. Tables of Deaths. Vol. II*, p. 144; *Census of Ireland, 1851. Part V. Tables of Deaths. Vol. I*, p. 406.
38. Christine Kinealy, *The Great Irish Famine: Impact, Ideology and Rebellion*, (Basingstoke, 2002), p. 147.
39. *Census of Ireland, 1851. Part V. Tables of Deaths. Vol. I*, p. 406.
40. There were seven British Army Barracks in Dublin in 1847: *Thom's Directory, 1847* (Dublin, 1846), p. 799.
41. *FJ*, 7 Oct. 1847.
42. Ibid.
43. *FJ*, 7 Oct. 1847.
44. Ibid., 23 Aug. 1845.
45. Ibid.
46. Georgina Laragy, 'Suicide and insanity in post-Famine Ireland', in Cox & Luddy (eds), *Cultures of Care*, pp 79–91; eadem, '"A peculiar species of felony": suicide, medicine and the law in Victorian Britain and Ireland', in *Journal of Social History* 46:3 (spring, 2013), pp 732–43.
47. Bailey, *'This rash act'*, p. 80. Bailey found that wealthier individuals were often more likely to have their suicides concealed by ambiguous verdicts.
48. Georgina Laragy, 'Locating investigations into suicidal death in urban Ireland, 1901–1915' in eadem, Olwen Purdue and Jonathan Jeffrey Wright (eds), *Urban Spaces in Nineteenth-Century Ireland* (Liverpool, 2018), pp 154–71.
49. *FJ*, 18 Jan. 1847. Bardin's name is spelled 'Barden' in the *FJ* in reporting around this case. However, in most other records related to the individual, his name is spelled 'Bardin'. It also appears as 'Bardon' on occasion. For the purposes of this article I am confining myself to 'Bardin'.
50. Details of the duties of the water-bailiff can be found at *Municipal Corporations (Ireland). Appendix to the First Report of the Commissioners. Report on the city of Dublin. Part I*, p. 16, H.C. 1835 [C 25], xxviii, 98.
51. *FJ*, 6 Mar. 1846. See also ibid., 9 Dec. 1845.
52. Ibid., 18 Jan. 1847.
53. Ibid., 9 Jan. 1847.
54. Ciarán McCabe, *Begging, Charity and Religion in Pre-Famine Ireland* (Liverpool, 2018), p. 128. St Nicholas Without, vestry minute books, 1820–50 (Representative Church Body Library). Bardin (spelled Bardon) is listed as a Roman Catholic and 'repealer' in the *Dublin Improvement Bill. Appendix to the Report of Abraham Hayward, Esq. Q. C., and Charles Peter Brassington, Esq., Land Surveyor, Surveying Officers*, p. 14, H.C. 1847 (275), xxvi, 142. See also: Stefanie Jones, 'Dublin reformed: the transformation of the municipal governance of a Victorian city, 1840–1860' (unpublished PhD thesis, Trinity College, Dublin, 2002), vol. 1, pp 39–40.
55. *FJ*, 14 Jan. 1847.
56. Ibid., 25 Jan. 1847.
57. Frank Cullen, *Dublin 1847: City of the Ordnance Survey* (Dublin, 2015), p. 85. It was finally removed in the later part of the century and converted into the present St Patrick's Park.
58. The other alleyways mentioned above were part of the block of housing facing Bardin's home.
59. *FJ*, 18 Jan. 1847. These are Bardin's words paraphrased at the inquest.
60. McCabe, *Begging, Charity and Religion*, p. 15; *FJ*, 6 Mar. 1846; see also *FJ*, 9 Dec. 1845. He sold tickets for dinners in aid of the St Nicholas of Myra Orphan Fund.
61. McCabe, *Begging, Charity and Religion*, p. 7.
62. 'City of Dublin', held by Ordnance Survey Ireland; published by University College Dublin Library http://digital.ucd.ie/view/ucdlib:40861, accessed 17 Feb. 2020.
63. Aesenath Nicholson, *Annals of Ireland* (1847), p. 45.
64. Nicholson, *Annals*, p. 45.
65. David Dickson, *Dublin: The Making of a Capital City* (London 2014), p. 317.
66. Raymond J. Raymond, 'Dublin: The Great Famine', in *Dublin Historical Record* 33: 3 (June 1980), p. 101; *Dublin, Part III, 1756 to 1847*, Irish Historic Towns Atlas (IHTA), no. 26, (Dublin, 2014),

p. 9, digital version https://s3-eu-west-1.amazonaws.com/assets.ria.ie/ihta/ihta-digital/towns-in-19th-century/Dublin+part+III/IHTA_26_Dublin_Part3_Text.pdf, accessed 19 June 2019.
67. Mary E. Daly, 'Famines and famine relief, 1740–2000', in Eugenio Biagini and Mary E. Daly (eds), *The Cambridge Social History of Modern Ireland,* (Cambridge, 2017), p. 43.
68. *FJ*, 9 Jan. 1847.
69. Christine Kinealy, *Apparitions of Death and Disease: The Great Hunger in Ireland,* (Harmen, CT, 2015), p. 17.
70. Dublin Corporation minutes, 21 Jan. 1847 (Dublin City Library and Archives, C2/A1/13).
71. Ibid. It is not clear whether he resigned from the committee entirely or purely from his role as a visiting officer.
72. Bardin owned a 'size, hair and neat's foot oil and bone factory' at 30 Patrick Street where he also lived. In 1854 Bardin's widow was listed at the same address from which she operated the same business so it is unclear the extent of Bardin's business failure: Thom's Directory, 1847 (Dublin, 1846), p. 798; Thom's Directory, 1858 (Dublin, 1854), p. 1409. He owned 30, 31 and 32 Patrick Street in 1847, and paid cess and minister's money on all three properties: (St Nicholas Without vestry minute book).
73. *FJ*, 18 Jan. 1847.
74. Ó Gráda, *Ireland's Great Famine: Interdisciplinary Perspectives* (Dublin, 2006), p. 218.
75. Ibid., p. 220.
76. MacSuibhne, *Subjects Lacking Words,* p. 10.
77. Fear of contagious disease did appear in discussions around burial during this period: *FJ*, 26 Apr. 1848.
78. Dominick LaCapra, *Writing History, Writing Trauma* (Baltimore, MD, 2014), preface, p. x.
79. Mac Suibhne, *Subjects Lacking Words*, p. 16.
80. *FJ*, 18 Jan. 1847.
81. McCabe, *Begging, Charity and Religion*, p. 8.
82. McLean, *The Event*, p. 95.
83. *FJ*, 18 Jan. 1847.
84. Thomas Laqueur, 'Bodies, details and the humanitarian narrative', p. 177. His death was reported in multiple newspapers, most of those lifting their piece from *Saunder's Newsletter.* The following papers published an account broadly similar; none deviated from the findings of the jury at the inquest, that the cause of the 'rash act' was the suffering he had witnessed as relieving officer: *The Pilot,* 1 Jan. 1847 (as Barden); *FJ,* 18 Jan. 1847 (Barden); *Liverpool Mercury*, 22 Jan. 1847; *Newry Telegraph*, 19 Jan. 1847; *Londonderry Sentinel*, 23 Jan. 1847; *Dublin Evening Mail*, 18, 21 Jan. 1847; *Clare Journal, and Ennis Advertiser*; 19 Jan. 1847.
85. *FJ*, 25 Jan. 1847: St Nicholas Without Relief Committee Report. Sums calculated from *FJ*, 14 Jan. 1847.
86. *FJ*, 15 Feb. 1847.
87. The population of St Nicholas' Without parish was 12,391 in the mid-1830s: Samuel Lewis, *A Topographical Dictionary of Ireland …* (2 vols, London, 18327), vol. 1, p. 556.
88. St Nicholas Without parish vestry minute book, 3 Feb. 1847.
89. St Nicholas Without parish vestry minute book: Figures of assessment for coffins for the poor are taken from multiple annual vestry meetings.
90. *FJ*, 1 Mar. 1847.
91. Ibid., 19 Mar. 1846; Kinealy, *Apparitions,* pp 16–17.
92. John Bardin bought a plot for his wife Alicia who died in 1833; her sister, Mrs Murray, was buried the following year in 1834; and Patrick Bardin's infant son Michael was buried there. In July 1846 Patrick's father John died aged 87 years and was laid to rest alongside his wife. The burial registers for Glasnevin Cemetery reveal Patrick was buried there just six months after his father: headstone, Glasnevin Cemetery, BA 10 (South); 'Registry of grants in Goldenbridge & Prospect Cemeteries, vol. 1, 1832–45'; Register of interments, Prospect Cemetery General Ground, vol. 4, 1844–9 (Glasnevin Trust).
93. Bardin is listed as a member of the Loyal Repeal Club: *FJ*, 11 Jan. 1842; *The Nation*, 4 Apr. 1846.
94. R. A. Houston, *Punishing the Dead: Suicide, Lordship and Community in Britain, 1500–1830* (Oxford, 2010), p. 270.
95. *FJ*, 27 Jan. 1847.

96. Dublin Corporation minutes, 8 May 1847 (Dublin City Libraries and Archives, C2/A1/41).
97. Eric Parisot, 'Framing suicidal emotions in the English popular press, 1750–80' in Heather Kerr, David Lemmings and Robert Phiddian (eds), *Passions, Sympathy and Print Culture: Public Opinion and Emotional Authenticity in Eighteenth-Century Britain* (London, 2016), pp 183–4.
98. Kelly, 'Suicide in eighteenth-century Ireland', p. 136.
99. Margaret Kelleher, *The Feminization of Famine: Expressions of the Inexpressible?* (Cork, 1997), p. 17.
100. The author would like to thank Dr David Murphy and Dr Aoife Bhreathnach for reading an earlier draft of this article.

'That They Might Obtain the Shelter of a Prison': Kilmainham Gaol and the Great Famine

1. John Howard, *The State of the Prisons* (London, 1777) and *An Account of the Principal Lazerettos in Europe; With Various Papers Relating to the Plague: Together With Further Observations on Some Foreign Prisons and Hospitals; and Additional Remarks on the Present State of Those in Great Britain and Ireland* (2nd edn, London, 1791). Howard issued a second and third edition of *The State of the Prisons* in 1780 and 1784 respectively, which included details of additional tours of inspection he made to prisons in Great Britain and Ireland.
2. Howard, *Account of the Principal Lazerettos in Europe*, p. 83.
3. These plans appear in an appendix in *Report from the Commissioners Appointed to Enquire into and Inspect the Conditions and Government of the State Prison and other Gaols in Ireland given to the House of Commons* (London, 1809).
4. & 2 Geo. IV, c. 57 (1821).
5. Under this legislation, the country was divided into a northern and southern circuit. The Inspectors-General alternated responsibility for one of these two circuits on an annual basis.
6. *Third Report of the Inspectors-General on the General State of the Prisons of Ireland, 1824,* p. 18, H.C. 1825 (493), xxii, 227 (henceforth cited as *I. G. Third Report, 1824).* Throughout this essay, the second and subsequent reference to each report of the inspectors-general will be cited in the following format: *I. G. Third Report, 1824.*
7. While reference will be made on the effect that the presence of convicts in the gaol had on the institution in terms of overcrowding, the focus of this article will be on Kilmainham Gaol as a local prison.
8. Geo. IV, c. 74 (1826).
9. *Eighth Report of the Inspectors-General on the General State of the Prisons of Ireland: 1830,* p. 25, H.C. (48), xxiv, 744.
10. *Twenty-Third Report of the Inspectors-General on the General State of the Prisons of Ireland, 1844: With Appendices*, p. 39, H.L. 1845 (37), xxvii, 265.
11. Randall McGowen, 'The Well-Ordered Prison: England, 1780–1865' in Norval Morris and Favid J. Rothman (eds), *The Oxford History of the Prison: The Practice of Punishment in Western Society* (Oxford, 1998), pp 90–2.
12. *I. G. Twenty-Third Report, 1844,* p. 39.
13. Ibid.
14. Ibid., p. 41.
15. *I. G. Twenty-Third Report, 1844,* p. v.
16. *Twenty-Fourth Report of the Inspectors-General on the General State of the Prisons of Ireland, 1845: With Appendices*, p. 5, H.L. 1846 (38), xxxviii.
17. *I. G. twenty-fourth report, 1845*, p. 6.
18. Twenty-Fifth Report of the Inspectors-General on the General State of the Prisons of Ireland, 1846: With Appendices, p. 6, H.L. 1847 (39), xxxix, 290.
19. Ibid., p. 10.
20. Ibid.
21. Ibid., p. 19.
22. The figures quoted are based on the totals for numbers of prisoners committed each year, inclusive of debtors, as recorded in the reports of the inspectors-general. In some cases these were recorded in the introduction to the report listing the figures for all the gaols in the country, in others they appear in

the individual section on Kilmainham Gaol. In the 1855 report the total prisoners committed is given as 1,977 (see *Thirty-Fifth Report of the Inspectors-General on the General State of the Prisons of Ireland, 1856: With Appendices*, p. viii, H.L. 1857, sess. II (33), xxxiii. However, the total for 1855 given in the 1856 report is 1,810 (see *Thirty-Sixth Report of the Inspectors-General on the General State of the Prisons of Ireland, 1857: With Appendices*, p. 289, H.L. 1857–8 (43), xliii, p.289.
23. *I. G. Twenty-Sixth Report, 1847,* p. 5.
24. Ibid., p. 5.
25. Philip Harling 'The Trouble with Convicts: From Transportation to Penal Servitude, 1840–67', in *Journal of British Studies* 53:1 (Jan. 2014), p. 88.
26. *Twenty-Eighth Report of the Inspectors-General on the General State of the Prisons of Ireland, 1849: With Appendices,* pp viii–ix, H.C. 1850 (311), xxxi. While acknowledging that some people did commit crimes during the Famine in the hope of securing a sentence of transportation and the alleviation of their stress, Nicholas Woodward questions whether it was a significant factor in the increase in sentence of transportation at that time: see Nicholas Woodward 'Transportation Convictions during the Great Irish Famine', in *Journal of Interdisciplinary History* 37:1 (summer, 2006), p. 64.
27. Attempts were made to set up alternative penal colonies in other outposts of the empire such as Bermuda, the Cape Colony and Gibraltar, but none of these proved viable alternatives: see Harling, 'Trouble with Convicts', pp 84, 89–93.
28. & 11 Vict., c. 84.
29. *Twenty-Sixth Report of the Inspectors-General on the General State of the Prisons of Ireland, 1847: With Appendices,* p. 8, H.L. 1847–8 (45), xlv.
30. Ibid., p. 6.
31. Ibid., p. 83.
32. Ibid., p. 30.
33. *Twenty-Seventh Report of the Inspectors-General on the General State of the Prisons of Ireland, 1848: With Appendices,* pp 5–6, H.L. 1849 (44), xliv.
34. *I. G. Twenty-Eighth Report, 1849,* p. xi.
35. *I. G. Twenty-Sixth Report, 1847,* p. 84.
36. Christine Kinealy, 'The Role of the Poor Law During the Famine', in Cathal Póirtéir (ed.), *The Great Irish Famine* (Dublin, 1995), p. 116.
37. *I. G. Twenty-Eighth Report, 1849,* p. x.
38. Ibid.
39. *Twenty-Ninth Report of the Inspectors-General on the General State of the Prisons of Ireland, 1850: With Appendices,* p. xv, H.L. 1851 (28), xxviii.
40. Ibid.; *I. G. Twenty-Eighth Report, 1849,* p. x.
41. *I. G. Twenty-Eighth Report, 1849,* p. viii.
42. *I. G. Twenty-Ninth Report, 1850,* p. xv.
43. *I. G. Twenty-Eighth Report, 1849,* p. 18.
44. *I. G. Twenty-Ninth Report, 1850,* p. xv.
45. Ibid., p. ix.
46. Newgate Prison on Green Street accounted for 1,574 prisoners in 1849, but was not in use in 1850.
47. *I. G. Twenty-Ninth Report, 1850,* p. xi.
48. Ibid., p. xv.
49. Ibid., pp xv–xvi.
50. *Thirtieth Report of the Inspectors-General on the General State of the Prisons of Ireland, 1851: With Appendices,* p. 32, H.L. 1852 (34), xxxiv.
51. Ibid., p. 33.
52. *I. G. Twenty-Eighth Report, 1849,* p. viii.
53. *I. G. Twenty-Ninth Report, 1850,* pp xix-xx. For the original report, see *Report from the Select Committee on Prison Discipline; Together with the Proceedings of the Committee, Minutes of Evidence, Appendix and Index,* p. iv, H.C. 1850 (632), xviii, 4.
54. *Thirty-Second Report of the Inspectors-General on the General State of the Prisons of Ireland, 1853: With Appendices,* p. xi, H.L. 1854 (43), xliii.
55. Ibid.
56. Elaine Farrell, *Women, Crime and Punishment in Ireland: Life in the Nineteenth-Century Convict Prison* (Cambridge, 2020).

57. *I. G. Twenty-Ninth, Report 1850,* p. xix.
58. *Thirty-First Report of the Inspectors-General on the General State of the Prisons of Ireland, 1852: With Appendices*, p. 21, H.L. 1852–3 (76), lxxvi.
59. *I. G. Thirty-Second Report, 1853,* p. xv.
60. & 18 Vict., c. 86 (1854).
61. & 22 Vict., c. 103 (1858).
62. Patrick Carroll-Burke, *Colonial Discipline: The Making of the Irish Convict System* (Dublin, 2000), p. 114.
63. Rebecca Sharon Lawlor, 'Crime in Nineteenth-Century Ireland: Grangegorman Female Penitentiary and Richmond Male Penitentiary, With Reference to Juveniles and Women, 1836–60 (M.Litt thesis, NUI Maynooth, 2012), p. 19.
64. *I. G. Thirty-Second Report,* 1854, p. xv.
65. *Thirty-Third Report of the Inspectors-General on the General State of the Prisons of Ireland, 1854: With Appendices*, p. x, H.L. 1854–5 (40), xl.
66. Ibid.
67. Interestingly, the proportionate rise in female criminality during the Famine period appears to have been confined to petty crime. Convictions for capital offences, which generally carried a sentence of convict transportation, rose significantly during the Famine for men and women. However, the proportion of men committing more serious crime and being sentenced to transportation actually increased, from 77% to 82% of the total: see Woodward, 'Transportation Convictions during the Great Irish Famine', pp 72–5.
68. Maria Luddy, *Prostitution and Irish Society 1800–1940* (Cambridge, 2007), pp 3–4.
69. Ibid., p. 27.
70. Dublin–Kilmainham General Prison Register 1838–40, 1840–43, 1843–5, 1845–8 and 1848–50, available at findmypast.ie (accessed 22 Dec. 2020).
71. Dublin–Kilmainham General Prison Register 1848-50, available at findmypast.ie.
72. In 1848 and 1849 the overall prison numbers for Kilmainham Gaol was not broken down by gender.
73. The overall figure for prisoners in Kilmainham for 1850, 1851 and 1852 are based on the numbers given in the individual reports on the gaol for those years; this is because those totals are broken down by gender.
74. In 1852, 1853 and 1854 the total figures for prisoners in Kilmainham which are broken down by gender do not include debtors. Inclusive of debtors, the totals for these years are 4,141, 3,001, and 3,013 respectively.
75. *I. G. Thirty-First Report, 1852*, p. 42; *I. G. Thirty-Second Report, 1853*, p. 8.
76. Dublin–Kilmainham General Prison Register 1848–50, 1850–53, 1853–8, 1858–63, 1864–7 and 1867–71, available at findmypast.ie (accessed 22 Dec. 2020).
77. Eliza Kenny attempted suicide on 4 Mar. 1844 (Dublin–Kilmainham General Prison Register 1843–5). Margaret Cardiff attempted suicide on 31 May 1853 and again on 13 July 1868 (Dublin–Kilmainham General Prison Register 1850–53 and 1867–71). At a meeting of the Rathdown Poor Law Guardians of 4 August 1869, the death of Margaret Cardiff aged 35 as a result of inflammation of the bowels was recorded (Rathdown Poor Law Union Board-Guardians Minute Book A 52, Mar. 1869 to Sept. 1869), all available at findmypast.ie (accessed 22 Dec. 2020).
78. *I. G. Thirty-First Report, 1852,* p. 40.
79. *I. G. Thirty-Fourth Report, 1855,* p. 4.
80. Luddy, *Prostitution and Irish Society*, pp 26–7.
81. Ibid., p. 23.
82. Farrell, *Women, Crime and Punishment*, p. 234.
83. *I. G. Thirty-Second Report, 1853*, p. 8.
84. *I. G. Thirtieth Report, 1851*, p. 23.
85. *I. G. Thirty-Ninth Report, 1860*, p. xiv.
86. Farrell, *Women, Crime and Punishment*, pp 6–7.
87. *I. G. Thirty-Fourth Report, 1855*, p. 4.
88. McGowen, 'The Well-Ordered Prison', pp 92–3.
89. Tim Carey, *Mountjoy: The Story of a Prison* (Cork, 2000), p. 124.

SECTION IV: THE FAMINE IN CULTURAL HISTORY

Dublin Fictions and the Economics of Famine Memory

1. See for instance what is probably the best-known Famine novel from the nineteenth century, Anthony Trollope's *Castle Richmond* (London, 1860), which runs the whole gamut. Chapter 25 in Joseph O'Connor's bestseller *Star of the Sea: Farewell to Old Ireland* (London, 2002) is another striking (and more recent) example, although it also has some more sordid elements lacking in early Famine fiction.
2. For an overview of the conventions of Famine fiction, see Marguérite Corporaal, Christopher Cusack, and Lindsay Janssen (eds), *Recollecting Hunger: An Anthology. Cultural Memories of the Great Irish Famine in Irish and British Fiction, 1847–1920* (Dublin, 2012).
3. See Christopher Cusack, 'Transformative nationalism and class relations in Irish Famine fiction, 1896–1909', in Marguérite Corporaal and Peter Gray (eds), *The Famine and Social Class: Conflicts, Responsibilities, Representations* (Oxford and New York, 2019), pp 151–69.
4. David Lloyd, 'The indigent sublime: spectres of Irish hunger', in *Representations* 92 (2005), p. 161.
5. *FJ*, 4 Jan. 1847, quoted in Ó Gráda, *Black '47*, p. 167.
6. See Ó Gráda, *Black '47*, pp 157–93.
7. See, for instance, Christopher Morash, *Writing the Irish Famine* (Oxford, 1995), or more recently, Marguérite Corporaal, *Relocated Memories: The Great Famine in Irish and Diaspora Fiction, 1846–1870* (Syracuse, 2017).
8. See also Christopher Cusack, 'Sunk in the mainstream: Irish women writers, canonicity, and Famine memory, 1892–1917', in Kathryn Laing and Sinéad Mooney (eds), *Irish Women's Writing at the Turn of the 20th Century: Alternative Histories, New Narratives* (Brighton, 2020), pp 37–48.
9. Peter Gray, 'The making of mid-Victorian Ireland? Political economy and the memory of the Great Famine', in Peter Gray (ed.), *Victoria's Ireland? Irishness and Britishness 1837–1901* (Dublin, 2004), p. 153
10. Bigelow, *Fiction, Famine, and the Rise of Economics in Victorian Britain and Ireland* (Cambridge, 2003), p. 112.
11. Lloyd, 'The indigent sublime', p. 154.
12. Ibid., p. 158.
13. David Lloyd, *Irish Culture and Colonial Modernity 1800–2000: The Transformation of Oral Space* (Cambridge, 2011), p. 22.
14. Gray, 'The making of mid-Victorian Ireland?', p. 152.
15. Ibid., p. 153.
16. William Barry, *The Wizard's Knot* (London, 1901), p. 178.
17. Alice Stopford Green, *Irish Nationality* (New York, 1911), p. 229.
18. James Connolly, *Labour in Ireland:* Labour in Irish history *and* The re-conquest of Ireland (Dublin, 1922), p. 170.
19. See also Marguérite Corporaal, 'Political economy? The economics and sociology of famine', in Matthew Campbell (ed.), *Irish Literature in Transition, vol. 3: 1830–1880* (Cambridge, 2020), pp 78–91.
20. Louis J. Walsh, *The Next Time: A story of 'Forty-Eight* (Dublin, 1919), p. 162.
21. Sarah Comyn, *Political Economy and the Novel: A Literary History of 'Homo Economicus'* (London, 2018), p. 1.
22. John Stuart Mill, *Essays on Some Unsettled Questions of Political Economy* (London, 1844), p. 137.
23. Comyn, *Political Economy and the Novel*, p. 14.
24. Lloyd, 'The indigent sublime', p. 161.
25. Lloyd, *Irish Culture and Colonial Modernity*, p. 139.
26. I have not been able to discover the author's identity, but a reviewer of her novel *An unnatural mother* appears to have been privy to it, stating that her 'real name is entirely racy of her native soil and of her Catholic creed': P. J. Lennox, review of *An Unnatural Mother*, in *Catholic University Bulletin* 18:6 (1912), p. 548.
27. See also Christopher Cusack and Lindsay Janssen, 'Death in the family: Reimagining the Irish family in Famine fiction, 1871–1912', in Yvonne O'Keeffe and Claudia Reese (eds), *New Voices,*

Inherited Lines: Literary and Cultural Representations of the Irish Family (Oxford and New York, 2013), pp 7–34.
28. 'Slieve Foy', 'Attie and his father: A tale of the poor', in *Stories of Irish Life, Past and Present* (London, 1912), pp 43–55.
29. Ibid., p. 44.
30. See Andrew Mangham's discussion of the links between political economy and physiology in *The Science of Starving in Victorian Literature, Medicine, and Political Economy* (Oxford, 2020).
31. 'Slieve Foy', 'Attie and his father', p. 50.
32. Ibid., p. 51.
33. Ibid., p. 52.
34. Ibid.
35. Ibid., p. 54.
36. Ibid., p. 52.
37. Ibid., p. 55.
38. After the first two pages, the Sullivan daughters disappear from the narrative and merit only a single brief reference once Sullivan has returned to the workhouse.
39. Colum McCann, *TransAtlantic* (London, 2014), p. 40
40. Ibid., p. 88.
41. Ibid., p. 44.
42. Ibid., p. 67.
43. Ibid.
44. Ibid.
45. Ibid., p. 42.
46. Ibid., p. 67.
47. Ibid., p. 75.
48. A similar contrast between city and country as perceived by a well-to-do individual travelling by coach across famine-stricken Ireland features in Conal O'Riordan's *Soldier's end* (London, 1938). Here too Dublin has its share of beggars, yet these are stereotypical urban destitutes 'spend[ing] their morning's treasure trove on gin' (p. 41). As in McCann's novel, the effects of the Famine become visible when main character Sir David Quinn travels to the south-west, encountering familiar scenes including evictions, dead women and children by the roadside, and labourers on public works projects 'lying dead with their pickaxes in their hands', with conditions getting worse as he approaches Munster (p. 63).
49. McCann, *TransAtlantic*, pp 41–2, 44.
50. See Margaret Kelleher, *The Feminization of Famine: Expressions of the Inexpressible?* (Durham, NC, 1997), p. 2.
51. McCann, *TransAtlantic*, 69.
52. Ibid., p. 69.
53. Ibid.
54. Ibid., p. 70.
55. Lloyd, 'The indigent sublime', p. 163
56. McCann, *TransAtlantic*, p. 71.
57. Patricia McFate, *The Writings of James Stephens* (New York, 1979), p. 133.
58. Joseph Lennon, 'The starvation of a man: Terence MacSwiney and Famine memory', in Oona Frawley (ed.), *Memory Ireland, vol. 3: The Famine and the Troubles* (Syracuse, 2014), p. 79. There are in fact many other examples of early twentieth-century Famine fiction.
59. Kevin Whelan, 'The memories of "The Dead"', in *Yale Journal of Criticism* 15:1 (2002), p. 61.
60. Stephens is not alone in transposing Famine memory to an Irish urban setting. James Joyce, for instance, used James Clarence Mangan's Famine writings as an example for his representation of urban destitution in *Ulysses* (1922). See James F. Wurtz, 'Scarce more a corpse: Famine memory and representations of the gothic in *Ulysses*', in *Journal of Modern Literature* 29:1 (2005), pp 102–17.
61. James Stephens [James Esse], *Hunger: A Dublin Story* (Dublin, 1918), p. 14.
62. Ibid., p. 9.
63. Ibid., pp 19–20.
64. Ibid., p. 20.
65. Ibid., p. 18.

66. Ibid., p. 21.
67. Ibid., p. 23.
68. Ibid., p. 25.
69. Ibid., p. 28.
70. See Kelleher, *The Feminization of Famine*, p. 84.
71. Stephens, *Hunger*, pp 13, 24, 27.
72. Ibid., p. 29.
73. Patrick Sheehan, *Glenanaar:A Story of Irish Life* (London, 1905), p. 199.
74. Emily Mark-FitzGerald, 'Famine memory and the gathering of stones: Genealogies of belonging', in *Atlantic Studies* 11:3 (2014), p. 430.
75. William J. Smyth, 'The province of Leinster and the Great Famine', in John Crowley, William J. Smyth and Mike Murphy (eds), *Atlas of the Great Irish Famine* (Cork, 2012), p. 333.
76. David Lloyd, 'Colonial trauma/postcolonial recovery?', in *Interventions* 2:2 (2000), p. 228.

'A Very Ready Sale': Exhibiting, Viewing and Selling Art in Dublin, 1845–49

1. Born in Dublin, Anna Maria Hall (1800 – 1881, née Fielding) was a novelist and writer, who often published as 'Mrs S. C. Hall'. Her husband, Samuel Carter Hall (1800 – 1889) was a journalist and editor of the *Art-Union Monthly*, which later became the *Art Journal* (1858). Together they are best known for their three-volume work *Ireland: Its Scenery, Character, etc.*, published between 1841 – 43, and which gives key accounts of life in Ireland prior to the Famine.
2. Mrs S. C. Hall, 'The Cry from Ireland', in *Art-Union Monthly* (Apr. 1847), p. 141.
3. Catherine Roach, 'An Ecosystem of Exhibitions: Venues, Artists, and Audiences in Early Nineteenth-Century London', in *British Art Studies* 14 (2019), p. 2 (https://doi.org/10.17658/issn.2058-5462/issue-14/croach/p2) (accessed 22 Feb. 2022).
4. For more on notable private collections in Dublin see, Fintan Cullen, *Ireland on Show:Art, Union and Nationhood* (Surrey, 2011), pp 7–8.
5. *A Brief Account of the Intended Academy of Fine Art to be Established in Dublin by Royal Charter*, 1820, quoted in John Turpin, *History of the Royal Hibernian Academy of Arts, Volume One, 1823 – 1916* (Dublin, 2018), p. 25.
6. Catherine Roach, 'An Ecosystem of Exhibitions', p. 12 (https://doi.org/10.17658/issn.2058-5462/issue-14/croach/p12) (accessed 22. Feb. 2022).
7. For more on panoramas in nineteenth-century Dublin, see Kevin Rockett and Emer Rockett, *Magic Lantern, Panorama and Moving Picture Shows in Ireland, 1786–1909* (Dublin, 2011).
8. See Philip McEvansoneya, 'John Constable and the Royal Hibernian Academy in 1834, with an unpublished letter to Martin Cregan', in *Burlington Magazine* 1255 (2007), pp 685–9.
9. Philip McEvansoneya, 'Ireland on show: art, union, and nationhood' in *Irish Studies Review* 21 (2013), p. 232.
10. Turpin, *History of the Royal Hibernian Academy of Arts*, p. 98.
11. For a full breakdown of the figures and number of works purchased, see Turpin, *History of the Royal Hibernian Academy*, pp 99–100. See also Eileen Black, 'Practical Patriots and True Irishmen: The Royal Irish Art Union, 1839–59', in *Irish Arts Review Yearbook* 14 (1998), pp 140-6.
12. *The Fourth Annual Report of the Committee of Selection of the Royal Irish Art-Union, or the Society for the Encouragement of the Fine Arts in Ireland by the Purchase and Diffusion of The Works of Living Artists: Being that for the Year 1843* (Dublin, 1844), p. 12.
13. The appropriateness and legality of art unions was called into questions because of the association of lotteries with gambling, and by extension, moral behaviour, and character. For a full account see Cordelia Smith, 'Art Unions and the Changing Face of Victorian Gambling' in Daniel Bivona and Marlene Tromp (eds), *Culture & Money in the Nineteenth Century:Abstracting Economics* (Athens, OH, 2016), pp 97–116.
14. A useful listing of some of the RIAU's purchasing and engraving activities during the period 1845–49 can be found in Walter Strickland, *A Dictionary of Irish Artists* (2 vols, Dublin, 1913), vol. 2, pp 659–63.

15. For more on these types of views, see Síghle Bhreathnach-Lynch, 'Framing the Irish: Victorian Paintings of the Irish Peasant', in *Journal of Victorian Culture* 2:2 (1997), pp 245–63.
16. Turpin, *History of the Royal Hibernian Academy of Arts*, p. 112.
17. Ibid., pp. 112–15.
18. Ibid., p. 113.
19. Margarita Cappock, 'Pageantry or Propaganda? The Illustrated London News and Royal Visitors in Ireland,' in *Irish Arts Review Yearbook* 16 (2000), p. 87.
20. *FJ*, 2 Aug. 1849.
21. *DEP*, 31 July 1849.
22. Ibid. 'Alderman Moon' was Sir Francis Graham Moon (1796–1871), a London-based print seller and publisher.
23. *DEPC*, 2 Aug. 1849. The painting referred to is Edwin Landseer, *Windsor Castle in modern times; Queen Victoria, Prince Albert and Victoria, Princess Royal* (1841–3, oil on canvas, Royal Collections Trust, RCIN 406903).
24. For more on the history of replicas, variations, copies and prints in the nineteenth century see: Julie F. Codell (ed.), *Victorian Artists' Autograph Replicas: Auras, Aesthetics, Patronage and the Art Market* (London, 2020); Patricia Mainardi, 'Copies, Variations, Replicas: Nineteenth-Century Studio Practice', in *Visual Resources* 15:2 (1999), pp 123-47 and Hélène Lafont-Couturier, 'La maison Goupil ou la notion d'oeuvre originale remise en question', *Revue de l'Art* 112 (1996), pp 59–69.
25. *The Pilot*, 6 Mar. 1848.
26. *FJ*, 11 Oct. 1847.
27. See Kathryn Milligan, 'Pier, Procession and Presence Chamber: Royal Visits to Dublin, 1821–1911', in M. Campbell and W. Durham (eds), *Making Majesty: The Throne Room at Dublin Castle, A Cultural History* (Kildare, 2017), pp 201–35.
28. Richard D. Altnick, *The Shows of London* (Cambridge, MA & London, 1978), p. 105; Roach, 'An Ecosystem of Exhibitions', p. 15. See https://doi.org/10.17658/issn.2058-5462/issue-14/croach/p15 (accessed 22. Feb. 2022).
29. See Christine Riding, 'Staging the raft of the Medusa', in *Visual Culture Britain* 5 (2004), pp 1–26; Cullen, *Ireland on Show*, pp 71–85.
30. *DEP*, 16 Aug. 1849.
31. 'Private View', *FJ*, 15 Oct. 1845, p. 2.
32. 'Landseer's Picture', *DEM*, 15 Oct. 1845, p. 3.
33. 'The Fine Arts', *Norfolk Chronicle*, 15 Nov. 1845, p. 5.
34. 'Landseer's Picture of "Horses Drinking in a Courtyard"', *FJ*, 2 Dec. 1846, p. 2.
35. Andrea Meyer, 'A View from Germany: Vernet, New Media, and the Remaking of History Painting', in Daniel Harkett and Katie Hornstein (eds), *Horace Vernet and the Thresholds of Nineteenth-Century Visual Culture* (Hanover, NH, 2017), pp 245–9. See also Melanie Vandenbrouck, 'Myth-making in Versailles: the French 'liberating mission' in Algeria and Horace Vernet's *Prise de la Smala d'Abd-el-Kader*', in *Immediations* 4 (2007), pp 93–109.
36. *FJ*, 26 Sept. 1848.
37. 'The Fine Arts. The Smahla of Abd-El-Kader', *DWR*, 30 Sept. 1848, p. 7.
38. For more on Vernet and Orientalism, see Julia Thoma and Melanie Vandenbrouck, 'From Battlefields to Scriptures: Horace Vernet's Vision of the 'Orient'', in Loïc Guyon and Andrew Watts (eds), *Aller(s)-Retour(s): Nineteenth-Century France in Motion* (Cambridge, 2013), pp 168–84.
39. *FJ*, 4 Oct. 1848.
40. Alfred Decaen after Horace Vernet, *Prise de la Smahla d'Abd-El-Kader* (1856, oil on canvas) (Musée Condé, Chantilly, PE629).
41. *FJ*, 26 June 1849.
42. The painting had been exhibited at the Royal Academy in the spring of 1849, and the noted firm of Paul and Dominic Colnaghi had commissioned a mezzotint of the scene from Samuel Reynolds in the same year. Hardinge served as the Chief Secretary for Ireland in 1830 before being appointed the Governor General of India in 1844. In December 1845, he accompanied Sir Hugh Gough (later memorialised by John Henry Foley in a controversial sculpture for the Phoenix Park), to the battlefield of Ferozeshah.
43. FJ, 13 Dec. 1849 & and *DWR*, 15 Dec. 1849.
44. *WDWM*, 7 Nov. 1846.

45. *FJ*, 1 Jan. 1840.
46. *WDWM*, 11 Apr. 1846.
47. *DWR*, 17 Jan. 1846.
48. *WDWM*, 17 Jan. 1846; *DEP*, 17 Feb. 1846; *FJ*, 27 Feb. 1846, p. 3.
49. *FJ*, 18 Jan. 1847.
50. *Art Union Monthly* (Mar. 1847), p. 100.
51. *DEPC*, 19 Jan. 1847.
52. *DEM*, 5 Mar. 1847.
53. *DEP*, 9 Mar. 1847.
54. *FJ*, 18 Mar. 1847.
55. *Art Union Monthly* (May 1847), p. 161.
56. J. Bruyn, B. Haak, S. H. Levie and P. J. J. van Thiel, *A Corpus of Rembrandt Paintings: 1625–1631*, vol. 1 (New York, 1982), p. 195.
57. *DEP*, 29 May 1847.

Epilogue: Famine Memory and the City

1. Edward Chandler, *Photography in Ireland: The Nineteenth Century* (Dublin, 2001), pp 10–12. The term 'calotype' refers to the original paper negative exposed in the camera; 'salted paper prints' (sometimes also referred to as 'calotype prints') are the printed positives on paper, made from the calotype negative.
2. In Chandler's opinion the photographs are unlikely to be Talbot's, since there is no record of him travelling to Ireland in the 1840s. Many early photographers sent their negatives to Lacock Abbey for printing; some of the Dublin calotypes can be identified as produced by the same camera and/or photographer, but authorship cannot reliably be established. Today the most comprehensive index of the Dublin negatives and positive prints (held in various collections) is the Bodleian Library's *William Henry Fox Talbot Catalogue Raisonné* (https://talbot.bodleian.ox.ac.uk/). The majority of the Dublin negatives and prints originally from the Talbot collection at Lacock Abbey are today distributed amongst the Talbot Collection of the British Library, and the National Science and Media Museum.
3. Emily Mark-FitzGerald, 'Photography and the Visual Legacy of Famine', in Oona Frawley (ed.), *Memory Ireland, Vol. 3: The Famine and the Troubles* (Syracuse, 2014), pp. 121–37.
4. For accounts of the manifestations of Famine memory in a variety of representational forms, see Marguerite Corporaal, Oona Frawley and Emily Mark-FitzGerald (eds), *The Great Irish Famine: Visual and Material Culture* (Liverpool, 2018).
5. *Illustrated London News*, 13 Aug. 1847, p. 108.
6. Ibid., p. 106.
7. Patrick Geoghegan, *Liberator: The Life and Death of Daniel O'Connell, 1830–1847* (Dublin, 2010).
8. Paula Murphy, 'Commemorating Daniel O'Connell', in *Nineteenth-Century Irish Sculpture: Native Genius Reaffirmed* (New Haven and London, 2010), pp 185–204.
9. For details of pre-1990s Famine commemorations, see Emily Mark-FitzGerald, *Commemorating the Irish Famine: Memory and the Monument* (Liverpool, 2013), pp 57–63.
10. Ibid., pp 233–40.
11. Ibid., pp 219–25, 238–9.
12. An exhibition commemorating Strzelecki was subsequently sponsored by the Embassy of Poland in Ireland: Peter Gray and Emily Mark-FitzGerald, *A Forgotten Polish Hero of the Great Irish Famine: Paul Strzelecki's Struggle to Save Thousands* (Dublin, 2019).
13. Despite its current location on Custom House Quay, Gillespie's *Famine* group was not designed for that location or intended to directly reference Dublin (see Mark-FitzGerald, *Commemorating the Famine*, pp 219–25). The *Jeanie Johnston* was built and designed in Tralee.
14. Peter Higginbotham's comprehensive site on British and Irish workhouses provides useful details of their history and present condition and uses: http://www.workhouses.org.uk. See also Frank Corrigan, 'Dublin workhouses during the Great Famine', *Dublin Historical Record*, 29:2 (1976), pp 59–65.

15. The earliest workhouse in the city was established by Act of Irish Parliament in 1703 to the south of St James' Street, which later became the Foundling Hospital and Workhouse in 1730. The South Dublin Union Workhouse was renovated by George Wilkinson in 1839, with a capacity of 2,000 inmates.
16. The predecessor of Dublin North Union was the northside 'House of Industry', founded in 1772 on Channel Row (north Great Brunswick Street). By the mid-nineteenth-century a large number of institutions came under its remit or were closely associated with the Union, including Richmond Hospital, Richmond Lunatic Asylum, Whitworth Hospital, Hardwicke Fever Hospital, the Bedford Asylum for Children, and Talbot Dispensary. The 1770s House of Industry was adapted for use as a workhouse by George Wilkinson and opened in 1840, with an identical capacity to Dublin South of 2,000 inmates.
17. Rathdown's workhouse (located in Loughlinstown) opened in 1841, with a capacity of 600 inmates.
18. Balrothery's workhouse (north-west of Lusk) opened in 1841, with a capacity of 400 inmates.
19. Peter Gray, *The Making of the Irish Poor Law, 1815–43* (Manchester, 2009).
20. Peter Gray, 'Conceiving and Constructing the Irish Workhouse, 1836–45', in *Irish Historical Studies* 38:149 (2012), pp 22–35.
21. The most comprehensively analysed to date is the North Dublin Union: see Timothy W. Guinnane and Cormac Ó Gráda, 'Mortality in the North Dublin Union during the Great Famine', in *Economic History Review* 55:3 (2002), pp 487–506.
22. Corrigan, 'Dublin workhouses', pp 61–2.
23. On the fate of these unions in the post-Famine period, see Virgina Crossman, *Politics, Pauperism and Power in Late Nineteenth-Century Ireland* (Manchester, 2006).
24. Jacinta Prunty and Sullivan (eds), *The Daughters of Charity of St Vincent de Paul in Ireland: The Early Years* (Dublin, 2014).
25. *Final Report of the Commission of Investigation into Mother and Baby Homes,* Department of Children, Equality, Disability, Integration and Youth, 2021, Chapter 13, 'Dublin Union/Pelletstown/St Patrick's, Navan Road/Eglinton Road', pp 1–111. Whilst the Commission's report provides key historical information on the running of Pelletstown and similar institutions across Ireland, it has been widely critiqued for its downplaying of witness statements, both those submitted as formal affidavits to the Investigation Committee, and those provided to the Confidential Committee (both part of the broader Commission): see for example Catriona Crowe, 'The commission and its survivors', *The Dublin Review* 83 (2021), pp. 60–96. The abbreviated witness summaries contained in the Pelletstown section of the Report bear out this criticism. Records of the Dublin Unions and their Boards of Guardians are held in the National Archives; Pelletstown archives are held by the Child and Family Agency (TUSLA), the Department of Health, and privately by the Daughters of Charity (*Final Report,* p.4).
26. A high cross monument in the former (now derelict) workhouse graveyard of Balrothery, erected by the Board of Guardians in 1918, is dedicated broadly 'to the memory of those whose remains lie interred in this cemetery'.
27. A competition run in 2011 by the Office of Public Works attempting to fulfil the 2009 Ryan Report's recommendation for a public memorial to the victims of abuse within residential care facilities collapsed under the weight of controversy in 2013: see Joanne Laws, 'Memorial to the Victims of Abuse While in Residential Care' (2013), www.publicart.ie.
28. The older Civic Museum (run by Dublin City Council) closed in 2003. The two primary Dublin-focused museums today are the Little Museum of Dublin (a small, eclectic independent museum, opened in 2011) and 14 Henrietta St (a site-specific house museum opened in 2018 by Dublin City Council).
29. Graeme Gilloch, *Myth and Metropolis: Walter Benjamin and the City* (Cambridge, 1997).
30. Breandán Mac Suibhne, *The End of Outrage: Post-Famine Adjustment in Rural Ireland* (Oxford 2017), p. 19.

Index